ENTERPRISE MOBILITY: APPLICATIONS, TECHNOLOGIES AND STRATEGIES

Tennenbaum Institute Series on Enterprise Systems

The mission of the Tennenbaum Institute is creation and dissemination of information, knowledge and skills to enable fundamental change of complex organizational systems. The IOS Press book series on Enterprise Systems is one of the ways that the Institute facilitates this dissemination of knowledge created by our many partners in academia, industry, and government as well as the Institute's faculty and staff.

The goal of each volume in the series is to bring together multi-disciplinary and transdisciplinary perspectives, empirical and axiomatic research, and design methods and tools within focus areas of particular importance to enable fundamental enterprise transformation in both private and public sectors. Focus areas of interest range from value creation and work processes to management decision making and social networks, all in the context of fundamental enterprise and organizational change. The objective is to address enterprise systems at all levels, ranging from technological systems to human and organizational systems.

The Institute is committed to attracting thought leaders from a wide range of disciplines, challenging them to communicate broadly, and helping them create works that can truly help those entrusted with transforming their enterprises. We intend these volumes to enable people to enhance value for all of their enterprise's stakeholders, ranging from shareholders and employees, to customers and other constituencies.

The Tennenbaum Institute is a unit of the Georgia Institute of Technology, Atlanta, Georgia, 30332, USA. For further information, please visit www.ti.gatech.edu.

Volume 2

Recently published in this series:

Vol. 1.   W.B. Rouse and A.P. Sage (Eds.), Work, Workflow and Information Systems

ISSN 1874-737X

Enterprise Mobility: Applications, Technologies and Strategies

Edited by

Rahul C. Basole, PhD.

Tennenbaum Institute, Georgia Institute of Technology,
760 Spring Street NW, Atlanta, GA 30332-0210, USA

IOS
Press

Amsterdam • Berlin • Oxford • Tokyo • Washington, DC

ISBN 978-1-58603-905-9

Published previously in the journal *Information Knowledge Systems Management* 7, 1–2 (2008), ISSN 1389-1995.

Publisher
IOS Press
Nieuwe Hemweg 6B
1013 BG Amsterdam
The Netherlands
fax: +31 20 687 0019
e-mail: order@iospress.nl

Distributor in the UK and Ireland
Gazelle Books Services Ltd.
White Cross Mills
Hightown
Lancaster LA1 4XS
United Kingdom
fax: +44 1524 63232
e-mail: sales@gazellebooks.co.uk

Distributor in the USA and Canada
IOS Press, Inc.
4502 Rachael Manor Drive
Fairfax, VA 22032
USA
fax: +1 703 323 3668
e-mail: iosbooks@iospress.com

Contents

Part V: Cases

Information Knowledge Systems Management 7 (2008) 1–7
IOS Press

Enterprise mobility: Researching a new paradigm

Rahul C. Basole
Tennenbaum Institute, Georgia Institute of Technology, 760 Spring Street NW, Atlanta, GA 30332, USA
E-mail: rahul.basole@ti.gatech.edu

Abstract: The proliferation of mobile information and communication technologies has led to a profound change in the way people work, communicate, and collaborate and conduct business. However, businesses today are just beginning to recognize the importance and potentially transformative impact of enterprise mobility. While the concept of enterprise mobility continues to emerge in the management and technology literatures, it is still not well understood. This special issue brings together global, multi-disciplinary perspectives from leading scholars and practitioners on the value and transformative impact of enterprise mobility on work, technology, and organizations, discusses critical enablers and strategies, and provides case study insights.

1. Introduction

The logic for enterprise adoption and use of mobile information and communication technologies (ICT), such as laptops, smart phones and other handheld devices, is well recognized. Any technology that can deliver tangible business benefits, by making information more accessible, is generally considered a good thing. Initial case studies have supported these propositions; commonly observed benefits of enterprise mobility include higher levels of end-user convenience, efficiency, productivity, decision-speed, and process improvement [8].

However, this was not always the case. When enterprises first began to evaluate and adopt mobile ICT, the underlying technology enablers were still fairly immature and often failed to deliver on the expected benefits. Similarly, enterprises were not adequately "ready" to embrace mobile ICT; they often lacked a technological infrastructure, business processes, human resources, leadership, and organizational culture that could facilitate and accelerate enterprise mobility implementations [9]. The predictable outcome was widespread disappointment. Many considered mobile ICT to be another hyped up technology with only little enterprise value.

Today, much has changed. The underlying technology has improved significantly. The central pieces of the mobile data equation, which we refer to as the mobile *DNA* (devices, networks and infrastructure, and applications), are all falling into place: devices are becoming more suited for mobile data use, wireless networks are maturing and becoming increasingly ubiquitous and capable of handling higher data throughput, and value-added mobile applications are rapidly emerging. Likewise, enterprises are realizing the long-term, strategic benefits that enterprise mobility can deliver: efficiencies, cost savings, new competitive advantages and core competencies – all capable of fundamentally transforming existing organizational, business model and strategy paradigms [5,13]. With these opportunities in mind, many enterprises are preparing for a mobile future.

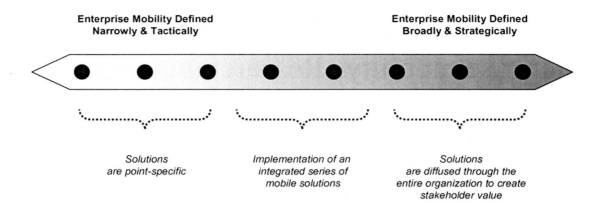

Fig. 1. The Enterprise Mobility Continuum.

The perfect storm of technology enablers and increasing levels of enterprise readiness has led to a growing number of organizations adopting, implementing and using mobile ICT in a wide variety of industries and contexts to varying extents [10]. The differences in these implementation levels can be generally attributed to where organizations place their view of enterprise mobility on the continuum (see Fig. 1) [3].

Some define enterprise mobility narrowly and tactically. In this view, point-solutions, such as mobile e-mail, dominate. These implementations tend to primarily focus on basic communication and productivity improvements. Others define enterprise mobility more broadly and strategically. In this instance, the focus is on strategic and large-scale enterprise wide implementations (e.g. mobile CRM) that enable organizations to create new core competencies, gain and sustain competitive advantages, and define new markets.

As the number of enterprises using mobile ICT increases, it becomes imperative to have a more complete understanding of what value and impact it has, what drives and enables it, and in what ways it can and will transform the nature and practices of work, organizational cultures, business processes, supply chains, enterprises, and potentially entire markets [4]. Enterprise mobility is therefore a topic of great interest to both scholars and practitioners [2].

Despite the importance of enterprise mobility as a topic area, the literature to date is relatively sparse [14]. Few papers have been published in premier management, information systems, engineering, and organization science journals. However, there are signs that this is changing. An online bibliographical database dedicated to the mobile business literature has emerged (www.m-lit.org) and some mobile communications journals (e.g. International Journal of Mobile Communications) have shifted their focus to include enterprise mobility related topics. An IEEE conference dedicated to mobile business was established in 2002 and has produced several research articles exploring issues related to enterprise mobility. In 2007, a research track on Mobile Enterprise and Workforce support attracted numerous papers that investigated technical, economic, and social issues of mobile ICT in enterprises. In summary, these activities provide an indication that there is a growing interest in the study of enterprise mobility by a broad community of scholars [11].

This volume aims to contribute to and extend both our *theoretical* and *practical* understanding of *enterprise mobility* by exploring the necessary strategic, technological, and economic considerations, adoption and implementation motivators and inhibitors, usage contexts, social implications, human-centered design issues, support requirements, and transformative impacts. The main objective of this special issue is to discuss applications, technologies, strategies, theories, frameworks, contexts, case studies, and analyses that provide insights into the growing reality of enterprise mobility for scholars and practicing managers.

2. Papers in this issue

This volume contains thirteen articles from leading scholars and practitioners and can be broadly categorized into five sections. The first section provides an introductory view to the evolution of enterprise mobility; the second section examines the changing nature of work, work practices, and the work environment; in the third section of this special issue, critical enablers of enterprise mobility are discussed; in the fourth section, authors explore strategic considerations; the last section provides insightful case studies of enterprise mobility across multiple domains. Together, the articles explore enterprise mobility across the entire continuum.

2.1. The evolution of enterprise mobility

The first paper, *"The Convergence of Wireless, Mobility, and the Internet and its Relevance to Enterprises"* by Andrew Seybold of Seybold Consulting, provides an introductory perspective on the historical evolution of mobile ICT, how mobile ICT have traditionally entered the workplace, and how this process is changing. In particular, Seybold describes the implications of converged communications for enterprises and provides suggestions on how to manage new communication requirements in the age of mobility.

The mobile telecommunications industry is characterized by a complex value network of incumbent and emerging players [6]. The second paper, *"Business Mobility: A Changing Ecosystem"* by Mary McDowell of Nokia, provides a catalyst's perspective on enterprise mobility solutions by exploring the structure and dynamics of the underlying business ecosystem, discussing the changing roles and relationships of key players, and projecting potential market growth opportunities. McDowell's observations suggest that a number of changes are occurring and even more are necessary in order for enterprise mobility to evolve to the point of fruition, where companies consider mobile solutions as key strategic investments. McDowell concludes with several insightful vignettes of large companies that have made significant steps toward strategic and holistic adoption of enterprise mobility.

2.2. The changing nature of work, work practices, and the work environment

Recent research has called for a re-emphasis on the nature of work [1]. The introduction of emerging and potentially disruptive ICT, such as mobile ICT, into organizations particularly raises the question of its transformative impact on work, work practices, and the work environment [7,12].

In their paper *"A Socio-Technical Perspective of Mobile Work"*, Leida Chen and Ravi Nath from Creighton University explore the salient characteristics of an effective mobile work environment by applying a socio-technical perspective to the study of mobile work. Through a structured interview approach with chief information officers, Chen and Nath identify the primary elements of the social and technical subsystems related to mobile work. They conclude that both social and technical systems are highly interdependent and must be jointly optimized to create effective mobile work environments.

Camille Venezia, formerly with Knoll Workforce Research, and Verna Allee and Oliver Schwabe of Value Networks investigate the challenges of workspace design for evolving mobile workers needs in the paper entitled *"Designing Productive Spaces for Mobile Workers: Role Insights from Network Analysis."* The authors argue that only a few companies have developed strategies for mobile work that take physical space, mobile devices, and office equipment requirements into consideration. In many cases, costly mistakes in design and implementation have been made. Using value network analysis, Venezia and her colleagues define the specific roles mobile workers play, map the ways they interact with others and explore how this interaction impacts technology and workspace needs. Their study sheds light on popular "myths" of mobile work and provides valuable insight for technology providers, workplace designers, and managers.

The paper *"Telecommuting and Corporate Culture: Implications for the Mobile Enterprise"* authored by Anthony Hoang, Robert Nickerson, Paul Beckman, and Jamie Eng from the San Francisco State University re-examines the impact of corporate culture on telecommuting and explores its implications for the mobile enterprise. The study presents findings from a survey with managers and business professionals. Specifically, Hoang and his colleagues find that corporate culture is still a strong deterrent to telecommuting in many organizations. Their results have important implications for organizations moving towards enterprise mobility.

2.3. Critical enablers of enterprise mobility

As work spaces and settings change, technologies enabling enterprise mobility must take changing user requirements and evolving use contexts into consideration. Judith Gebauer from the University of Illinois, Urbana-Champaign, addresses this issue by investigating the salient functional and non-functional technology requirements of mobile professionals that lead to increased adoption, use and user performance in her paper *"User Requirements of Mobile Technology: A Summary of Research Results."* Based on results of a series of research studies, the author concludes that (i) user-perceived technology maturity is a critical factor to explain and predict mobile technology use, (ii) users require basic communication and productivity-related functionality for particular tasks, and (iii) mobile technology has a considerable impact on job performance and personal life.

Given the unique characteristics of mobile devices, many design and use issues emerge that do not exist in traditional desktop systems. In the paper, entitled *"Mobile Interaction Design: Integrating Individual and Organizational Perspectives"*, Peter Tarasewich from Suffolk University, Jun Gong from Google, and Fiona Fui-Hoon Nah, and David DeWester from the University of Nebraska identify potential issues and problems with the design and use of mobile information systems by examining both personal and organizational perspectives of two critical enterprise mobility enablers, namely mobile devices and applications. Their study concludes with a set of guidelines that can assist organizations in making decisions about the design and implementation of mobile technologies and applications in organizations while taking user, data, security, and other contextual issues into consideration.

Mobile applications are one of the key enablers of enterprise mobility. In many instances, enterprises have simply extended their existing business applications to the mobile domain. More recently, mobile work specific applications have emerged. The paper, *"A Comparative Anatomy of Mobile Enterprise Applications: Towards a Framework of Software Reuse"* by Patrick Brans, formerly with Sybase, and Rahul Basole of the Tennenbaum Institute at the Georgia Institute of Technology, explores the rapidly evolving domain of mobile enterprise applications. The authors discuss how mobile applications have traditionally been developed and in what ways established software reuse principles can facilitate and enhance development. Brans and Basole suggest a methodology for identifying reusable mobile application components and develop a taxonomy of mobile applications, with a particular focus on field office applications.

In contrast to individual consumers, enterprises are much more concerned about the security of sensitive and critical corporate data. Given the inherent vulnerability of mobile devices and the data that resides on them, the success of enterprise mobility is largely dependent on providing adequate security levels. The paper "*Protecting Data on Mobile Devices: A Taxonomy of Security Threats to Mobile Computing and Review of Applicable Defenses*," by Jon Friedman and Daniel Hoffman of Fiberlink, provides a broad overview of mobile device security, develops a multi-categorical threat taxonomy and discusses technologies and methods that can be applied against each threat type.

2.4. Strategic considerations

The mobile ICT landscape is complex, characterized by continuously evolving technologies and emerging standards. Organizations often face tremendous challenges when making strategic decisions in this uncertain environment [4]. Thus, a third theme that is important in understanding enterprise mobility relates to the plethora of strategic considerations firms and solution providers must take into account in order to successfully operate in this complex and dynamic environment.

Christina Loh, Andrew Stadlen, John Moses, and Conor Tuohy from Palm Enterprise and Rahul Basole from the Tennenbaum Institute at the Georgia Institute of Technology provide a unique empirical study on the determinants and challenges of enterprise mobility support in their paper "*Enterprise Mobility and Support Outsourcing: A Research Model and Initial Findings*." The authors argue that the evolution of the wireless industry and the rapid proliferation of a mobile workforce has left many businesses at a disadvantage. Mobility support is highly complex and often given only little attention. Mobile network operators often tend to act as the primary point of support contact for enterprises. However, the support received is often below expectations and leaves businesses searching for alternate sources. Using a large-scale survey of executives and IT managers, Loh and her colleagues provide insight into what types of support strategies companies are pursuing and organizational receptiveness towards mobility support outsourcing.

The paper "*Enterprise Mobile Product Strategy using Scenario Planning*" by Sami Muneer and Chetan Sharma of SAP and Sharma Consulting, respectively, investigates the challenges companies face when evaluating enterprise mobility technologies. Muneer and Sharma argue that when planning for a long-term product roadmap, companies have to consider a myriad of evolutionary trends and forecasts to determine the probable list of product functionalities and their introduction timing in the lifecycle of the product. Drawing on the scenario-planning methodology, their paper suggests how to formulate a product strategy and roadmap.

2.5. Case studies

Eusebio Scornavacca and Stuart Barnes of the University of Wellington, New Zealand, and Norwich Business School at the University of East Anglia, respectively, examine "*The Strategic Value of Enterprise Mobility: Case Study Insights*." Using the Mobile Enterprise Model, a framework for understanding the potential of mobile applications in organizations, Scornavacca and Barnes find that most organizations focus on process and mobility, rather than overall market impact. The primary benefits organizations gained included efficiency and effectiveness. Scornavacca and Barnes conclude that most organizations are merely in the empowerment phase and that there are significant opportunities for mobile enterprise applications to provide considerably more benefit for their organizations.

Carsten Sørensen, Jan Kietzmann, Gamel Wiredu, Silvia Elaluf-Calderwood, Kofi Boateng, and David Gibson from the London School of Economics conclude this volume with an excellent summary of lessons learned through multiple case studies on the use of mobile ICT in enterprises in their paper "*Exploring Enterprise Mobility: Lessons From the Field.*" Sørensen and colleagues explore key challenges in the application of mobile information technology to improve organizational efficiency based on findings from 11 empirical studies. Their results indicate that there is not a clear linear relationship between the introduction of mobile ICT and the consequences in terms of increased organizational agility through enterprise mobility. Sørensen and colleagues also argue that the resulting benefits of mobile ICT are context-dependent and that organizations must carefully experiment to investigate how to yield the most benefit. The practical examples presented in the vignettes and discussed in the analysis provide management with excellent tangible examples of enterprise mobility placed in a theoretical context.

3. Conclusions

The emergence of mobile ICT within the enterprise has resulted in a paradigm shift of how business is conducted now and in the future. Business professionals, mobile workers, and field staff can now remain as productive outside the office as they are within the office. Mobile ICT provide workers the means to access and utilize work-critical data and information wherever and whenever they need it. However, these benefits represent only the tip of the iceberg. Enterprise mobility solutions have the potential to fundamentally transform organizations, supply chains, and markets.

As mentioned at the outset of this article, the literature on enterprise mobility is relatively sparse when related to the breadth and importance of the area. In order to address this gap, the material that follows purposely includes both practitioner and academic perspectives. Taken together, the thirteen articles in this special issue represent a significant step forward in our collective theoretical and practical understanding of enterprise mobility and set the stage for numerous future research opportunities.

Acknowledgements

The editor of this special issue would like to express his sincere gratitude to all contributing authors and thank the many reviewers who generously contributed their time to this volume by carefully reading the manuscripts and providing helpful criticism. He would also like to thank Dr. William B. Rouse, who facilitated the idea of this special issue and who has always been a great supporter of interdisciplinary and forward-looking research that is so well represented by the accepted manuscripts.

References

[1] D.E. Bailey and S.R. Barley, Return to work: Toward post-industrial engineering, *IIE Transactions* **37**(8) (2005), 737–752.
[2] S.J. Barnes, Enterprise Mobility: Concept and Examples, *International Journal of Mobile Communications* **1**(4) (2003), 341–359.
[3] R.C. Basole, *The Emergence of the Mobile Enterprise: A Value-Driven Approach*, Proceedings of the Sixth International Conference on Mobile Business, Toronto, Canada, 2007.
[4] R.C. Basole, *Modeling and Analysis of Complex Technology Adoption Decisions: An Investigation in the Domain of Mobile Information and Communication Technologies*, Unpublished Dissertation, Georgia Institute of Technology, 2006.
[5] R.C. Basole and W.B. Rouse, *Towards the Mobile Enterprise: Readiness and Transformation*, Encyclopedia of Mobile Computing and Commerce, 2007.
[6] R.C. Basole and W.B. Rouse, Complexity of Service Value Networks: Conceptualization and Empirical Investigation, *IBM Systems Journal* **47**(1) (2008), 53–70.

[7] R.C. Basole and R.A. DeMillo, in: *Enterprise IT and Transformation*, W.B. Rouse, ed., Enterprise Transformation: Understanding and Enabling Fundamental Change (Chap. 11), New York: Wiley, 2006.

[8] R.C. Basole, *The Value and Impact of Mobile Information and Communication Technologies*, Proceedings of the 2004 IFAC Symposium, Atlanta, Georgia, 2004.

[9] R.C. Basole, *Strategic Planning for Enterprise Mobility: A Readiness-Centric Approach*, Proceedings of the 2007 Americas Conference in Information Systems, Keystone, Colorado, 2007.

[10] M. Lattanzi, A. Kohonen and V. Gopalakrishnan, *Work Goes Mobile: Nokia's Lesson from the Leading Edge*, New York: Wiley, 2006.

[11] K. Lyytinen and Y. Yoo, The Next Wave of Nomadic Computing: A Research Agenda for Information Systems Research, *Information Systems Research* **13**(4) (2002), 377–388.

[12] W.B. Rouse, A Theory of Enterprise Transformation, *Systems Engineering* **8**(4) (2005), 279–295.

[13] W.B. Rouse, ed., *Enterprise Transformation: Understanding and Enabling Fundamental Change*, New York: Wiley, 2006.

[14] E. Scornavacca, S.J. Barnes and S. Huff, Mobile Business Research, 2000-2004: Emergence, Current Status, and Future Opportunities, *Communications of the AIS* **17** (2006), 635–646.

Rahul C. Basole is a Research Scientist in the Tennenbaum Institute at the Georgia Institute of Technology. His research focuses on modeling, visualization, and analysis of complex systems, innovation strategy and management, emerging IT, and applied decision analysis. In his current role, Dr. Basole conducts research on the complexity of value networks and eco-systems with a particular focus on the mobile business, healthcare, biotech, and services domain. Dr. Basole has received several best paper awards and his work has been extensively published in books, prestigious research journals, and conference proceedings. In previous roles, he was the CEO, Founder, and VP Research of a Silicon Valley-based wireless research and consulting firm, the Director of Research and Development at a leading software firm, and a Senior Analyst at a leading IT management consulting firm. Dr. Basole is a member of the Institute for Operations Research and Management Sciences, the Decision Sciences Institute, and the Association for Information Systems. He currently serves as a director or advisor for several technology firms. He received a B.S. degree in industrial and systems engineering from Virginia Tech, has completed graduate studies in engineering-economic systems, operations research, and management information systems at Stanford University and the University of Michigan, and received a Ph.D. degree in industrial and systems engineering from the Georgia Institute of Technology, concentrating in IT and operations management.

Part I: Introduction

Information Knowledge Systems Management 7 (2008) 11–23
IOS Press

The convergence of wireless, mobility, and the Internet and its relevance to enterprises

Andrew M. Seybold
Andrew Seybold Inc., 315 Meigs Road, A-267, Santa Barbara, CA 93109, USA
E-mail: aseybold@andrewseybold.com

Abstract: Convergence will have an effect on every aspect of an enterprise. Exactly what is convergence and how will we get there? This paper examines how new technologies have traditionally entered the workplace, how this process is changing and the implications for enterprises as they enter a new world of converged communications. Part of the convergence experience is to make information easily available no matter what type of device we are using or where we are. Convergence, based on a set of smart networks, smart devices and a new approach to the Wireless Internet, will help us manage all of our telecommunications requirements on an ongoing basis.

Keywords: Convergence, wireless, telecommunications, Internet, enterprise

1. Introduction

Convergence (converged environments/networks) defines a multi-media environment and/or network where signals regardless of type (i.e., voice, quality audio, video, data, etc.) and encoding methodology may be seamlessly exchanged between independent endpoints with similar characteristics. Convergence in this case requires the overall environment to have two primary characteristics: (1) the intelligence to provide translation between disparate signal types and multipoint routing to establish connectivity between requested endpoints and (2) the ability to dynamically allocate required bandwidth to support endpoint requirements for each requested session. Convergence as defined by this is independent of signal format and transport media.

The telecommunications industry has a vision of convergence that is the marriage of a number of different networks that provide access to voice, data, audio and video services [30]. In its ultimate form, this convergence will rely on smart devices over smart networks and today it is assumed that it will also be based on Internet Protocol or IP transport from end to end. The use of IP as the transport renders the combining of different networks and different types of data easier and the vision includes not only a seamless flow of information, but also a common billing scheme that provides a single bill for all of the various telecommunications services.

There are a number of unanswered questions surrounding convergence – how long it will be until we are able to deliver the vision of total convergence, whether convergence is more about the integration of telecommunications technologies or about bundling services to make it less desirable and more difficult for customers to move to another service provider or if it is a combination of both of these.

What are the advantages to the network provider and to the customer? Is convergence a win-win proposition or simply a ploy by the networks? The evolution of telecommunications from its infancy to today when it is an integral part of our lives at home, at the office and on the road has occurred in a short period of time and further evolution continues to advance quickly. In this paper we will explore how the ideas behind convergence will affect where we are heading.

2. History

For many years, new technologies were developed for and deployed by enterprise customers. Many of these new technologies and the resultant devices entered the workplace surreptitiously, being purchased by employees with their own money because of their strong belief that the technology would help them be more efficient in their jobs while the corporate powers were slow to accept and adopt new technologies and devices.

This was true of the first Personal Computers to appear on corporate desktops, the first notebook computers and, in wireless, the first one-way and then two-way pagers and cell phones.

Historically, new technologies were first adopted by individuals who recognized how these new products and services could help them better perform their jobs, make their life easier and help them move ahead in the corporate world. These early adopters [11], as they are known, were also the first to embrace email services such as those offered in the late 1980s and early 1990s by MCI, CompuServe and others.

With the exception of the first Personal Computers, products were initially engineered and designed with the corporate buyer in mind because enterprises had the funds to invest in new technologies. Today, enterprise customers are more willing to engage with new technologies and devices but are still considered to be "slow adopters," requiring vendors to engage in prolonged sales cycles and drawn-out pilot projects and tests.

Wireless technologies were first adopted by individuals and companies primarily for business uses. In the 1970s and into the 1980s, the first wireless devices to be used in a business environment were one-way pagers [15]. These pagers were first introduced to provide alerting services for doctors on call and service technicians in the field. They soon spread to sales professionals who wanted their customers to be able to reach them quickly.

In 1990, with the advent of wide-area paging services, there were 22 million pagers in use and that number grew to more than 61 million by 1994. As the industry grew, so did the number of ways to access someone's pager, first by dialing a number and leaving a message and then by computer access. After the invention of the two-way pager, messages could be sent and received by other pager customers or via a computer terminal.

In the early stages of cellular deployment in the United States and elsewhere (1981–1989), cell phones were bulky and usually mounted in vehicles, and the cost of ownership and operation was high. As wireless service providers attracted more customers, handheld cell phones became available and pricing for their use declined rapidly.

The cellular networks were first built out to cover business and industrial areas of major cities, then the major highways [32]. Little if any coverage was provided into areas where people lived. Cellular handheld phones were expensive to purchase and use and were considered to be a business tool.

During the first fourteen years of cellular service in the United States, network operators were able to attract only 60 million customers nationwide and the majority of these customers used their cellular phones solely for business.

Also during this period of time, starting in 1982, many enterprises were installing their first voicemail systems [31] for their wired phone systems and the combination of voicemail and the availability of cellular phone service began driving additional enterprise acceptance of wireless. At the same time, the first handheld cellular phones began appearing in the market, led by the Motorola DynaTAC. The availability of voice mail and handheld cellular phones was a combination most corporations could relate to and they were able to make a business case for their use. Sales staff in the field could use their cellular phones to access their voice mailbox and retrieve their messages without having to return to the office, and they could use their cellular phones to respond to the phone messages they retrieved.

Then, in 1995, the average monthly cost of operating a cellular phone dropped below the $50 per month critical price point and within only three years, the cellular user population doubled from 60 million to 120 million customers [18]. With this rapid growth of the cellular industry, new wireless tower sites were built out and coverage in the United States as well as around the world continued to expand and improve. This is when people began using their cellular phones during leisure time for personal matters as well as during the workweek for work-related activities.

Toward the end of 1994 and into 1995, the US Government's Federal Communications Commission (FCC) decided that having only two wireless operators competing for business did not provide enough competition in the marketplace, so it authorized additional spectrum known as the PCS or Personal Communications Spectrum to be auctioned to enable new companies to provide additional types of wireless services and more competition [1].

The vision for the PCS spectrum was perhaps the first mention of what we today consider to be the convergence of wired and wireless communications. The FCC's statement was that this new spectrum would permit new companies to enter the market and to develop new networks that would be able to track our location and route calls to us depending upon where we were. If we were in our car, we might receive both our business and personal calls, and if we were inside our house, we would receive only our personal calls and business calls would be directed to our voicemail, and so forth. While this was a great vision, the reality was that the technologies needed to enable this type of service were not yet available [12]. As a result, the new networks built out on the PCS spectrum merely mimicked the existing networks. However, because the number of wireless network operators was increased from two per area to four or five per area, competition caused the price of wireless services to continue to decline, which meant more people could afford wireless voice services.

This is how the United States' two largest wireless operators – AT&T Wireless and Verizon Wireless – came to use a combination of both sets of spectrum while other operators including Sprint Nextel and T-Mobile use only PCS spectrum. The timing of these auctions coincided with new technologies that were becoming available. Until this point in time, most cellular networks, at least those in the United States, used a technology known as analog or AMPS [16]. This type of service mimicked the wired phone service where each caller is assigned a specific pair of wires during a call. In the case of wireless, callers are assigned one specific radio channel for as long as they are on the call. If they move from one location to another during the call, the tower their signal is reaching may change, but the call is still occupying one radio channel.

With the advent of wireless digital technologies came the ability to provide more service to more customers using the same amount of spectrum. A variety of digital technologies were deployed and they all provided more capacity using the same amount of radio spectrum. The introduction of digital wireless also added a new dimension to our wireless capabilities. We now had the ability to send and receive text messages, and over the next few years we also gained the ability to use the wireless networks to send and receive packets of data.

The first wireless data networks in the United States became commercial in the early 1990s. There were three networks – two standalone data-only networks and one that made use of the cellular radio channels. Data speeds were in the 10–20 Kbps range and data was used primarily for dispatch of service fleets, public safety departments and, over time, for two-way messaging services for corporate customers [17].

Just as the combination of voice mail and cellular phones resulted in a useful tool for corporations, so too did the advent of the worldwide Web (the Internet) and the ability to send and receive data via wireless devices. Email had been around for a long time in the academic community and then commercially even before the Internet became viewed as a business tool [8]. Now email flourished and instead of being a remote service you subscribed to, it became a service run by your corporation that connected you to all of the others in your company as well as people from other companies. Again, email was seen as a business tool and it was not until much later that email became as popular with consumers as it is today.

Once again, the marriage of two existing technologies – email and wireless – drove the adoption of new devices and technologies. The first wireless email system of record was launched in 1991 by a company called RadioMail [13] and first went commercial in 1992. This system used an HP handheld computer (HP95LX), an Ericsson wireless modem in a carrying case and RadioMail service. You could not use your existing email address for RadioMail, you had to have a second address such as andy@radiomail.com, but you could forward your existing email to your RadioMail account and check your email periodically during the day.

Then in 1999, the first small pager-like email device, called the BlackBerry, was introduced by Research In Motion (RIM) [14] and wireless email began to develop as a major growth area for wireless.

By the late 1990s and early into 2000, corporations and individuals were struggling to keep up with all of their communications services. Typically, we had a home phone number, an office phone number and a mobile phone number. Each of these had a voice mailbox for taking messages and we had to manage all three of these during our normal workdays. Many of us also had a fax machine and one or more email addresses, perhaps one for work and one we used on a personal level. We could also have been using text messaging services, and Instant Messaging (IM) was growing in popularity.

As an industry, we had been struggling with how to manage all of our telecommunications resources for many years. While we were more connected than ever before, we were connected in so many different ways that there was still the possibility that we would miss a very important message or voice mail [4].

New technologies have been introduced into the wireless world that give us faster access to data services, and now we are able to connect our notebook computer directly to our corporate network (using data encryption and other security measures) at about the same speed as our current home DSL or cable service.

The network operators, starting early in this decade, invested billions of dollars into what is known as third-generation technologies or 3G [20]. These technologies provide for more voice call capacity and high-speed data using the same spectrum that was used for the earliest systems. As these 3G systems were built out, network operators once again turned to the corporate world for their first customers.

As before, corporations were slow to adopt these new technologies. For the most part, they were concerned about the security of their data, the cost of the systems and the cost of providing customer support. The uptake for these 3G systems in the corporate world was, therefore, painfully slow and the network operators began turning directly to their consumer customers [23]. They had to start generating revenue on these new networks and since corporations were not willing to take the risk, network operators began offering products and services such as ringtones, games, music downloads and even video, all aimed at the consumer marketplace.

For the first time in the history of wireless, the migration to a new technology was not being driving by the corporate world but by teens, moms and families who quickly embraced these new entertainment options.

While there were corporate devices in the marketplace – PC Cards for data use, smartphones and BlackBerrys – more emphasis was being placed on the consumer customer than the corporate customer. Starting in late 2006, network operators began to see a decent return on their capital investment from the consumer applications and services they were offering and now they are returning to paying more attention to business customers [24].

3. Today

Today's business community is facing new telecommunications challenges. The Internet has become deeply ingrained in our society, and most corporations use the Internet not only for their own Websites but also as a conduit to conduct business around the world. Email has become as important, if not more so, than voice communications, and yet we are still faced with the same problems surrounding interoperability that we faced more than a decade ago.

The telecommunications industry has recognized this and is working toward providing solutions to many of these issues. The word being used to describe the steps that have been taken and those that will follow is "convergence." In the case of telecommunications, convergence has come to mean that we are heading for a world where all of our communications channels will be interconnected, all of our information will be available via a number of different routes and channels and all of our messages, both voice and data, will be available to us in a single place [9].

Just as the FCC had a vision a decade ago when it auctioned the PCS spectrum, we have a vision about where convergence will ultimately take us. The wired and wireless industries are being brought together by the Internet, not necessarily the Internet itself, but the Internet Protocol or IP. Our historically switched wired and wireless networks are replacing their switches with IP routers and smart computer back-end systems, and all new wireless technologies will support IP over the airlink. The ultimate vision is that we will have an all-IP world, which will make it easy to connect and interconnect different types of communications into a synergistic set of services [7].

Our wireless phone will become only one of the many devices we will use to access our voice and data resources, whether they are for business or leisure, and our device will also be our command-and-control center [19]. Just as we use a remote control today to change channels on our TV, our wireless device will enable us to interact and control many of the devices and services around us. We will be able to access our banking services, use our phone for purchasing services and materials, check the status of our home, check the location of our children and, of course, take charge of our business life no matter where we are.

The expanded vision of convergence includes our primary wireless device being our gateway into the business world. As we approach a computer – any computer – it will communicate with our wireless device and that computer will become "our" computer for the period of time we are using it. We will be able to access all of our corporate data services, check the status of a shipment for our client and, since our wireless device will know where we are and what we are doing, it will work with the smart IP-based networks to manage our wired and wireless phone calls, voice mails, emails and other communications. When we are in our office, calls will be directed to both our wireless phone and our desk phone. When we are at home, they will be directed both to our home phone and our wireless phone or, more likely, we will be using our wireless phone as our home phone and our business calls can be directed to our voicemail.

We will be able to read or listen to our voice mail, read or listen to our email and respond to both either in written or spoken form. We will be able to use our wireless command-and-control device to route any data, say a PowerPoint presentation, to anyone anywhere in the world and to interact via voice, text and email with groups of co-workers or family and friends. We will be able to receive updates regarding our appointments and travel services as situations change.

The convergence that will make all of this and more possible, will include location-based services – the ability to know where you are and what you are doing. This is not a big brother type of scenario, but one where your location is important when it comes to the information you are receiving or have access to.

This convergence is also the convergence of wireless and wired services including cable, DSL and fiber, and access to multiple networks with the ability for your device to determine the most appropriate network for the task you need to perform at the time you need to perform it.

We will have access to all of the information we want and need no matter where we are including traffic reports [26], turn-by-turn directions and company data access as well as entertainment in the form of mobile TV [10], audio and live news and information we have requested that will be sent directly to us.

We will have a single phone number that will serve all of our needs and we will have a multiplicity of devices, some designed for specific functions and some that will serve multiple purposes [29]. Voice and data will be interchangeable and we will be able to access the Internet and other information by typing or speaking commands. We will be able to download entertainment to one device and redirect it to others, and we will be able to receive updates on subjects and issues we are interested in. All of this will be automatic and will be accomplished by the smart networks communicating with our smart devices.

This vision is easy to articulate and there is more to it than I have described here, but as you can see, we are truly headed toward a converged world. Some elements of this convergence are already available today, and the reason we are heading in this direction is at least twofold. First, this convergence is intended to make our lives easier and more productive. Second, network operators believe bundling a number of different services such as wired, wireless, TV, mobile TV, data, email, etc., and having all of these services tightly integrated and on a single bill, will result in more customer loyalty. Once they have captured us as a customer, we will not be as willing to move to a different provider.

4. Starting small

As with all visions, while it is easy to verbalize where we are heading, it is more difficult to detail the timeframe and to understand the steps we will have to take in order to achieve the vision. Certain elements are available today and many companies are working diligently at implementing more of the services and features discussed above, but as with any market-driven set of technologies, different companies will be providing different solutions to achieve the same goal: common telecommunications services across all types of communications networks.

Let's explore some of the moves toward convergence that are available today. Convergence is coming at us from the consumer side outward and from the corporate side as well. On the consumer side, Verizon Wireless and AT&T Wireless are already offering bundled services that include home phone service, high-speed Internet access, multiple TV channels and, in some cases, wireless voice and data services all bundled together and all on a single bill. For the most part, today these services are standalone services. It is the bundling of the service charges and the discount that is offered if you subscribe to two or more services that represent the beginnings of convergence. This first, early type of convergence is driven by pricing and the assumption that if you receive this type of service bundle you will remain a customer for a longer period of time.

Next in the world of wireless networks is the beginning of a trend that will continue both for consumers and in the business world. T-Mobile has a product called HotSpot @Home [25]. This is a Wi-Fi router installed in your home and connected to your existing DSL or cable service. You need to subscribe to the HotSpot @Home service in addition to your standard T-Mobile wide-area voice and data service and you need a handset that works on both the T-Mobile network and Wi-Fi. Once you have such a device and you enter your house, HotSpot @Home will transfer your voice and data services to the Wi-Fi connection and your phone will switch to Wi-Fi mode, at which time T-Mobile will integrate your Wi-Fi connection into its wide-area network.

The advantage for customers is that they receive wireless coverage inside their home where they might not have T-Mobile coverage, and T-Mobile keeps you as a customer. Once you are at home, you are not using the wide-area network and more bandwidth is freed up for other customers. This system also works with T-Mobile's hotspots at Starbucks and other locations, and it can be configured to take advantage of Wi-Fi hotspots in other locations as well. This service could also be used inside a business, but so far, T-Mobile is not going after that market.

The other method being deployed to provide in-building coverage uses what is called a Femto Cell [5]. A Femto Cell is a small, self-contained cell site designed to extend coverage of the wide-area network inside a home or small business. Sprint Nextel has launched the first Femto Cell service in the United States in several markets. Its Femto Cell costs the customer a onetime fee and can handle up to three phone calls at the same time. The current version of the Sprint Femto Cell does not support data services.

While these two different types of services may be aimed at adding coverage inside buildings, they are a part of the move toward convergence. Since the ultimate vision of convergence is that we will all carry a smart device that can be used anywhere, both Wi-Fi and Femto Cells will play a role in this convergence over time. Part of the objective of having full convergence is that we should be able to live in an always on, always connected world. Today, as we all know or will discover, we live in an always on and sometimes connected world. Femto Cells and Wi-Fi access points tied into wide-area networks are one more piece of the convergence puzzle.

In the business environment, a number of different techniques are being used to provide the first steps toward convergence. As more companies replace their traditional PBX systems with Voice over IP (VoIP) PBX systems made by Cisco and a growing number of other companies [2], these PBX systems based on the Internet Protocol can be easily incorporated into a wide-area wireless network. This integration provides several advantages. First, when a desktop extension is dialed either from inside the company or outside, the call will be directed to both the desktop phone and the individual's cell phone.

Next, it is possible to combine both the wireless network's voice mail and the company's voice mail into a single voice mail system that can be accessed via wired or wireless phones.

It is also possible with this type of integration to provide direct extension dialing from the wireless phone when it is within range of the PBX system in the office. That is, you would be able to dial a four-digit extension rather than a ten-digit number followed by the extension after the system answers, just like on your office desk phone. You also have access to all of the other features and functions provided by the PBX system including conference calls, call forwarding and any other built-in functions.

There are several companies working with corporations to provide wide-area voice and data access inside corporate buildings and on enterprise campuses. Some of these systems will require wide-area network Femto Cell-like radios to be installed in the corporation, some will make use of the existing wired network with Wi-Fi extensions and some will be a combination of both. One of the advantages of this type of system is that it can provide access to both voice and data and the data can be sent over the company's high-speed connection to its destination without having to use the wide-area network. Again, this frees up some of the wireless network operator's limited bandwidth for other customers.

On our way to full and complete convergence, there are many steps to be taken. Convergence, or the idea of combining various telecommunications systems and functions, is not new. However, until now, each network and type of network has been different enough that tying them together has been difficult to impossible. With the advent of IP back-end solutions for both the wired and wireless worlds (as well as the cable industry) [22], some of these issues are being resolved and the ability to work cross-platform is becoming easier.

Convergence is a vision that will provide advantages to both the customers and the network operators as it is being implemented over the course of the next five to ten years. Customers will benefit by being able to combine various mailboxes into a common and easily accessible single solution that can be accessed via voice or data services. Services will be less expensive by virtue of being bundled with a common bill for multiple services and, over time, the system will provide for the ability to modify the services to fit a specific set of needs or requirements. Network operators will have customers who are less likely to churn off their systems as well as the opportunity to sell the customers more services across the various platforms, thus ending up with a larger percentage of customers' telecommunications and entertainment budgets.

The advantages of convergence for a corporation are better overall communications for its workforce, fast response to its customers, cost savings on a per-person basis and the ability to provide a single secure point of access to all employees. Again, the advantages for network operators include customer longevity and the ability to up-sell additional services.

Convergence is also about these new services. Wireless network operators are concerned about being relegated to the role of wireless pipes with others being paid for the information that flows over their wireless networks. The wired telecommunications community has essentially been relegated to the role of a pipe already while the content providers are making money.

Convergence, it is hoped, will provide both the wired and wireless operators opportunities to sell additional services and increase their revenue per customer in both the consumer and business communities.

5. The Internet and convergence

Perhaps one of the most misunderstood elements of the convergence trend is how the Internet will play into our overall telecommunications future. At the moment, those who are talking about taking the Internet wireless are envisioning just that – whatever we can do on our desktop computers today as far as Internet access goes, we should be able to do with wireless devices with smaller screens and smaller keyboards. Thus this aspect of convergence is generally assumed to be simply part of the information that will become available to us as we move toward a more converged world.

The reality will have to be very different for a number of reasons. First is the fact that wireless spectrum is a finite resource – we cannot make any more of it, we can only use what we have more efficiently. However, we are restrained by laws of physics that cannot be broken. Next is the fact that wireless bandwidth is shared bandwidth, regardless of whether it is wide-area bandwidth or a single Wi-Fi access point.

As an example, an access point located at a Starbucks is connected to the Internet via what is called a T1 line. The total data capacity of this line is 1.54 Mbps. Therefore, the total data speed available from this access point is 1.54 Mbps and not the Wi-Fi data rates that can be considerably higher. The T1 line is referred to as the choke point in a system. The maximum amount of data available for a given site is not necessarily based on the data speed and capabilities of the wireless link, it could also be limited by the backhaul to move the data to the Internet.

If you are the only customer in the Starbucks who is making use of the Wi-Fi access point you will have access to all 1.54 Mbps of data speed. However, if there are nine other customers all using the same access point, you will be sharing the total available bandwidth with them. This does not mean you will only receive one-tenth of the bandwidth since you are using a packet-data system as are the nine others who are also using the access point. Your packets are co-mingled on the data channel and most likely you will be operating at a speed of about half of the total available or around 700 Mbps, which is still fast enough to complete your work. However, if three or four of the other customers making use of this one access point are using it to stream IPTV or some other form of video, you will find that your data speed will be much slower.

The same thing applies to a wide-area network. Each cell site is divided into sectors (usually three) and you share all of the bandwidth available in that one sector. This bandwidth is also limited by the amount of bandwidth available to carry the data from the cell site back to the network. But now, instead of sharing your data connection inside a store the size of Starbucks, you will be sharing your data access with anyone using the network who is also in the same cell sector (some cell sectors cover several miles). In addition, the further you are from the cell site, the slower your data speed will be [27].

These types of shared bandwidth issues are generally not a problem when you are on a dedicated wired connection from a DSL line, but if you use a cable modem, you have exactly the same problem since your data speed is dependent upon how many other customers in your neighborhood are making use of their cable modems, and for what purposes. If you do make use of a cable modem, you have probably experienced this phenomenon of data speed fluctuation, but it will be more pronounced using a wireless modem.

The next difference between the Internet and a wireless network has to do with network management. In a wireless network there is always a network operations center that is manned on a 24 × 7 basis. There are software packages that are running and constantly checking the status of the network – how much voice and data is being used, where there might be a slowdown and even if someone is using their wireless connection to download a lot of video or other high-bandwidth content. The center has the capability to look at every cell site in the network as well as every device on the network. It can see the status of the network at all times and has the capability to turn off a customer who is using too much data for too long a period of time.

The network operation center's job is to load balance the demand on the network in order to be able to serve as many customers as possible. This type of management is becoming easier as the newer technologies offer quality of service (QoS). QoS enables the network operator to assign data speeds and customer access on a tiered or priority basis, which we believe will result in new pricing models for various levels of QoS. In the meantime, it is at the network operations center where the health of the network is constantly monitored and changes are made as necessary to continuously optimize the available bandwidth.

Another issue with wireless networks is that there are only two ways to add bandwidth. The first is to have more spectrum available at a cell site so if that site becomes heavily used, the network operator can add more radio channels and provide more bandwidth. The second and more common way to gain additional capacity is to build more cell sites closer together. This is an intensely time-consuming and expensive proposition. On average in the United States, it takes most wireless network operators about three years and a few $100K to build out a new, large cell site. Many cities and counties are slow to respond to a request for a permit and even slower when they hold public hearings on the proposed cell site [21].

There are other issues with the bandwidth available on a wireless network, but these are the major ones when it comes to bandwidth constraints. Turning to the Internet, we see that it is an unmanaged network that no one has any real jurisdiction over, and while its bandwidth is limited – and the Internet is becoming busier – it is far easier to add access and bandwidth to an Internet site than it is to build a new cell site. eBay, for example, can add a few more servers and then run another fiber connection from the servers to an Internet portal and it is finished.

Because it is so easy to add bandwidth for the Internet, those in the Internet and computer communities who believe we can simply move today's Internet experience to our wireless devices do not understand these issues nor do they understand that when we are out of our offices and away from our desks we simply do not have the time to duplicate our desktop Internet experience on our wireless devices. Finally, they seem to think that the Internet is a destination. In reality, it is another network connected to thousands of different destinations including back to our own corporation's data stores.

Part of the convergence experience as we progress is to make information easily available no matter what type of device we are using or where we are. Therefore, it is my belief that we need a new Internet experience to go along with our converged world. This new, wireless Internet would be smart, making use of smart devices across smart networks that are IP-based. Instead of having to initiate a search for some information we might want or need, our existing applications should be smart enough to understand what it is we are looking for and then use the network to find this information without any action on our part. Here is one way it might work: Today, if you have a flight to New York in your calendar on your desktop and you are using a smartphone, chances are that data is sent to your smartphone and displayed on a calendar there. If you want to check on the flight, you have to exit your calendar, open your browser, type in the URL to your airline, usually click on several windows to drill down to the page where you enter the date and time of the flight and what you get back is a snap-shot in time of the status of your flight.

What if once it was entered into your calendar, the smart network would continue to check on the flight in the background, providing you with gate changes, upgrade request information and perhaps even placing a weather icon on your calendar telling you the weather conditions at your destination? Next, you have entered information on the calendar concerning a rental car and a hotel location and sometime during your travels, turn-by-turn directions would be automatically acquired and added to your calendar. Further, if your plane was running late, the system would notify the rental car company, your hotel and even your client if you were going to be late for a meeting [3].

There is a big difference between the Internet Wirelessly and the Wireless Internet. In the process of converging our communications links, we also need to address smarter ways to access our data on a variety of different devices. The smaller screens and keyboards of our wireless devices require a rethinking of our access requirements.

6. Moving forward with your own convergence strategy

While there is a vision of where we will end up when we truly have total convergence of all of our telecommunications needs, it will not be smooth sailing between now and then. There will be mistakes along the way, and there is really no market research for where we are heading. Moreover, convergence means different things to different people and groups of people. If you are an enterprise IT professional, you may or may not care about convergence extending beyond your corporate requirements to those of your workforce for their own use.

However, one thing that has been proven over the course of the past few years is that field workers and business professionals who are given wireless access to all of their voice and data services tend to work longer hours and be more productive during the hours they are working. In that case, it makes sense for corporations to take into consideration both the corporate and personal needs of the employees when it comes to converged services.

For a corporation, the first step toward full convergence that makes sense is to integrate your PBX with your wireless service providers' networks. If you have an IP PBX, this is not a difficult task and can be accomplished using a system integration house such as IBM IGS or directly by the network provider. You do not need to have a single wireless network operator since your PBX can be integrated with several networks almost as easily as one. Verizon Wireless, AT&T Wireless and Sprint Nextel all advertise their ability to do this type of integration. There are also a number of companies that specialize in this type of integration and a quick search on Google will provide a listing of these companies. Be sure to check out references prior to signing a contract with any company. Also, do not be talked into a long-term contract with today's pricing plans. Wireless voice and data pricing will be changing over the course of the next few years [28] and it should be possible to have your PBX and wireless services fully integrated and have a contract that entitles you to price breaks over time.

The benefits of this first level of integration, as discussed above, include direct extension dialing even when using the wide-area wireless network, common voice mailboxes, both phones ring when there is an incoming call and the wireless handset can make use of all of the PBX's features such as conference calling and common address book access.

Another strategy for voice and data integration is to make use of your existing local-area network and add Wi-Fi access points, then purchase combination Wi-Fi/wide-area phones. The issue with this option at the moment is that VoIP over Wi-Fi is not ready for full commercialization. The T-Mobile HotSpot @Home technology does not use VoIP, but rather standard GSM wide-area wireless voice that is wrapped in an IP "blanket" and meets the UMA standard (Unlicensed Mobile Access).

The bottom line with convergence is that it will become easier over time and you will be able to achieve higher levels of integration as IP back-end systems are more widely deployed.

Do not start on a convergence project simply because it is the next big thing in telecommunications. You need to have a business plan and model that shows a positive return on investment over a relatively short period of time [6]. We are in the early stages of convergence and there are many different approaches today with more on the way. Convergence can save you money, it can make your voice and data services more effective for your workforce and it can move you ahead of your competitors.

Remember too that it is good for your wireless network operator since you will be less likely to change wireless networks when they have been integrated with your PBX system. Another area of convergence for data that is worth exploring is to have your wireless network operator install microcells inside your facility that will give you wide-area coverage inside a building for both voice and data services but not interconnection between your PBX and the wireless network.

7. Conclusions

"Convergence" has become a buzzword in the telecommunications industry. It is the merger of a number of different technologies and one of the few advances that benefits both wireless network operators and their customers.

One of the reasons Verizon Wireless did not split into two separate companies (one serving the wired customer base and one serving wireless customers), and that the new AT&T combined several wired phone companies with its wireless company (Cingular), is because both companies believe in the power of convergence and are working toward this goal. Sprint Nextel has chosen to offer its own version of convergence using cable company partners and its new WiMAX network offerings, however, it appears as though its focus at the moment is aimed more toward the consumer than the enterprise customer. Other companies can put together convergence packages for enterprises, but those that offer all of the services under a single company name will continue to have an advantage because of the level of integration in their back-end plant facilities.

The industry has a vision of what the final outcome of convergence will be, including the ability to use multiple networks and multiple devices and to have the same level of service across a broad range of technologies. The vision is based on a set of smart networks and smart devices that will help manage all of our telecommunications requirements on an ongoing basis, saving time and money in the process.

But we are still in the early stages of the convergence process and much work remains to be done before we reach the goal of a ubiquitous, converged world. New technologies are coming online in the 2009/2010 timeframe, IP systems are replacing today's switched networks and, as we head toward an all-IP world, voice and data services will be co-mingled. With voice over IP, when it is truly ready for wireless commercialization in a few years, the cost of delivering both voice and data will be less, the cost of the services to the customer will be less and the integration or convergence of voice and data services will be easier. In the meantime, decision makers are urged to move forward cautiously and make sure all of their questions and concerns are being addressed.

8. Summary

The convergence of communications systems, both voice and data, holds two major implications for the corporate world. The first is a cost savings, as part of the early convergence momentum is to combine wired, wireless and broadband services into a single bill that is discounted if a customer chooses to subscribe to all of these services from the same vendor.

However, the most important aspect of telecommunications convergence is that it centralizes all forms of communications – voice, data, video and other services – and it simplifies the management of telecommunications resources since there is now a single point of focus for both voice and data messages. Corporate employees can stay more organized and save time when accessing voice, data or even video capabilities.

This paper explains first, how new technologies were the purview of corporations but are now being implemented for consumers first and business customers second. However, telecommunications providers still realize that their highest value revenue comes from corporations and they have now begun to refocus their attention on the business market.

The implications of this for corporations are that the pace of telecommunications convergence will quicken, and pricing for services will continue to drop. This also means that corporations need be mindful of several facts: that technology is changing rapidly, the migration from 2G to 3G wireless networks happened in half the time it took to migrate from 1G to 2G, and the move toward the fourth generation of wireless technology is happening even more rapidly.

This does not mean corporations should take a wait and see attitude, rather it means they should make sure their providers are giving them terms that are flexible and do not tie the corporation to fixed pricing for service levels for long periods of time. We are headed toward an all IP world where all voice, data and video will be handled as bits on many different networks and routed to the appropriate device, over the appropriate network at the appropriate time. We will experience various levels of difficulties as we advance toward this goal, but we can lessen the grief for ourselves and our companies by understanding that these changes are coming and avoiding being locked into one set of technology solutions going forward.

References

[1]   Broadband PCS Auction Rules, *Mobile Phone News*, 1994.
[2]   Cisco Systems White Paper. IP Communications: Considerations and Benefits.

[3]   B.L. Dewey, Active Content. *Andrew Seybold's Outlook*, October 1999.
[4]   B.L. Dewey, Universal Access (p. 15). *Andrew Seybold's Outlook*, May 1999.
[5]   Femtoforum, www.femtoforum.org.
[6]   I. Hayes, *Just Enough Wireless Computing,* Yourdon Press Computing Series, 2002.
[7]   G. Henderson, *IMS: The Catalyst for Service Convergence Across Wireless & Wireline Networks,* TMCnet, 2005.
[8]   B.M. Leiner et al., *A Brief History of The Internet,* The Internet Society, October 1998.
[9]   MIT Enterprise Forum of the Northwest, Implications of Convergence in the Wireless Industry, 1998.
[10] A.A. Reiter, Jeff Pulver says real-time personal mobile broadcasting is coming of age in 2008. February Reiter's Mobile TV Report, 2008.
[11] E.M. Rogers, *Communications Technology*, The Free Press, 1986, 138.
[12] A.M. Seybold, Cellular as a PCS System, *Andrew Seybold's Outlook on Communications and Computing*, July 1995, 1.
[13] A.M. Seybold, Wireless Services Part II, *Andrew Seybold's Outlook on Mobile Computing*, August 1993, 13.
[14] A.M. Seybold, Mobiltorial, June *Andrew Seybold's Outlook*, 1993, 1999, 17, 22.
[15] A.M. Seybold, *Using Wireless Communications in Business,* New York: Van Nostrand Reinhold, 1994, 111.
[16] A.M. Seybold, *Using Wireless Communications in Business,* New York: Van Nostrand Reinhold, 1994, 142.
[17] A.M. Seybold, *Using Wireless Communications in Business*, New York: Van Nostrand Reinhold, 1994, 32–36, 51.
[18] A.M. Seybold, Wireless Data University (slide 156). Source CTIA, 2004.
[19] A.M. Seybold, How Many Screens. *Wireless Week*, 2005.
[20] A.M. Seybold, March Andrew Seybold University, 2005.
[21] A.M. Seybold, *The Big Question: Why Do We Need More Cell Sites?* White Paper, 2005.
[22] A.M. Seybold, Improve IMS – Don't Replace It. *Commentary*, July 2006.
[23] A.M. Seybold, The Six Myths of Wireless Data: Merrill Lynch Q-2-07 Report Data. Andrew Seybold University, 2006/2007.
[24] A.M. Seybold, Andrew Seybold University (slide 154), 2007.
[25] A.M. Seybold, Convergence T-Mobile Style. *Tell It Like It Is*, November 2007.
[26] A.M. Seybold, Real-Real-Time Traffic Information. *Commentary*, November 2007.
[27] A.M. Seybold, Taking the Internet Wireless. *Commentary*, September 2007.
[28] A.M. Seybold, Sprint Says It, Verizon Does It! *Commentary*, February 2008.
[29] A.M. Seybold, Wireless: 300 Percent Penetration. *Tell It Like It Is*, January 2008.
[30] S. Shepard, *Telecommunications Convergence, 2/e How to Bridge the Gap Between Technologies and Services.* McGraw-Hill, 5.
[31] The History of Voice Mail (undated). *Everything Voicemail*.
[32] US International Trade Commission. *Global Competitiveness of US Advanced Technology Industries: Cellular Communications* DIANE Publishing, 1993, 2–3.

Andrew M. Seybold is one of the world's leading authorities on technology and trends shaping the world of wireless mobility. With more than forty years of experience in the computing, wireless communications and mobility industries, Mr. Seybold is a respected analyst, consultant, commentator and active participant in industry trade organizations. As such, his views have influenced strategies and shaped initiatives for telecom, mobile computing and wireless industry leaders worldwide. Mr. Seybold has and does serve on a number of advisory boards including Motorola's prestigious Visionary Research Council. He is widely known throughout the wireless communications industry for his keen perspective as well as his track record for accurately predicting trends in mobile wireless technology and convergence. Mr. Seybold is a frequent speaker at leading industry events and at corporate events for Fortune 1000 companies and was elected a Fellow in the Radio Club of America (2000) for his contributions to the wireless data industry. Mr. Seybold provides consulting, education, newsletters, and speaking services to the wireless and mobility industries as well as to organizations making use of the technologies to enhance their own businesses – his worldwide consulting client base reads like a who's who of these industries. Mr. Seybold has published three books, and regularly writes for leading industry publications as well as producing his weekly *Commentary* e-newsletter and *TELL IT LIKE IT IS* blog. Mr. Seybold produces a number of conferences and events throughout the year including Andrew Seybold Wireless University sessions held in conjunction with the CTIA on a twice-yearly basis. Oft quoted, and sought after as a speaker, Mr. Seybold is regarded as one of the driving forces in the wireless and mobility industries today and over the years has become known for telling it like it is, and being able to distinguish fad from trend.

Information Knowledge Systems Management 7 (2008) 25–37
IOS Press

Business mobility: A changing ecosystem

Mary McDowell

Nokia Corporation, 102 Corporate Park Drive, White Plains, New York, 10604, USA

Abstract: This paper examines the evolution of the still-nascent business mobility ecosystem and its key drivers, such as consumer behavior, that shape the segment. It also explores the changing roles and relationships of the ecosystem's key players; projections for growth in business mobility; and the value or ROI of business mobility. It offers advice to businesses that are considering business mobility solutions. And it points out a number of changes that members of the business mobility ecosystem will need to make in order for business mobility to evolve to the point of fruition, where companies are willingly ready to purchase solutions as a strategic investment, and where the solutions are as solid but also as flexible and easy to buy and integrate in a heterogeneous, global market. Lastly, the paper takes a look at a few large companies that have made significant steps toward strategic and holistic adoption of business mobility.

Keywords: Business mobility, ecosystem, mobile growth drivers, ROI

1. Introduction

While early cell phone adopters used hand-held devices for communicating with their managers, coworkers, suppliers and customers, the devices were insufficient for conducting meaningful business in a secure mobile environment. There was no e-mail component, no scheduling capabilities, no way to manage a personal computer's address book, and – most important – no network security.

Nonetheless, opportunities for personal use got people excited about wireless communication, and helped build a critical mass of consumers hungry for more mobile applications – especially e-mail, gaming and other favorite electronic activities. Consequently, unlike more traditional rollouts of technology in business settings, the end user has always been at the forefront of mobility.

Individual consumer demand has sparked the widespread use of mobile technology in ways that enterprise demand might never have. Today, we see how the Internet and Web 2.0 capabilities such as FaceBook and Second Life have created a cultural and generational gulf between "digital natives" and "digital immigrants." Now, business users, who are also everyday consumers, are insisting on Web 2.0 or Web 2.0-like tools and services in their business lives.

Exploring the evolution of the still-nascent business mobility ecosystem, this paper examines:

- The foundations of business mobility and its key drivers, such as consumer behavior;
- The changing roles and relationships of the ecosystem's key players;
- Projections for growth in business mobility;
- Return on investment in business mobility; and
- Three case studies of business mobility today.

2. The foundations of business mobility

What was it that attracted early adopters to mobile communication? Probably *not* that it enabled their managers to interrupt weekends and vacation days with calls to beaches, backyards and soccer fields. In fact, personal applications were the big attraction: the ability to be in touch with their families throughout the day; to be able to call for emergency road service without leaving their cars; to check sports scores and stock prices; to phone home from the grocery store because they forgot their shopping lists; and to exchange text-messages with friends and family.

The mid- to late-1990s saw the growing trend toward wider corporate distribution of mobile phones to employees – or the decision to support a wider range of models, with the aim of improving productivity and efficiency. This opportunistic adoption may be considered the first phase of business mobility. At the time, analysts and academic researchers predicted enormous growth in years to come [7]. Today, such growth is occurring.

Eventually, enterprises started taking a greater interest in mobile applications after individual consumers demonstrated a strong desire to go wireless – and after applications for reading e-mail remotely on PDAs were introduced. Executives immediately saw the benefit of being able to read e-mail away from the office and the PC, and demanded that their IT departments supported the PDA-based solutions. That spurred greater interest among knowledge and other mobile workers.

Today, businesses are integrating mobile technologies in varying forms and complexities within their IT infrastructures – and the workforce is increasingly reaping the benefits. Similar to the way in which consumers' Web 2.0 behaviors have led to the rise of social networking tools and blogs within the enterprise, the demand for mobility is largely driven by end-user enthusiasm and engagement.

While consumer demand drives business mobility, it is not the same consumer demand that historically drove mobility among individual consumers. Local area networks (LANs), wide area networks (WANs) and smart-phones bring the promise of business mobility closer to reality, but organizations moving toward mobility will demand more from the business mobility ecosystem – and ecosystem members will have to collaborate in new ways, compete against one another at times, rethink their revenue models and in some cases, retool their strategic objectives.

2.1. Driving mobile growth

According to a recent Gartner study "until 12 months ago, wireless e-mail had been a sort of 'elite group' application, most often deployed for and used by executives in large organizations. During the last year, this situation changed: a 'democratization' process has begun that will bring wireless e-mail to many mobile devices, and business and consumer users will adopt it massively. There are 15 million business e-mail users worldwide (that is, about 2 percent of total business e-mail accounts); by year-end 2010, the number of wireless e-mail business users will grow to 130 million (0.7 probability). By yearend 2010, the total number of wireless e-mail users, including business users and consumers, will exceed 350 million worldwide (0.7 probability)" [2].

E-mail is the predominant gateway to business mobility because the practicality of mobile access to e-mail is so obvious. Mobile e-mail, like land-line e-mail, doesn't have an easily quantifiable return on investment. It is hard to tell how much more productive or valuable it makes an employee. Nonetheless, generally speaking, most of us would agree that mobile e-mail is an important business tool. Already, many organizations – especially those with an employee population working in the field – could barely function without it. And many who choose not to implement it will find themselves at a competitive disadvantage in the coming months and years.

Increasingly, businesses that have discovered the value of mobile e-mail realize it is only the tip of the iceberg and are looking to mobilize other mission-critical applications such as field repair or delivery – which do have a direct and measurable ROI.

Peppard and Rylander [9] predicted that in the future, handheld mobile devices connected to telecommunications networks will be a critical way to gain access to content in digital format. However, a number of concerns still limit a wider adoption of wireless e-mail. Unsurprisingly, security tops the list. The inherent complexity of mobile technologies – in particular, the continuous introduction of new products and the lack of standardization in the space, together with the significant impact on IT departments in terms of management and security – raises many issues that have influenced enterprises to put off making key strategic decisions in this area. But ease of discovering, buying and implementing solutions are also barriers to more widespread adoption.

Mobile devices will continue to be the vehicle for communicating in a number of methods and accessing a variety of business and personal services and capabilities. These devices will likely continue to become even more highly intuitive with interfaces that support a wide array of services as well as productivity and personal applications and tools (e-mail, calendars, cameras, music players, etc.). In this respect, in order to keep current with Web 2.0 technology and user expectations, devices need to offer a combination of beauty and brains, all the while delivering an uncompromised user experience. Services and applications should be easy to discover, purchase and use. That means not only designing mobile device interfaces to support current and future services, but making it simple to integrate services and applications such that the experience is easy for the end user as well as the IT manager.

3. Ecosystem members and their changing roles

In a recent analysis, the telecommunications and software consulting firm Ovum found that mobile applications face slow growth despite the segment's most successful vendors having been in business for five or more years [3]. There have been significant hurdles to overcome. However, conditions are now ripe for growth – and for this market to extend itself beyond a niche market and early users – from opportunistic toward strategic and ultimately holistic adoption.

When considering drivers of mobile growth, Ovum attributes investment by carriers and other players in the ecosystem. Carriers have begun to take the mobile application space seriously and are creating the structures that are necessary to enable rapid growth of mobile applications. Carriers are forming partnerships with software vendors, offering incentives and training their sales teams and actively pursuing the opportunity. Since carriers are generally the major sales channel for mobile solutions, this is beginning to provide a major piece of the puzzle for greater corporate adoption of mobile applications.

Superficially, the business mobility ecosystem may appear familiar – device manufacturers, network operators, systems integrators, IT providers and value-added resellers (VARs), each specializing in a product or service that, when combined, enable mobile communication. But their relationships to one another are changing. For example, in a dramatic and potentially industry-changing development, Internet carriers are joining the business mobility ecosystem as the Internet replaces mainframes and operating systems as the primary platform through which data travels. Roles are shifting, revenue models changing, new business models emerging [1,7], new risks emerging and new opportunities are presenting themselves in a more complex, open, competitive and heterogeneous environment.

In the past, device makers limited themselves to manufacturing and selling mobile devices and appealing to end-users through usability and aesthetics; and they partnered with network operators to offer mobile solutions.

Today, differentiation at the device level is based on a combination of elements. While integrating more advanced technologies such as dual-mode (cellular and wireless LAN, for example) is one obvious path for remaining competitive, the look and feel of the device is as important as what is under the cover. Users want devices that are smart, intuitive, suited to both business and personal use, and look good. This remains true in both mature markets such as Western Europe and the US, and in rapidly emerging markets such as India and China, where lower price points do not necessarily negate the value of aesthetic appeal to end users. A variety of models with a range of features and price points is also critical. Whereas in 2006 India was still considered largely an entry market, it is emerging as a market with higher average selling prices and replacement purchases. Rural, central Africa is in large part bypassing traditional wire line and personal computing infrastructures and leap-frogging to adopt the latest wireless technologies; mobile devices are used for a variety of applications ranging from simple telephone communication to determine latest livestock selling prices for remote farmers, to banking their income.

As important as the device's looks and intelligence are, its accessibility in the market and its ability to support a variety of applications are paramount.

Traditionally, the market's primary players had a fairly straightforward arrangement: device makers built the hand-held units, and operators or retailers put them into the hands of end-users. For example, in Europe where the global system for mobile communications (GSM) standard has prevailed for years, customers have traditionally had more choice in devices and increasingly in service providers, because virtually all handsets were compatible with the GSM standard. In the U.S. sales were primarily through operators – and devices were often branded or co-branded by operators. Retail purchase choice was limited to the devices that were compatible with the operator's network standard.

In that model, network operators such as AT&T, Verizon and Sprint shared the space: they built and maintained networks on which mobile data traveled, each with their own standard. Each member of the ecosystem had a role, a revenue model and its own unique value on the supply chain. Overall, the ecosystem was relatively uncomplicated: members – each with their own set of core competencies – brought the fruits of their efforts to the table and cooperated with one another to sell to consumers.

3.1. New relationships, new rules, new complexities

As business mobility becomes a necessity, and as convergence becomes a reality, the ecosystem is becoming more complex, as well – and the relationship between members more delicate. In some markets, the retail shop is the dominant route to market, as well as the service and repair point. In others, carrier branded or co-branded sales remain prominent, with the carrier increasingly becoming a solution provider, offering integrated applications.

In the business mobility ecosystem, device makers can no longer rely on sales of just one model to maintain market share. They have more partnerships, more competition from inside the ecosystem, heavier demand for new products and services that meet a variety of end-user needs and more complexity in their device sales. These manufacturers may be involved with multiple partners, including carriers, VARs, IT integrators – in sales training, support, even helpdesk operations. Their involvement will require new commitments, new investments and new revenue sources – and in some cases, willingness to both partner with and compete with the other members in the ecosystem.

As the demand for mobility solutions grows at the individual user level as well as at the business level, virtually all players in the business mobility ecosystem will be faced with the challenge of offering a variety of more personalized solutions. Two paradigms are emerging; first is the need for virtually all resellers to offer flexible, easy-to-use solutions at the device level. This means the ability to offer multiple services with an intuitive user experience, on multiple devices from multiple vendors. Unlocked will take on a new meaning, where consumers and business users alike will demand an uncompromised user experience.

At the same time, emerging solutions that support multiple radio technologies and emerging standards and applications will be an increasingly important part of the mix. Such is the influence of the many forms of convergence, too: fixed-mobile convergence (FMC), voice and data, personal and professional applications.

For example, Voice-Over-Internet Protocol (VoIP) routes phone calls through the Internet, not through cell towers. The inevitable convergence of Internet, cell, cable and land-line services created more opportunities, but it also created the prospect of lost revenues in traditional business models. As business mobility increasingly becomes a necessity, it adds further complexity to the ecosystem. The result: wide-open market opportunity for all players, new business models, and wide-open competition across the converging Internet, carrier, hardware, and software players in the expanded ecosystem.

Not all businesses and business users have the same needs. Corporations are heterogeneous; a holistic adoption of business mobility will require a seamless integration of features on a single screen. The newest mobile devices are "unlocked" and able to be used in multiple solutions with hundreds of VARs, network integrators, carriers and other members of the business mobility ecosystem. In some ecosystems, VARs continue only to sell products. For now, their models are not changing. Others are moving toward a solutions model where they provide not only handsets to corporate or individual consumers, but a range of services as well.

3.2. Challenges to ecosystem revenue models

Business mobility market participants already collaborate in numerous ways in the development of products – and they cooperate to offer simplified solutions to the enterprise. Carriers are important both as customers and as channels for applications and software and solutions developers and hardware manufacturers. System integrators also are key partners in the value chain because they select hardware and develop the software and service packages that become long-term licensing and service agreements for applications developers and carriers.

While revenue sharing does occur, there is currently a natural division of revenue between implementation services (hourly or project fees for integrators and consultants), software licenses, hardware purchases and carrier services. As the business mobility market matures, however, the lines between these streams will blur. For example, more software will be delivered as a service by various players (including hardware vendors, carriers and system integrators) and more hardware will be delivered pre-configured or easily configurable with applications. In many cases, enterprises are already acting as their own system integrators, and – in a few cases, such as in the utilities industry – as their own network operators.

Openness and standards will remain important as the converging mobility, Internet, IT, entertainment, software, and other industries continue to broaden the ecosystem.

Clearly, mobile access to the Internet means more than simply retooling Web sites so they look better on mobile devices. What mobile users really respond to is not some stripped-down version of the Internet, but a fourth screen that more closely resembles what they are used to experiencing on their PCs or TVs, such as the ability to read an entire Web page on a small device – or even watch a movie or TV show or play a game.

But are corporations actually moving toward a holistic approach to mobility? While many workers are no longer tethered to land lines, *business mobility* means more than just a cell phone connection and remote e-mail.

4. Business mobility: A priority for many organizations

In a recent Forrester survey, respondents said they expected mobile voice, equipment and data services spending to grow to 29 percent of telecom and networks budget – up from 26 percent in 2006 [8]. According to Forrester, enterprises are bullish on spending: 63 percent plan to increase mobile data spending and 56 percent expect to increase voice spending. Almost half of the survey respondents ranked setting a mobile strategy and policy as a priority for 2007. Meanwhile, centralizing management of mobile devices is a priority for 41 percent of the respondents. Interestingly, less than a third of the respondents ranked either of these as a low priority – suggesting that mobility is important for most enterprises.

One potential stumbling block: without a strategy, firms will continue to cobble together "one-off" solutions and never experience the true value of mobility. For vendors to be successful in the mobility space, they will need to demonstrate how they can help clients build and execute a business mobility strategy that integrates mobility with the customer's existing wired infrastructure, incorporates both voice and data, and extends beyond basic (cell phone, e-mail, contacts) access to provide end users access to their information and one another in a secure, "always-on" environment and with a user experience that is without compromise.

Rather, today's mobility offers connectivity to a limited set of users with a relatively small number of applications. Going forward, vendors will need to help their enterprise customers identify which applications or processes make the most "mobile sense." By creating case studies and implementation guides, vendors can help firms use mobility to improve business processes with lessons learned from early mobility pioneers such as FedEx and BP.

Consulting firm PricewaterhouseCoopers (PwC) projects the business mobility market in the U.S. will surpass $100 billion in 2009 [10]. PwC believes the most successful business mobility businesses will have an open model that encourages innovation through strategic alliances and partnerships. The model it envisions demonstrates a willingness to sacrifice short-term control in favor of long-term growth. For example, application developers may compete directly with one another in customizing a solution for one company or a set of companies with similar interests, while simultaneously partnering to develop a high-volume, packaged solution offered through a carrier.

Ultimately, PwC believes the business mobility market will enable business transformation on a grand scale to a large customer base. Mature, standardized applications and pervasive high-speed connectivity to employees, vendors, customers and other enterprises will impact a wider array of business processes than ever before and generate new mobile business models reminiscent of today's Enterprise Web 2.0.

5. Return of Investment (ROI) of business mobility

How is the value of business mobility measured? A recent industry study conducted by the Economist Intelligence Unit (EIU), a leading global research and advisory firm, polled senior-level decision makers at global 1,000 companies to find out how their organizations were using business mobility. The survey revealed that far from being deployed in "bleeding-edge" technology firms or relegated to niche or vertical industries, business mobility is now broadly applicable to companies across industries [5].

From revenue gains to improved workforce agility, collaboration, and the ability to attract and retain top talent, the power of mobility can be applied in many ways to drive value to the enterprise. Taking a closer look at the ROI of business mobility, following are highlights from the EIU study, including direct quotes from some of the surveyed executives.

5.1. Key indicators of ROI

Over time, the population of mobile workers has steadily expanded. According to the EIU study, nearly 40 percent of executives surveyed said that at least one in five of their company's workforce could be considered a "mobile worker," spending an average of one day per working week away from the office.

As business mobility makes headway into organizations and more advanced applications and processes are mobilized, the reasons behind companies' mobility adoption can vary from traditional ROI benefits to more contemporary values such as employee retention.

EIU survey respondents were asked to consider several ROI measures and state whether their organizations currently used them or planned to do so within the next two years. After reduced physical infrastructure costs, executives most frequently said they would be looking for better collaboration with customers and better access to colleagues or external partners as key indicators of ROI.

Goals related to work-life balance have also entered into executives' ROI calculations, where mobility is a means to attract and retain top performers by offering greater flexibility and empowering employees to work remotely. Almost one-third of surveyed organizations already track work-life balance programs; about one-quarter plan to do so within two years.

Aligned with these results, surveyed executives were also asked to identify the top three challenges to their future competitive strategies:

– The need to attract and retain talent within their firms;
– The ability to respond more quickly to customer needs; and
– The need to quickly identify and communicate any noticeable changes in customer behavior.

In addition to driving bottom-line results, the EIU survey shows that organizations are increasingly focusing on new and sometimes non-financial measures of ROI.

5.2. Hard benefits

Some of the traditional ROI measures for mobility include reduced real estate costs, faster sales cycles, lower costs associated with remote training and overall financial performance. For package delivery leader UPS, for example, business profitability is top of mind when decision-makers there evaluate the effectiveness of their mobility strategy – and the nature of the logistics business makes mobility standard operating procedure at all levels of the organization. At UPS, the "sales force is highly mobile, which has significantly improved the bottom line. Mobility has allowed salespeople to skip going into the office to print out their daily or weekly call list with all the other documentation. Because of this real-time effect, (sales people) can do bids on the fly now" [5].

Organizations like UPS expect business mobility to yield a rich payoff, and mobile solutions are used throughout the company. In fact, UPS views mobility as part of the normal business day and does not differentiate between drivers or corporate managers. According to the company, "everyone is mobile" [5].

5.3. Soft benefits

Three-quarters of EIU survey respondents pointed to human factors such as attracting the best talent, improving customer service and building brand reputations as reasons for deploying mobility [5].

With a large and distributed sales force that is constantly exchanging information with its customers, mobility could not be more important to pharmaceutical leader Novartis. Each day, the company supports several thousand field employees in North America, realizing the benefits and operational gains offered by business mobility. The company invested very early in wireless capabilities for the sales force and found that from a "productivity viewpoint, it was a big win" [5].

In addition to mobilizing its field sales force, Novartis has also applied mobility to employees across the business as a means to attract and retain top talent by offering better work-life balance. Giving employees more control over how they want to work – in an office environment, at home, or a mixture of the two – has become a competitive advantage for the company.

Novartis also provides its field-based employees with high-speed Internet access at home. This allows sales representatives to upload their daily work faster, and enables the company to offer online training on drug products, regulations, medical procedures and other issues.

Far from being ends in themselves, such mobility initiatives are viewed as keys to staying competitive. Asked to identify the main competitive factors pushing their organizations toward greater mobility, surveyed executives cited factors involving person-to-person contact among colleagues or with customers as being greater concerns than traditional benchmarks such as reduced downtime or lower physical infrastructure costs [5].

5.4. A new approach to business mobility

When organizations first started giving mobile devices to their employees, most believed only special-ized workers at technology companies would benefit from having such tools. Mobilizing a workforce was perceived to be costly, complex and a security nightmare.

However, the EIU survey suggests that these beliefs are largely becoming relics of the past, putting to rest some of the old myths that once called into question the promise of a mobilized workforce, namely, that:

- Mobilized workers were a specialized subgroup of employees who represented a small fraction of any organization's overall workforce;
- Mobilizing an organization's workforce was always a costly endeavor that might not be offset by the savings from resulting efficiencies and benefits; and
- Employees using mobile solutions could not securely connect to the company network to access corporate data, making them a threat to the integrity of a company's most critical information.

Surveyed executives decisively rejected these assertions, along with the belief that mobile work means being "always on" and a threat to work-life balance [5]. At the same time, they revealed mobility is not without its hurdles, although most seemed focused on cultural and managerial issues rather than business ones. The single largest obstacle cited by executives was the challenge of learning to manage a mobile workforce. Even so, less than 20 percent of those surveyed selected that answer. Closely related to managing mobile workers was maintaining a cohesive organizational culture across scattered workforces.

The survey shows that executives are coming to grips with other dimensions of the organization that might benefit from greater mobility. For example, executives pointed to the need to identify new business processes and applications to mobilize as significant tasks for the future.

6. Business mobility applications: Some examples

As ecosystem members jockey for new footing, and as devices and networks emerge promising more robust and secure mobile environments, embedded or easily downloaded applications, how are leading-edge organizations moving toward true business mobility? Here are examples of how three organizations are using business mobility applications to improve efficiencies, increase effectiveness, and maintain their competitive edge.

6.1. Mobility in the media

Recently, a European news agency made a shift toward mobility so it could gather and transmit news more efficiently. Based in Munich, Germany, Bayerischer Rundfunk (BR) has been the state broadcaster for Bavaria since 1948 and was a founding member of the Association of Public Broadcasting Corporations in the Federal Republic of Germany (ARD) in 1950. It is currently the fourth-largest ARD member organization, with about 2,900 employees. There are more than 6.3 million radios and nearly 5.4 million televisions registered in its geographic area.

BR runs its own five radio stations and its own TV channel, and contributes to the joint ARD channel Erstes Deutsches Fernsehen. Structurally, BR is broken down into legal, radio, TV, administrative and technical directorates.

Mobility is of key importance to most media operations because information needs to be researched, gathered and transmitted quickly. This applies in particular to the journalists from BR who report from all over the world. They need to send their reports to the editorial teams as quickly as possible, and the administrative staff needs to be accessible when they are away from the office – which occurs frequently.

BR sought a unified and flexible system for its mobile communications. A number of requirements from various departments had to be considered. For instance, mobile synchronization of contact and calendar details was necessary to maximize standardization between the IT system and the mobile devices. Another requirement was that employees had to be able to send and receive e-mail.

The IT department had its own requirement: the operating system had to be open and capable of being integrated into the existing IT architecture easily. The essential applications include receiving e-mail, managing appointments and using the latest address files available. BR's IT infrastructure is based on Microsoft Exchange, a groupware solution that permits comprehensive and varied tasks, such as e-mail and appointment management and the creation of address books.

Employees of BR now have mobile access to their e-mail, appointments and contact details. The staff uses a total of 200 hand-held devices controlled via two servers. Reporters can e-mail up-to-date reports using their mobile devices. Regardless of whether they are at receptions or on a press trip, or if a court reporter wants to send an initial report to the editorial team while a case is in session, the mobile solution enables reporters to extend the information "edge" that the broadcaster enjoys.

The new solution offers many advantages: an up-to-date appointment calendar, an accessible personal phone list, the sending and receiving of e-mail, and – most important for business mobility – integration into the IT architecture. For example, reporters can use their mobile devices to transmit and transfer data in real time. It is also important for staff at the technical directorate to be highly accessible since the IT systems cannot be "down" in a media environment.

There is an alert function running for this reason. This function enables the technical directorate staff at BR to be advised quickly if problems arise. BR management believes it is particularly important for staff to be accessible at all times, and have a high level of acceptance for the application, since central communication functions can be used via mobile devices.

6.2. A single, integrated platform

In addition to media companies, the technology sectors, including telecommunications, have led the way as consumers of business mobility products, including VoIP and security features such as encryption. In most other industries, the first business mobility products were mobile voice and wireless e-mail access via laptop or PDA. Adopted quickly by financial services and professional services firms, today these industries are expanding mobile access to other types of applications and being joined by companies from other sectors such as manufacturing, healthcare, pharmaceutical, biotech and utilities.

The ultimate goal for business mobility: an integrated platform for mobile applications that extend far beyond e-mail – with Internet access, and with ability to support a variety of devices (to suit the end users' preferences) and a variety of applications and services. As in the case of BR, ultimately, business mobility will mean being able to operate a business or do a job using just one remote device – and being able to send/receive attachments, work around a virtual private network (VPN), add a firewall, etc., all on just one screen without compromising security – seamlessly integrating personal life and office life.

Another organization sought an end-to-end global enterprise security solution for its entire enterprise network. Andritz Oy develops high-tech production systems and industrial process solutions for various standard and highly specialized products in five vertical markets: Pulp and Paper, Rolling Mills and Strip, Processing Lines, Environment and Process, Feed and Biofuel, and Hydro Power.

Andritz Group employs 10,000 people at more than 100 worldwide locations. The company manages 35 production facilities and 120 global affiliates and distribution firms, requiring extensive IT and communication resources. Andritz Group sought a collaborator that could provide a comprehensive enterprise offering with the ability to manage and protect a global network and enable mobile employees with the tools and resources necessary to do their jobs effectively and efficiently. Andritz Group's Finnish subsidiary, Andritz Oy, was tasked with implementing a global enterprise security solution.

In addition, the company needed to outfit approximately 800 of its 1,100 employees in Finland with mobile business devices featuring specific applications that allow them to perform necessary tasks in the field. Through a three-way consultation process involving Nokia, Andritz Oy, and reseller Nordic LAN WAN, the companies implemented an end-to-end enterprise solution to meet the customer's needs and expectations. The devices are easy to use, deploy and manage over the air. The solution features wireless e-mail and other mobile business applications; firewalls and VPNs for multiple layers of protection; and professional services and support to help Andritz Oy during the process.

In order to protect their global enterprise network and extend their network perimeter, Andritz deployed nearly 100 firewall/VPN appliances, which combine enterprise-class reliability, market-leading software and a hardened operating system on purpose-built, high-performance platforms. This allowed Andritz to integrate security features into the network and easily deploy and manage those systems. To help provide secure communication and access to information and resources for mobile employees, Andritz deployed Nokia SSL VPN and Nokia IP VPN solutions, which enable authenticated, controlled access to business applications, data and resources from a desktop, notebook, or handheld device. These solutions helped Andritz increase productivity by connecting mobile employees to the enterprise and one another via mobile devices, while protecting proprietary company information and assets.

Because constant communication between on-the-go employees worldwide is necessary, Andritz needed to provide them with reliable devices as well as the necessary tools and applications to communicate easily and perform their jobs effectively.

To accomplish this, Andritz outfitted its mobile employees with hand-held devices, each equipped with a solution involving mobile e-mail, calendar, and contacts, yielding several benefits for Andritz, including:

an easy-to-use interface (essential for going beyond phone calls and e-mail to performing complicated tasks in the field); corporate e-mail compatibility with a variety of e-mail solutions; simple, no-nonsense management of personal information; straightforward text and messaging features enabling instant communication among mobile employees; ease of integration with Andritz's existing infrastructure, leading to fewer disruptions and distractions – and a quicker return on investment; and GSM global connectivity, offering flexibility and cost savings for employees who travel.

The deployment of an end-to-end enterprise offering for Andritz provides a strong base from which Andritz can work with its present and future partners to build out more business mobility projects.

6.3. From three phones down to one

Business mobility holds promise for more than just the technical and media sectors. HSB Stockholm, for example, is a Swedish housing cooperative established in 1923. HSB Stockholm builds, manages and actively strives to create good housing for its members. With more than 155,000 members in the Stockholm area alone, it is one of the major players in its field; nationally, every tenth Swedish home was built by HSB.

With more than 390 tenant-owner associations within its organization, HSB Stockholm receives between 4,000 and 5,000 phone calls every day. And it makes between 3,000 and 4,000 outgoing phone calls. In essence, telephony communication is a critical function for HSB Stockholm's success. Employees manage issues over the phone regarding everything from leaking pipes to building projects costing many millions of euros. Easy telephony and employee availability are key elements to keeping members satisfied and maintaining a steady growth of business.

How employees use telephones differs widely depending on their function within the organization. Some are based at the office, while others roam the Stockholm area visiting member associations and checking the progress of building projects on site. HSB Stockholm previously depended on DECT phones to achieve in-office mobility for its employees. That meant that some employees had up to three phones: a stationary office phone, a DECT phone, and a mobile phone. As the DECT phone system was approaching the end of its life-cycle, HSB Stockholm had to make a decision: either invest more in the DECT system or invest in a mobile communication system for its existing Alcatel switches. The first option would have meant additional costs for new DECT phones and extra base stations. And it still could not guarantee 100 percent in-office coverage.

In the fall of 2006, HSB Stockholm decided to try Nokia Intellisync Call Connect for Alcatel, a solution that integrates mobile devices with the company's fixed telephony infrastructure. It extends desk phone features with one business number to the mobile device. The solution also simplifies the corporate telephony architecture and facilitates in the elimination of overlapping devices, meaning that HSB Stockholm employees could start using their mobile devices as primary business tools.

The solution entails an installable client software application, which manages interoperability with the Alcatel OmniPCX call control platform and provides an intuitive user interface to manage call routing preferences and access in-call services from the private branch exchange (PBX). Some of the most important features used by HSB Stockholm personnel include do-not-disturb, hold/resume, call transfer, consultation call, swap, conference call and private/business modes.

The solution routes the mobile calls made in business mode via Alcatel OmniPCX. The receiving party will see only the desk phone number instead of the mobile phone number. This means that the mobile phone number can be kept for private use. External callers will use the same desk phone number to call in, and the solution manages routing to the mobile device according to user-defined rules. After successfully testing the devices, HSB Stockholm decided to invest in 40 licenses. Over time, they plan to invest in an additional 100 licenses. The DECT phone system was shut down completely in September 2007. Management calls the solution "very intuitive." Users hardly need to read the manual to use the application. The ease-of-use means that employees are more available and more productive.

The prior use of multiple phones was a challenge for achieving effective communication. With the new solution, employees save time and hassle, needing only one hand-held device by their side. Also, DECT phones did not give the employees at HSB Stockholm full coverage in the seven-story office building. With their new device, personnel are now free to roam the office while remaining connected to the GSM or 3G net. However, possibly the most important benefit of such an integrated solution is the increased functionality and user-friendliness of the application. Instead of having to press long and complicated "short" number sequences for different commands, users now only need to choose one of the intuitive icons displayed on the user interface – for example, to transfer or put a routed call on hold.

HSB management sees significant benefits to the new solution. Most important is the ability of employees to stay in touch with members effectively and with greater efficiency.

7. Conclusion

Over the last several years, the pace of mobile innovation has objectively increased, but remarkably little of it actually reaches the broader U.S. mobile user market in a meaningful way [6]. The mobile ecosystem as it currently exists is simply too much of a barrier. Many organizations are currently addressing mobility opportunistically rather than strategically or holistically. Moving to a holistic approach will require members of the business mobility ecosystem to show the IT managers and the business leaders measurable ROI or demonstrate real business value. Without an ROI, IT may not buy in; consequently, without new ways of thinking about revenue splits, there could remain an economic barrier to entry, network coverage may not improve significantly, and usage will likely never move much beyond opportunistic.

A move toward holistic use will also require applications to be simplified, while still supporting multiple device models as well as single mobile device models with multi-channel distribution capabilities and open and extensible and middle-ware.

Similarly, without a compelling, market-driven vision for business mobility, the mobility landscape will remain scattershot, individually-driven – possibly strategic, but not transparent and holistic. This new vision will require ecosystem members to reposition themselves and realign with the understanding that they will cooperate with one another *and* compete against one another.

7.1. Vision and bold experimentation

There are several recommendations for business mobility ecosystem members [4]. These recommendations include:

- Investing to become "a knowledge bank" of business mobility services and solutions: more papers, articles, analyst reports and industry recommendations will appear in coming months;
- Being prepared to provide a seal of approval for mobile applications: the solution provider landscape is crowded and confusing for enterprise buyers – a laundry list of possible partners is even less helpful than providing no direction at all;
- Identifying partners to facilitate a go-to-market strategy: reach out to other value-chain participants to gain greater customer visibility and improve product positioning; and

– Evaluating integrated channel partnerships similar to those formed between the wireless e-mail providers and carriers.

The market could see additional acquisitions. Until recently, a robust go-to-market ecosystem was the missing link in the business mobility value chain. Bringing together a universe of leading channel and operator partners will unlock the true potential of business mobility.

References

[1] R.C. Basole and W.B. Rouse, Complexity of Service Value Networks: Conceptualization and Empirical Investigation, *IBM Systems Journal* **47**(1) (2008), 53–70.
[2] M. Basso and K. Dulaney, *Magic Quadrant for Enterprise Wireless E-Mail Software,* 4Q06 (ID Number: G00144613). Stamford, CT. Gartner Research, 2007.
[3] J. Dawson, *Beyond E-Mail: Mobile Application Lessons from the US Market,* London, UK, Ovum, 2007.
[4] N. Dyer, *Carriers Are Best Positioned in the Enterprise Mobility Value Chain,* DecisionNote Trend Analysis. Boston, MA. Yankee Group Research Inc., 2005.
[5] Economist Intelligence Unit, *Business mobility and the agile organisation: The quest for competitiveness,* 2007.
[6] S. Ellison, *Vendor Needs and Strategies: A 10-Point Strategy for Google to Transform the Mobile Ecosystem and Dominate the Third Screen (IDC #208673),* Framingham, MA, IDC, 2007.
[7] F. Li and J. Whalley, Deconstruction of the telecommunications industry: from value chains to value networks, *Telecommunications Policy* **26** (2002), 451–472.
[8] M.D. Lopez, Buyers Yearn for Enterprise Mobility Leadership. *Trends*, Cambridge, MA. Forrester Research, Inc., 2007.
[9] J. Peppard and A. Rylander, From Value Chain to Value Network: Insights for Mobile Operators, *European Management Journal* **24**(2–3) (2006), 128–141.
[10] PricewaterhouseCoopers, *How to realize the full potential of enterprise mobility,* 2007.

Mary McDowell is Executive Vice President and Chief Development Officer of Nokia's Corporate Development Office, responsible for optimizing Nokia's strategic capabilities and growth potential. She oversees Corporate Business Development, Corporate Strategy, Mobile Software Sales and Marketing, Nokia IT, Office of the Chief Technology Officer, Operational Excellence and Quality, and Solutions Portfolio Management. She has been a member of the Nokia Group Executive Board since 2004.

McDowell joined Nokia in 2004 as Executive Vice President and General Manager of Enterprise Solutions, with responsibility for the development and manufacturing of Nokia's range of enterprise products and solutions. This included the Nokia Eseries mobile business device range, mobility software, and security and mobile connectivity solutions. Prior to joining Nokia, McDowell served as Senior Vice President and General Manager of Industry-Standard Servers at Hewlett Packard and Compaq. McDowell had worldwide P&L responsibility for the multi- billion dollar ProLiant server business, the world's largest server franchise, which held the number one position for over a decade. A 17-year veteran of HP-Compaq, she has a track record of success in building new business and is widely respected as an industry innovator. McDowell holds a bachelor's degree in computer science from the University of Illinois.

Part II: The Changing Nature of Work, Work Practices and Work Environment

Information Knowledge Systems Management 7 (2008) 41–60
IOS Press

A socio-technical perspective of mobile work

Leida Chen[a,*] and Ravi Nath[b]

[a]*Department of Information Systems & Technology, College of Business Administration, Creighton University, Omaha, NE 68178, USA*
E-mail: leidachen@creighton.edu

[b]*Department of Information Systems & Technology, College of Business Administration, Creighton University, Omaha, NE 68178, USA*
E-mail: rnath@creighton.edu

Abstract: Developing an effective mobile work environment is one of the major challenges that many organizations are facing today. Organizations need to understand the myriad of issues that will determine the success of mobile work. These issues can be best studied from the socio-technical perspective in order to gain a holistic understanding of mobile work. The premise of the socio-technical theory is that the social and technical systems are interdependent and must be jointly optimized in order to determine the best overall solution for the organization. Based upon the information gleaned from structured interviews conducted with the Chief Information Officers (CIO) of ten organizations, this study identifies the primary elements of the social and technical subsystems related to mobile work. Additionally, the study provides a list of recommendations for organizations in order to improve their mobile work environment using the socio-technical perspective.

Keywords: Mobile work, organizational culture, socio-technical perspective, wireless technology

1. Introduction

Advances in information technology (IT) have forever transformed the way work is performed. The last few years witnessed unprecedented emancipation of office workers, changing workplace culture, emergence of global workforce, and proliferation of virtual collaboration [21]. Today, one of the greatest challenges enterprises are facing is how to build an effective workforce in a technology-rich, dynamic business environment. Business and IT executives alike need to be aware of the impact of technology on the working style of their growing mobile workers. Mobile workers are defined as employees that use computer and communication devices to access remote information from their home base, workplace, in transit, and at destination [25]. These workers are characterized by a high level of mobility or greater distance from the traditional office, or both. Chen and Corritore [8] used the term "nomadic worker" to describe mobile employees who perform anytime anywhere work. By this definition, mobile workers not only include employees who work remotely but also employees who demonstrate a high level of mobility within the workplace.

The number of mobile workers is on the rise. It is predicted that there will be 61 million mobile workers by 2009 [32]. A 2006 survey found that 44 percent of companies planned to increase their population of telecommuters in the future [6]. While mobile work practices are widespread today, managing and

---

*Corresponding author.

supporting mobile workers have lagged in many organizations. Many companies have not been able to reap the full benefits of this flexible work arrangement because they do not provide sufficient support for creating a successful mobile workforce [34]. One study found that only about half of companies had a policy for managing mobile workers [6]. Therefore, to create a successful mobile workforce, companies must play an active role in fostering an environment that is conducive to effective mobile work.

The concept of mobile work has received increasing research interest in recent years. However, to the best of our knowledge, no comprehensive framework exists that incorporates key issues related to corporate support for mobile workers. It is clear that creating an effective mobile work environment embodies not only technical issues but also social and cultural issues. This study will attempt to fill this void by employing a socio-technical perspective to develop a framework for studying the interaction between the underlying technical and social subsystems of mobile work. The main objectives of this study are:

- to investigate the prevailing practices in supporting mobile workers.
- to identify the major concerns and critical success factors in mobile work.
- to identify the elements of the social and technical subsystems for mobile work.
- and, to provide companies with recommendations for creating an effective mobile work environment.

This study seeks to provide insights into the above mentioned issues by interviewing chief information officers (CIOs) of companies using a structured-interview approach. This paper is organized as follows. The next section will examine the existing literature on mobile work and summarize the main issues explored by the literature. This is followed by a discussion on the socio-technical theory and its applicability to this study. The subsequent section will discuss the research methodology employed. Then based upon the interviews with the CIOs, key elements of the technical and social subsystems with regard to mobile work and workers are provided. Finally, the article concludes with recommendations for organizations on creating an effective mobile work environment and implications of our findings for information systems researchers and practicing managers.

2. Literature on mobile work

The early works on mobile work focused on the new mobile or nomadic computing technologies that made mobile work possible. Such technologies are often seen as both the driver and enabler of organizational transformation, and research in area mostly focuses on how technologies are likely to change the ways organizations accomplish work [33]. Mobile workers are supported by the nomadic computing environment in which nomads have access to computing resources, communication capabilities, and services that are transparent, integrated, convenient, and adaptive [25]. Mobile and wireless technologies extend work beyond the office, and they provide flexibility with respect to both timing and location of work. These technologies support a wide range of employees from field technicians to executives. Key benefits of this computing environment include improved employee productivity, quick response to inquiries, enhanced customer services, and empowerment of field employees [11,18]. Studies also suggest that the value of these technologies lies in their ability to relieve humans from spatial and/or temporal constraints of work [2] and is a function of the user's immediacy of information needs and user mobility [9]. One of the key technical issues discussed in the literature is security. It is widely acknowledged that serious weaknesses exist in the current security policies for mobile workers. A survey conducted by Cisco Systems revealed that a large percentage of mobile workers have not taken the necessary steps to protect their computers and data [39]. Another study [19] found that most executives ranked security the number one obstacle for mobile workers, much higher than other concerns such as cost and the complexity of mobile data solutions.

The social impacts of mobile work practice and the technologies that support mobile work have also gained a lot of research attention. Some studies have focused mostly on the potential negative effects of technologies on employees' quality of life and job performance such as danger (competence-incompetence paradox), anti-social behaviors (engagement-disengagement paradox), distraction, and infringement on work-life boundaries (empowerment-enslavement paradox) [16,17,23,24,28,31]. Jessup and Robey [24] underscored the importance of social issues when studying nomadic computing environments. They claimed that new technologies that enable mobile work practices will inevitably have social consequences at the individual, team and organizational levels. Individuals must redefine what social norms, work and supervision are in this new computing-enhanced environment; teams must find new ways to make themselves efficient with new work cultures and practices. Organizations are urged to redefine social boundaries in this technology-rich environment. Other studies have found that nomadic computing may infringe on employees' work-life boundaries [2,17,23,31]. Specifically, Jarvenpaa et al. [23] described how anytime anywhere work had become "all the time, everywhere work" for some mobile workers. The ease of access to information and people made possible by new technologies is raising organizations' expectation to receive immediate responses from their employees. Researchers predict that the spillover from work to personal life can have long-term negative effects on employees and will eventually lead to a decrease in productivity [13,17].

Recently, a number of studies focused on the cultural aspect of mobile work. Chen and Nath [10] coined the term "nomadic culture" to describe a collection of artifacts, values, and basic assumptions that provide nomadic workers with the flexibility to work anywhere and anytime they need to. In organizations with nomadic culture, same or comparable access to information, support mechanisms, and opportunities are available to nomadic workers regardless of their time and location of work. These organizations not only provide their employees with nomadic computing capabilities, but they also design their business processes, operational procedures, organizational structure, and reward systems around the needs of nomads. Based on the culture model proposed by Schein [36,37], another study operationalized the theory of nomadic culture by identifying the underlying assumptions, espoused values, and artifacts of nomadic culture [8]. This study posits that companies with nomadic culture held the basic assumptions that employees are trustworthy, responsible, and self-directed and that technology is important and has a positive impact on the organization. These assumptions influence a set of employee-oriented (ability to work anytime anywhere is desirable, effective supervision of nomadic workers is possible, and virtual workgroups are effective) and technology-oriented (IT makes employees more effective, and proactively sensing and responding to new technologies are important) espoused value. The assumptions and values are ultimately reflected in the artifacts of organizational support for nomadic workers. The study also found that nomadic culture led to a higher level of employee job satisfaction. This is consistent with the anecdotal evidences observed in many organizations. For example, Best Buy, whose result-only work environment initiative was considered the most resolute among large companies, reported record job satisfaction and productivity among its mobile workers [14].

3. The socio-technical perspective

The socio-technical theory was first conceived at the Travistock Institute in London in the middle of the 20th century [12]. The socio-technical theory implies that any organization or organizational work system consists of two interdependent subsystems – the social and the technical subsystems. The

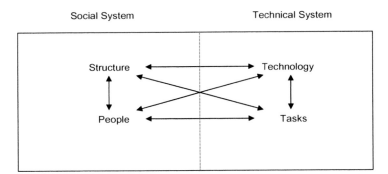

Fig. 1. The Interacting Variable Classes Within a Work System (adapted from Bostrom and Heinen [4]).

technical subsystem is concerned with "the processes, tasks, and technology needed to transform inputs to outputs," and the social subsystem is concerned with "the attributes of people (e.g. attitude, skills, values), the relationships among people, reward systems, and authority structures" [4, p. 17]. Bostrom and Heinen [4] provided the above diagram (Fig. 1) to describe the interacting variable classes within a work system – technology, tasks, structure and people. The socio-technical theory posits that social and technical systems cannot be viewed as independent of each other. The interaction and compatibility between the technical and social systems determine the effectiveness of a work system.

The premise of the socio-technical theory is that the social and technical systems are interdependent and must be jointly optimized in order to determine the best overall solution for the organization. The socio-technical perspective believes that computer-related technology is essentially neutral and that failure to recognize the social system associated with the design and use of technology is the reason why many computer-based information systems fail [4]. The traditional MIS approach focused on the optimization of the technical subsystem and the adaptation of the social system to it. In contrast, the socio-technical theory believes that any redesign of an organization's work system must consider the impact of each subsystem on the other and that the requirements of these two subsystems must be met simultaneously [33].

Research in MIS has always been concerned with the interaction between the technical and social subsystems. The socio-technical approach has been widely accepted as the preferred method for computer-based system analysis, organizational work design, studying the diffusion of new technologies, and measuring information systems quality (e.g. [7,15,30,35,38]. The principles of the socio-technical perspective can also be extended to provide practical recommendations for the design of a flexible, technology-rich work environment. The socio-technical perspective implies that when an organization makes a work process change, both technical and social dimensions must be considered to find the best overall solution. Under the socio-technical perspective framework, the technical and social aspects of the change are jointly optimized. In other words, we should not only be concerned with how technologies transform the way enterprises accomplish work but also the technologies' implications for social and organizational norms in this technology-rich environment. The understanding of these issues will allow organizations to successfully redefine how people should act, interact, and be organized to accomplish work in the new work environment.

In this study, we identify the key elements of both the technical and social systems relevant to mobile work through in-depth interviews with chief information officers (CIOs). The identification of these key elements will allow us to investigate how the technical and social systems can be jointly optimized to create an environment that supports effective mobile work while suppressing the dysfunctional aspects of this new work environment.

Table 1
Interview questions

1. What different types of mobile workers are supported? What are the specific tasks being supported (e.g. virtual team work, remote access from the field, etc.)?
2. Do you have a dedicated IT group supporting mobile workers?
3. What is needed in you organization in order to have success with mobile workers (This includes technical, managerial, organizational, and cultural issues.)?
4. What technologies and technical infrastructure are provided to support mobile workers? What are the main technical issues your organization faces in supporting mobile workers (e.g. security, bandwidth, connectivity, etc.)? How are they addressed?
5. Do you feel that your organization's culture is conducive to effective mobile work? How can it be improved?
6. Does your organization have any formal process by which mobile workers receive appropriate training (both technology-related and non-technical such as work-life balance, danger, antisocial behaviors, distraction)?
7. Has the proliferation of mobile workforce raised any significant issues between the worker and his/her supervisor(s)? Has it led to changes in the ways that mobile workers are evaluated and rewarded?
8. How do you measure success for your mobile work program (e.g. efficiency, effectiveness, retention, job satisfaction, ROI, etc.)?
9. Do you have any corporate-level policy for telecommuters, flexible-work arrangements, and mobile workers?
10. What are the main concerns of mobile workers (e.g. technology-related concerns, work-related concerns, time-commitment concerns, expectation to be reachable anytime anywhere, etc.)?
11. On a scale of 1 to 5, how successful is your organization's support for mobile workers?

1	2	3	4	5
Not Successful	Marginally Successful	Somewhat Successful	Successful	Highly Successful

4. Research methodology

To ascertain the perspectives of chief information officers' (CIO) regarding current practices in mobile work, social and technical support mechanisms for mobile workers, and major concerns related to mobile work and workers, CIOs of ten organizations in a large Midwestern city in the United States were interviewed. These interviews were conducted in person by the researchers using a structured-interview approach. The initial set of interview questions was formed by studying the literature in mobile work, mobile work culture and other pertinent issues surrounding the mobile work environment in organizations. Subsequent brainstorming by researchers resulted in a set of ten questions that were used during the interviews. Table 1 lists these questions. Also included was a general question asking CIOs to rate their organization's success with mobile work and workers using a five-point Likert scale (1 = not successful; 5 = highly successful).

Interviews lasted between 45 and 90 minutes. All interviews were tape-recorded with interviewee consent and were then transcribed. Profiles of the ten organizations where the interviews were conducted are provided in Table 2.

5. Results

The organizations in our study represent diverse industries – transportation, manufacturing, financial services, insurance, etc. They also vary considerably in size with the largest having 52,000 employees and the smallest having 55. The percent of mobile workers range from 15% to 80% of the total work force. In addition, all CIOs rated their success with mobile workers at 3 (successful) or higher.

The transcripts of the interviews were carefully studied by the researchers and the findings are summarized below. They are presented as four cohorts of issues dealing with people, technology, task, and

Table 2
Profiles of sampled Organizations (n = 10)

Industry	# Employees	% Mobile workers	Mobile success (1–5)
Transportation	52,000	80%	4
Technology Services	55	25%	4
Utility	2,700	20%	3
Asset Management	400	15%	4
Insurance	4,000	15%	3
Engineering Services	6,700	45%	3
Credit Services	950	80%	3
Manufacturing	3,000	15%	4
Financial Services	6,500	30%	5
University	1,000	60%	3

SOCIAL SUBSYSTEM	TECHNOLOGY SUBSYSTEM
People: • Types of Mobile Workers • Generational Gap • Social/Behavioral Issues	**Technology:** • Connectivity • Bandwidth • Security • Supporting Mobile Workforce • Limitations of Technology • Keeping Pace with Mobile Workers Demand for Technology
Structure: • Evaluating Mobile Workers • Measuring Success of Mobile Work • Organizational Culture • Other Management Issues	**Task:** • Types of Tasks Performed by Mobile Workers • Dealing with Regulations

Fig. 2. Mobile work: Socio-technical perspective.

structure. Figure 2 lists the elements of the social and technical subsystems of mobile work uncovered during the interviews.

5.1. People

The people aspect of the socio-technical theory pertains to employees and the knowledge, skills, attitudes, values and needs they bring to the workplace. The interviews revealed that the companies support a variety of mobile workers and that the number of mobile workers is expected to increase steadily in the future. Also, the organizations are witnessing a generational gap between younger and older employees in terms of their attitude towards technology, technology needs, and technical skills. This gap suggests that a one-size-fit-all model for supporting mobile workers is not likely to be successful. Social/behavioral issues associated with mobile workers are also discussed.

5.1.1. Types of mobile workers

The results showed that the percentage from one organization to another of employees who are mobile varied widely– ranging from 15% to 80% of the total employees. The percent of remote workers or telecommuters was substantially smaller (less than 2 percent on average). However, CIOs reported that their companies planned to expand the number of remote workers in the future. Besides the commonly cited reasons of organizational flexibility, efficiency, and enhanced quality of work life for remote work, organizations are also positioning remote work as a strategy for recruiting hard to find talent and as a means for "business continuity" in case of a pandemic or a disaster at the work place. As work becomes highly specialized, companies need to be more flexible about where their employees work. Many organizations reported that they accommodate remote employees in order to acquire specific skill sets that are not available locally. One CIO noted that "the flexibility of working at home is a selling point in the tight labor market." Another trend reported by the CIOs is the increasing globalization of mobile workers who travel to or work in foreign countries. These mobile workers face a very different set of technology and task requirements compared to domestic mobile workers.

Sales & Marketing and Information Technology are the two areas where most mobile workers can be found. These jobs can easily be performed remotely with the help of technology and, in some cases, they can be performed more effectively in the field (e.g. client site) than in the office. Traveling executives are another group of employees who work remotely. They want to stay connected and have access to critical enterprise data during their trips. Other types of mobile workers are more industry specific. For example, in an insurance company, underwriters and claim examiners spend a large percentage of their time at client sites. In a bank, financial officers need to approve wire transfers when they are away from the office in order to speed up customer service. In a number of organizations, mobile technology has trickled down from supporting information workers to clerical workers. Originally provided to information workers and executives, mobile work technologies are now seen among clerical jobs. In the case of a railroad company, mobile repair crews use mobile devices to report and download daily work orders.

5.1.2. Generational gap

Most of the CIOs interviewed agreed that a generational gap exists between younger and elder employees. Overall, younger employees are viewed to be more receptive to new technologies and mobile work practices and handle mobile work better because they are accustomed to the technology rich environment. They are more comfortable communicating via electronic channels such as emails and text messages. A number of CIOs felt that a mobile work environment is crucial in recruiting a younger workforce. One CIO commented that "the new workers, between 18 and 30, are looking to come to work in environments where it's exciting. If they don't see any technology, they're not going to be really attracted to this company for very long because it is not going to be viewed as progressive." The CIOs acknowledged that the younger generation of workers is changing the way they think of mobility. Keeping up with younger workers' technology needs and making the work environment attractive to them are becoming major challenges that companies are facing today.

Among older employees, some resistance was witnessed initially when mobile technologies were first introduced in the workplace. Traditionalists voiced their skepticism about the usefulness of mobile devices and mobile work practices. However, in most organizations, employees started to see the value of mobile devices soon after they used them. They found that it was a more efficient way to manage their work. Resistance from management was also seen in some organizations as managers did not think that the employees needed to be mobile to perform their job and that mobility increased the difficulty in managing the employees.

5.1.3. Social/Behavioral issues

Mobile workers face work-life balance issues and feeling of isolation. This finding is consistent with the existing literature, and most CIOs felt that these issues need to be addressed urgently. One CIO noted that "the job is no longer from 8:00 to 4:30 everyday, it's somewhat around the clock. Each individual has to be able to balance that. I think some people will be able to do that while others are going to need more guidance on how to achieve that balance." Addiction to mobile devices was suggested as one of the primary reasons for work-life imbalance. Many CIOs remarked that the work life balance issue is something that the organization and managers need to be sensitive about. It was suggested that to combat this problem, employees need to learn to prioritize and take control. One CIO pointed out that "mobile workers should focus on setting their priorities and not let them be dictated by 'my boss is sending me another email'."

Creating a sense of belonging sometimes can be a challenge with the mobile workforce. One CIO noted that "mobile workers question whether they are part of the team or not. How do you develop camaraderie remotely?" Another CIO commented that "mobile workers don't participate. They miss out on a lot of the intangible stuff that we do." Mobile workers have feelings of isolation as they lose the support network that traditional workers have in the office; therefore, it is important for managers to understand the signs of these symptoms and find ways to address them.

Furthermore, CIOs agreed that training on social aspects of mobile work would help alleviate some of the aforementioned social issues. Nevertheless, only one of the organizations interviewed has formal training on non-technical issues for mobile workers. The CIO of the organization noted that "we touch on the proper ways to use a mobile device in a setting with the customer and not let it become a barrier or distraction. Our organizational development team provides a broad array of training on antisocial behaviors and work-life balance. Culture and teamwork just keep getting reinforced all the time through all of our team-oriented training."

5.2. Structure

The structure construct of the socio-technical theory investigates broader organizational issues such as reward systems and authority structure. Issues relating to this construct include how to evaluate the performance of mobile workers, how to measure the success of mobile work, what policies need to be developed to manage mobile work, what impact organizational culture has on mobile work, and what management issues an organization faces in the mobile work environment.

5.2.1. Evaluating mobile workers

The mobile work environment creates new challenges in evaluating employee performance. All the CIOs agreed that in order to measure the performance of mobile workers, managers must set clear expectations and goals. "Part of employee evaluation is sometimes how they interact in groups or meetings," commented one CIO, "I think it's important that managers are setting expectations that can be measured outside of visual credits." Most organizations stated that they had not adjusted the ways that employees were evaluated for mobile workers. For non-professional jobs, employee evaluation remains metric-oriented, but for professional jobs, as one CIO commented, "there is a bit more of an artistic talent that has to go into that thought process so each one is different." Some viewed this as a potential problem. "We're so locked into measuring our results by hours that you're on the job that we have to change some of these measurements. We have to learn to measure the information workers in terms of their output other than time that they spend at work physically," commented one CIO.

Treating mobile workers fairly during evaluation was perceived as a potential issue by some. One CIO noted that "you really have to be sure that you're treating those employees the same and getting their input on everything with regards to employee evaluations or promotion possibilities. I can see that as being a potential issue in my organization." However, some CIOs felt that positive reinforcement and constant feedback instead of rigid performance evaluation rules worked better in this flexible work environment. One CIO mentioned that, "we want to honor mobile workers on the basis of the positive things that they are doing ... We provide constant feedback on the performance without saying 'if you don't meet that quota, then we're going to take you into the performance appraisal room and show you what you need to be doing.' This is old school management technique."

5.2.2. Measuring success of mobile work

While anecdotal evidence has shown that people are more effective and responsive due to mobile technologies and work environment, most organizations admitted that they were not good at measuring success of mobile work. However, the CIOs acknowledged the importance of measuring success. Measures currently used in our sample of organizations include return on investment (ROI), cost of operation, customer satisfaction, and employee retention. However, none of the organizations employ a comprehensive way to measure all the tangible and intangible aspects of mobile work. One CIO raised an interesting point that measuring success of mobile work is not a priority at this point in his organization: "Right now we really don't want to go down that path. We want people to adopt the technology, to learn it, and not live in fear that they're being constantly measured."

5.2.3. Organizational culture

The extent to which organizations supported mobile workers and their work largely depended upon the culture of the organization and their employees. Organizations need to answer the question of whether they are comfortable with employees not physically being in a space eight hours a day, 40 hours a week. Consider the following comments from two CIOs: "We're a sales-based company so that mentality of the freedom of being on the road and doing what you have to do is pretty much ingrained into our culture;" "The culture is conducive to mobile work because it's sort of a way of life that's happened with us and we can't operate without it." In these organizations, mobile work is more enthusiastically embraced by the management and employees. Employees tend to have high expectation about technology and ask for more mobile applications, more connectivity, and higher speeds. These companies tend to make significant investment in supporting and promoting mobile work, and they have developed more comprehensive policies on managing mobile workers. Employees are viewed as capable, motivated, and trustworthy. This is how one CIO described his organization: "We find that our mobile workers are really smart people and that we can turn them lose on a project and they can make it on their own and get it done as opposed to constantly standing over their shoulder saying: you need to do this next for the next five minutes." On the other extreme are the comments of the CIO of another company that reflect a controlling and inflexible culture: "Our culture says, 'be at your desk, work.' We have a very strong 40 hour mentality. I tell my people, 'you can't work from home, we don't have a work-from-home policy.' You will see managers walking around just to see who is here. This is the culture." In these organizations, mobile work initiatives are not supported by the management and employees tend to resist new technologies and changes in the workplace. Nearly all CIOs noted that the right organizational culture and work environment are the keys to success in mobile work.

5.2.4. Other management issues

A number of additional management issues germane to mobile work and workers were identified during the interviews. These issues and relevant comments from the CIOs are listed in Table 3.

5.3. Technology

The technology construct of the socio-technical theory deals with the devices, tools and techniques needed to transform inputs into outputs. A number of technical issues exist in supporting mobile workers.

Table 3
Other management issues

Issue	Description	Selected comments
Resistance from management	Some managers are uneasy about the new mobile work environment. The mobile work environment requires managers to learn new ways to manage mobile workers. For some managers, the problem is to "let go." Exercising too much control can frustrate mobile workers and create a non-trusting work environment.	"There's some nervousness among supervisors. They say, 'I'm not seeing John everyday so is John really doing what he says he's doing?' There're definitely some cultural shifts for us."
Resistance from tenured workforce	Tenured workforce is uneasy about the changes in the workplace and the new requirements of their jobs. They view the introduction of technology a threat to their job security. All CIOs agreed that top management commitment is essential to making this cultural shift.	"It is a challenge to get tenured people to take the mobile tools out of the office and actually use them in customers' presence as opposed to coming back with their yellow pad and re-keying it all back in."
New skills for managing mobile workers	Managers need to clearly communicate their expectations to mobile workers and put standards in place. They need to help mobile workers deal with behavioral issues that may come with mobile work. They also need to keep mobile workers informed and communicative.	"With mobile work, you end up encourage a lot of autonomy in people. But if you didn't try to put standards in place, it's hard to get consistency across the whole organization." "We are trying to be cognizant of the behavioral issues with those mobile workers, making sure there is an expectation that they are in the office periodically, and they are part of team activities so they don't develop isolationist kind of behaviors." "We have to make sure we have conference calls in on staff meetings so everybody knows what's going on. We have to make sure all of our documentation can be delivered electronically so we can email it to them."
Tendency to manage and lead by emails	Managers sometimes still need to manage people in the old-fashion ways even though the environment has become technology rich. A common mistake that managers tend to make today is managing and leading through emails.	"You need to sit down and talk with your employees about what are causing them difficulties. If you don't do that, you're going to have more and more management issues down the road because I don't think you can effectively manage or lead people through emails."

As one CIO commented, to be successful in supporting mobile workers, the organization needs to have "the willingness and patience to deal with the technology; be able to accept those things that aren't perfect yet, and be able to say we're going to work through all of them." The technical issues include connectivity, bandwidth, security, supporting mobile workforce, limitations of technology, and keeping pace with mobile workers' demand for technology.

5.3.1. Connectivity

Connectivity is the frequently cited technical issue faced by companies when it comes to supporting mobile workers. Wireless coverage can be spotty and unpredictable in some areas, and no commercial network seems to have the perfect solution to provide connectivity in every situation. Due to poor coverage, employees who travel frequently to rural areas often cannot access real time information from the company. Consequently, companies have to work with multiple wireless providers in order to have connectivity for all territories. One CIO said that his company had to build its own communication infrastructure to give its employees access, which can be an expensive endeavor. Vendors' restrictions on the types of mobile devices that will work on their network create an additional layer of complexity. For example, certain mobile devices and air cards only work with certain networks. Most CIOs expressed their desire to be able to have a limited number of network vendors, a limited number of wireless plans, and consistency from a cost perspective. Another issue related to coverage is managing user expectations. One CIO noted that "users take for granted that it's always going to work. There are times when we're not in a range of wireless, so when that happens, people get pretty agitated and say: how am I supposed to do my work?" Finally, supporting mobile workers who travel internationally causes additional complexity.

5.3.2. Bandwidth

Bandwidth requirements depend on the types of applications used by mobile workers and the number of mobile worker supported by the organization. Most organizations have sufficient bandwidth for emails and routine business transactions; whereas, an engineering firm where mobile workers send large architectural designs over the network on a regular basis may experience frequent bandwidth shortage. While business continuity was mentioned frequently as one of the motives for experimenting with mobile work, most companies admitted that they were not prepared to handle a large number of mobile workers in case of a pandemic or terrorist attack.

5.3.3. Security

Security was the top technical issue mentioned during the interviews. The mobility of employees and a variety of devices create a number of security threats to company's data and equipment. Nevertheless, the security threats have not deterred companies from experimenting with mobile technologies. One CIO commented that "it's a risk that we're willing to take, as a business, to extend the technologies and still keep advancing." All companies studied have taken steps to address security threats in its support for mobile workers. Besides security measures commonly applied to desktop computers, the five most common approaches that specifically addressed mobile work security threats employed by companies were:

– Company issued equipment only for data access by mobile workers.
– Encryption of data on mobile devices.
– Virtual Private Network (VPN) access for mobile workers.
– Remote data erase if mobile device is lost or stolen.
– Storing and managing sensitive data centrally instead of storing locally on mobile devices.

All interviewed CIOs agreed that it is extremely difficult to control and manage security with mobile workers. Some comments that allude to this are: "users choose to use their laptops in risky ways such as connecting to an unsecured wireless connection at the airport," "users don't password protect their mobile devices," and "everyone wants convenience but they don't want to go through the security aspect of it. They don't value the security aspect until they lose something." Therefore, educating mobile workers about security and strictly enforcing security policies are essential in enhancing security awareness among mobile workers.

The human aspect of security was also discussed during the interviews. Many companies have shifted their focus on security from protecting their perimeter from the hackers to information theft by internal employees. Random monitoring of mobile workers' activities is a common practice in many companies. One CIO of a financial firm noted that "we randomly monitor what you (employees) are doing in the office and out of the office. We have spent a great deal of money in what I would call big brother type of things to monitor internally." Some companies have strict policies against using company issued equipment for non-work related purposes.

As companies extend their networks beyond organizational boundaries, security issues are also becoming more complicated. The CIO of one insurance company which shares customer information with its independent brokers posed the following questions: "What about client information that's on the laptops of brokers who are not employees of the company? Who is responsible for its security?" The CIOs also suggested that having a business continuity plan in place and evaluating security risks are keys to recovering from security breaches or disasters.

5.3.4. Supporting mobile workforce

All CIOs interviewed agreed that a mobile workforce requires a lot of support, especially technical support. The support responsibilities and functions including initial setup, training, and troubleshooting usually fall on the shoulders of IT infrastructure teams and helpdesks. None of the organizations interviewed currently has an IT group that is solely dedicated to supporting mobile workers. However, some CIOs commented that sometime in the near future this will have to happen. Not having a dedicated mobile work support group is limiting the organization's ability to provide and expand services to mobile workers. One CIO pointed out "that's probably why we haven't put more applications on some of the smaller devices because it's complicated and we don't have the staff to support them." The level of support required also depends on the technology sophistication of the mobile workforce. "Sometimes you've got to show people how to use things five, six times or every time they travel. There are certain people that are technology adverse, especially older employees," said one CIO. Training of mobile workers is one way to help reduce heavy support load from IT departments. It was also noted by several CIOs that younger employees are more accustomed to self-service; therefore, well prepared online help menus and documents are crucial to supporting younger mobile workers.

Supporting mobile workforces has put additional strain on IT departments' resources in many organizations. Due to the nomadic nature of mobile workers, companies are creating new support mechanisms that are outside of the normal channels. IT departments are struggling with the question of how to provide support more efficiently. One CIO commented that "there's a difference between the knowledge base and the doer base. The doer base is an issue for us." Some CIOs also pointed out that it is always difficult to support the international mobile workforce because your support center may not coincide with a mobile worker who is in a different time zone. Getting support to mobile workers whenever and wherever they need it is a top concern of the CIOs. Having a 24/7 around the clock support center to support mobile workers is desired by many organizations; however, most companies are constrained by lack of resource to do so.

5.3.5. Limitations of technology

A number of limitations in existing technology are hampering organizations from supporting mobile workers effectively. Incompatibility between older and newer technologies and between technologies implemented by different vendors is a major technical issue. The CIO of an insurance company which has independent brokers who work with multiple insurance companies noted that "we each have different standards in regards to encrypting information. It would be nice to have a standard out there which right now isn't there. So from that perspective, we're still trying to sort through as an industry." Most business applications today are not designed to function on mobile devices properly due to processing and throughput requirements and screen size limitation. One CIO noted that in his organization "applications are the same whether you're on a mobile device or you're on a 19" LCD screen, so from a convenience standpoint, there's a deficiency in the apps that are supporting mobility. It's just not there yet."

5.3.6. Keeping pace with mobile workers' demand for technology

Keeping up with mobile workers' demand for new technologies and controlling the cost of supporting mobile workers is one of the main concerns of many organizations. One CIO noted that "the whole computing environment that they live in at home and in society has raised their expectations an awful lot. You can have Microsoft Vista running on your computer at home. Well, we're not going to deploy it here for probably two years because we have too many other things that we have to consider." Another CIO noted that "mobile workers want new gadgets every six months not every two three years. The technology outlives the demand or the desire for the technology." Controlling costs associated with supporting mobile work has become a major issue for some organization. A number of CIOs pointed out that "finding out where the bang for the buck is" is the key to keeping the cost in check.

5.4. Task

The task construct of the socio-technical theory studies the specific tasks supported by information technology. The relevant task issues in mobile work are tasks performed by mobile workers and dealing with regulations and industry-specific rules.

5.4.1. Types of tasks performed by mobile workers

A wide array of tasks are performed by mobile workers ranging from email to "just about everything you do at work". The most common task supported is email, followed by access to enterprise transactional systems. Some organizations provide key status information to executives on their mobile devices and access to monitoring systems to IT professionals. Virtual team work in the form of teleconferencing and webminar is also supported by some companies. Other tasks are mostly organizational specific. For example, an engineering design firm supports mobile workers to plan projects and markup designs. Another organization which operates a number of rural clinics supports remote diagnosis by doctors.

The types of tasks performed by mobile workers differ drastically from one organization to another. During our interviews, some CIOs felt that tasks performed by mobile workers had to be a very specific. One CIO equated those tasks to jobs that organizations would consider outsourcing: "if you can package it up in this black box, that's the kind of things you should be able to outsource or do remotely." The nature of the job plays an important role in determining who gets to work remotely and who does not. The CIOs of these organizations noted that mobile workers in their organizations were likely to have well-defined jobs whose efforts were quantifiable. One CIO admitted that he did not assign tasks that are directly related to organizational goals to his mobile workers. However, this view was not shared by other organizations whose cultures were more conducive to mobile work.

5.4.2. Dealing with regulations

Certain regulations and industry specific rules also affect the extent to which mobile work is encouraged in some organizations. One CIO stated that "in the collection business, it's hard to have mobile workers because there are so many regulations around being able to control what people say on the phone and being able to record it." The CIO of a company whose employees are mostly unionized noted that "we run into some of the union rules here if we ask the employees to fix a problem from home, off hour, on weekend, or at night." One CIO explained the issue caused by having out-of-state sales force: "if you allow work at home outside of the states you have your main presence in, you are subject to sales tax in those states. That's going to deter any company from doing it much." Another CIO raised an issue the company was facing with regard to government contracts: "We have a lot of flexibility, but there is still a large focus on working fixed hours. There is the importance of being able to record time because we do a lot of government contracts. This becomes an issue if you're working irregular hours."

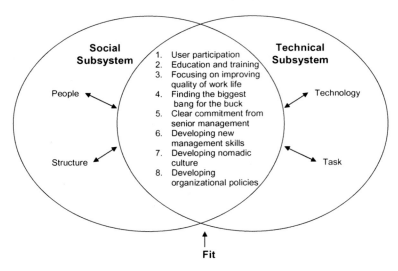

Fig. 3. Recommendations for a socio-technical approach to managing mobile work.

6. Recommendations for a socio-technical approach to managing mobile work

The interviews with CIOs uncovered many key socio-technical issues relevant to mobile work. In many organizations, the difficulty for creating an effective mobile work environment lies in managing the interface between the technical and social subsystems. When properly managed, the interface provides a fit between the two subsystems. Managers should be concerned with the fit between the two subsystems because the imminent technological changes brought by mobile work will likely cause some misalignment. Similarly to other technology-led organizational changes, the misalignment between the technical and social subsystems will lead to negative outcomes such as low morale, decreased productivity, low quality of work, increased conflict and even sabotage, waste, job stress and duplication of effort [27]. It is apparent that successful mobile work can only be designed and managed using a socio-technical approach. This approach requires us to manage not only the social and technical subsystems separately but the interface between the two subsystems as well. Based on the socio-technical theory and insights gleaned from the interviews, a number of recommendations for organizations to support and manage mobile work using a socio-technical approach are outlined in Fig. 3 and discussed below. These recommendations aim to improve the management of the interfaces among the primary social and technical constructs: people, structure, technology, and task.

6.1. Recommendation 1: User participation

One of the key characteristics of the socio-technical perspective is active participation from the user community during the design of both technological and organizational changes [27]. User participation has been consistently found in MIS research to influence the success and acceptance of a wide range of information systems that have led to organizational changes (e.g. [20,22,40]). The mobile work landscape has significantly changed and broadened due to both business needs and technology advancements. One theme that emerged repeatedly during our interviews was that there was not a "one-size-fits-all" solution for all mobile workers. Organizational designers and technologists need to be sensitive to the unique needs of different types of mobile workers. Table 4 is a sample worksheet that can help organizations in

Table 4
Mobile worker needs worksheet

	Fixed Work Hours			Flex Time			On Call / 24/7		
	E	I	C	E	I	C	E	I	C
Local/Office									
Remote Site									
Home									
Travel									
International									

E – Executive; I – Informational Worker; C – Clerical Worker.

understanding the needs of their mobile workers. Mobile workers can be categorized according to their work location (local/office, remote site, home, travel, or international), work hour (fixed, flex time, or call/24/7), and type of job (executive (E), informational worker (I), or clerical worker (C)). For success, each type of mobile workers faces different social and technical issues and requires different technical and organization solutions. Active user participation in requirement determination, technology selection, and policy making will help ensure that the mobile work environment is user-oriented and can meet the social and technical needs of users well.

6.2. Recommendation 2: Education and training

Education and training are two important elements in managing the interface between users and technology. A survey of HR professionals found that mobile workers were not receiving the same level of training and mentoring opportunities as other employees in organizations [?]. Deficiency in employees' skills in the enabling technologies is likely to affect the outcomes of mobile work and their attitudes toward the new work environment. Training has been consistently found in MIS research to improve technology acceptance through its effect on computer self-efficacy (e.g. [1,3]); therefore, technology-related training is helpful in encouraging employees, both young and elder, to experiment with mobile work technologies and reducing user resistance due to low computer self-efficacy. As the literature in mobile work suggested, while mobile work offers unprecedented freedom and potential for efficiency, it has produced numerous side effects such as danger, anti-social behaviors, distraction , and infringement on work-life boundaries [17,23,28]. In the case of Best Buy's mobile work initiative, it was pointed out that educating managers and employees about the new location-agnostic work is imperative for success [14]. Training on how to cope with the social paradox presented by nomadic technologies and new work arrangements will enable employees to work effectively and, at the same time, minimize the negative effects.

6.3. Recommendation 3: Focusing on improving quality of work life

In addition to improving performance, technologies and policies implemented for mobile work, companies should also focus on improving the quality of work life for employees. This includes developing humanistic policies that respect mobile workers' privacy and need for flexibility, establishing evaluation measures that focus on performance, investing in technologies that help mobile workers be more successful, assisting mobile workers avoid dysfunctional social and behavioral issues, and relieving mobile workers from their frustration with technical problems. Mobile workers require a higher degree of corporate support than traditional workers. Organizations should develop a holistic support plan and infrastructure that effectively addresses the key concerns of mobile workers. While most organizations have a plan for technical support, few organizations have formalized non-technical support such as training on how to build camaraderie among virtual team members and how to deal with social/behavioral problems that are likely to surface with mobile work. Behavioral problems such as work life balance can be just as, if not more, distressing to mobile workers as technical issues such as connectivity and bandwidth. Therefore, a holistic plan is necessary in order to improve mobile workers' quality of life in parallel with performance enhancement.

6.4. Recommendation 4: Finding the biggest "bang for the buck"

In an age where organizations are given the mandate to do more with less, resources for various organizational initiatives are scarce and must be utilized wisely. In most organizations, mobile work began as grass root initiatives. Like most other grass root initiatives, mobile work projects often lack strategic visions and long term planning in many of the organizations that we studied. As a result, the solutions are fragmented, and the return on investment mediocre. For example, one CIO commented that "we've taken an approach of a step at a time to support mobile workforce. The best way to improve it would be for us to look at it strategically." Planning mobile work strategically will allow the organization to take a top-down approach to better align business needs and IT investments. It will also allow the organization to develop a holistic game plan that addresses the socio-technical issues related to mobile work. Strategic planning helps the organization determine where the most "bang for the buck" is in mobile work. For an organization to succeed in its quest for agility, one key is to identify the right investment opportunities for mobile work that will deliver superior returns and improve the quality of work life for employees, and that means investing in the right technology to support the right tasks performed by the right people in the right organizational environment.

6.5. Recommendation 5: Clear commitment from senior management

Mobile work is a growing trend in the workplace. The key drivers for this include: gen Xers and gen Yers entering the workforce, globalization, and advancement in mobile technologies. Therefore, it is imperative that organizations adapt to this new paradigm. It would be unwise for organizations to resist these changes as they will inevitably face issues such as failure to recruit or retain high quality employees, inflexible work environment, and stagnant productivity growth. It is important to convey this message to senior management and make them understand the implications of mobile work on the organization's competitiveness. Senior management commitment has consistently been found in MIS research to influence IS success (e.g. [5,26]). Garnering strong senior management commitment will help secure the technological and organizational resources to support mobile work. Without sufficient resources, the major paradigm shifts in technology and organization to support mobile work will not succeed. Senior management commitment will also help set the tone for the organization to cultivate the right cultural environment for mobile work success.

6.6. Recommendation 6: Developing new management skills

Managers need a new skill set to manage a mobile workforce and be comfortable with the flexibility of it. Two areas are especially notable: redefining evaluation and reward systems and redefining the role of supervisors.

Traditionally, due to limited visibility of mobile workers in the office, their promotability becomes limited. Studies have found that remote workers felt that their career path was limited due to their remote work practice even though their performance had improved [29]. To create an effective mobile work environment, organizations must "demolish decades-old business dogma that equates physical presence with productivity" [14]. In order to effectively motivate mobile workers, managers need to develop and use valuation criteria that focus on performance outcomes rather than time spent at the office. Such a focus does not address the where and when of working, or the 'with whom' of working, but only the outcomes of the work. In a technology rich environment, managers must resist the urge of evaluating and rewarding employees based on simple measure of the behaviors and appearance of mobile workers (e.g. How long is the employee connected to the Internet? How many email messages has the employee sent?) [24].

The roles of supervisors in the mobile work environment also need to be redefined. While studying the effect of nomadic work on employee satisfaction, Chen and Corritore [8] realized that the role of supervisory activities in a mobile work environment was more complex than previously anticipated. In a flexible work environment, successful employees are self-motivated and prefer to be self-directed. They turn to their managers for support rather than supervision. Thus, the role of supervisors needs to be shifted from supervision to facilitation. Chen and Corritore's (2008) research also found that simply moving to a mobile work environment without reevaluating the supervisor-subordinator relationship might lead to lower employee satisfaction.

6.7. Recommendation 7: Developing nomadic culture

An effective mobile work environment requires an organizational culture that is conducive to mobile work. Chen and Corritore's [8] research on nomadic culture provided some actionable recommendations for enhancing an organization's culture for supporting mobile workers. For an organization interested in cultivating nomadic culture, besides providing the obvious artifacts (e.g. technologies, policies, and training), it is critical that the organization develop the underlying assumptions and values among its leadership and employees since these assumptions and values will ultimately determine the artifacts and how artifacts are implemented. Two categories of assumptions and values, employee-related and technology-related, were found to be important. Cultivating these values is the key to creating a sustainable competitive advantage based on mobile work-enabling technologies. The positive assumptions and values will eventually lead to more wide-spread and enthusiastic support for nomadic work throughout the organization. As a part of a socio-technical approach, nomadic culture urges organizations to not simply supply their employees with nomadic computing capabilities but focus on designing their business processes, operational procedures, organizational structure, and reward systems around the needs of nomads [10].

6.8. Recommendation 8: Developing corporate policies about mobile work

Developing policies about mobile work was pointed out often during the interview as a key to success in both managing and supporting mobile workers. Nevertheless, none of the organizations studied has a comprehensive policy regarding mobile work. Some organizations have a formalized policy on telecommuting which determines who is qualified to work from home and whether the company or the employee is responsible for the costs related to establishing a home office. Some organizations have policies on the proper and secure use of company assigned computing equipment and data. A significant percentage of the organizations do not have any formal policy on mobile work. They claim to handle issues regarding mobile workers "on a case-by-case basis".

Some organizations choose to maintain a certain level of flexibility in their policies. One CIO noted that "our policy is pretty flexible, and we rely on the person being accountable. If that person can't be accountable and get their work done, then they lose the privilege. We don't punish all because of one." While a flexible policy might be sufficient and conducive to experimentation during the initiation stage, a comprehensive policy is required as more and more social, organizational, and technical issues related to mobile work start to surface. Organizational and divisional level policies will help managers become more effective and maintain a high level of consistency throughout the organization. A wide range of issues related to flexible work arrangement, performance evaluation, compensation, employee monitoring, and security, need addressing in the mobile work environment. And this will require establishing a set of formalized corporate mobile work policies. These policies should focus on identifying humanistic ways of utilizing the new technology-rich and flexible work environment. They should be viewed as tools for protecting the organization (e.g. protecting information security) and its employees (e.g. protecting employees' personal boundary) and maintaining consistency and fairness in mobile work. The policies should also help provide incentives for employees and managers to utilize new technologies and seek opportunities for performance improvement in the new work environment.

7. Conclusion and directions for future research

This study examined how organizations manage and support mobile work from a socio-technical perspective. The structured interviews uncovered a wide array of social and technical issues relevant to mobile work. The interviews suggested that organizations should employ a socio-technical approach to managing mobile work. Based on the issues gleaned from the interviews and socio-technical theory, this study makes eight recommendations to organizations that want to enhance its mobile work environment. In addition to providing normative recommendations to practitioners, this study has made significant theoretical contributions to the study of mobile work. It has demonstrated the appropriateness of utilizing the socio-technical theory for studying the mobile work phenomenon and identified key relevant socio-technical issues. The findings of this study provide future research in this area with a solid theoretical framework. One specific interesting avenue for future work would be a broader survey of organizational mobile work practices and issues in order to triangulate and expand the findings of this research. As an exploratory study, this research uses a qualitative research methodology to identify potential issues related to mobile work. A quantitative research methodology such as a survey study can be useful in identifying issues from a larger population of organizations and mobile workers. Furthermore, in-depth case studies of organizations with mobile workers are needed to further validate the proposed socio-technical approach and discover organizational-specific issues.

References

[1] R. Agarwal, V. Sambamurthy and R.M. Stair, Research report: the evolving relationship between general and specific computer self-efficacy – an empirical assessment, *Information Systems Research* **11**(4) (2000), 418–430.

[2] S. Balasubramanian, R. Peterson and S.L. Jarvenpaa, Exploring the implications of m-Commerce for markets and marketing, *Journal of the Academy of Marketing Science* **30**(4) (2002), 348–361.

[3] J.C. Bedard, C. Jackson, M.L. Ettredge and K.M. Johnstone, The effect of training on auditors' acceptance of an electronic work system, *International Journal of Accounting Information Systems* **4**(4) (2001), 227–250.

[4] R.P. Bostrom and J.S. Heinen, MIS problems and failures: A socio-technical perspective PART II: The application of socio-technical theory, *MIS Quarterly* **1**(4) (1977), 11–28.

[5] S.A. Brown, N.L. Chervany and B.A. Reinicke, What matters when introducing new information technology, *Communications of the ACM* **50**(9) (2007), 91–96.

[6] CA Magazine, Checking in on the mobile office, *CA Magazine* **136**(8) (2006), 12.

[7] P. Carayon and B. Karsh, Sociotechnical issues in the implementation of imaging technology, *Behavior & Information Technology* **19**(4) (2000), 247–262.

[8] L. Chen and C. Corritore, A theoretical model of nomadic culture: assumptions, values, artifacts and the impact on employee job satisfaction, *Communications of AIS* (2008), forthcoming.

[9] L. Chen and R. Nath, A framework for mobile business applications, *International Journal of Mobile Communications* **2**(4) (2003), 368–381.

[10] L. Chen and R. Nath, Nomadic culture: cultural support for working anytime, anywhere, *Information Systems Management* **22**(4) (2005), 56–64.

[11] L. Chen and R. Nath, An empirical examination of the impact of wireless local area networks on organizational users, *Journal of Electronic Commerce in Organizations* **4**(2) (2006), 62–81.

[12] A. Cherns, The principles of sociotechnical design, *Human Relations* **29**(8) (1976), 783–792.

[13] N. Chesley, Blurring boundaries? Linking technology use, spillover, individual distress, and family satisfaction, *Journal of Marriage and Family* **67**(5) (2005), 1237–1248.

[14] M. Conlin, Smashing the clock, *Businessweek* (December 11, 2006), 60–68.

[15] J. Cooper, N. Gencturk and R.A. Lindley, A sociotechnical approach to smart card systems design: an Australian case study, *Behavior & Information Technology* **15**(1) (1996), 3–13.

[16] K.C. Cousins and D. Robey, Human agency in a wireless world: patterns of technology use in nomadic computing environments, *Information & Organizations* **15**(2) (2005), 151–180.

[17] G.B. Davis, Anytime/Anyplace Computing and the Future of Knowledge Work, *Communications of the ACM* **42**(12) (2002), 67–73.

[18] M. Drew, Bringing enterprise mobility to industry, *Manufacturers' Monthly* (December, 2006), 28.

[19] T. Ernest-Jones, Pinning down a security policy for mobile data, *Network Security* **6** (2006), 8–12.

[20] J. Hartwick and H. Barki, Explaining the role of user participation in information system use, *Management Science* **40**(4) (1994), 440–465.

[21] R.D. Hof, Technology on the March, *BusinessWeek* **4047** (2007), 80–83.

[22] B. Ives and M. Olson, User involvement and MIS success: a review of research, *Management Science* **30**(5) (1984), 586–603.

[23] S.L. Jarvenpaa, K.R. Lang and V.K. Tuunainen, Friend of foe? The ambivalent relationship between mobile technology and its users, in: *Designing Ubiquitous Information Environment: Socio-Technical Issues and Challenges*, C. Sorensen, Y. Yoo, K. Lyytinen and J. DeGross, eds, Springer, New York, 2005, pp. 29–42.

[24] L.M. Jessup and D. Robey, The relevance of social issues in ubiquitous computing environments, *Communications of the ACM* **45**(12) (2002), 88–91.

[25] L. Kleinrock, Breaking loose. *Communications of the ACM* **44**(9) (2001), 41–45.

[26] W. Lewis, R. Agarwal and V. Sambamurthy, Sources of influence on beliefs about information technology use: an empirical study of knowledge workers, *MIS Quarterly* **27**(4) (2003), 657–678.

[27] N. Margulies and L. Colflesh, A socio-technical approach to planning and implementing new technology, *Training and Development Journal* **36**(12) (1982), 16–29.

[28] C.A. Middleton and W. Cukier, Is mobile email functional or dysfunctional? Two perspectives on mobile email usage, *European Journal of Information Systems* **15**(3) (2006), 252–260.

[29] M. Olson, New information technology and organizational culture, *MIS Quarterly* **6**(4) (1982), 71–92.

[30] S.C. Palvia, R.S. Sharma and D.W. Conrath, A socio-technical framework for quality assessment of computer information systems, *Industrial Management & Data Systems* **101**(5) (2001), 237–251.

[31] E. Prasopoulou, A. Pouloudi and N. Panteli, Enacting new temporal boundaries: the role of mobile phones, *European Journal of Information Systems* **15**(3) (2006), 277–284.

[32] RCR Wireless News, Ranks of mobile workers continue to grow, *RCR Wireless News* **24**(16) (2005), 30.

[33] W.B. Rouse and M.L. Baba, Enterprise transformation, *Communications of the ACM* **49**(7) (2006), 67–72.

[34] N. Sale, The way we will all work, *Global Telecoms Business* **93** (2007), 66–67.

[35] S. Sawyer, J.P. Allen and H. Lee, Broadband and mobile opportunities: a socio-technical perspective, *Journal of Information Technology* **18** (2003), 121–136.

[36] E. Schein, Coming to a new awareness of organizational culture, *Sloan Management Review* **25**(2) (1984), 3–16.

[37] E. Schein, *Organizational Culture and Leadership*, 2nd ed., Josey-Bass, San Francisco, 1992.

[38] A.B. Shani, R.M. Grant, R. Krishnan and E. Thompson, Advanced manufacturing systems and organizational choice: sociotechnical system approach, *California Management Review* (1992), 91–111.

[39] VARBusiness, Mobile users pursue risky business, *VARBusiness* **22**(22) (2006), 51.

[40]   B.H. Wixom and H.J. Watson, An empirical investigation of the factors affecting data warehousing success, *MIS Quarterly* **25**(1) (2001), 17–41.

Lei-da Chen is an Associate Professor of Information Systems and Technology in the College of Business Administration at Creighton University. His research and consulting interests include electronic commerce, mobile e-commerce, and diffusion of information technology in organizations. Dr. Chen has published over 50 professional articles in refereed journals and national and international conference proceedings. He is also the co-author of a book entitled *Mobile Commerce Application Development*.

Ravi Nath is the director of the Joe Ricketts Center and the holder of the Jack and Joan McGraw Endowed Chair of Information Technology Management in the College of Business Administration at Creighton University. Before joining Creighton University, he was on the faculty of business administration at the University of Memphis where he served as the Associate Dean for Academic Programs and Director of the Ph.D. program in Management Information Systems. Dr. Nath has a Masters degree from Wichita State University and a Ph.D. degree from Texas Tech University. He spent the 1991–1992 academic year lecturing and conducting research in Zimbabwe as a Fulbright Scholar. He has published over 80 research papers in the area of Electronic Commerce and Information Systems in various national and international journals. Dr. Nath serves on the Board of Directors of several for-profit and non-profit organizations.

Information Knowledge Systems Management 7 (2008) 61–75
IOS Press

Designing productive spaces for mobile workers: Role insights from network analysis

Camille Venezia[a,*], Verna Allee[b] and Oliver Schwabe[c]
[a]*Formerly with Workforce Research, Knoll, Inc., 3304 Bryker Drive, Austin, TX 78703, USA*
E-mail: camille@veneziaenterprises.com
[b]*Value Networks, LLC, 1012 Folsom Street, Suite 386, San Francisco, CA 94103, USA*
E-mail: verna.allee@valuenetworks.com
[c]*Value Networks, LLC, 1012 Folsom Street, Suite 386, San Francisco, CA 94103, USA*
E-mail: oliver.schwabe@valuenetworks.com

Abstract: Workspace design has not been keeping up with the evolving needs of mobile workers. Although the economic benefits of mobile work have been expanding for companies, few companies have mobile worker strategies that seriously address how new ways of working require different kinds of physical space, mobile devices, and office equipment. Popular mobile worker "myths" about the work they do, what they need when they are in the office, and even gender and age have led to costly mistakes in office design and installations and technology purchases. This paper presents findings from a mobile workforce study, in which value network analysis was used to define the roles mobile workers play, map the ways they interact with others and explore how this interaction impacts technology and workspace needs. The insights gained from this approach are helping workplace designers, technology providers, and workspace managers better meet the real needs of workers and use resources more effectively.

Keywords: Mobile workforce, mobile worker roles, value network analysis, knowledge management, workplace collaboration, physical work environments

1. Introduction

Over the past decade, the number of workers who spend a significant portion of their time away from traditional assigned office space has substantially increased. Many workers today conduct their work day "on the road," from hotel rooms and client offices, or from places within their facility other than their assigned desk. This is now referred to as *virtual work* or *mobile work*. For the purpose of understanding physical workspace needs, we define mobile worker as *an employee who has choices concerning how, when and where they work.* This definition encompasses various terms associated with this type of work including: Remote worker, distance worker, far-flung team member, telecommuter, teleworker, virtual and distributed worker.

In some contexts, mobile work is more narrowly defined as work conducted through the use of mobile devices. However, mobile technologies are only some of the enablers of mobile work. Equally important is the *physical* environment that supports the use of mobile technologies, although this has received

---

*Corresponding author.

considerably less attention in the literature about mobile work. This study demonstrates the importance of flexible workspace arrangements for the success of mobile workers. Further this study addresses how different worker roles require different kinds of supporting technologies. These role-based findings overturn a number of popular myths about mobile workers. The results of this study have significant implications for workspace solution designers, technology providers and managers who support mobile workers.

2. Background

A recent benchmark study from Nemertes Research [27], based on discussions with 120 IT executives at companies of various size and focus, revealed that a staggering 83% of the participating organizations now consider themselves to be virtual, with workgroups spread across multiple locations and geographies. Fully 91% of the study's company employees do some work outside of traditional headquarter locations, and 96% use some form of real-time collaboration tools (e.g., instant messaging, Web conferencing, audio/video conferencing).

Yet, the Nemertes study [27] found that only 43% of the identified global organizations had a mobility strategy and another 26% currently were developing one. Among US-based companies involved in the study, only 35% had a strategy, and another 16% had one in development; thus, almost half of US enterprises had no organization-wide strategy for supporting the needs of the mobile workforce. Even more telling, only 15% of all organizations interviewed had a specific mobility budget.

2.1. Addressing mobile worker dissatisfaction

Mobile work practices, once regarded as alternatives, are proven as ways to save money, access required skill sets, and increase productivity [12]. The economic benefits of mobile work and mobility resources have been well established in the BOSTI study [9], the Hudson Institute workforce study [23], studies by the Center for Workplace Preparation [21], the workforce agility study [5], and the study by Knoll Workforce Research [24]. Despite these proven benefits, companies have been cutting budgets (if they ever have one for mobile work) and other support [31].

This lack of support impacts many areas of support, including the provision of physical workspaces appropriate to the needs of mobile workers. The result is that people have expressed disenchantment with the value of their company's primary workplace and stated that their corporate office architecture is unproductive, underutilized, and misaligned with the needs of the evolving workforce [10,20]. Mobile workers feel marginalized when they do not have the best mobile devices for their needs. This study demonstrates that they also feel isolated and unsupported in the way they are assigned space and equipment.

The premise of this research is that the shift to greater mobility and the associated changes in workspace and technology usage are affecting diverse roles, work activities, interpersonal collaboration, and worker satisfaction. In particular we sought to understand how various types of mobile workers communicate, both socially and professionally. According to our study respondents, it is no longer enough to provide a one-size-fits-all package for mobile devices, equipment, and workspaces. Workers have become more discerning about exactly what they need to support their work and are frustrated when their unique needs are not met.

2.2. Findings as an outgrowth of previous study: Unassigned space does not work

A previous study of flexible and mobile work strategies demonstrated the failings of unassigned work spaces [24]. In-depth field interviews were conducted with real estate and human resource decision makers within five Global 100 companies representing five different industries. This was a qualitative study from the organizational or leadership perspective. The findings revealed that, after companies conducted workspace usage analyses and realized a large percentage of workstations were vacant, a common solution was to create unassigned space for a percentage of the workplace or a portion of the company's real estate portfolio. Real metrics were produced and real dollars saved in terms of space management. However, management also acknowledged that achieving anticipated value from mobile worker programs had been elusive.

Many managers executing unassigned workspace strategies encountered obstacles and resistance. Workers felt marginalized, especially due to being assigned undesirable seating areas, which were sometimes completely separate from the work group to which they belonged. After that initial study the question remained unanswered: *Why has the unassigned space strategy had such minimal success in supporting new work patterns and mobile work?* This question begged for investigation into the drivers and influencers, not only of the mobile strategists and workspace designers, but of the workers themselves.

Therefore, the 2006 study focuses on the worker perspective of how they perceive their work now, along with what works, doesn't work and what's needed in the way of physical space and technology support. Ultimately, the study's goal was to understand more fully how today's mobile workers affect space utilization.

2.3. Collaboration and human networks

The 2006 study was conducted from the employees', rather than management's, perspective. The starting point involved considering the different ways people might interact with each other, knowing that collaboration is an increasingly vital feature of business life. Particularly in knowledge-intensive work, creating an informational environment that helps employees solve increasingly complex and often ambiguous problems holds significant performance implications.

One approach to improving collaboration is to formally support knowledge networks that harness the power of a company's natural communities of mutual interest, which have emerged spontaneously in the digital age. These networks, sometimes call "communities of practice," boost the value of the informal networks that in many companies already exist among groups of professional or managers with common interests rooted in similar job, skills, or needs of knowledge. Investing in and formalizing the roles of such networks can encourage people with common interest to collaborate with relatively little ambiguity about decision-making authority. In vertical or matrix organizational structures, such ambiguity generates internal organization complication and tension [14].

Usually, when considering where people turn for information or knowledge, the logical sources people think of are databases; the Web; intranets and portals; and other, more traditional repositories (e.g., file cabinets, policy and procedure manuals). However, research has shown that a significant component of one's information environment consists of the relationships that a person can tap for various informational needs. For example, a study conducted by Allen and Henn [3] at the Massachusetts Institute of Technology found that engineers and scientists were roughly five times more likely to turn to a person for information than to an impersonal source, such as a database or a file cabinet.

With a growing understanding of this, interest in understanding human networks and in applying classic network analysis techniques to organizational issues has been increasing in recent years. Universities and the private sector are looking more deeply into these ideas. The University of Virginia Network Round Table, for example, has involved more than 40 large companies in learning about the latest developments in organizational network analysis [14]. The technology and methodology is easy to use because algorithms and virtually free applications exist. These tools enable one to see the informal knowledge sharing networks and communication links that complement the formal organization. A similar approach could be useful in understanding the key roles, relationships, and interactions of mobile workers.

3. Research approach

The present study was conducted on the premise that mobile workers depend upon a web of relationships (i.e., a network) to fulfill their tasks. Workers seek to be effective in the different purposeful value creating networks to which they belong. A *value network* is any web of relationships that generates economic or social value through complex, dynamic exchanges of both tangible and intangible benefit [2]. Value creating networks operate both internally across the organization and also extend externally to partners, stakeholders, and the industry. This perspective of how organizations work has been growing in management awareness since the late 1990s, not only in the United States but in Europe and other countries, as well [1,11,28,32,33].

3.1. Value network analysis

In contrast to organizational network analysis, which focuses on knowledge sharing between individuals, *Value network analysis* [2] attempts to determine the value generating interactions between people in a network. It is a lens for exploring the otherwise hidden relationships, processes, and deliverables that underpin high-performing workgroups. People who play roles in a network take the assets they control and convert them into negotiable forms of value, which can be extended or offered to others in the network. Value network analysis, therefore, examines (a) the actual value-adding roles people play and (b) the specific value deliverables they convey to others. Value is considered in both tangible (contractual) and intangible (informal) terms.

- *Tangible value* is generated through contracted or mandated activities that contribute directly to economic gain or expected services. Tangible value is generated in the type of activities typically tracked in a value stream or in business processes (e.g., Six Sigma, LEAN).
- *Intangible value* normally lies concealed. It includes the value generated by informal, non-mandated activities that help deepen business relationships and contribute directly to operational effectiveness. Through the value network lens, the mission-critical support that builds relationships and keeps things running smoothly becomes apparent.

Other mobile worker surveys have focused solely on outputs and formal reporting relationships and on uses of technology, rather than on value creation or professional interaction [6–8,16]. In contrast, the perspective of value network analysis [2] was selected as the key tool with which to define the roles and relationships of mobile workers in this study. This type of analysis gives executives the information they need to foster collaboration at critical junctures, and to tap the talents and expertise of mobile workers more effectively.

Specifically, the fresh perspective of value network analysis introduced several important elements into the design of this study:

- This research looked at the relationships and roles of mobile workers, not just their functions or tasks.
- It assumed a strategic view of mobile workers as a cornerstone for the increasingly agile, globally networked organizations that are becoming the norm in every industry.
- This approach made it possible to expose critical working relationships, environmental conditions, infrastructure, and motivators.
- Finally, it made possible conclusions about how to best support mobile workers, based on understanding how such workers interact, communicate, and collaborate, which determine how they use space, technology, and collaborative tools.

This awareness of the importance of connectivity and intangibles also surfaced in the study during the interviews. For example, Joel Ratekin from the Corporate Real Estate group at Capital One told us, "Who you know determines what you know. Before moving a group into a mobile program, we need to find out how connected they are. We have plenty of tools to measure the tangibles, but if a work group becomes mobile and we fail to understand the intangibles involved, these could erode without us knowing until it's too late."

3.2. Survey methods

A total of 557 respondents participated in a survey designed to gather data for the research analysis. They came from 84 different organizations. Of the total, 246 respondents came from a large multinational conglomerate, and 311 respondents came from mixed companies.

The survey instrument was designed with value network analysis questions that focused on the type of value being created, the level of value as perceived by the worker, and the type of value output generated. The question set included respondents' background information as well as questions regarding: roles; technology use; space needs and work habits, especially as related to working with others; and general feelings about being a mobile worker.

The survey asked respondents not only to define their own roles, but also to describe the roles with which they interacted and how they believed their value was perceived by others. Respondents made their choices from a drop-down list of 27 roles, which were compiled from common management taxonomies (Table 1). These questions about roles allowed for a finer level of granularity in the way respondents described their work and business relationships. The instrument also provided a way to discover whether different roles carried the same technology requirements.

4. Results and findings

4.1. Myth busters

This study found that a number of commonly held myths about mobile workers, if they were ever true, were simply not supported by the findings. The following are the most compelling and significant assumptions debunked by the study.

4.1.1. Assumptions about Age and Gender

There has been a common assumption that mobile workers are either female or young technology workers and that they are performing individual, low-skill-based work tasks [13,26]. In fact, the study provided a high level of consistency in answering the question, who is the mobile worker? The male-to-female ratio was 65/35, and the majority of respondents characterized themselves as follows:

Table 1
Role choices for respondents (listed in alphabetical order)

Administrator	Developer	Partner
Advisor	Evaluator	Problem solver
Buyer	Influencer	Producer
Client	Innovator	Regulator
Competitor	Investigator	Researcher
Comptroller	Leader	Seller
Contractor	Marketer	Service provider
Coordinator	Mentor	Subject matter expert
Designer	Other expert	Trouble shooter

- Mature: 65% were older than 40
- Family-oriented: 82% were married or living with a partner
- Hardworking: 75% worked more than 40 hours per week

4.1.2. Assumptions about roles and professional stature

Traditionally, it has been assumed that only specialist workers (e.g., salespeople, auditors, consultants) spend significant periods away from the office [4]. However, the present study found that all levels of staff work outside the office. In fact, most of the mobile workers surveyed occupy professional, managerial, or executive positions. Almost half (48.6%) of the workers perceived themselves as occupying leadership roles; the breakdown of their most common responses was as follows:

- Leaders (13.3%)
- Consultants (13.1%)
- Problem solvers (8.2%)
- Coordinators (7.5%)
- Subject-matter experts (6.5%)

Not only were these mobile workers higher level professionals than most people might have assumed, but they were working on specific issues and projects with clients as active consultants and problem solvers, rather than in service support or sales roles.

These mobile workers were serious, career-oriented employees: 67% were employed in an organization with a formal mobile work program and had long-term employment at their company. As many as 30% had been employed for 6 to 10 years, and more than 20% had spent 16 to 20 years or longer at their organization.

4.1.3. Assumptions about the need for a productive workspace

There has been a tendency to think that mobile workers are constantly on the move, either in a car or on an airplane [19,30]. However, this study found that only some mobile workers are really physically mobile; a great many actually can be found in the same location on a daily basis. The primary difference is that their location is typically a home office rather than a traditional workplace.

Many mobile workers feel they do their best task-focused activity work at home. More than 60% of survey respondents reported being most productive at home, with as much as two-thirds of their home work time spent on individual or independent work. They also indicated they found other places, sometimes outside the traditional office, to be more productive when something really needs to get done. They also expressed that the office was usually not well conceived regarding the new roles it is increasingly being asked to fulfill. Increasingly, respondents indicated, people are using restaurants and coffee cafes to meet with others.

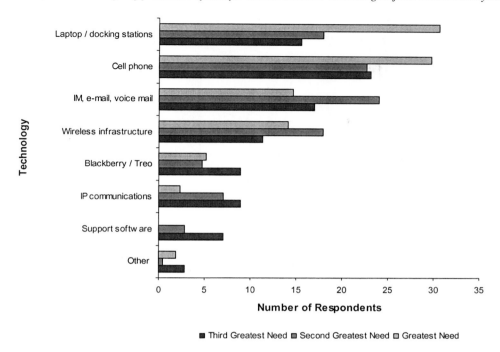

Fig. 1. An example of the top three mobile technology needs of respondents from a mix of industries.

Mobile workers expressed a compelling need for team space; 75% of the respondents said they come into the office for face-to-face meetings. Survey comments validated the experience that team rooms are sorely missing and often architecturally not enabled appropriately. A disparity exists between needed work settings and the types of spaces provided to mobile workers. More than 50% of the mobile workers surveyed stated they really need conference room space at their employer's office, but are having trouble getting it. Less than 5% of respondents had assigned collaborative workspaces. The survey results revealed that mobile worker role profiles vary with respect to office infrastructure and technology needs, but overwhelmingly show the same unmet requirements for meeting space.

4.1.4. Assumptions about technology needs

There also has been an assumption that the basic functionality of mobile devices and the mix of technologies needed are very similar for all mobile workers [18,25]. However, aside from the "big three" (i.e., laptop, cell phone and interpersonal communication), this study revealed very different technology needs among the respondents, based on the varied roles mobile workers play.

Collaborative technology is a must-have for mobile workers: 90% of mobile workers in this survey said they need mobile teleconferencing and collaborative technology capabilities. In general, being mobile means a heavy reliance on technology for achieving peak performance, for feeling organized, and for meeting personal necessities. Not surprisingly, all respondents described their top three needs for mobile devices as (a) a laptop and docking station; (b) cell phone and (c) instant messaging, voice mail, and e-mail (Fig. 1). However, simply having these devices did not prevent most workers from feeling a disconnect between what was provided to them (or allowed for in their budget) and what they really need to be productive.

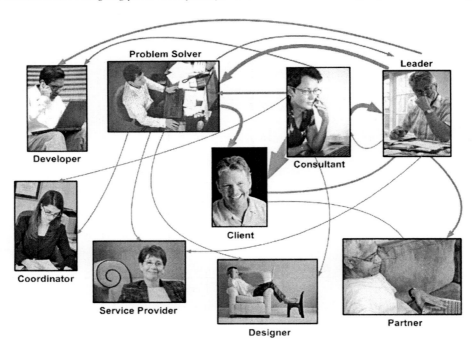

Fig. 2. Typical frequency of interactions between roles – *the thicker the line, the greater amount of interaction.*

4.2. Role implications for workspace and product designers

The data collected for this study made it possible to profile the three most common leadership roles assumed by mobile workers (i.e., problem solvers, consultants, and leaders) in terms of their work habits, technology needs, and workspace requirements. For example, the survey responses suggested that a problem solver has a much richer and more stable environment than a consultant, although the consultant has a more focused value network and tends to work in a variety of settings.

The pattern of interactions between individuals with various roles is as interesting as the roles themselves. Figure 2 shows the typical interactions problem solvers, consultants, and leaders have with people in some of the other most common roles.

This study suggests that technology and workspace designers need to pay more attention to the idea that a role drives behavior, and therefore also determines the kind of support required to work effectively. For example, if two people hold the same job title but perceive their roles differently, they are likely to end up doing different things during the course of the day. Thus, the environment needs to be different for both to be productive in their respective ways.

This study found the key differentiator for what technologies and workspaces a mobile worker requires is not age; rather, *it is entirely a matter of the worker's role.* Recognizing that the typical mobile worker is an older professional is one clue that these workers are not all alike and that their needs can be very different. Yet, companies tend to have set packages of technology and equipment that are available for mobile workers, without considering the need to support multiple roles.

The three sections that follow discuss the role profiles of problem solvers, consultants, and leaders. The study findings suggest a number of recommendations for technology and workspace designers. The role characteristics for each group, as well as the home and office needs associated with its roles, are summarized in Table 2.

Table 2
Roles and needs of problem solvers, consultants, and leaders

	Role characteristics	Home needs	Office needs
Problem solver	– Multiple issues at once – Many single interactions – Paper and filing: "keeping things straight" – Use of reference material – Predominately working at home	– Bookcase – Computer and Internet – Mailing service – Professional copying – Office-like seating – Remote printing	– Printing/faxing – Mailing service – Professional copying – Space for individual interactions – Collaboration on the fly – Day care
Consultant	– Small number of projects – Fewest number of contact points – Communications with clients and leaders – "Road warrior"	– Smart phone – Video conferencing – Remote printing	– Space to display or present to small groups and individual team meetings & updates – Booths – Concierge
Leader	– Many frequent interactions – Immediacy – Speed/convenience – Confidentiality	– Immediate access – Directories – Concierge – Representative space – Transportation	– Formal conferencing – "Iconic"/branded spaces – Group settings – Confidential – Dry cleaning – Day care – Concierge/dining

4.2.1. Problem solvers

According to the survey, the majority of problem solvers were home based. These problem solvers typically have many single contacts a day. They resolve a spot issue, then move on to the next task. In this way, they handle multiple issues at once, but engage in single interactions. Primarily, they are involved in transferring expertise. One unique quality of the problem solvers is that they indicated a high requirement for paper and filing. They work with multiple people at once and need to remember relevant information about these individuals. Because this information often resides in a binder or book or manual, the problem solvers need reference materials close at hand.

At home

Technology and workspace designers should keep in mind that problem solvers need a regular office at home that is set up for doing computer work and accessing reference material. They need an ergonomic chair, a substantial desk, a bookcase, a computer, and paper storage and filing spaces. Other needs that emerged from the survey data are access to offsite printing and postal services, and a high quality Internet link of some kind. In essence, problem solvers' home needs are very similar to their office needs.

At the office

When problem solvers visit their offices, they do the same thing they did from home; that is, they have many single contacts to solve single problems. They meet with people about specifics and also engage in back office services of printing, faxing and mailing. They often find they have a great deal time between meetings, and may find themselves asking, "What will I do with this time?" Some elements can be provided at the office to help problem solvers work effectively and achieve a greater life/work balance. Daycare is one example; if the person is on the road or at the office for a long period of time, but normally works from home, he or she may need childcare support at home or the office when they are not at home.

4.2.2. Consultants

A consultant has a very different profile from that of a problem solver. The data from this study showed that consultants have the lowest number of contact points but the highest frequency of interactions; thus, they engage with a small group of people several times a day. Additionally, the people with whom they talk are not necessarily people internal to the team or company, but rather clients or leaders. So, compared with problem solvers, consultants were much more physically mobile. Like road warriors, the consultants travel from site to site or city to city, supporting small groups of people. They are also project focused. Projects have a finite time, so they typically work with small teams and have a high degree of interactions.

At home

It is important for technology and workspace designers to realize that consultants have relatively less concern about furniture and more concern about their technology budget. Compared with the other roles examined in this study, consultants expressed the greatest need for mobile devices: cell phone, laptops, smart phones, and teleconference and video conference capability. They did not mention many specific needs for furniture.

At the office

When consultants come into the office, their foremost needs are to display and present; therefore, they should have access to display boards, big screens, and meeting or presentation rooms. Typically, they work with small groups or individuals, not large gatherings. So, for example, when they meet to update team members, they need an allocated team space or casual café or coffee booth.

4.2.3. Leaders

The leaders in this study fell in the middle between the problem solvers, who had many single interactions, and the consultants, who had few but frequent contacts. So, if a problem solver had 25 contact points and a consultant had 5, the leader had 10. These interactions are numerous and frequent, which requires a steady flow of information. Therefore, immediacy, speed, convenience, and confidentiality are important to the leaders.

At home

Technology and workspace designers need to recognize that leaders are most concerned about services and about having immediate access to the people with whom they work. At home, they need a representative space where people can come to visit; this is not necessarily the home office, but rather a professionally presentable place within the home. In addition, leaders need such services as concierge, travel and transportation, and a way to hold meetings that are private or confidential. For them, having *secure* technologies is an important concern.

At the office

For the office, leaders expressed the need for formal, iconic conferencing spaces that are representative of the culture of the company. They need both a large, public group gathering place and the ability to go from that space to an adjacent one that is much more confidential. Balancing the life/work equation is important to leaders, so they need access to dry cleaning, daycare, concierge, and dining. Technologies that are most helpful to leaders are those that help manage contacts and schedules, rather than large amounts of documentation.

5. Discussion

5.1. Challenges for the office landscape

To rationalize their property portfolios, property and facility managers are under pressure either to make better use of existing resources to free up space or to grow without taking on any more space. However, many are not adjusting the office footprint to meet the needs of workers. A Silicon Valley consultant reported that when she visits large companies, many offices have a central "dead zone" with empty cubicles, while the few meeting rooms around the edges are overbooked. Company cafeterias have become ad hoc meeting spaces because rooms are not available.

Another issue is the reluctance on the part of property managers to let go of floor space "just in case" it is needed. One survey respondent reported, "My company is not providing enough support for mobile workers. Although the mobile work program is supported on a corporate level, our site manager isn't bright enough to use it to effectively reduce our office footprint, so he's stuck with the bill for the full footprint *and* reimbursement for home expenses."

What can be done? To begin with, a portion of the real estate saving dollars should be reinvested in a realistic mobile worker budget that addresses diverse technology and equipment needs. Respondents in this study asked for layers of hyperconnectivity. When asked why he did not need an assigned workstation, one respondent replied, "Equipment doesn't care where it's located. We can be connected through technology." Therefore, a real estate strategy must serve the work being done and accommodate the need for different work settings, along with saving space.

5.2. Consider shared office space

The idea of slashing costs by sharing office infrastructure has been around since the 1980s, but sharing office space also carries the stigma of not being a "real" worker. Today, wireless and economic globalization has given companies more options that do not entail workers being tied down to long-term office leases, and shared office space strategies are becoming outmoded by technology. In total, the Office Business Center Association International estimated that 4,000 shared office business centers exist throughout North America and 5,500 around the globe [29].

5.3. Reconsider the mix of work settings being offered

Plan a more holistic view that goes beyond corporate guidelines and standards. Consider the linkage between the workplace and a particular engagement. Begin by determining the time spent within the organization in team or group work compared with time spent in individual work [17]. Then assess the need for different types of work settings required for different roles, and create welcoming places where people want to be.

5.4. Rethinking space design

The findings indicate that organizations should consider undertaking a thorough review of their typical space profile and reassign space in greater alignment with the needs and expectations of an increasingly mobile population. Based on respondents' answers to the survey, there are several ways to create a more accommodating and effective workplace.

1. Address requirements of older and younger mobile workers for greater effectiveness at their workplace and home:

    – Mobility resonates particularly with older workers. Those who want to extend the number of years they remain in the workforce find traditional workplace policies inadequate for working at home. They feel the standard provisions (e.g., inflexible work hours, workspace as entitlement, commuting to one location, treating employees as costs) inhibit their effectiveness.
    – Younger mobile workers view mobile work as directly correlated with improved quality of life, which allows for greater flexibility with their time.
    – Mobility is a solution to increase productivity when employees are faced with temporary health issues or health restrictions related to aging and disability [22].

2. Provide corporate workspaces that allow for mobility of work and mobility of the workplace, not only the mobility of people. Workplaces must be highly portable, with the necessary technology, equipment, and support tools.

    – Enable mobile workers to work where and when they like, at any hour or day of the year; manage people by objectives rather than by their presence
    – Support working collaboratively at *any* time and *any* place
    – Be more context aware; enable workers to switch easily between collaborative work settings and individual, task-focused activities
    – Have plug-and-play capability available; primary workplace and home locations need high-quality workspaces with technology access for collaboration and virtual conferencing
    – Facilities operators should seek priority agreements with service providers for services at other locations, including residences

3. Provide work environments and service centers in addition to workstations, including the following:

    – Spaces free from interruption (this is both a cultural and design issue)
    – Informal areas where people can meet and engage with each other
    – Back-office services that facilitate copying, printing, and mailing
    – Team communication centers, both physical and virtual
    – Learning and development activities to identify and support people playing key roles in improving knowledge networks
    – Non-traditional areas for "hanging out" or informal meetings (e.g., booths near coffee bars)
    – Concierge support services, dining areas and gaming areas
    – Wireless and teleconference capability; new technology for video conferencing
    – Private space/studios (i.e., not private offices), including some with homelike environments

5.5. A final word on technology

Providers of mobile devices and technologies can easily fall into the trap of designing for stereotypes of mobile workers instead of looking at the real users of mobile technologies. It is not sufficient to just observe how people physically interact with a device when addressing design; the context of the work itself must be considered. Older workers are just as at home with mobile technologies as are younger users, although the needs of the former may be quite different because their roles are different. Technology package providers and designers need to take this into account.

6. Conclusions

Mobile worker programs must provide resources for the primary role an individual is assuming, which is *not* that of mobile worker. When mobile workers can concentrate on assuming their *primary* roles, their performance is highest. The formal organization needs to be regarded as a resourcing model to support key roles in identified work activities and the value networks that "float" between the lines of the organizational chart. But this cannot be done without a clear mobile worker strategy and a budget to implement it.

Mobile workers need productive workspaces at home, as well as places to work and meet in the office setting. Different roles require different types of technology, workspace design, meeting spaces, and services. Equipment and workspaces must fit unique needs in terms of supplies; technical support and training; places to send mail; and places to meet and socialize with colleagues, customers, and clients. Social or organizational network analysis can be used to help to improve knowledge flows, and to locate expertise by focusing on individual communication flows. Value network analysis can help people better support key roles and organize projects and activities that cross internal and external organizational boundaries. Evaluating mobile worker roles creates new business opportunities for infrastructure and technology providers and transforms the provisions of space and services.

References

[1]   V. Allee, Reconfiguring the value network, *Journal of Business Strategy* **21**(4) (2000), 36–39.
[2]   V. Allee, *The Future of Knowledge: Increasing Prosperity through Value Networks*, Burlington, MA: Butterworth-Heinemann, 2003.
[3]   T.J. Allen and G. Henn, *The Organization and Architecture of Innovation: Managing the Flow of Technology*, Burlington, MA: Butterworth-Heinemann, 2006.
[4]   J.H.E. Andriessen and M. Vartiainen, *Mobile Virtual Work: A New Paradigm,* Berlin, Germany: Springer, 2005.
[5]   R.M. Beatty, & Saratoga/PricewaterhouseCoopers LLP, *Workforce agility: The new frontier for competitive advantage,* 2005. Available at http://www.convergys.com/employeecare_workforce-agility.html.
[6]   F. Becker, K.L. Quinn and L.V. Callentine, (1995). *The ecology of the mobile worker.* Ithaca, NY: Cornell University International Workplace Studies Program. Available at http://72.14.253.104/search?q=cache:i5689LRhG60J: iwsp.human.cornell.edu/pubs/pdf/Ecology_of_Mobile.pdf+%22The+ecology+of+the+mobile+worker%22+becker&hl= en&ct=clnk&cd=3&gl=us.
[7]   F. Becker, C.M. Tennessen and L.M. Dahl, *Managing workplace change.* Ithaca, NY: Cornell University International Workplace Studies Program, 1997. Available at http://iwsp.human.cornell.edu/pubs/pdf/Managing_Workplace_Change.pdf.
[8]   Booz Allen Hamilton & INSEAD. *Innovation: Is global the way forward?* (2006). Available at http://www.boozallen.com/media/file/Innovation_Is_Global_The_Way_Forward_v2.pdf.
[9]   M. Brill, S. Weidemann, & BOSTI, *Disproving Widespread Myths about Workplace Design*, Jasper, IN: Kimball International, 2001.
[10] J.K. Chan, S.L. Beckman and P.G. Lawrence, Workplace design: A new managerial imperative, *California Management Review* **49**(2) (2007), 6–22.
[11] C.M. Christensen, *The Innovator's Dilemma: The Revolutionary Book That Will Change the Way You Do Business,* New York: Collins Business Essentials, 1997.
[12] M. Conlin, Square feet. Oh, how square! *BusinessWeek*, July 3, 2006. Available at http://www.businessweek.com/magazine/content/06_27/b3991073.htm.
[13] J.H. Coplan, . Help for moms who want to work at home. *BusinessWeek*, August 23, 2000. Available at http://www.businessweek.com/smallbiz/content/aug2000/wf000823.htm.
[14] R.L. Cross and A. Parker, *The Hidden Power of Social Networks: Understanding How Work Really Gets Done in Organizations,* Cambridge, MA: Harvard Business School Press, 2004.
[15] R.L. Cross, R.D. Martin and L.M. Weiss, Mapping the value of employee collaboration. *The McKinsey Quarterly* **3** (2006). Available at http://www.mckinseyquarterly.com.
[16] Deloitte. *Virtual Workplace Survey*, 2005. Available at https://ias.deloitte.co.uk/Surveys/VirtualWrkplc.nsf.

[17]   P. Evans and B. Wolf, Collaboration rules, *Harvard Business Review* **83**(7) (2005), 96–104.

[18]   J.D. Fay, Managing the mobile workers: There are new solutions for managing mobile resources, *Transport Technology Today* **26**(3) (January 1, 2003), 26–28.

[19]   P. Gogoi, Welcome to the Gen Y workplace. *BusinessWeek*, May 4, 2005. Available at http://www.businessweek.com/bwdaily/dnflash/may2005/nf2005054_4640_db_083.htm.

[20]   C.E. Grantham, J.P. Ware and C. Williams, *Corporate Agility: A Revolutionary New Model for Competing in a Flat World*, New York: AMACOM/American Management Association, 2007.

[21]   C. Healy, *A business perspective on workplace flexibility: When work works, an employer strategy for the 21st century*. Center for Workplace Preparation, 2004. Available at http://www.familiesandwork.org/3w/research/downloads/cwp.pdf.

[22]   J.W. Hedge, W.C. Borman and S.E. Lammlein, *The Aging Workforce: Realities, Myths, and Implications for Organizations*, Washington DC: American Psychological Association, 2006.

[23]   W.B. Johnston and A.E. Packer, *Workforce 2000: Work and Workers for the 21st century*, Indianapolis, IN: Hudson Institute, 1987.

[24]   Knoll Workforce Research. Time as a new currency: Flexible and mobile work strategies to manage people and profits, 2005. Available at http://www.knoll.com/research/downloads/KnollTimeCurrency.pdf.

[25]   J.L. Koch and D. Caldwell, *Mobile computing and its impact on the changing nature of work and organizations*, Working paper, Santa Clara University, Santa Clara, CA, 1999.

[26]   M.A. Naylor, There's no workforce like home. *BusinessWeek*, May 2, 2006. Available at http://www.businessweek.com/technology/content/may2006/tc20060502_763202.htm.

[27]   Nemertes Research. *Nemertes benchmark: Building a successful virtual workplace*, 2007. Available at http://www.nemertes.com/networking_telecommunications/nemertes_benchmark_building_a_successful_virtual_workplace.

[28]   R. Normann and R. Ramirez, From value chain to value constellation: Designing interactive strategy, *Harvard Business Review* **71**(4) (1993), 65–77.

[29]   Office Business Central. *OBC industry facts*, 2007. Available at http://www.obcai.org/index2.cfm?section=resources&content=indfacts.

[30]   K. O'Hara, M. Perry, A. Sellen and B.A. Brown, Managing information on the move, in: *Wireless World: Social and Interactional Aspects of the Mobile Age*, B. Brown, N. Green and R. Harper, eds, The Hague, Netherlands: Springer Verlag, 2001, pp. 180–194.

[31]   B.S. Sellers and S.A. Thomas, Managing the cost of real estate. *The McKinsey Quarterly* **4** (2007). Available at http://www.mckinseyquarterly.com.

[32]   C.B. Stabell and O.D. Fjellstad, Configuring value for competitive advantage: On chains, shops, and networks, *Strategic Management Journal* **19** (1998), 413–437.

[33]   D. Tapscott, D. Ticol and A. Lowy, *Digital Capital, Harnessing the Power of Business Webs*, Boston: Harvard Business School Press, 2000.

**Camille Venezia** is a recognized leader in Corporate Mobile Work Strategy and former Director of Workforce Research in the Global Business Division of Knoll, Inc. She has 25+ years of industry experience, with a background in sociology and master's in organization development and human resource management. She is a LEED Accredited Professional, a certified Value Network Practitioner and Professional/Executive Coach. Her area of focus is organizational change issues critical to the emerging workforce, including worker productivity and innovation, employee attraction and retention, changing workforce demographics, and business strategy execution. Ms. Venezia has conducted research with leading Global and Fortune 500 companies and the Architectural and Design communities to understand relationships between sustainable workforce performance, organizational structures, and physical environments. She conducts management seminars and consults with major corporations executing network organizational structures, mobility and flexibility strategies, and sustainability practices. She lectures at leading industry organizations, including the International Interior Design Association (IIDA) and International Facility Management Association (IFMA), has published in and serves as a member of the Editorial Advisory Board for the *Journal of Corporate Real Estate*, and has published in CoreNet Global Leader journal and *Interior and Sources* magazine.

Verna Allee is the President of Value Networks LLC and founding sponsor of the Value Networks Consortium. Value Networks LLC is the leading provider of value network visualization and analysis applications. Customers include Cisco, Boeing, SAP, Scottish Enterprise, Telenor and Hydro Aluminum in Norway, Rolls Royce Marine Engine, Knoll, Kimberly-Clark, AgResearch (New Zealand), Mayo Clinic, Environment Canada, The Institute of Public Health Ireland, GAN-Net, and GRI (Global Reporting Initiative). Ms. Allee is a Fellow of the World Business Academy, advisor to the European Commission and was a member of the Brookings Institution Task Force on Intangibles in the late 1990s. She is on a number of Advisory and Editorial Boards including Hazel Henderson's Ethical Business television series, Inside Knowledge and IC (Intellectual Capital) Magazine. She is visiting professor at the Marshall School of Business at the University of Southern California (Los Angeles), Greenwich University (London), Hanken Swedish School of Business (Helsinki), and the University of Waikato (New Zealand). Her publications include numerous articles and book, including The Future of Knowledge: Increasing Prosperity through Value Networks (2003) The Knowledge Evolution (1997), co-editor with Dinesh Chandra of What is True Wealth and How Do We Create It? (2003).

Oliver Schwabe is owner and managing director of Eurofocus International Consultants Ltd (founded 1991). Mr. Schwabe has been working in the consulting and coaching environment since 1985. In the role of co-founder and Chief Technology Officer for the Silicon Valley based network intelligence company Value Network LLC, he also leads the development of the patented GenIsisTM Application Suite, a portfolio of leading middleware applications designed to apply value networks principles and organizational network analysis techniques in industrial contexts. Mr. Schwabe also regularly assumes the role of interim manager or project manager for small to medium size enterprises. Furthermore, he is a founding member of the Value Networks Industry Consortium (www.vncluster.com), is the Fellow for Product Development for Entovation International, is featured on the Entovation Global Knowledge Leadership Map, and teaches around innovation, organizational development, and system dynamics at various universities in Europe and the USA. Mr. Schwabe has a BSc in Human Resources Management, an MSc in Strategic Management, an MBA in International Business, and a DBA in E-Business and Knowledge Management.

Information Knowledge Systems Management 7 (2008) 77–97
IOS Press

Telecommuting and corporate culture: Implications for the mobile enterprise

Anthony T. Hoang[a], Robert C. Nickerson[b,*], Paul Beckman[c] and Jamie Eng[d]
[a]College of Business, San Francisco State University, San Francisco, CA 94132, USA
E-mail: anthony_hoang@yahoo.com
[b]Department of Information Systems, College of Business, San Francisco State University, San Francisco, CA 94132, USA
E-mail: RNick@sfsu.edu
[c]Department of Information Systems, College of Business, San Francisco State University, San Francisco, CA 94132, USA
E-mail: pbeckman@sfsu.edu
[d]Department of Decision Sciences, College of Business, San Francisco State University, San Francisco, CA 94132, USA
E-mail: jeng@sfsu.edu

Abstract: Enterprise mobility includes at home work often called telecommuting. Although telecommuting has been highly touted for a number of years, its adoption has seen varying levels of success. Earlier studies indicated that corporate culture might be a deterrent to the acceptance of the practice. The purpose of this research is to re-investigate the impact of corporate culture on telecommuting. This paper reports the results of a survey of business professionals and managers regarding perceptions of corporate culture toward telecommuting. The main conclusion of the paper is that corporate culture is still a deterrent to telecommuting in many organizations. The results have implications for management, workers, and organizations moving toward a more mobile enterprise.

Keywords: Telecommuting, telework, work at home, corporate culture, mobile enterprise

1. Introduction

Enterprise mobility takes on many forms including employees using smart phones to check email, "road warriors" placing orders through mobile sales systems, executives holding videoconferences while traveling to distant locations sites, and knowledge workers collaborating with coworkers while working at their homes. Businesses in many cases encourage such use of remote applications by their employees, but, at the same time, they express concerns about employees working away from their regular place of work. Questions arise about monitoring employee activity, measuring employee productivity, and ensuring task completion, among others. With current technology many employees are able to work

---

*Corresponding author.

just about anywhere, including an airport, a hotel room, a café, a park, and their home. They can also work just about anytime; they are not tied to a nine-to-five workday. Whether using wired or wireless technology, employees have many opportunities for remote work. Indeed, today an employee's proximity to his or her office is often less important than a reliable internet connection.

One of the earliest forms of remote work involved employees working from their homes using communications technology (originally slow speed dial-up modems) to connect to their distant offices. Whereas today's DSL and cable connections are dramatically faster, the fundamental approach to working at home has not changed: employees still perform their regular work tasks at their homes while connected electronically to their offices. This alternative form of work has historically been called telecommuting and has seen many variations of use and importance over the years. Today, however, with the anyplace and anytime nature of mobile technology, telecommuting has become more common and more important to the organization. The general purpose of this research is to see where telecommuting stands in today's enterprises.

Telecommuting has potential benefits for the economy in general and for companies in particular. The National Technology Readiness Survey (NTRS) estimated that the U.S. economy could save $3.9 billion per year if workers with the choice to telecommute would do so [34]. Gomes [14] reported on a survey by Korn/Ferry International that revealed that 78% of managers think employees are equally productive when they work away from their offices.

Despite its apparent benefits, telecommuting acceptance has not caught up with expectations. The U.S. Department of Labor [3] disclosed that the percentage of workers working at home in 2004 remained essentially the same as in 2001 (roughly 15%). Korzeniowski [25] reports that the growth rate for telecommuting as projected by International Data Corporation will be less than 2% through 2009. A recent study conducted by Telework Exchange and the Federal Managers Association [51] found that only 35% of federal government managers endorse telecommuting. Rockridge Associates Incorporated and the University of Maryland [34, p. 7] discovered that only 2% of workers telecommuted full time in 2005 while 9% telecommuted part time.

These studies indicate that telecommuting has not become widely accepted. The reasons for this fact are not clear, but corporate (organizational) culture has been suggested as one. The Korn/Ferry International survey cited earlier [14] indicated that 61% of the managers believe that telecommuting could hurt employees' careers. A 1995 study by Haworth reveals that the primary barrier to telecommuting is corporate culture [20, p. 6].

Motivated by these findings, this research examines whether corporate culture is an obstacle to the progress of telecommuting. To investigate this question, a web-based survey of 78 working professionals and managers was conducted. This paper presents the results of that survey. The results of this survey have implications for organizational management, individual workers, and, ultimately, enterprise mobility. It also has implications for future research on mobility of the workforce.

The next section of this paper reviews the literature related to enterprise mobility, corporate culture, and telecommuting including its short history and its current state, and discusses the role of corporate culture in telecommuting. The following section presents our research methodology and the analysis of results. The next two sections discuss our results and their organizational implications. The final section concludes the paper.

2. Literature review

2.1. Enterprise mobility

Enterprise mobility has been investigated by MIS researchers from various perspectives over its brief history. These researchers have examined the topic theoretically, conceptually, and empirically. Even the terms used in enterprise mobility research have changed over time.

Lyytinen and Yoo [28] claim that enterprise mobility, which they say is supported by "nomadic computing", is being driven by the three primary changes of "knowledge intensity, globalization, and virtualization" in the business environment. These three factors require workers to be able to access organization information globally. This requirement will subsequently require changes in how organizations are designed and how they operate. They ultimately conclude that past IT research assumptions must change due to the nature and use of mobile devices and global access to information. New assumptions about the use of IT in mobile enterprises will lead to new research directions such as leadership in the design and development of "nomadic information environments" and the recognition that as information and technology become more mobile the more social impacts will affect their use. This has great importance on organizations wishing to become mobile enterprises through processes such as telecommuting, as social effects of distant workers will have to be considered along with technological effects.

In another research direction, Kakihara and Sørensen [24] consider the concept of mobility from a purely theoretical perspective. By focusing on the interactions that people perform and not on the technology they use, these authors break down the concept of mobility along the three dimensions of space, time, and context. They also ignore the purely "geographical" nature of mobility and instead focus on the interactions individuals perform with one another. Using an analogy to topology and fluid flow, the authors suggest that "social space behaves like a fluid" wherein mobile technologies produce and systematize useful fluid work settings and situations. From the perspective of a mobile enterprise, telecommuting alters all three of the "space, time, and context" dimensions of work as compared to a "traditional" office information worker. Hence this fluid flow model could be a useful analogy for investigating telecommuting.

Pica et al. [37] extend beyond Kakihara and Sørensen's view of mobility as interaction in proposing a more comprehensive theory for studying mobility inside organizations and across roles. These authors propose that mobility is tightly linked to work conditions and those studying enterprise mobility need to recognize this particular impact as well as the impact of the information with which employees work. Task-technology fit plays an increasingly important role but must also consider the changing environments in which the technology is injected, as mobility implies changing work locations and situations. The authors claim that "the use of mobile devices can not be analyzed separately from the work context." This has important implications for the mobile enterprise, as the authors claim that the value and usability of mobile technologies should not be evaluated purely from an analysis of the functions of those technologies. Therefore, telecommuting in the mobile enterprise must be examined in the larger work context in which it is implemented and not merely associated with the functions that it supplies.

Finally, Scornavacca et al. [46] examined 235 research papers in the field of mobile business and assessed the past, present, and future of this field of study. Their goal was to summarize the state of mobile business research and to provide guidance on useful future research directions. The authors noted the increasing trend through the previous five years of not only the number of articles related to mobile business but also the increasing number of journals and conferences. The authors show that the number of papers doubled each subsequent year over their period of analysis. They also note that the focus of research has been largely on consumer-oriented issues even though business applications of mobile technology are expected to grow twice as rapidly as consumer applications. The authors further note that the research focus has slowly changed from earlier conceptual studies to later empirical studies. Their suggestions for future research are in the areas of: business and organization applications instead of consumer applications, empirical research instead of conceptual research, and development of theory. The research project described in this paper attempts to follow all three of these suggestions by collecting empirical survey data about organizations and developing fundamental theories about the impact of corporate culture on telecommuting in the mobile enterprise.

2.2. Corporate culture

The concept of using corporate culture to analyze organizations was examined in a research paper by Smircich [49] wherein she found five primary research themes: comparative management, corporate culture, organizational cognition, organizational symbolism, and unconscious processes and organization. She proposes that researchers of corporate culture select their research directions based on their own assumptions on organizations and "cultural perspective". The result of this premise is that those examining corporate culture will delve in different directions, unearthing knowledge that will yield variant results depending on which of the five research themes drives that researcher and that research stream. She concludes by echoing earlier research [38] that organizational research study is moving from an area dominated by the "open systems" metaphor to one accepting of the "culture" metaphor. This implies that studies of enterprise mobility should incorporate the concept of corporate culture and not merely the concept of the organization as a system.

Barney [2] found that three attributes of a firm's culture must exist for that firm to create a sustainable competitive advantage. Those three attributes are: 1) the culture must be valuable, meaning that it provides mechanisms that lead to better financial performance, 2) the culture must be rare, meaning that it is not commonly evident in firms in that industry, and 3) the culture is not "perfectly imitable", meaning that other firms lacking that culture cannot easily adopt or replicate it. The author does not imply that organizations with these cultural features will automatically have a sustainable competitive advantage because there may be other characteristics of the firm that negate the value of these cultural attributes. This premise has significant impact for those firms that wish to become mobile enterprises. This is so because if the characteristics of an organization's culture that allow adoption or promotion of mobility (such as telecommuting) are not financially valuable, rare, and difficult to imitate, then enterprise mobility will not result in a sustainable competitive advantage.

Denison [7] examined the difference between research on corporate climate and research on corporate culture. One of his premises is that some quantitative survey methods used to examine corporate culture are in opposition to the foundations of original culture research methods. Furthermore, those same quantitative survey methods are strikingly similar to methods used in earlier corporate climate research. He then contrasts the differences and similarities between these two research approaches quite succinctly as "If researchers carried field notes, quotes, or stories, and presented qualitative data to support their ideas, then they were studying culture. If researchers carried computer printouts and questionnaires and presented quantitative analysis to support their ideas, then they were studying climate." He concludes by speculating that the difference between the two is a matter of interpretation rather than actual phenomenon. This implies that it is appropriate to study enterprise mobility either from an organizational climate perspective or from a corporate culture perspective (as was taken in the research project described in this paper).

In the third edition of his book, *Organizational Culture and Leadership* [44], Edgar Schein defines the culture of a group as "a pattern of shared basic assumptions that was learned by a group as it solved its problems of external adaptation and internal integration, that has worked well enough to be considered valid and, therefore, to be taught to new members as the correct way to perceive, think, and feel in relation to those problems." He also points out that for corporate cultures to succeed and continue, groups may have to remove ineffective leaders. Those leaders are ones who do not lead the organization to success because they did not fit the culture or because they were unsuccessful at changing a dysfunctional culture. This implies that there are corporate cultures that may be more or less successful at promoting enterprise mobility and/or telecommuting because of the ways that those organizations create, evolve, and infuse their culture. Furthermore, leaders of organizations that successfully become mobile enterprises must ensure that their corporate cultures are able to evolve and instill the acceptance of work mobility, whichever means the organization chooses for that mobility (via telecommuting or other distant-work processes).

Building on this concept of corporate culture and how it can be a large determinant on the ability of a corporation to adopt some useful tool or process, Hatch and Schultz [19] examined how firms try to apply corporate branding. They propose a model to aid management in best aligning corporate branding with the existing corporate culture, strategic vision, and corporate image. The model suggests that the organization's ability to link and promote the interplay between these three elements will determine its success at corporate branding. The authors further believe that corporate branding is a dynamic process that must be continually monitored. As the organization changes, so must the process of corporate branding; it must also be adopted, accepted, and promoted through the entire organization. The corollary to telecommuting is that for an organization that wishes to become a mobile enterprise by adopting telecommuting to succeed, the organization may have to continually monitor the adoption and usage of telecommuting and make it a corporate-wide endeavor.

2.3. Telecommuting

In a research article on transportation alternatives, Jack Nilles coined the term "telecommute" [32, p. 4]. He defined telecommuting as information industry workers performing work "using communications and computer technologies at locations much closer to their homes" and described it as a way to reduce commuter traffic. In the research project, he and his team examined telecommuting in an insurance company on the west coast of the United States in order to study its feasibility. The publication of this influential study became the inspiration that spawned a large body of research in this area. Fittingly, Nilles has been universally recognized as the "father" of telecommuting research [21].

Since Nilles' paper, various definitions for telecommuting have emerged. Mokhtarian et al. [31] explain telecommuting as:

> "... salaried employees of an organization replace or modify the commute by working at home or a location closer to home than the regular workplace, generally using ICT to support productivity and communication with the supervisor, co-workers, clients, and other colleagues."

Potter [39] takes a broader view and describes telecommuting as a new paradigm where a "boundary-less organization" brings work to workers to be performed at the location that makes the "most sense." This view, however, involves modes of remote work that have only recently become technologically feasible (e.g., working in a café with a Wi-Fi hotspot). Since we are concerned with the impact of corporate culture on telecommuting, we choose to follow Nilles' original concept and restrict our definition to the work-at-home situation, which is the oldest form of telecommuting. We use this definition of telecommuting in this paper, as over time corporate culture is likely to have the most impact on it.

Various other terms referring to this form of workplace arrangement are used in businesses today including telework, work-at-home, e-work, distributed work, flexiwork, and flexiplace. Although the definitions of the different terms vary somewhat, the underlying premise is essentially the same.

In general, a telecommuter (or teleworker) is an individual who telecommutes. This term, however, is ambiguous. Garrett and Danziger [13] explore the taxonomy of a telecommuter; aside from distinguishing between a part-time and a full-time telecommuter, the authors categorize the subject into three types: Fixed-Site teleworker, Flexiworker, and Mobile Teleworker. Consistent with our chosen definition of telecommuting, this research defines a telecommuter as a full-time or part-time fixed-site (home) telecommuter.

The practice of telecommuting in the 1970's was mainly experimental when Nilles performed his original research [32] and the U.S. economy was more manufacturing-based than it is today. In the 1980's, the number of information workers in the U.S. jumped to over 50% [54, p. 1]. Personal computers and network connections from the home emerged. These developments increased opportunities for telecommuting. In 1984, telecommuting gained visibility when residents in the Los Angeles area used telecommuting to avoid traffic congestion caused by the Olympic Games [10]. Ramsower [41, pp. 12–14] further described telecommuting in the early 80's as "increased dramatically". He cited estimates from a popular magazine that almost "six hundred workers in thirty-five organizations were telecommuting." The motivations were varied: tapping into home-based workers in response to worker shortage, reducing office space, and reducing auto driving.

In the late 1900's, the concept of a "virtual society" emerged. Igbaria et al. [22] anticipated the traditional society transitioning into a "virtual society" by four driving forces: global economics, political policies, "enlightened and diversified population", and information technology. Telework (telecommuting) was mentioned as one "arrangement" for the up-coming "virtual society." Technological barriers to telecommuting began to disappear with advances in information and communication technologies: high-speed internet access began to replace low-speed modem connections and virtual private networks reduced concern over security vulnerability. By the end of the 1990's, Telecommute America reported over 11 million U.S. workers telecommuted [22]. A recent statistic from the U.S. Department of Labor showed that almost 14 million Americans work at home [3].

2.4. Advantages and disadvantages of telecommuting

Telecommuting attracts enormous interest for its impact on society, businesses, organizations, and individual workers. Its potential advantages are appealing, but its disadvantages can be detrimental. Harpaz [18, pp. 74–80] focused on the advantages and disadvantages of telecommuting, relating them to the individual, the organization, and society. Table 1 summarizes the potential advantages and disadvantages identified by Harpaz [18, pp. 74–78].

2.5. Telecommuting trends

Recent trends could be disappointing for telecommuting advocates and enthusiasts. A Gartner research report calls the phenomenon "The Quiet Revolution" [23]. Their data showed that the trend of U.S. telecommuter's growth rate is declining from a high of 25% growth in 2003 to less than a 5% growth in 2007 (measured as the number of workers who telecommute more than 8 hours per week). Jones [23] attributes the spike after 2001 to the terrorist attack of September 11, 2001. The Dieringer Research

Table 1
Potential advantages and disadvantages of telecommuting [Adapted from [18, pp. 74–78]]

Level	Advantages	Disadvantages
Individual	– Autonomy/Independence – Flexible working hour – Improved time management – Savings in travel time and expenses – Flexible in caring for family members	– Impaired feeling of belonging – Feeling of isolation – No separation between spheres of work and home – Required self-discipline – Lack of professional support – Impaired career advancement – Over-availability syndrome – Legal issues
Organization	– Increased productivity – Increased available of human resource – Significant decrease in absence levels – Savings in direct expenses – Increased motivation and satisfaction – Create a positive image of the organization	– Difficulties in application of centralized management – Required investment in new work and management methods – Possible harm to organizational commitment and identity – Costs involved in transition to telecommuting – Legal issues
Society	– Improvement in the quality of the environment – Decrease in traffic – Solutions for population with special needs (disabled workers) – Savings in infrastructure and energy	– Creation of a detached society – Flexible working hour – Improve time management, professional flexibility

Group conducted a survey for the WorldatWork association and found that only about 8% of workers have the opportunity to work at home one day each month [56]. The same report shows that there were about 14.7 million full-time telecommuters in the U.S. in 2006 (out of almost 150 million total workers in the U.S.). The National Technology Readiness Survey reports that only 2% of full-time employees in the U.S. telecommuted in 2005 [34]. Citing from the forecast by International Data Corporation (IDC) of just 2% growth rate for telecommuting through 2009, Korzeniowski [25] entitles his article "Telecommuting Climate Getting Chilly." In the same article, Merle Sandler from IDC commented that "there hasn't been as much growth in telecommuting as some observers had expected."

One possible conclusion from the literature is that telecommuting is still in its infancy. Nevertheless, interest in the topic of telecommuting is on the rise. Siha and Monroe [48, pp. 470–471] conducted an empirical review of literature on the topic of telecommuting (telework) and found that the number of publications is in the thousands. Their results indicate that workforce issues (46.8%) and organizational issues (30.5%) are perhaps more influential on telecommuting than technology issues (12.8%) and other issues (9.8%).

2.6. Telecommuting drivers

The intent of the original research on telecommuting by Nilles was to promote an option for reducing vehicle travel with the purpose of conserving energy [32]. This desire to reduce traffic from public roads has recently intensified. The "2005 Urban Mobility Report" prepared by the Texas Transportation Institute disclosed a staggering statistic on traffic congestion in the U.S. According to the report, the cost of traffic congestion for the U.S. economy in 2003 was over $63 billion [45]. Aside from the traffic congestion problem, automobile travel contributes to the degradation of air quality. The Clean Air Act Amendments of 1990 partially addresses this issue by requiring large organizations in polluted areas to reduce daily vehicle commuting by 20% [48, p. 456]. Another law that encourages telecommuting is the Americans with Disabilities Act. This law requires organization to "make reasonable accommodations for disabled employees" [22]. Government policies and the desire of workers to reduce the stress of commuting are among the factors that drive telecommuting.

Changes in family structure and in the demographics of the American workforce in the last decades add to the attractiveness of telecommuting. The emergence of the dual-earner family where two adults are employed has become the norm in today's society [6, p. 3]. According to the U.S. Department of Labor (2006 statistic), among the 35 million married-couple families (with children under 18 years of age), 61% of those are dual-earner families [5]. Women have been entering the work force *en masse* [36]. Labor statistics of 2005 show that participation of women in the labor force increased to 59% [4], and 70.5% of mothers work [5]. Consequently, work-life balance becomes a challenge. The inherent flexibility of telecommuting makes it appealing for workers with family and life responsibilities.

The changing nature of the economy is another driving force for telecommuting. The U.S. economy has been transforming from an industrial to a service economy from the beginning of the 1980s [6, p. 3]. The nature of the workforce in the service industry is primarily information or knowledge workers, in which work can be done with information and communication technologies; the need for being in the office decreases as a result. Also, globalization trends have increased the complexity of the business organization and lead to the "increased specialization in white-color work force" [36]. Attracting and retaining these specialized workers is a challenge for organizations, and thus telecommuting can be used to accommodate scarce and skillful human resources.

The heightened concern for emergency-response at the turn of the century raised the importance of telecommuting to the next level. The tremendous disruptions caused by the terrorist attack of September 11, 2001, Hurricane Katrina, the threat of the bird flu pandemic [9, p. 53], and severe weather conditions are among the many reasons that compel public and private organizations to rethink their operational structure and arrangements to prepare for the worst. For example, telecommuting was a necessity after the 1989 Loma Prieta earthquake in San Francisco for the EPA to respond to the emergency [55]. Operation continuity is vital for many organizations and telecommuting is a viable arrangement and strategy for crisis management.

Advances in information and communication technologies are another driver for telecommuting. The improvement of information technologies prompts organizations to re-examine and re-design their structure and policies (such as the use of telecommuting as a workplace alternative) in order to enhance operational effectiveness and to remain competitive. However, some authors dispute the notion that technology is a driver for organizational arrangement change. Christensen [6, p. 3] believes that the movement of workers to a home-based arrangement "will have more to do with prevailing conditions in the economy and the family than in the availability of computer technology." Huws et al. [21, p. 219] argue that technology is the enabler, but the future of telecommuting will not be determined by technology:

> "Telework will not be simply determined by information technology and its potential for transforming the nature and location of information-processing work . . . The determining factor is [therefore] not the technology itself . . . rather, it is a matter of assessing economic, social and political trends."

Olson [35, p. 72] states that technology developments will create the necessary supporting need for the "new form of work" (telecommuting) but the need for organizations to "search for alternative means of adapting to the change" will be determined by developments in economic and demographic structures. The position of Gordon [15, p. 73] on the future of telecommuting is that technology plays an important role but by itself is not adequate for widespread workplace decentralization. Nevertheless, advances in technology will continue to be vital for telecommuting.

2.7. Telecommuting deterrents

Telecommuting has its share of critics. The tradeoffs and drawbacks of telecommuting could lead to the hesitance or reluctance of organizations and/or workers to adopt this form of work arrangement. The many barriers and deterrents to telecommuting since its inception still exist in today's environment and could explain the slow progress of the phenomenon.

In 2001, the U.S. government's General Accounting Office (GAO) prepared a report specifically to identity the potential barriers to telecommuting that private companies face. The study conducted for the report identified the following barriers [12]:

- Employers concern about the challenge of privacy issues in monitoring data used and access by remote workers, the security implication of proprietary and sensitive data at an offsite location, and the economic implication of widespread implementation of telecommuting
- Health and safety rules could expose the organization to lawsuit threat and additional liability
- The complexity of tax laws and the uncertainty of whether additional tax burden will be incurred (e.g., tax implications of telecommuters working in one state with a primary residence in another state)

The vulnerability to legal risks associated with remote workplace is a deterrent to telecommuting. Furthermore, the reluctance to fully and officially endorse telecommuting may deter workers from choosing this mode of work.

The outsourcing/offshoring phenomenon, in terms of workforce reduction by organizations, could be another deterrent for telecommuting. The pressure for cost-cutting is a high priority for many organizations in today's economic climate, partly due to increased foreign competition as a result of globalization. Reducing labor costs by outsourcing/offshoring has been a popular choice for many companies. The effect is increased domestic layoffs. In 2004 alone, the number of layoffs associated with outsourcing/offshoring was over 73,000, according to Mass Layoff Statistics data from the U.S. Department of Labor [30]. Realizing that their jobs can be expendable [50, p. 17], workers may be hesitant to telecommute because of the perceived fear that out-of-sight employees are more likely to be the next layoff target. This phenomenon is evident in the result of an empirical research study by Lim and Teo [26, p. 578], which discovered that "individuals with higher levels of perceived job insecurity . . . will have a less favorable attitude towards teleworking."

The social relation aspect of human nature could be another major reason for the reluctance to telecommute. It may seem that the motivation to work is primarily a paycheck, but Ramsower [41, p. 3] disputes this notion:

"The days when it was believed that the primary motivation to work was monetary are past. People work because of social and achievement needs, and telecommuting may in fact be very detrimental to satisfying such a need through work."

Social relation has also been identified to be "a major source of job satisfaction" [27]. Root [42, p. 25] believes that "social processes and collaboration efforts are at the heart of most work activities," and attributes "interpersonal communication and informal social relationship" to the success factors for individual workers. Terveen and McDonal [52, p. 401] summarize the social aspect of human nature as:

"People are social creatures – fundamentally so. We look to other people for a multitude of purposes: dating and eventually marriage, pursuing shared interests, addressing community issues, solving technical problems, or maybe just having a good conversation."

Grantham [17, p. 73] conducted a case study on the virtual office and found that 72% of individuals consider relationships with their co-workers as important or very important. The social isolation imposed by telecommuting could therefore be a major deterrent of remote working.

2.8. Telecommuting and corporate culture

Also considered to be one of the main deterrents to telecommuting are the inherent characteristics of the organization. Corporate (organizational) culture has a profound influence on telecommuting and vice versa. Many aspects of telecommuting are considered to be somewhat incompatible with current corporate cultures in which management style is still ingrained with traditional practices.

As revealed by a Haworth and IFMA survey, corporate culture is the top barrier to telecommuting [20]. Nilles also conceded that telecommuting has not lived up to its expectation and attributes the slow progress to the still existing traditional manufacturing-style management of the "information factory" [33]:

> "Most offices are, in effect, information factories. As everyone 'knows,' the information workers all have to report to the information factory in order to do their work. That's the way we've always done it. It is very difficult to get managers of organizations to think about working in other ways".

Olson [35, p. 80] provides further detail on the traditional workplace as a central location where employees come and occupy as a group, and work in a typical nine-to-five schedule; this traditional work place is where work performance and organizational procedures are "critically" bound. Gordon [15, p. 3] describes the traditional organization as a "100-year old tradition" of central work place where customs and routines are set based on the "daily two-way journey." It is clear that for telecommuting to become common, this traditional way of work and organizational practices will require changes, but, as Gordon [15, p. 73] points out, "old habits last a long time," and, in the assessment by Nilles [33], getting managers or the organization to change is very difficult.

Corporate culture is defined by Martin [29, p. 3] as encompassing perceptions, beliefs, values, memories, and experiences. The difficulty for telecommuting is that the lack of social interaction imposed by it could impair individuals' ability to learn those beliefs, values, and perceptions. Olson [36, p. 131] shares an intriguing view of the corporate culture:

> "In general, organizational culture is geared around the 'place'; when an employee walks in the door of the building, he or she is 'owned' by the organization until the end of day. In corporate culture, working nine-to-five is subordinate in importance to 'being there' ".

Olson [36, p. 131] further explains that in a corporate culture, there are "organizational symbols" that employees observe and acceptable norms that employees learn, such as "how much one can [goof off,] when coffee breaks take place, how punctual one should be at a meeting, what clothes are appropriate."

The importance that corporate culture places on visibility could indeed impede telecommuting. The assumption that the performance evaluation system used by today's managers is primarily based on "results" may be just an illusion. Ellison [11, p. 23] notes that managers have been relying on "visual cues" to evaluate employees and that shifting to a "manage-by-results" system would be challenging. The observation from Olson [36, p. 131] is that "no matter how much it is stated that good performance is rewarded, the real key to promotability is visibility" and that conformity to the organizational norms must be displayed to the managers in order to be rewarded. The unfortunate irony for telecommuting is that the telecommunication medium is inadequate to completely substitute visibility and face-to-face interaction; it is noted by Ramsower [41, p. 9] that the "bandwidths" of other modes of communication are insufficient to deal with "body language, subtle meanings, and implied gestures."

Another aspect in corporate culture is the notion of "control" that has been ingrained in management philosophy for a long time. Gordon [15, p. 74] believes that "the fear of loss of control" could be the chief reason for the resistance to embrace telecommuting. Gordon further explains that the management philosophy in today's corporate culture still resembles the legacy practice of substituting "observation for

Table 2
Telecommuting frequency

Frequency	N	%
Full-time	13	16.67%
Most days of a week	7	8.97%
A few time a week	8	10.26%
A few time a month	29	37.18%
Rarely	21	26.92%

management" in which close observation was necessary to ensure performance of factory workers [15, p. 74].

Clearly, social presence or physically "being there" is instrumental to the current corporate culture. Shifting the culture to a new paradigm that is less reliant on face-to-face interaction could be extremely challenging and could take a long time.

3. Research and analysis

In order to assess the current impact of corporate culture on telecommuting, an anonymous web-based survey was developed to gather data from working professionals and managers. The questionnaire in the survey consisted of 20 statements describing corporate culture or behavior that would presumably affect attitudes toward telecommuting. An initial set of statements was derived from the literature review. Interviews with several telecommuting employees of a high-tech company were then conducted to review the questions and to provide additional questions.

The design of the questionnaire in the survey used a common approach in which some statements are written in a positive fashion and some are written in a negative form (for example, see Alghazo [1]). Part 1 consisted of ten statements portraying organizational culture or behaviors in a fashion presumably favorable to telecommuting (positively-framed statements). Part 2 consisted of ten statements portraying organizational culture or behaviors in a fashion presumably incompatible or unfavorable to telecommuting (negatively-framed statements). All statements are listed in the Appendix. Respondents were asked to evaluate each statement based on the current corporate culture or organizational environment (as they know it), rather than on the ideal condition, and to indicate the strength of their agreement on a seven-point Likert scale (from "strongly disagree" to "strongly agree" with a neutral of "neither agree nor disagree") with each statement. The survey also included an open-ended question and several questions to categorize the respondents.

Invitations to participate in the web-based survey were sent via email to 132 working professionals and managers in several high-tech companies. Seventy-eight responses were received for a 59% response rate. Thirty respondents provided additional comments to the open-ended question. Seventy-one (91.0%) of the respondents came from North America, 2 from (2.6%) from Europe, and 5 (6.4%) from Asia.

Table 2 shows the frequency of telecommuting by the respondents. The respondents were divided into two groups based on their telecommuting practices: predominant-telecommuting workers consisting of respondents who telecommute full-time or most days of a week (20 respondents or 25.6%) and occasional-telecommuting workers consisting of respondents who rarely telecommute, telecommute a few days a month, or telecommute a few days a week (58 respondents or 74.4%).

Statements 9 and 10 from the negatively framed statements in Part 2 were excluded from the analysis because several respondents commented that those statements did not appear to be correlated with whether the corporate culture is favorable or unfavorable to telecommuting. The analysis of the remaining 18

Table 3
Analysis of unfavorable and favorable responses

	Item	Unfavorable %	Favorable %	Respondents' perception	
				Unfavorable	Favorable
Part 1 Positively framed statements	1	47%	44%	X	
	2	27%	60%		X
	3	46%	38%	X	
	4	64%	33%	X	
	5	56%	35%	X	
	6	33%	49%		X
	7	73%	17%	X	
	8	44%	37%	X	
	9	54%	33%	X	
	10	59%	32%	X	
Part 2 Negatively framed Statements	1	62%	22%	X	
	2	37%	49%		X
	3	92%	3%	X	
	4	58%	28%	X	
	5	55%	31%	X	
	6	56%	31%	X	
	7	59%	31%	X	
	8	86%	4%	X	
Total				15 (83%)	3 (17%)

statements involved assigning the scores 1 to 7 to the responses, with positively-framed statements assigned 1 for "strongly disagree" to 7 for "strongly agree" and negatively-framed statements assigned 7 for "strongly disagree" to 1 for "strongly agree". Reversing the scores of some questions so that "favorable" responses are always assigned the highest score is the recommended technique for analysis of Likert scale data [8].

To assess the reliability of the questionnaire, Cronbach's alpha was calculated on the Likert scales of the 18 statements used in the questionnaire. An alpha of .934 indicated a high degree of reliability.

Because the Likert scale in this questionnaire represents ordinal data, the recommended measure of central tendency is the median [8]. For all 18 statements and all respondents, the median is 3. The interquartile range (IQR), which is a measure of dispersion for ordinal data, for all data is 3.

To attain an indication of favorability, the data was analyzed in several ways. First, the responses for each statement were aggregated into two groups. For positively-framed statements all "agree" responses ("somewhat agree", "agree", "strongly agree") were combined into a "favorable" group, and all "disagree" responses ("strongly disagree", "disagree", "somewhat disagree") were combined into an "unfavorable" group. An inverse process was used for negatively-framed statements. The percentages of responses in both groups were compared to provide an indication of the respondents' "favorability" perception. Table 3 gives the percentage of responses to each statement that were "unfavorable" and "favorable" along with the respondents' perception. This table also indicates whether the overall perception was unfavorable or favorable for all items.

Next, the median score for each respondent for all 18 statements was compared with a neutral score of 4, which corresponds to the response of "neither agree nor disagree." Table 4 gives the number and percentage of respondents whose median score was higher than the neutral score, at the neutral score, and lower than the neutral score, along with the median and the interquartile range of the responses to the 18 questions in each category (higher, neutral, lower). The table also gives the median of the medians and the interquartile range of the medians for each category.

Table 4
Median scores of respondents compared to neutral score

Score	N	%	Median of Responses	IQR of Responses	Median of Medians	IQR of Medians
Median higher than neutral	19	24.4%	6	2	6	1
Neutral medians	9	11.5%	4	2	4	0
Median lower than neutral	50	64.1%	3	2	2.5	1

Table 5
Analysis by category of telecommuters

Category	N	%	Median of Responses	IQR of Responses	Median of Medians	IQR of Medians
Predominant-telecommuting workers	20	25.6%	5	3	5	2.125
Occasional-telecommuting workers	58	74.4%	3	2	3	1.875

Table 6
Analysis by percentage of response of the predominant- and occasional-telecommuting workers

	Item	Predominant-telecommuting workers				Occasional-telecommuting workers			
		Unfavorable	Favorable	Respondents' perception		Unfavorable	Favorable	Respondents' perception	
		%	%	Unfavorable	Favorable	%	%	Unfavorable	Favorable
Part 1	1	35%	65%		X	52%	36%	X	
Positively	2	20%	80%		X	29%	53%		X
framed	3	40%	55%		X	48%	33%	X	
Statements	4	30%	70%		X	76%	21%	X	
	5	30%	70%		X	66%	22%	X	
	6	15%	75%		X	40%	40%	(neutral)	(neutral)
	7	60%	20%	X		78%	16%	X	
	8	25%	60%		X	50%	29%	X	
	8	40%	50%		X	59%	28%	X	
	10	25%	60%		X	71%	22%	X	
Part 2	1	35%	55%		X	71%	10%	X	
Negatively	2	0%	100%		X	50%	31%	X	
Framed	3	100%	0%	X		90%	3%	X	
statements	4	20%	65%		X	71%	16%	X	
	5	15%	70%		X	69%	17%	X	
	6	40%	50%		X	62%	24%	X	
	7	25%	65%		X	71%	19%	X	
	8	80%	10%	X		88%	2%	X	
Total				3 (17%)	15 (83%)			16 (89%)	1 (6%)

To determine whether there is a difference in perception between the predominant-telecommuting group and the occasional-telecommuting group, an analysis was performed of the results broken down by the two categories; the results are provided in Table 5. This table shows the number and percentage of respondents in each category and the median of the responses to the 18 statements in each category along with the interquartile range of the responses in each category. The table also shows the median of the medians and the interquartile range of the medians for each category. Finally, the analysis of the percentage of responses in the "favorable" and "unfavorable" group for the predominant-telecommuting workers and occasional-telecommuting workers is shown in Table 6.

Respondents were also asked to indicate the importance of the option to telecommute to their potential employment opportunity consideration. Table 7 shows this result.

Table 7
Importance of telecommuting when considering employment opportunity

Level of importance	N	%
Not Important	20	25.64%
Important	28	35.90%
Very Important	20	25.64%
Absolutely Important	10	12.82%

4. Discussion

The median score for all respondents of 3, which is below the neutral score of 4, indicates that the respondents' perception of the corporate culture's favorability to telecommuting is negative. Further evidence of this can be seen in Table 4 in which almost two-thirds of the medians are less than the neutral score of 4. In addition, Table 3 shows that over 80% of the statements received unfavorable responses. These results collectively suggest that corporate culture is indeed a barrier to telecommuting. Responses to the open-ended question support this conclusion as in the following examples: "Telecommuting is highly discouraged within the management team." "My organization strongly opposes telecommuting." When the sample is broken down into the predominant-telecommuting group and the occasional-telecommuting group, however, the results reveal that the predominant-telecommuting group has a more positive perception of the corporate culture's favorability to telecommuting than that of the occasional-telecommuting group as shown in Tables 5 and 6. The predominant-telecommuting group perceives that the current corporate culture is favorable to telecommuting while the other group indicates the opposite. A possible explanation could be that the respondents who practice telecommuting extensively might have already adjusted to the new work arrangement and accepted the ramifications. As one respondent stated: "Even though this survey asks questions that look negative, it should be noted that I made the conscious choice to telecommute knowing these ramifications."

Consistent with other findings from the literature [3,34,43,56], the results from this study show that the prevalence of telecommuting is at the low end. As shown in Table 2, only about 17% of respondents are full-time telecommuters. This low percentage of full-time participation in telecommuting could provide additional evidence that corporate culture is still incompatible with this form of enterprise mobility. Additionally, remarks from some respondents imply that the organization's attitude toward telecommuting is still somewhat skeptical, as in the following examples: "One big disadvantage of telecommuting is that you miss out on the spontaneous hallway conversations." "There is too much synergy lost by not being able to walk to someone's desk and chat about an idea or problem." "It is true that not being in the office often would be difficult to attain a management position."

In spite of the generally unfavorable corporate culture toward full-time telecommuting, some corporate cultures appear to be highly receptive to part-time or occasional telecommuting. The high percentage of respondents falling into the occasional telecommuter category (about 56% in Table 2) reflects this finding as do comments from several respondents such as: "In my organization, there is great acceptance of occasional work from home." "Telecommuting at my company is generally well supported and accepted as an alternative to coming to the office daily. As long as an individual can be in the office regularly (several days for week) for meetings and face-to-face interactions then it can work fine and is supported."

The data from Table 7 reveal that respondents have a fairly high preference for the option to telecommute: 74% of the respondents stated that if a new employment opportunity is being considered, offering the option to telecommute by a prospective employer would be an important, very important, or absolutely important determinant in making their employment choice. It is unclear, however, whether the preference is for full-time or part-time telecommuting. Based on the comments provided by participants, it can be speculated that part-time telecommuting would be the preference for the majority of the participants. This suggests that offering some form of telecommuting could be a tool for an organization to attract and retain talented workers and hence promote enterprise mobility.

The survey also reveals that visibility is still very much part of the corporate culture. When asked to evaluate the question stating that visibility is NOT important for attaining a management position (Part 1, statement 10), the "Strongly Disagree" rating scale received the highest number of response (24%), followed by the "Disagree" rating scale (18%) and then the "Somewhat Disagree" rating scale (17%). This finding suggests that some level of visibility in the organization is still instrumental for career advancement, and therefore part-time telecommuting is perhaps more suitable for current corporate culture. Although the findings suggest that current corporate culture is unfavorable to telecommuting, the notion of trust does not appear to be an issue. By a large margin (60%), respondents believe that current corporate culture has a high level of trust and confidence in telecommuters and they would be committed and motivated, and will fulfill their daily responsibility remotely (Part 1, statement 2).

Consistent with findings by Grantham [17, p. 73], relationships with colleagues are perceived by the vast majority of the respondents to be instrumental to their success and achievement. 92% of the respondents agree that relationships with co-workers are an important determinant for their accomplishment (Part 2, statement 3). This finding may also reveal another disadvantage for full-time telecommuters in that building relationships with co-workers can be a challenge due to the lack of face-to-face interaction.

Several respondents commented that the emergence of distributed teams is changing the corporate culture in their organizations and this new management style is more conducive to managing telecommuters. It should be noted, however, that there is a distinction between telecommuting workers and distributed workers; distributed workers may be located remotely but may not necessarily be telecommuters.

5. Organizational implications

The results of this research have important implications for organizations. The negative corporate perceptions of telecommuting could portend poorly for the future of enterprise mobility in general. If, as the research indicates, telecommuting is viewed unfavorably by many corporations, enterprise mobility, which is often much less controlled than telecommuting, may have a questionable future. At the same time, those employees who regularly engage in telecommuting have a positive perception of it. Thus we might hypothesize that those employees engaged in other forms of enterprise mobility might also think positively of these work alternatives. Given these conflicting results, organizations may need to examine their policies regarding mobility in general and telecommuting in particular, decide what forms of work are consistent with the organization's goals and corporate culture, and determine how best to encourage or discourage mobility, including telecommuting, among employees.

Although the incidence of full-time telecommuting is low, part-time telecommuting is common among employees and seems to be accepted in many organizations. This revelation indicates that part-time telecommuting is accepted in most current corporate cultures. It further suggests that multi-workplace arrangements for individual workers could become the dominant trend in years ahead. As a consequence, organizational managers need to consider how this form of telecommuting, and other part-time forms of mobility, should be integrated into their organizations.

The results of the survey showing that a high percentage of workers desire some form of telecommuting need to be considered when designing the work environment. Innovation in workplace design may need to include tradeoffs between high-mobility features and fixed office space allocation. In addition, the increasing need for flexibility in dual-career families [6, p. 3] plus the trend toward higher specialization for businesses [35, p. 73] imply that offering a telecommuting option to support enterprise mobility is important for attracting and retaining workers with specialized skills and talents. Indeed, organizational managers need to consider all workplace options in order to manage the best new employees, especially those from the internet-savvy "millennial" generation [40].

Although telecommuting can offer an attractive workplace arrangement for individual workers to achieve work-life balance, the social isolation effects of telecommuting could lead to lessened career development opportunities. The results of this research suggest that visibility is still instrumental in today's corporate culture. Perhaps, the notion that "visibility is promotability" [36, p. 131] should be reconsidered when selecting the appropriate mode of telecommuting for an organization seeking true enterprise mobility. Enterprise mobility may be of value to the organization but its benefits may come at the expense of individual worker's careers.

Finally, organizations must consider how employees interact and work with each other in deciding on the role of telecommuting in particular and enterprise mobility in general. Because relationships with colleagues are considered so important to employees, organizational managers need to ensure that whatever mode of work is used encourages relationship-building. With the increased use of virtual teams by organizations, this imperative becomes even more important.

6. Conclusion

Despite the many potential benefits and advantages of telecommuting as portrayed in the literature ([47, pp. 21–34] [16, pp. 10–26] [32]), the progress of telecommuting appears to be moving at a slow pace. The findings from Haworth and IFMA [20, p. 6] and others [33] [11, p. 23] [15, p. 74] indicate that traditional corporate (organizational) culture was one of the major barriers to telecommuting, deterring the adoption of this new form of workplace arrangement. Although this research was limited by a small (n = 78) convenience sample, the results obtained indicate that corporate culture is indeed still a deterrent to telecommuting. At the same time, however, part-time telecommuting is readily accepted in organizations. In addition, employees who telecommute look upon the practice favorably, and most employees view the option to telecommute as desirable when considering employment opportunities. Thus, although our major conclusion about corporate culture and telecommuting is negative, our other conclusions indicate the practice has a certain place in today's organizations.

The vision of a predominantly virtual society by Igbaria et al. [22] in which work is done primarily in a virtual setting, such as provided by telecommuting, has yet to materialize. The prediction by futurist Alvin Toffler of the emerging "electronic cottage" in which "office towers may, within our lifetimes, stand half-empty, reduced to use as ghostly warehouses or converted into living-space" [53, p. 181], appears to remain an illusion. What has evolved seems to be the prevalence of occasional telecommuting in which the balance between reaping the benefits of telecommuting and conforming to corporate culture's tradition can be achieved.

Another important conclusion of this research is that as mobility becomes more of an option within the enterprise, organizations need to understand its role in general and that of telecommuting in particular. The major implications of this research for organizations were examined in the previous section. Organizations need to ask questions such as: Will our company allow or even encourage employees to work from home and still provide them with a career path equivalent to that of static employees? With changing technology and changing employee attitudes and lifestyles, will our organization be willing to alter its culture so that telecommuting becomes a more accepted practice? This research indicates corporate culture is a deterrent to telecommuting, and thus the answers to these and similar questions today may be negative. In the future, however, these questions will need to be continually addressed as the mobile enterprise evolves.

Future research in this area should concentrate on expanding the sample size and type of respondents. The sample size of this research was somewhat small and was convenience-based. A larger group of randomly selected respondents will yield greater statistical relevance to any conclusions. Future research could also delve more deeply into different types of corporations with different histories and corporate cultures. The current research did not attempt to collect data on or analyze telecommuting with regard to either of these variables. It is very possible that organizations in differing industries, with different histories, and/or different cultures, will have different impacts on attitudes toward telecommuting. Some of these underlying variables may drive an organization's perception on telecommuting.

From a broader perspective, research that examines the impact of corporate culture on other forms of enterprise mobility is recommended using the approach in this paper. With the increased mobility of employees today using a variety of technologies and modes, organizations need to understand how their culture impacts employees individually and the organization as a whole. These future avenues of research will add to the knowledge base of corporate culture and its impact on enterprise mobility.

References

[1] I.M. Alghazo, Student attitudes toward web-enhanced instruction in an educational technology course, *College Student Journal* **40**(3) (September 2006), 620–630.

[2] J. Barney, Organizational Culture: Can It Be a Source of Sustained Competitive Advantage? *Academy of Management Review* **11**(3) (1986), 656–665,

[3] BLS (2005). Work At Home In 2004. Bureau of Labor Statistic. U.S. Department of Labor. Sept. 22, 2005. <http://www.bls.gov/news.release/pdf/homey.pdf> (Accessed on Mar 11, 2007).

[4] BLS (2005). Women In the Labor Force. Bureau of Labor Statistic. U.S. Department of Labor. May 13, 2005. <http://www.bls.gov/bls/databooknews2005.pdf> (Accessed on Mar 11, 2007).

[5] BLS (2006). Employment Characteristics of Families in 2006. Bureau of Labor Statistic. U.S. Department of Labor. April 27, 2006. <http://www.bls.gov/news.release/pdf/famee.pdf> (Accessed on Mar 11, 2007).

[6] K.E. Christensen, *The New Era of Home-Based Work*, Boulder and London: Westview Press, 1988.

[7] D. Denison, What IS the Difference Between Organizational Culture and Organizational Climate? A Native's Point of View On a Decade of Paradigm Wars, *Academy of Management Review* **21**(3) (Jul 1996), 619–654, ABI/INFORM Global.

[8] D.A. de Vaus, *Surveys in Social Research*, London: George Allan & Unwin, 1986.

[9] D. Dunn, Prepare for the Worst, *Information Week* (June 5, 2006), 53–56.

[10] S. Ellis and R. Webster, Information Systems Managers' Perceptions of the Advantages and Disadvantages of Telecommuting, *ACM SIGCPR Computer Personnel* **18**(4) (Oct 1997).

[11] N.B. Ellison, *Telework and Social Change: How Technology is Reshaping the Boundaries between Home and Work*, Westport, London: Praeger, 2004.

[12] GAO. (2001). Telecommuting: Overview of Potential Barriers Facing Employers. July 11. Briefing for the U.S. House of Representatives Majority Leader Dick Armey. General Accountant Office. <http://www.gao.gov/new.items/d01926.pdf> (Accessed Mar 16, 2007).

[13] R. Garrett and J. Danziger, Which Telework? Defining and Testing a Taxonomy of Technology-Mediated Work at a Distance, *Social Science Computer Review* **25**(1) (2007), 27–47.

[14] L. Gomes, Technology Journal – Talking Tech: Telecommuting paradox: Bosses say it works but might hurt employee, *Wall Street Journal* (*Europe*) (Jan 25, 2007), 34, Brussels.

[15] G.E. Gordon, Corporate Hiring Practices for Telecommuting Homeworkers, in: *The New Era of Home-Based Work*, K.E. Christensen, ed., Boulder and London: Westview Press, 1988, pp. 65–78.

[16] G.E. Gordon and M.M. Kelly, *Telecommuting: How to Make It Work for You and Your Company*, Englewood Cliffs, New Jersey: Prentice-Hall, Inc., 1986.

[17] C.E. Grantham, Working in a virtual place: a case study of distributed work. *Proceedings of the 1996 ACM SIGCPR/SIGMIS conference on Computer personnel research*, SIGCPR '96. April 96: ACM Press, 1996.

[18]   I. Harpaz, Advantages and disadvantages of telecommuting for the individual, organization and society, *Work Study Journal* **51**(2) (Apr 2002), 74–80, MCB Up Tlt.

[19]   M. Hatch and M. Schultz, Bringing the corporation into corporate branding, *European Journal of Marketing* **37**(7/8) (2003), 1041–1064.

[20]   Haworth and IFMA. *Alternative Officing Research and Workplace Strategy.* Haworth Incorporated and International Facility Management Association (IFMA), 1995.

[21]   U. Huws, W.B. Korte and S. Robinson, Telework: Towards The Elusive Office. *Empirical Information System Series.* New York, Brisbane, Toronto, Singapore: John Wiley & Sons, 1990.

[22]   M. Igbaria, C. Shayo and L. Olfman, On becoming virtual: the driving forces and arrangements. *Proceedings of the 1999 ACM SIGCPR conference on Computer personnel research,* SIGCPR '99. April: ACM Press, 1999.

[23]   C. Jones, *Teleworking: The Quiet Revolution,* (2005 Update). Gartner, Incorporated Sept 14, 2005. ID Number: G00122284.

[24]   M. Kakihara and C. Sørensen, Mobility: An Extended Perspective. *Proceedings of the Hawai'i International Conference on System Sciences,* 2002.

[25]   P. Korzeniowski, Telecommuting Climate Getting Chilly. *E-Commerce Times.* Dec 22, 2005. <http://www.ecommercetimes.com/story/47786.html> (Accessed on Mar 11, 2007).

[26]   V.K.G. Lim and T.S.H. Teo, To work or not to work at home – An empirical investigation of factors affecting attitude toward teleworking, *Journal of Managerial Psychology* **15**(6) (2000), 560–586.

[27]   E. Locke, The Nature and Causes of Job Satisfaction, in: *Handbook of Industrial and Organizational Psychology,* M.D. Dunnett, ed., Rand McNelly, 1976, pp. 1297–1349.

[28]   K. Lyytinen and Y. Yoo, The Next Wave of Nomadic Computing: A Research Agenda for Information Systems Research, *Information Systems Research* **13**(3) (Dec. 2001), 377–388.

[29]   J. Martin, *Culture in organizations: Three perspectives,* New York: Oxford University Press, 1992. Cited in Ellison, 2004.

[30]   MLS, 2006. Mass Layoff Data Indicate Outsourcing and Offshoring Work. *Monthly Labor Review.* Aug 2006. Bureau of Labor Statistic. U.S. Department of Labor. <http://www.bls.gov/opub/mlr/2005/08/art1full.pdf> (Accessed Mar 18, 2007).

[31]   P. Mokhtarian, I. Salomon and S. Choo, Measuring the Measurable: Why can't We Agree on the Number of Telecommuters in the U.S.? *Quality & Quantity Journal* **39**(4) (2005), 423–452.

[32]   J. Nilles, *The Telecommunications-Transportation Tradeoff,* New York, London, Sydney, Toronto: Wiley-Interscience, 1976, 1–6.

[33]   J. Nilles, Thoughts on the Future of Telecommuting. Fleming LTD. *Telework Consulting.* Jan 1998. <http://www.davidflemingltd.com/commentary/Jack%20Nilles.htm> (Accessed on Mar 4, 2007).

[34]   NTRS. 2006. 2005/2006 National Technology Readiness Survey – Summary Report. Jul 12, 2006. Rockridge Associates. University of Maryland <http://www.rhsmith.umd.edu/ntrs/NTRS-2005-06.pdf> (Accessed on Feb 20, 2007).

[35]   M.H. Olson, New Information Technology and Organizational Culture, *MIS Quarterly* **S6** (1982). Research Program of the Society for Management Information Systems (Dec 1982): pp. 71–92.

[36]   M.H. Olson, Corporate Culture and the Homeworker, in: *The New Era of Home-Based Work,* K.E. Christensen, ed., Boulder and London: Westview Press, 1988, pp. 126–134.

[37]   D. Pica, C. Sørensen and D. Allen, On Mobility and Context of Work: Exploring Mobile Police Work, *Proceedings of the 37th Hawaii International Conference on System Sciences,* 2004.

[38]   L. Pondy and I. Mitroff, Beyond open system models of organization, in: *Research in Organizational Behavior,* (Vol. 1), L.L. Cummings and B.M. Staw, eds, Greenwich, CT: JAI Press, 1979, pp. 3–39.

[39]   E.F. Potter, Telecommuting: The Future of Work, Corporate Culture, and American Society, *Journal of Labor Research* **24**(1) (2003), 73–84.

[40]   C. Raines, 2002. Managing Millenials. Excerpted from C. Rains, *Connecting Generations: The Sourcebook for a New Workplace,* Crisp Publications, 2003. <http://www.generationsatwork.com/articles/millenials.htm> (Accessed on February 23, 2008).

[41]   R.M. Ramsower, *Telecommuting: The Organizational and Behavioral Effects of Working at Home,* UMI Research Press. Ann Arbor, Michigan, 1985.

[42]   R.W. Root, Design of a Multi-Media Vehicle for Social Browsing, *Proceedings of the 1988 ACM conference on Computer-supported cooperative work,* CSCW '88: ACM Press, 1988.

[43]   C.P. Ruppel and S.J. Harrington, Telework: An Innovation Where Nobody is getting on the Bandwagon, *ACM SIGMIS Database* **26**(2–3) (May 1995), ACM Press.

[44]   E. Schein, *Organizational Culture and Leadership,* San Francisco: Jossey-Bass, 2004.

[45]   D. Schrank and T. Lomax, The 2005 Urban Mobility Report, Texas Transportation Institute, The Texas A&M University System, 2005.

[46] E. Scornavacca, S. Barnes and S. Huff, Mobile Business Research Published in 2002–2004: Emergence, Current Status, and Future Opportunities, *Communications of AIS* **17** (2006), Article 28.

[47] L. Shaw, *Telecommute! Go to Work without Leaving Home*, John Wiley & Sons, Inc., 1996.

[48] S.M. Siha and R.W. Monroe, Telecommuting's past and future: A literature review and research agenda, *Business Process Management Journal* **12**(4) (2006), 455–482.

[49] L. Smircich, Concepts of Culture and Organizational Analysis, *Administrative Science Quarterly* **28**(3) (Sep. 1983), 339–358, Organizational Culture.

[50] W.E. Snizek, Virtual Office: Some Neglected Considerations, *VIEW Point* **88**(9) (Sep. 1995), Communication of the ACM.

[51] Telework Exchange and FMA. 2007. Telework Exchange and Federal Managers Association Study Reveals Only 35 Percent of Managers Believe Their Agencies Support Telework. TeleworkExchange. Jan 22, 2007. <http://www.teleworkexchange.com/managementstudy/TANDBERG-Disruptive-Study-Press-Release_012207.pdf> (Accessed Mar 16, 2007).

[52] L. Terveen and D.W. McDonal, Social matching: A framework and research agenda, *ACM Transactions on Computer-Human Interaction (TOCHI)* **12**(3) (2005), ACM Press.

[53] A. Toffler, *The Third Wave*, New York: William Morrow And Company, Incorporated, 1980.

[54] USDOT, 1992. TDM Status Report: Telecommuting. Federal Transit Administration. U.S. Department of Transportation. August 1992.

[55] E. Weiner and R. Stein, The Evolving Federal Role In Telecommuting. *Telework Exchange* (Feb. 2005). <http://www.teleworkexchange.com/federal-role-in-telecommuting.doc> (Accessed on March 15, 2007).

[56] WorldatWork. 2007. Telework Trendlines for 2006. A report by WorldatWork based on data collected by The Dieringer Research Group. <http://www.worldatwork.org/Content/research/image/Trendlines_2006.pdf> (Accessed on Mar 15, 2007).

Appendix: Survey statements

PART 1

1. *My organization fully embraces, promotes, or encourages telecommuting (or work-at-home).*
2. *I believe my organization has a high level of trust and confidence in telecommuters that they would be committed, motivated, and will fulfill their daily responsibility remotely.*
3. *When my company designs, upgrades, or implements organizational solutions or processes, accommodating telecommuters (work-at-home users) is usually mentioned and considered to be an important aspect of the project.*
4. *I believe, in my organization, the reduced physical visibility of a full-time telecommuter does NOT inhibit his/her career goal achievement.*
5. *My organization provides most of the essential resources (such as paid internet connection, peripheral devices) for telecommuter to work effectively.*
6. *I believe telecommuters and office workers in my organization receive the same level of coaching and development opportunity.*
7. *In my organization, social events such as holiday parties or company celebration events are usually organized in a way that it would accommodate telecommuters or remote workers. (e.g. setting up a webcam and phone bridge for remote workers to participate virtually).*
8. *I believe, in my organization, office workers do NOT have an advantage over telecommuters when it comes to performance evaluation and/or promotion consideration.*
9. *I believe negative perception of telecommuters or work-at-home employees does NOT exist in my organization.*
10. *I believe, in my organization, physical visibility is NOT important for attaining a management position.*

PART 2

1. *My organization's culture is still predominantly office-centric and thus being a telecommuter is a disadvantage.*
2. *If I become a telecommuter, it could limit or delay my access to important resources (human and non-human), and that would be a barrier to my success.*
3. *Relationship with co-workers and other colleagues in the organization is an important determinant for my success and achievement.*
4. *In my organization, it is likely that telecommuters could be inadvertently overlooked for important career-helping assignments, and thus it could be a disadvantage for me if I become a full-time telecommuter.*
5. *If I am a full-time telecommuter (not "being there" often enough), my perceived value to the company is likely to be reduced in the view of others external to my team/group.*
6. *I am NOT confident that there is no negative perception of telecommuters in my organization.*
7. *It is likely that the awareness of my ability and expertise (from other groups within the company) will be reduced if I telecommute full-time, and that could limit my career's growth potential*
8. *The spontaneous and informal interaction/contribution is highly valued in my organization.*
9* *The extra energy required for demonstrating my performance and accomplishment is a burden for me (if I telecommute full-time)*
10* *The acceptance level of telecommuting in my organization is unpredictable or unclear.*

∗Statement 9 and 10 from part 2 of the survey were excluded from the analysis.

Anthony T. Hoang has more than ten years of experience working as an IT professional for a high-tech company in the San Francisco Bay Area. His specialization is in the end user computing area, which includes enterprise desktop management, application and operating system deployment, and web-base applications. He received his MBA from San Francisco State University and he holds a B.S. in Computer Science also from San Francisco State University.

Robert C. Nickerson is Professor and Chair of the Department of Information Systems and Director of the Center for Electronic Business in the College of Business at San Francisco State University. His areas of specialization include wireless/mobile systems, electronic commerce systems, global information systems and technology, database design models and methodologies, and collaborative computing. In addition to publishing numerous research papers in these and other areas, he is the author of fourteen major textbooks on information systems, computers, and programming. He has been on the editorial board or guest editor of several journals. He is a regularly invited professor at the University of Paris Dauphine, the University of Nice-Sophia Antipolis, and the University of Mannheim, and he has been an invited speaker at other European universities and research institutes. He holds a Ph.D. in Information Sciences from the University of California at Santa Cruz, an M.S. in Business Administration from the University of California at Berkeley, and a B.S. in Industrial Engineering and Operations Research also from the University of California at Berkeley.

Paul Beckman is an Associate Professor of Information Systems in the College of Business at San Francisco State University. His areas of research interest are community wireless networks, wireless mesh networks, universal design for learning (UDL), and applications of social network analysis. He has published refereed journal articles in the fields of management information systems and industrial engineering/human factors. His research has also been published in the conference proceedings of ICIS, HICSS, AMCIS, DSI, and several other academic conferences in the areas of management information systems and industrial engineering. In 2003, he was named the inaugural Teaching Professor of the Year in the College of Business at San Francisco State University. He also has several years of industry experience as a systems analyst at Hewlett-Packard San Diego Site and as a consultant at Hewlett-Packard Boise

Site, both in support of manufacturing information systems. His academic degrees are: University of Minnesota: B.S. (Geology), B.S. (Geophysics); Purdue University: M.S.M. (Management Information Systems), M.S.I.E. (Human Factors), Ph.D. (Management Information Systems).

 **Jamie Eng** is Professor of Decision Sciences in the College of Business at San Francisco State University. Her area of specialization is data analysis with applied research papers in various fields. She holds a D. Sc. and M. Sc. in Biostatistics from Harvard University and a Sc. B. from Massachusetts Institute of Technology.

Part III: Enablers

Information Knowledge Systems Management 7 (2008) 101–119
IOS Press

User requirements of mobile technology: A summary of research results

Judith Gebauer
College of Business, University of Illinois at Urbana-Champaign, 350 Wohlers Hall, 1206 South Sixth Street, Champaign, IL 61820, USA
E-mail: gebauer@uiuc.edu

Abstract: As advanced mobile technology becomes more widespread, the impacts on professional environments and on the personal lives of individual users continue to increase. Devices, such as smart cell phones, personal digital assistants (PDAs), and laptop computers can free their owners of the need to remain close to a wired information system infrastructure that is provided in a stationary office environment, and provide the opportunity to perform tasks in a wide variety of use contexts. With changes in use context, however, come changes in requirements, such as the need to limit weight and size of a device. In order to achieve success in the form of adoption, use, and positive impacts on user performance, a thorough understanding is needed about the functional and non-functional technology requirements of mobile professionals. In this paper, we summarize the results of a series of research studies that we conducted to explore the technology requirements of mobile professionals. The research studies included a content analysis of online user reviews, two empirical surveys, and a series of user interviews. Our research findings indicate that (1) user-perceived technology maturity is a critical factor to explain and predict the use of mobile technology by mobile professionals; (2) mobile technology needs to be available in a broad variety of use-situations; (3) users require basic communication and productivity-related functionality, in particular to support non-routine and supervisory task profiles; and (4) mobile technology can have considerable impacts on the job performance and on the personal lives of its users. Our findings have implications for the design, management, and research of mobile information systems.

Keywords: Mobile workforce, user mobility, technology maturity, task-technology fit, user satisfaction

1. Introduction

In the current paper, we focus on technology that is employed to help improve the productivity of business users in need to perform general business tasks while being away from a stationary office environment (mobile professionals), most notably based on communication and information access functionalities. We summarize the results of four research studies that we conducted in an effort to address the following three research questions: What are the technology needs of mobile professionals?; What are the success factors of mobile technology in support of mobile professionals?; and To what extent can established information system theories be applied to innovative technology in support of mobile professionals?

Continuously increasing in technical sophistication as well as diffusion, mobile devices, such as smart cell phones, personal digital assistants (PDAs), and portable computers enable business users to perform work-related tasks without the need to stay close to a wired information system infrastructure. For companies as well as individuals to fully benefit from the – oftentimes considerable – investments in the new technology, researchers and managers need to develop a thorough understanding about the requirements and impacts that are associated with the technology and its use. Furthermore, in order to determine the applicability of the results of previous research and theories of information systems it is important to consider carefully the idiosyncrasies of the mobile technology, such as form factors and user mobility.

As one established theory that is concerned with the success of information technology, the theory of task-technology fit (TTF) suggests that a match between business tasks and technology is important to explain and predict use and performance impacts [18]. The applicability of TTF to mobile technology, however, is not necessarily straightforward. For example, usability studies [28] suggest that the use-context may have a non-trivial effect on the conditions of fit between task and technology: First, it can be observed that form factors, such as weight and size of a device, play a more prominent role in mobile than in non-mobile use contexts [9,30]. Second, functional requirements may shift as business tasks are often performed differently in mobile versus non-mobile use contexts [10,28,36]. Thirdly, appropriation may differ to the extent that mobile technology may be used differently and for different reasons than seemingly comparable non-mobile counterparts [24,33]. As a result of such observable changes of business tasks, technology requirements and use patterns, we need to assess the applicability of previously established information system theories to mobile technologies and mobile use contexts, and to carefully determine the needs for theory adjustments and extensions [19,23].

The studies that are presented in the current paper employ a mixture of quantitative and qualitative research methodologies that include two empirical surveys, a content analysis of user-reviews, and a series of interviews, and were conducted over a five-year period (2002–2007). Our iterative approach reflects the complexities of a multi-faceted field of study, whereby the results from the earlier studies served to inform the design of the later studies. In addition, the multi-part research program allowed for the triangulation of conceptual insights based on the application of established information system theories and of practical insights based on real-world data, thus supporting us in our effort to straddle academic rigor and practical relevance [25].

Epistemologically, we applied two distinct research approaches. We deduced insights about the conditions of use and impacts of mobile technology by applying elements from the technology adoption model (TAM) and TTF. With a focus on behavioral aspects of information systems, both theories seek to explain and predict system adoption and use. In addition, we applied an inductive, phenomenological approach, where we synthesized detailed user-indicated requirements in an effort to explain and predict user satisfaction. This second approach is largely in line with information system theories that focus on user beliefs and attitudes of technology as an object [7,34], and more specifically with frameworks that have been developed by scholars of requirements engineering and usability research.

In the following, we first position our research program by sketching out its theoretical background. We then summarize the objectives, methodologies, and results of the four, related research studies that we conducted between 2002 and 2007. We conclude the paper with a discussion of our findings and the implications for research and management.

2. Theoretical background

The success of information systems has long been discussed by scholars of two distinct research streams that have only recently been integrated and reconciled [34]. The two research streams assess information system success with (1) behavioral measures, such as technology acceptance and use; and based on (2) technology-oriented measures resulting in user satisfaction, respectively. Both have been applied to mobile technology.

2.1. Focus on behavior: Understanding technology use and performance impacts

In the technology acceptance literature, most notably TAM, the research objective is to explain and predict system success based on measures of user behavior, such as system adoption and use [6,31]. Among the most salient findings of TAM are the identification of user-perceived usefulness and ease of use as the main predictors of intention to use and actual use of an information system [5,6]. Applications of the technology acceptance model to technology innovations, such as the World Wide Web [22,26] and Internet-shopping [15,16] largely supported the suggested relevance of both usefulness and ease of use.

Despite many extensions that have been reviewed and discussed at length elsewhere (e.g. [31]), scholars of TAM usually offer little insights into the antecedents of user-perceived usability and ease of use, nor are they concerned with the wider reaching consequences of system use, for example from an organizational level [2]. TTF – in particular its notion of the "technology-to-performance chain" [17, 18] – complements TAM well [11]: TTF it is concerned with the extent to which technology meets task-related requirements (fit), a construct that is conceptually related with TAM's construct of user-perceived usefulness. In addition, TTF reaches beyond TAM's use-construct as a dependent variable, and emphasizes the importance of adequate task-support as a condition of positive impacts on the performance of individuals [18] and groups [37].

For mobile information systems, TTF has been shown to be generally relevant [10], but more specific questions regarding the applicability of TTF to mobile information systems remain unanswered. Given its primary focus on user behavior, TTF generally offers little practical guidance for the design of a technology or task to achieve an optimal level of fit. An exception is presented by Zigurs and colleagues who developed [37] and later tested [38] a specific theory that detailed the requirements of group support systems to fit group tasks of varying complexity.

2.2. Focus on technology: Understanding user satisfaction

A second stream of research that is concerned with information system success focuses on user beliefs and attitudes about the technology as an *object* [34]. Scholars are concerned with explaining and predicting user satisfaction, and, thus, focus on identifying and analyzing design attributes and characteristics of information technology that may be associated with system quality [7,34]. While typically less of a direct predictor of actual use [8] the satisfaction literature offers more practical design guidelines than the acceptance literature has typically been able to provide. In the current paper, we consider ideas from two related approaches, namely requirements engineering and usability studies.

Requirements engineering is an essential element of software design and development, whereby the careful specification of requirements is considered critical to ensure a high level of software and system quality [35]. Requirements engineers often distinguish between functional and non-functional requirements [32]. Functional requirements pertain to the particular behaviors of a software system that are inherent in the different functions that the system can perform. To the extent that functional requirements determine what the system can do they also determine the extent to which user tasks can be supported.

In contrast, non-functional requirements support the functions of a system in a more general sense, and relate to the operation of the system. Typical non-functional requirements, sometimes also referred to as "ilities", are reliability, scalability, usability, system performance, and costs. To the extent that non-functional requirements relate to the conditions of the use context they may impose constraints on the design and implementation of the system.

As the main focus of requirements engineering is on technology per se, the approach is well complemented by research and practice that focus on usability as an important aspect of human-computer interaction. Within the broader context of product development, usability is associated with the ease with which people can employ a tool or other human-made object in order to achieve a particular goal [27]. Usability studies typically include aspects related with the psychology and physiology of the user, and with the specific use context [29]. Among the goals of usability experts are the elegance and clarity with which the interaction between a user and a computer program is designed.

Despite the popularity of mobile technology, difficulties with achieving high levels of usability have long been reported, in particular for applications that extend basic voice communication to provide Internet access and more complex data processing functionality [10,24,33]. For example, Buchanan et al. [3] found mobile Internet technologies based on the Wireless Applications Protocol (WAP) standard to provide a poor user experience based on the fact that they were difficult to use, and lacked flexibility and robustness. The authors provided suggestions of how to improve effectiveness and usefulness on a small screen with a user-centered approach. In an effort to help overcome design constraints and to provide adequate support for various tasks related with mobile consumer electronic commerce, Chan et al. [4] developed guidelines for content presentation, search, and navigation systems. Insights about the specific needs of mobile business users have been provided by Perry et al. [28]. In an interpretive research study of mobile workers who traveled internationally from the U.K., the authors analyzed context and activities, and emphasized the use of various electronic and non-electronic information and communication tools and technologies. Functional requirements that were identified in the study included: support for planful opportunism to make sure that documents and information were available during a trip in the appropriate form when and where needed; effective use of "dead" time to avoid work overload when returning to the office; use of the mobile phone as a device "proxy" based on the flexibility that was provided with the phone and that allowed the mobile worker to call the home office to access information system resources and ask to act on their behalf: "While it may not be the perfect tool, the [mobile] phone allows the mobile worker to achieve important goals without investing a lot of effort in locating or carrying specialized information or communications appliances with them" (p. 340); and use of technology for remote awareness monitoring for both the traveler and the colleagues back at the stationary office.

The importance of the use context for mobile Internet applications was confirmed in a usability research study by Kim et al. [21] who emphasized that different use contexts present unique usability problems. Related are frameworks that conceptualize different forms of mobility, depending for example on the range within which a technology user typically moves, and the resulting requirements for collaborative technology [24]. Zheng and Yuan [36] discussed the requirements of information systems that support stationary versus mobile work with a conceptual framework that takes into consideration the worker, task, context and technology.

2.3. Relationships between theory approaches

Both, TAM and TTF underscore the general need for usefulness and ease of use in an effort to achieve adoption, use, and performance impacts. The research results provide a general background and justification for the importance to design, implement and use systems that fit user tasks and levels of proficiency. Typically focused on mature technologies, neither TAM nor TTF are very specific regarding the antecedents of usefulness or ease of use. Requirements engineering and usability studies provide a complementary research setting that focuses more explicitly on the design and development of innovative systems and technology.

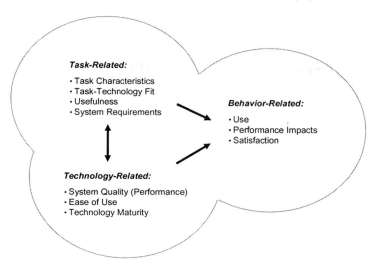

Fig. 1. Research constructs.

The research approaches that we just discussed also complement each other well because they collectively address three key elements related with information system success: task, technology, and user behavior (Fig. 1). Both TAM and TTF offer explanations for behavioral attitudes and beliefs that are related with system use and the resulting consequences on user performance. TTF, in particular in combination with conceptual elements from requirements engineering and usability, contributes insights about usefulness as one of the important antecedents of use. Usefulness and task-technology fit are conceptually related, inasmuch as in both cases the focus is on the potential of a technology to support a given task. TAM's second main antecedent of technology use – ease of use – is conceptually related with usability, as well as the assumed consequence of user satisfaction. Usability studies and requirements engineering – in particular regarding non-functional requirements – provide a framework to study user beliefs and attitudes about technology as an object. Figure 1 roughly positions the conceptual constructs with respect to the three themes of task, technology and behavioral consequences that are discussed in more detail when we present the four research studies in the next section.

3. Research studies

We conducted four research studies in an effort to improve our understanding about the requirements of business users of mobile technology, technology success factors, and impacts on user satisfaction and performance. In addition, we sought to assess the applicability of established information system theories. As mentioned earlier, we focused on mobile technology in support of general business tasks to be performed by business users who are away from a stationary office environment. We assessed systems with functionality to enable and support communication, information access, and productivity. Dependent variables in our studies included (1) user satisfaction, and (2) use and subsequent performance impacts. Explanatory variables included (1) the fit between the technology and the task profiles of its users, and (2) the extent to which the technology meets user expectations of functional and non-functional requirements. The four studies included (1) an empirical survey of mobile e-mail in a single company [11]; (2) a content analysis of online user reviews of various mobile technology devices [9, 14]; (3) an empirical survey of various mobile technology devices [12,13]; and (4) a series of interviews with business users of mobile technology. An overview of the objectives, data collection processes, and results of the four studies follows. For additional details that have been omitted in the current paper due to space restrictions, including information about constructs, questionnaires, and results of various validity tests, we kindly direct the reader to the referenced individual papers upon which the summaries are based.

3.1. Study #1: Empirical survey of mobile e-mail

In our first study, we surveyed the target users of mobile e-mail applications at a Fortune 100 provider of communication technology. The research objective was to contribute to the understanding of the success of mobile information systems as measured by use and performance impacts, and based on a behavioral research model that joined elements from TTF and TAM. To account for the idiosyncrasies of the mobile technology artifact, we included user mobility and technology maturity in the research model.

3.1.1. Data collection

The company operates in a number of global, dynamic, and highly competitive markets, and considers as much as thirty percent of its professional staff to be mobile. Survey data were collected at two separate times and included a total of 55 responses (30 users and 25 non-users of mobile e-mail). In 2002, we obtained data from 27 respondents that had expressed an interest to participate in mobile trial applications that were conducted in various parts of the company. We monitored the rollout of the trial applications that were in effect until early 2003. In 2005, we conducted a follow-up interview with a project director to assess the current state of mobile e-mail use in the company and to discuss the experiences with the trial applications in retrospect. For the second part of the survey, we collected a total of 28 responses from the same company at the end of 2006/beginning of 2007.

The 2002-3 trial applications were accessible via cellular phones and were based on WAP Docomo, and iDEN technologies. Login procedures required a combination of login name, password, pin, and/or a physical access card. In comparison, the 2006–2007 survey referred to the use of operational (= commercially available) mobile e-mail systems, whereby respondents indicated the use of a variety of state-of-the art smart cell phones and personal digital assistants. Figure 2 provides an overview of the research model that underlied study #1. In this study, task-technology fit was predetermined based on a presumed need for mobile e-mail to support business tasks that are characterized by medium levels of non-routineness (according to media-richness theory), and high levels of interdependence, time-criticality, and travel-related mobility.

3.1.2. Results

The data that were collected during study #1 were analyzed with structural equation modeling and the partial least square estimation method. The results of the separate analyses for the situations of pre-adoption (non-users) and post-adoption (users) are presented in Figs 3 and 4, respectively. More detailed information about the research model, hypothesis building, survey constructs, and the results of various validity tests is provided by Gebauer [11].

For both groups of users and non-users, the formative second order construct of task-technology fit was related significantly with three of the four suggested first order-constructs, indicating considerable statistical stability of the predetermined construct of fit. Only the path between mobility – measured as travel frequency and distance – and fit was not significant for either group (or for both groups combined).

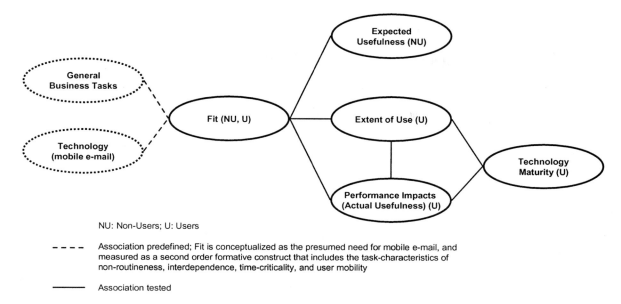

NU: Non-Users; U: Users

- - - - Association predefined; Fit is conceptualized as the presumed need for mobile e-mail, and measured as a second order formative construct that includes the task-characteristics of non-routineness, interdependence, time-criticality, and user mobility

———— Association tested

Fig. 2. Research model, combined for non-users (NU) and users (U) (study #1) [11].

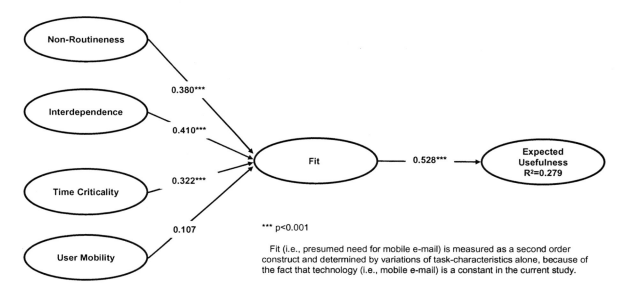

*** p<0.001

Fit (i.e., presumed need for mobile e-mail) is measured as a second order construct and determined by variations of task-characteristics alone, because of the fact that technology (i.e., mobile e-mail) is a constant in the current study.

Fig. 3. Survey results (study #1): non-users (n = 25) [11].

For non-users, we found support for the hypothesized positive association between fit and user-indicated expected usefulness. For the user group, we found support for the hypothesized positive associations between extent of use and actual usefulness, between technology maturity and extent of use, and between technology maturity and actual usefulness. Not supported were two suggested associations, namely the associations between fit and extent of use, and between fit and actual usefulness.

Two of our findings are particularly remarkable. First, user-perceived technology maturity – measured based on service quality and stated need for improvement – had by far the strongest explanatory power

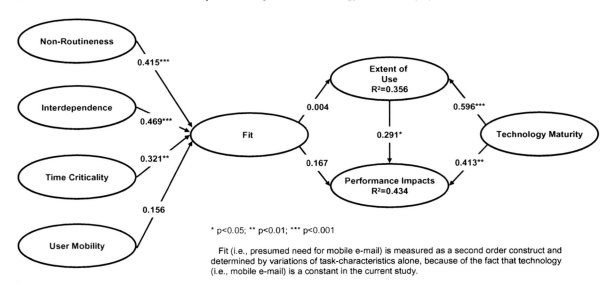

Fig. 4. Survey results (study #1): users (n = 30) [11].

in the model. While task-technology fit was related with expected usefulness for non-users, actual use and impacts of the technology on the performance of individual users were most strongly associated with user-perceptions of technology maturity. The quantitative results are further supported by numerous open and at times rather lengthy comments that we received from the survey participants, as well as by our own observations and by additional insights and documents that were provided to us by our corporate contacts. In all, the survey data indicate that only once (potential) users perceive the technology to be mature, will they be willing to try let alone use it, even in the case of a good presumed fit with individual task-profiles. Our results further suggest maturity to be a moving target, given that the issue of maturity (or rather the lack of it) was equally important at both points in time that we collected data (2002 and 2006) – even though participants explicitly acknowledged progress of the underlying technology. We conclude that technology maturity needs to be understood from the perspective of the user, and there appears to be a need to include user expectations into the analysis. [1]

Our second remarkable finding is related with the construct of mobility that was based on travel, including travel frequency and distance. In the current model, mobility contributed very little to explain fit – or any other variable. As a construct, and in line with earlier discussions [20,24,36], mobility turned out to be more complex than what we attempted to capture in study #1.

3.2. Study #2: Content analysis of online user reviews

In our second research study, we sought to obtain information from users on their belief sets regarding task-related requirements of mobile technology, and regarding the extent to which appropriate technology contributed to overall user evaluation (= satisfaction), use, and user performance ([9], see also [14]). In

---

[1]Unfortunately, because of limited statistical power as a result of the small sample size in study #1, we cannot derive meaningful conclusions regarding the suggested – yet insignificant – associations between fit, use, and performance impacts. While our interpretations of the survey data, user comments, and additional information that we analyzed all give us reason to believe that the expected relationships between fit and user behavior were overpowered by a user-perceived lack of technology maturity, statistical evidence alone is insufficient to draw such conclusions in the current study.

this study, we did not use a predefined survey, but applied a phenomenological, inductive approach that relied on the interpretation of online user reviews. Since the reviews were essentially unsolicited, we assumed that the comments would be particularly helpful in identifying requirements that are important to individual users. We intended to develop a realistic set of indicators with high practical relevance for design- and development-related decisions, and that would also help us assess the applicability of behavioral theories, such as TTF and TAM, to mobile technology.

3.2.1. Data collection

We gathered data from www.cnet.com, an online media website that allows its visitors to publish technology reviews. The site provided a large amount of relevant data that were readily available, as well as a homogeneous publishing environment. We analyzed reviews of four technology products, namely a smart cell phone, two personal digital assistant (PDA) devices, and an ultra-light laptop (Fig. 5). The devices were selected based on (1) the capability of the device to support business users, as stated in technology reviews that were published in the trade-press (online and offline) and as based on reported market share; and (2) popularity in the CNET online community, as indicated by the number of posted reviews, the number of site visitors who indicated the review to be useful, the number of comments on the reviews, and replies to comments. To ensure comparability of the technologies, we focused on devices that were introduced into the market during 2005, followed by reviews that were posted in 2005 to early 2006. For each of the four devices, we analyzed between 19 and 44 reviews in the order that the reviews were listed on the website, which by default was according to the number of visitors who indicated they found the respective review useful.

Three researchers collaborated to develop a database of coded user reviews, whereby we reiterated two steps over a period of several months: (1) development and refinement of a classification scheme that included the identification and description of comment categories; and (2) coding that included the classification and rating of the user reviews according to the classification scheme. Ratings ranged from very negative to very positive on a five-point scale. The content analysis resulted in a scheme of 49 categories as described in more detail in [14]. For the respective devices, the scheme included a number of functionalities, and four groups of non-functional features, namely portability, operation, usability, and network accessibility. We also recorded information about user satisfaction (= overall evaluation), and information about previous experience with the device and technology.

3.2.2. Results

When analyzing the content of online user reviews of mobile technology devices, we soon found that there was limited overlap between the user reviews and the suggested theory-based elements: Most of the essential theory components were hardly discussed in the reviews, including user-tasks, actual use, and impacts on task-performance. In contrast, many of the issues that were of concern to the reviewers were not part of the respective theories, such as detailed information about the technical performance of the devices. In other words, our content analysis yielded little information about behavioral aspects, such as the use and performance-related consequences of mobile technology, but provided us with a rich and detailed set of technology characteristics (technology as an object) that contributed to user satisfaction. In fact, the scheme that emerged resembled categorization schemes that have been developed by scholars of requirements engineering and usability.

We analyzed the data set with structural equation modeling, using partial least squares estimation to assess the impacts of the five factors and two control variables that were identified in the content analysis, on the overall evaluation of the mobile devices (Fig. 6). The results of the data analysis indicated that

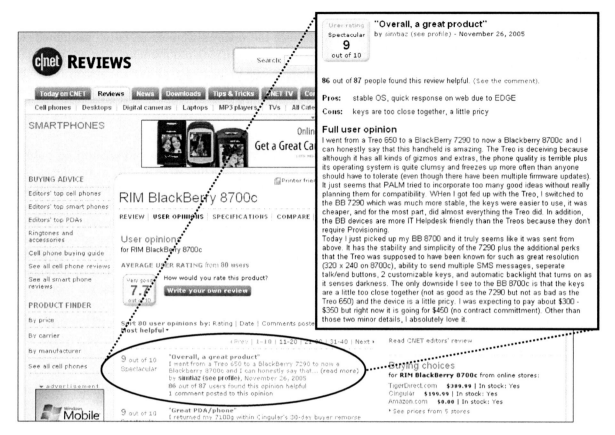

Fig. 5. Example review for study #2 (source: CNET.com).

as much as 66.2% of the variance of overall evaluation could be explained by the five factors (Fig. 6). For four of the factors, we found a significant positive relationship with overall evaluation, whereby functionality had the strongest influence on overall evaluation, followed by performance, usability, and portability. The relationship between network and overall evaluation, however, was not significant. Regarding the control variables, we found the results to vary significantly according to device, but not according to the indicated level of user experience. In particular the items associated with portability provided us with notable insights about the various use situations in which the reviewers expected the mobile devices to be available for service – an important extension of mobility construct that we applied in study #1.

3.3. Study #3: Empirical survey of mobile technology users

For study #3, we built on the insights derived in study #2 in an attempt to reconcile task-related aspects with technology characteristics, and the resulting impacts on user satisfaction [12,13]. The categorization scheme developed in study #2 provided the basis for a survey of mobile technology users that we administered in September 2006 (see Gebauer and Tang [13] for additional details about the survey, including survey questions). In this study, we were particularly interested in the associations between task profiles and the five user-indicated categories of functional and non-functional requirements

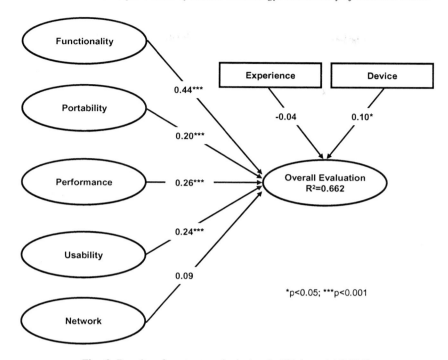

Fig. 6. Results of content analysis (study #2) (n = 144) [14].

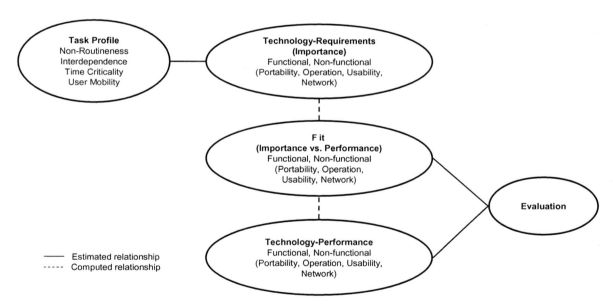

Fig. 7. Research model (study #3) [12].

that we had identified in study #2. In addition, we sought to explore the extent to which a match between user-indicated technology-requirements and user-indicated technology performance impacted user satisfaction (Fig. 7).

3.3.1. Data collection

The surveys were presented to a random sample of 2% of unique visitors at www.cnet.com. All participants were given the opportunity to participate in the drawing of a cash prize of $1,000. According to the cooperation partner who administered the survey, acceptance rates were average with about 6%, followed by a slightly lower than usual completion rate (40% vs. 50–70%), which might be attributable to the comparatively extensive length of the survey. We retained 216 qualified and complete responses from online visitors of the site who indicated to be employed, over 18 years of age, and who used a wireless device for work-related purposes. The survey data were analyzed with structural equation modeling and partial least squares estimation.

3.3.2. Results

We tested the conceptual model in two steps (see Gebauer and Tang [12] for additional details about the data analysis). First, we assessed the association between the task characteristics of non-routineness, interdependence, time-criticality, and user mobility on the one hand; and user-perceived requirements of mobile technology on the other hand. In line with the findings from study #2, user-perceived requirements were grouped into the factors of (1) functionality, including basic communication functionality, advanced data processing functionality, and leisure-related functionality (camera, video, music player); (2) portability and availability of the device in many different use-context situations; (3) operation-related features and versatility of the device; and (4) usability. Second, we assessed the extent to which a user's overall satisfaction with the devices was associated with (1) the user-perceived performance of the devices; and with (2) the extent to which user-indicated requirements differed from the user-perceived performance.

As a result of the first step in our analysis, we found that the overall the explanatory power of task characteristics for user-indicated technology requirements was limited, as indicated by the rather low R^2-values. In addition, only a small number of individual relationships were statistically significant (Fig. 8): Users who indicated their profiles to include highly interdependent tasks and users who indicated to be highly mobile also indicated the need for portable and widely available mobile technology. In addition, users who indicated their task profiles to be characterized by high non-routineness and time-criticality also indicated a strong need for highly operational and versatile technology. None of the other suggested associations was statistically significant at $p < 0.05$. In the current survey, technology functionality and usability were features that users indicated to be important *independent* of individual task profiles.

In the second step of our analysis, we found overall evaluation of the mobile technology to be explained to a large extent by a number of technology performance indicators that were most notably associated with the factors of usability, portability, and functionality, whereby the latter exhibited a negative path coefficient that was strong in particular for leisure related functionality (Fig. 9, left-hand side). In contrast to our findings in the first step of our analysis, the latent construct of operations and versatility was not linked significantly with overall evaluation of the technology. Our results become more poignant when we concentrate on the extent to which user-indicated requirements are met by the technology, and measured by the difference between actual perceived performance and stated requirements ("fit") with respect to the various functional and non-functional features (Fig. 9, right-hand side): In this case, both portability and usability have good explanatory power for overall evaluation, whereas functionality and operation have not. We also found indications of an interesting saturation effect: In situations where user-indicated requirements are lower than user-perceived performance ("under-fit"; expectations are not met) the difference between requirements and fit had significant explanatory power for overall evaluation, especially for usability-related measurement items. However, in situations where user-perceived actual performance of the technology was higher than the user-indicated requirements ("over-fit"; expectations are over-fulfilled), the link between the difference and overall evaluation was statistically insignificant.

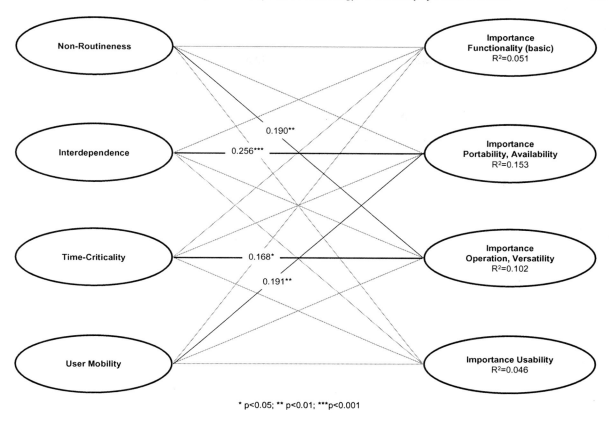

Fig. 8. Survey results (study #3): association between task profiles and user-indicated technology requirements (n = 216) [12].

3.4. Study #4: Interviews of mobile professionals

For our fourth research study, we conducted interviews with sixteen business users of mobile technology. In an effort to complement and extend our earlier studies, we hoped to obtain insights about both technology- and behavior-oriented aspects of mobile technology use. We also wanted to follow up on some of the open questions that we had identified earlier, most notably regarding the roles of user mobility and technology maturity, and the link between task profiles and technology requirements.

3.4.1. Data collection

The participants came from high-technology companies, and worked either in supervisory roles or in technical staff positions. The interviews were conducted during the summer of 2007 and included questions about the task and mobility profiles as well as the use-patterns of mobile technology, including smart phones, PDAs, and laptop computers. Again, we focused on various functions and features of the mobile devices that the participants indicated to be important as well as on the performance of the devices with respect to the functions and features. We also asked about differences in the way that tasks were performed depending on whether the user was mobile or not. Lastly, we asked the interviewees to indicate their level of satisfaction with the mobile devices they were using and the impacts of the technology on their individual performance.

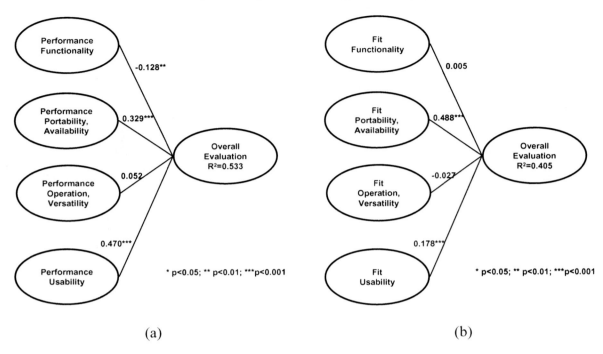

Fig. 9. Survey results (study #3) (n = 216): (a) Association between performance and user satisfaction (overall evaluation of the technology); (b) Association between the difference of indicated technology requirements and technology performance (= fit) and user satisfaction (overall evaluation of the technology) [12].

3.4.2. Results

Several findings emerged from our interviews that complement our earlier results. First, we gained additional insights about the concept of mobility. Several interviewees pointed out that mobility was not necessarily associated with specific geographical locations and long-distance movement, such as travel, but was more generally characterized by the possibility to "roam freely" during regular work hours, as well as during off-hours – all while continuously staying connected. For several interviewees, mobility included any situation where a user is away from his or her desk in a stationary office (and sometimes even situations when *at* the desk), such as meetings, commute, breaks, and when spending time at home after hours. The interviews were largely in support of earlier concepts of user mobility [24,36] and also confirmed the finding from our first study that a mobility construct that is based on travel alone is insufficient to provide insights about the technology needs of mobile professionals. Rather, mobility appears to be associated with the level of independence and flexibility that users gain with respect to any type of physical location and the possibility to change location frequently.

A consultant: "For me, mobility means the ability to work from anywhere and anytime. And when I work from home or remotely, I am not stuck to the house. The PDA gives me a lot of flexibility."

A software engineer: "At work, I have both a desktop and a laptop. I use the laptop at meetings and while changing office locations as I work at other company offices, and move around locations almost every other day. About one third of my time is spent at these meetings and different locations. I use my laptop to take notes, review documents and show people demos or data. Without the laptop it would be very difficult and inconvenient to do so."

Second, we found that users valued highly the convenience, flexibility, and timeliness that are provided by technology that is consistently available in many different use contexts. Interviewees indicated a reduction of stress just from being able to "check on things", to communicate swiftly, and to resolve issues on short notice.

A director of marketing: "One Friday night when I was out, I checked my email and found that one of the engineers had emailed me about some issues. Knowing about the message helped me to go back home, login and resolve the problems. Without the PDA I would not have known about it, so this way, I could respond and react faster."

Others, however, provided evidence for the suggested paradoxical nature of mobile technology (Arnold, 2003), as they indicated that being more accessible has contributed to an increase in workload, and at times has a negative effect on the balance of work and personal life.

Third, we found the need to keep connected to be especially strong for people with supervisory task profiles. PDAs appear to be the mobile device of choice for managers in particular.

A director of operations: "My job is very supervisory. As I am constantly delegating work when I am out of office I need to be constantly informed about the status. Without the PDA, I would have to use different devices like phones and pagers. But still I would not get email. Email is a huge deal in my job function, especially since even the pages are sent via email now."

In contrast, members of the technical staff appear to be much more willing to "let the office be", once their regularly scheduled work hours have ended, and to use laptops to support their work.

A senior software engineer: "I almost never work from home in terms of coding or my actual job. I work from home only when I have conference calls with a team in another time zone. At the most, I work from home about one to two hours a week, using a laptop."

Fourth, with respect to the functionality that mobile users value most, we found a predominant need for communication, including phone and e-mail, as well as a need for productivity tools that included scheduling functionality via a calendar, and contact management via an address book. The finding mirrors Perry et al.'s (2001) conclusion that users view the mobile phone as a versatile tool that can be used as a proxy in many different situations.

An engineering manager: "I am extremely forgetful and used to miss many meetings and tasks. It was chaos, because I was confused all the time. So, I bought the PDA specifically for this purpose. Now, I can schedule meetings and make notes more effectively. Even when I bump into somebody in the elevator and he wants to schedule a meeting, I can do that without any problem, as I have the PDA with me."

Lastly, the interviewees further confirmed the importance of portability, for example in terms of weight, size, and battery life; and usability (ease of use) that we also identified as important aspects of mobile technology in our earlier studies.

4. Conclusions

In the current paper, we have presented the results of four research studies that we conducted between 2002 and 2007 on the requirements of mobile technology in support of users who perform general business tasks. Our intention was to inform researchers and managers that are concerned with the development, implementation, and use of mobile information systems. Figure 10 provides an overview of the results as it positions the main constructs of the four studies in approximate relation with the three themes of tasks, technology and user behavior (compare with Fig. 1). In addition, we indicate with checkmarks ($\sqrt{}$) the extent to which supportive evidence for the suggested relationships was found in the various studies.

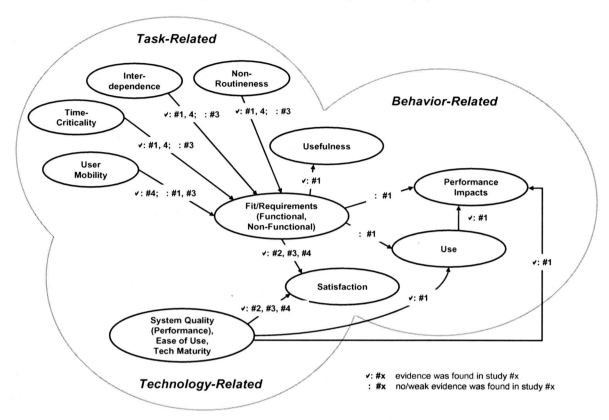

Fig. 10. Summary of results (studies #1–4).

Four findings stand out because of their statistical significance and their consistency over time. First, we found user-perceived technology maturity and system quality (technology performance) to be an important factor that can explain and predict not only the satisfaction of mobile professionals with the technology, but also its use and performance impacts. We conclude that technology providers, managers, and researchers need to take into very careful consideration the ease of use of the technology (usability), and more specifically the effort it takes a business user to set up and actually use the systems. Besides the perspective of the individual user *per se*, expectations also play a role, inasmuch as technology maturity can become a moving target that dynamically "adjusts" as the sophistication of the technology progresses.

Second, regarding the predominant technology requirements of the participants in our research studies, we found a strong need for the technology to be available in a broad variety of use-situations and contexts. The importance of portability of the devices in terms of size, weight, battery life, and availability of service independent of location was emphasized strongly and repeatedly.

Third, following the fulfillment of fundamental needs, such as ease of use and portability, straightforward communication and productivity-related functionality appear to be most valued, in particular in support of non-routine and supervisory task profiles. For many professionals, mobile technology has long become a proxy device that complements stationary office technology and that enables and possibly even deepens a high level of interdependence with team members and business partners.

Fourth, mobile technology can have considerable impacts on task procedures and job performance, but also on the personal lives of its users [1,33]. Convenience, timeliness, and flexibility are among the impacts of mobile technology that were mentioned most often by the participants in our research studies, and that lead to reported considerable increases in efficiency and effectiveness. We found an overall positive attitude of users regarding the technology-enabled blurring of the distinction between professional and personal lives. The majority of the users of mobile technology that participated in our research studies valued high the possibility to be kept "in the loop" while having the opportunity to be physically away from the office – during the work day as well as during off-hours – and be able to react flexibly and timely to important situations that may occur on short notice. Still, a smaller number of users (and non-users) voiced concerns about unwanted intrusion and added workload as a result of increasing accessibility.

Our results have implications for the behavioral and technology-oriented information system theories that provided the background for our studies. In applying TAM to mobile technology, we found that for technology that is characterized by ongoing developments, such as mobile technology, user perceptions of ease of use can have a stronger impact on adoption and use than what is typically assumed for technology that has progressed further. Similar to the situation for inexperienced users that has been examined by scholars of TAM, a situation of immature technology can bring into focus the need to carefully consider the ease of technology use, in addition to its usefulness.

Regarding TTF, we found the theory to be generally applicable to mobile technology insofar as a presumed need for mobile technology appeared to be associated significantly with user-expected usefulness of mobile email applications. We were surprised however, to find limited empirical support for the suggested links between task-technology fit and actual use and performance impacts. Our conclusions are two-fold: First, we found evidence for subtle changes in the way that tasks are performed in mobile versus non-mobile use environments. As some researchers have pointed out before us [28], mobile technology is often used as a proxy to complement more stationary technology. In a mobile use environment, the strongest needs appear to be for basic communication (phone, email) and productivity support (scheduling, contacts), rather than for more complex applications that would be appropriate to perform "back in the office" [24,33]. Second, we found a need to include into the analysis non-functional features, such as usability, portability and availability, in addition to functionality that has typically been the main focus of scholars of TTF.

We found categorization schemes and frameworks that have been developed by scholars of requirements engineering and usability to provide useful starting points for the exploration of the needs of a mobile workforce. In particular, the characterization of technology based on functional and non-functional features proved helpful to assess the suitability of mobile technology for use in many different contexts. In line with other scholars, such as Benbasat and Barki [2], and Wixom and Todd [34], we suggest the need for a thorough and explicit integration of elements from technology-oriented research disciplines, such as requirements engineering and usability, with elements from behavioral theories, such as TAM and TTF, when seeking to explain the use and impacts of *novel* applications, such as the ones based on mobile technology.

Important research opportunities remain in order to develop a deeper understanding about the needs of a mobile workforce and in order to more fully realize the benefits that are expected from the use of mobile technology. We see a need to assess in more detail the subtle changes that occur when users start to adapt their work-related tasks to mobile environments [36]. In addition to the need to understand changes in the way that mobile individuals perform their tasks, it will be important to assess changes that relate to the interactions between the mobile professional and other members of a work-team, including changes in the way that assignments are shared and allocated [24]. We also found a need to assess in more detail the aspect of user mobility and its various implications for technology requirements. Mobility appeared to be a complex and multi-dimensional construct that needs to be explored in greater depth before a mobile workforce can be supported most effectively with novel technology [20].

Acknowledgements

We thank the many participants in our studies and our corporate partners who have contributed their time and insights upon which the current paper is based. We also thank Shantala Balagopal for her help with the interviews, and acknowledge support from the College of Business at the University of Illinois.

References

[1]   M. Arnold, On the Phenomenology of Technology: The "Janus Faces" of Mobile Phones, *Information and Organization* **13** (2003), 231–256.

[2]   I. Benbasat and H. Barki, Quo Vadis, TAM? *Journal of the Association for Information Systems* **8**(4) (2007), 211–218.

[3]   G. Buchanan, S. Farrant, M. Jones, H. Thimbleby, G. Marsden and M. Pazzani, Improving Mobile Internet Usability, in: *Proceedings of the Tenth International World Wide Web Conference*, V.Y. Shen, N. Saito, M.R. Lyu and M.E. Zurko, eds, ACM, New York, 2001, pp. 673–680. Available at http://www10.org/cdrom/papers/230, August 15, 2007.

[4]   S.S. Chan, X. Fang, J. Brzezinski, Y. Zhou, S. Xu and J. Lam, Usability for Mobile Commerce across Multiple Form Factors, *Journal of Electronic Commerce Research* **3**(3) (2002), 187–199.

[5]   F.D. Davis, Perceived Usefulness, Perceived Ease of Use, and User Acceptance of Information Technology, *Management Information Systems Quarterly* **13**(3) (1989), 319–339.

[6]   F.D. Davis, R.P. Bagozzi and P.R. Warshaw, User Acceptance of Computer Technology: A Comparison of Two Theoretical Models, *Management Science* **35**(8) (1989), 982–1003.

[7]   W.H. DeLone and E.R. McLean, Information System Success: The Quest for the Dependent Variable, *Information Systems Research* **3**(1) (1992), 60–95.

[8]   D. Galletta and A. Lederer, Some Cautions on the Measurement of User Information Satisfaction, *Decision Science* **20**(3) (1989), 419–439.

[9]   J. Gebauer and M. Ginsburg, Exploring the Black Box of Task-Technology Fit: The Case of Mobile Information Systems. *Communications of the ACM* (forthcoming).

[10]   J. Gebauer and M.J. Shaw, Success Factors and Impacts of Mobile Business Applications: Results from a Mobile E-Procurement Study, *International Journal of Electronic Commerce* **8**(3) (2004), 19–41.

[11]   J. Gebauer, M.J. Shaw and R. Subramayam, Once Built *Well*, They Might Come: An Empirical Study of Mobile E-Mail. University of Illinois at Urbana-Champaign, College of Business Working Paper 07-0117, 2007, http://www.business.uiuc.edu/Working_Papers/papers/07-0117.pdf.

[12]   J. Gebauer and Y. Tang, User-Perceived Requirements of Mobile Technology: Results from a Survey of Mobile Business Users. *Proceedings of the 6th Workshop on e-Business (WeB 2007)*, Montreal/Canada; also University of Illinois at Urbana-Champaign, College of Business Working Paper 07-0116, 2007, http://www.business.uiuc.edu/Working_Papers/papers/07-0116.pdf.

[13]   J. Gebauer and Y. Tang, Applying the Theory of Task-Technology Fit to Mobile Technology: The Role of User Mobility, *International Journal of Mobile Communications* **6**(3) (2008), 321–344.

[14]   J. Gebauer, Y. Tang and C. Baimai, User Requirements of Mobile Technology: Results from a Content Analysis of User Reviews, *Information Systems and e-Business Management* (forthcoming).

[15]   D. Gefen and D. Straub, The Relative Importance of Perceived Ease of Use in IS Adoption: A Study of E-Commerce Adoption, *Journal of the Association for Information Systems* **1**(8) (2000).

[16]   D. Gefen, E. Karahanna and D.W. Straub, Trust and TAM in Online Shopping: An Integrated Model, *Management Information Systems Quarterly* **27**(1) (2003), 51–90.

[17]   D.L. Goodhue, Comment on Benbasat and Barki's "Quo Vadis TAM" Article, *Journal of the Association for Information Systems* **8**(4) (2007), 219–222.

[18]   D.L. Goodhue and R.L. Thompson, Task-Technology Fit and Individual Performance, *Management Information Systems Quarterly* **19**(2) (1995), 213–236.

[19]   I.A. Junglas and R.T. Watson, The U-Constructs: Four Information Drives, *Communications of the Association for Information Systems* **17** (2006), 569–592.

[20] M. Kakihara and C. Sørensen, Expanding the 'Mobility' Concept, *SIGGROUP Bulletin* **22**(3) (2001), 33–37.

[21] H. Kim, J. Kim, Y. Lee, M. Chae and Y. Choi, An Empirical Study of the Use Contexts and Usability Problems in Mobile Internet. *Proceedings of the 35th Hawaii International Conference on System Sciences*, Big Island, Hawaii, 2002.

[22] A.L. Lederer, D.J. Maupin, M.P. Sena and Y. Zhuang, The Technology Acceptance Model and the World Wide Web, *Decision Support Systems* **29** (2000), 269–282.

[23] K. Lyytinen and Y. Yoo, Issues and Challenges in Ubiquitous Computing, *Communications of the ACM* **45**(12) (2002), 63–65.

[24] P. Luff and C. Heath, Mobility in Collaboration. *Proceedings of CSCW 98,* Seattle Washington, USA, ACM, 1998, 305–314.

[25] R.O. Mason, MIS Experiments: A Pragmatic Experience, in: *The Information Systems Research Challenge: Experimental Research Methods*, (Vol. 2), I. Benbasat, ed., Harvard Business School Research Colloquium, Harvard Business School, Boston, Mass, 1989, pp. 3–20.

[26] J.-W. Moon and Y.-G. Kim, Extending TAM for a World-Wide-Web Context, *Information & Management* **38** (2001), 217–230.

[27] J. Nielsen, *Usability Engineering*, Morgan Kaufmann Publishers, 1994.

[28] M. Perry, K. O'Hara, A.Sellen, B. Brown and R. Harper, Dealing with Mobility: Understanding Access Anytime, Anywhere, *ACM Transactions on Computer-Human Interaction* **8**(4) (2001), 323–347.

[29] B. Shneiderman, *Software Psychology: Human Factors in Computer and Information Systems*, Cambridge, MA: Winthrop Publishers, 1980.

[30] O. Turel, Contextual Effects on the Usability Dimensions of Mobile Value-Added Services: A Conceptual Framework, *International Journal of Mobile Communications* **4**(3) (2006), 309–332.

[31] V. Venkatesh, M. Morris, F. Davis and F. Davis, User Acceptance of Information Technology: Toward a Unified View, *Management Information Systems Quarterly* **27**(3) (2003), 425–478.

[32] K. Wiegers, *Software Requirements*, Second edition, Seattle, WA: Microsoft Press, 2003.

[33] G.O. Wiredu, User Appropriation of Mobile Technologies: Motives, Conditions, and Design Poperties, *Information and Organization* **17** (2007), 110–129.

[34] B.H. Wixom and P.A. Todd, A Theoretical Integration of User Satisfaction and Technology Acceptance, *Information Systems Research* **16**(1) (2005), 85–102.

[35] E. Yourdon, *Modern Structured Analysis*, Englewood Cliffs, NJ: Yourdon Press, 1989.

[36] W. Zheng and Y. Yuan, Identifying the Difference Between Stationary Office Support and Mobile Work Support: A Conceptual Framework, *International Journal of Mobile Communications* **5**(1) (2007), 107–122.

[37] I. Zigurs and B.K. Buckland, A Theory of Task-Technology Fit and Group Support System Effectiveness, *Management Information Systems Quarterly* **22**(3) (1998), 313–334.

[38] I. Zigurs, B.K. Buckland, J.R. Connolly and E.V. Wilson, A Test of Task-Technology Fit Theory for Group Support Systems, *Database for Advances in Information Systems* **30**(3–4) (1999), 34–50.

Judith Gebauer is currently an Assistant Professor of Business Administration at the University of Illinois at Urbana-Champaign, College of Business, and a 2007-2008 Fellow at the University of Illinois Center for Advanced Study. She has been a post-doctoral research fellow and Lecturer at the University of California, Berkeley, Haas School of Business, and holds both master and doctoral degrees from the University of Freiburg in Germany. Her research focuses on the design and management of business information systems. Current research projects address issues related to mobile information systems, information system flexibility, and information system-based product modularization. Her papers have been published or have been accepted for publication in such journals as *Journal of the Association for Information Systems, Communications of the ACM, International Journal of Electronic Commerce, Information Systems Management, Information Systems and e-Business, Electronic Markets – The International Journal, Information Technology and Management, Informatik Forschung und Entwicklung*, and *International Journal of Mobile Communications*. She is also a co-chair of the Association for Information Systems Special Interest Group on e-Business. For additional information, please visit www.judithgebauer.com.

Information Knowledge Systems Management 7 (2008) 121–144
IOS Press

Mobile interaction design: Integrating individual and organizational perspectives

Peter Tarasewich[a], Jun Gong[b], Fiona Fui-Hoon Nah[c] and David DeWester[c]

[a]*ISOM Department, Sawyer Business School, Suffolk University, 8 Ashburton Place, Boston, MA 02108 USA*
E-mail: tarase@suffolk.edu
[b]*Google, 1600 Amphitheatre Parkway, Mountain View, CA 94043 USA*
E-mail: jungong@google.com
[c]*Department of Management, University of Nebraska – Lincoln, Lincoln, NE 68588 USA*
E-mail: fnah@unlnotes.unl.edu, ddewester@unlnotes.unl.edu

Abstract: While mobile computing provides organizations with many information systems implementation alternatives, it is often difficult to predict the potential benefits, limitations, and problems with mobile applications. Given the inherent portability of mobile devices, many design and use issues can arise which do not exist with desktop systems. While many existing rules of thumb for design of stationary systems apply to mobile systems, many new ones emerge. Issues such as the security and privacy of information take on new dimensions, and potential conflicts can develop when a single mobile device serves both personal and business needs. This paper identifies potential issues and problems with the use of mobile information systems by examining both personal and organizational perspectives of mobile devices and applications. It provides a set of guidelines that can assist organizations in making decisions about the design and implementation of mobile technologies and applications in organizations.

1. Introduction

Mobile computing continues to provide organizations in a wide variety of industries with an increasing number of information systems implementation approaches and alternatives (e.g. [5,11,49,67,79]). Hundreds of mobile applications and technologies have been developed, but it is often difficult for an organization to determine whether or not they will benefit from such innovations, or what limitations and problems they may encounter. Since mobile devices can potentially be used in any context and are often constrained by their relatively small form factor, new design and use issues arise with mobile applications that do not exist with desktop systems. While many rules of thumb for designing mobile information systems carry over from stationary systems, many new ones emerge, and issues such as the security and privacy of information take on new meanings and dimensions. There are also potential conflicts when a single mobile device or system serves both personal and business needs; mobile devices that are well accepted by individuals may not be suitable for the corporate world. For example, organizations need to be concerned about achieving the right balance of controlling and empowering employees with the appropriate level of access to organizational data, and maximizing the continuity of organizational processes and activities while managing any disruptive activities arising from the use of mobile computing in organizations.

The goal of this paper is to identify the potential issues and problems with mobile interface design and use in organizations, and present a set of general guidelines that can be used by organizations to assist decision making about the design and implementation of mobile technologies and applications. First provided is an overview of current mobile device input/output interaction technologies, along with the challenges they pose to organizations. Oftentimes, mobile device interface design is more restrictive than desktop interface design due to factors such as relatively limited computing and communication power, smaller platform sizes, always-changing context, and user attention being split between multiple tasks.

Next, the paper addresses security and privacy issues related to the use of mobile computing by organizations. While mobile computing can facilitate access to organizational data, security and privacy concerns must be taken into account to achieve the appropriate balance of access control. The portable nature of mobile devices makes them more vulnerable to loss, abuse, and theft than systems that remain behind locked doors. If wireless networks are used, data is also susceptible to unintended interception or theft by third parties. Security and privacy of stored or transmitted data is often maintained through methods (e.g., encryption) that keep it from being read by any unauthorized parties. But in a public setting, information displayed to a user (e.g., client data viewed on a laptop while on an airplane) may potentially be overseen by competitors or thieves. Furthermore, the classification of information as "private" may not be absolute. Privacy levels from organizational and personal perspectives may differ, which can potentially lead to conflicts when a device supports both personal and business use.

Finally, this paper provides guidance to organizations on how to design, implement, and manage mobile applications on both individual and enterprise levels. While many general rules of thumb for interface and interaction design exist, there have been no similar guidelines provided to enterprises. Most of the existing guidelines are derived from the perspective of an individual's use of mobile applications in dynamic contexts. But there are unique needs and concerns that must be considered for successful organizational use of mobile applications, that is, notions that go beyond individual use and may sometimes even conflict with personal use. We present a set of guidelines that are grounded in previous research, and provide examples where appropriate.

2. Mobile device interaction and challenges to organizations

Handheld mobile devices, including personal digital assistants (PDAs) and cell phones, have become increasingly prevalent. Given the unique constraints of mobile devices, a well-designed and usable interface is critical in order for employees of organizations to accept the use of mobile technology [31, 54,88]. Some of the most challenging issues facing mobile interface designers include [28]:

- Constantly changing context of usage, e.g., business executives who are always on the move
- Limited user attention given to the device and application, e.g., using the device when walking
- Mobile device user's hands are typically occupied with other physical tasks, e.g., holding a briefcase or shuffling paperwork
- High mobility during tasks, as well as the need to adopt a variety of positions and postures, e.g., activities of maintenance crew
- Interacting with devices while in motion (at high speed), driven by external environment, e.g., in a public transport system such as a subway or train

Other organizational issues also arise, including adherence to policies and standards, security and privacy of proprietary information, and the potential conflicts of using a single mobile device for both personal and business activities. To address these problems and challenges, the stage is set by providing a brief review of existing input/output interaction methods with mobile devices as well as security and privacy issues in the mobile environment. Mobile device interface design is generally more restrictive and problematic than desktop interface design because of constraints such as limited computing power, dynamic (and potentially unsecured) contexts, smaller platform sizes, and limited user attention [22,68].

2.1. Input interaction

Input interaction refers to the different ways in which users can enter data or commands. Commonly used technologies for input interaction with mobile devices include keyboards, keypads, styluses, buttons, cameras, microphones, scanners, and sensors (including those that determine the location of the device).

The standard QWERTY keyboard found on typewriters and personal computers is being used on laptop computers and handheld devices such as Blackberries. The problem with using this full keyboard on these devices is that users must adjust to smaller keys, which may even require users to learn to type messages with both thumbs. Smaller keys pose data entry problems and increase error rates. On the other hand, devices such as phones and handhelds usually rely on a limited keypad for input because of limited device space. As such, data entry can be very cumbersome for organizational use and adoption.

Most phones use a standard 12-button numeric keypad, with each of the keys from 2 through 9 corresponding to three or four English letters. Some common approaches for entering text using a keypad require pressing keys multiple times for each desired letter. Other approaches use dictionaries of words and linguistic models to "guess" the word intended by a series of keystrokes. Mackenzie and Soukoreff [46] provided an excellent review of existing mobile text entry methods, including small keypad based methods and stylus based methods, such as handwriting recognition, soft keyboards, and gesture input methods (e.g., Graffiti, Jot).

As another alternative, keyboards (or other key configurations) can be created virtually on a screen. These "soft-keyboards" use a stylus to press the virtual keys and are often implemented as text entry options on PDAs and smart phones. Another way to eliminate the use of a keypad for text entry is to attach a temporary full-size or miniature keyboard to the device being used. Full-size virtual keyboards (www.virtual-laser-keyboard.com) can also be projected on any flat surface using a laser connected to the mobile device. A potential problem for mobile workers who use any of these input technologies is the learning curve required to use the system effectively.

Mobile device input can also be achieved through mouse buttons, thumbwheels, and other special-purpose buttons. Pagers may only have three or four buttons which can be used for text entry purposes [45]. Mobile phones often have dedicated buttons with labels such as "call," "ok," and "clear" in addition to a numeric keypad. Mouse buttons are toggle switches that allow one-dimensional cursor movement. Small joysticks, which allow two-dimensional cursor movement, are sometimes found integrated into the keyboards of laptop computers, and more recently on mobile phones. Handheld devices usually have a mouse button and a few other special-purpose buttons, but no keyboard or keypad. Some handheld devices also feature a built-in thumbwheel, but the location of the wheel can limit which hand can hold the device during operation. Even newer interfaces for text entry can be found on the Apple iPhone and Bang & Olufsen's Serene mobile phone (which arranges a traditional keypad in a circle, similar to older rotary phones).

Using human speech as input to mobile devices is also becoming increasingly practical as voice recognition technology continues to improve. Voice input allows those users who cannot type or use a stylus to interact with a device. It may also be a viable interface alternative for devices too small for buttons or for those without a screen. One novel application of voice input and recognition for mobile phones can be found in GOOG-411 (www.google.com/goog411), which finds and connects a user with a local business that meets their needs. However, voice input suffers from possible privacy, confidentiality, and social issues. For example, users may feel uncomfortable speaking input aloud instead of typing or writing it, certain places (e.g., libraries) might restrict the use of voice input to maintain a quiet environment, and it may be risky to say certain information aloud if it can be overheard by those who could steal or misuse it (e.g., competitors, thieves). Furthermore, voice input may not work well (or at all) in noisy environments, limiting its use by mobile workers in certain contexts.

With the shrinking size of camera lenses and the increasing sophistication of digital photography, video is becoming more common as a form of input with mobile devices. Video might also be used as input through the recognition of hand gestures or facial expressions. For example, MouthType [42] is a system that uses a camera to recognize the mouth shape for text entry purposes. Of course, with small cameras also come additional concerns over corporate security, since photos can be taken virtually unnoticed.

Similarly, scanners and sensors are also becoming part of the wireless environment. Scanners can be used for reading text, bar codes, or other symbols. Wireless devices that scan UPC symbols or read RFID tags as input could be part of in-store mobile commerce applications used for comparison-shopping or for purchasing merchandise without the need of a cash register and sales attendant. Delivery companies routinely use barcode scanning to track real-time shipment status in the field, and there is a trend toward the use of RFID tags for this purpose as well. Inventory and supply chain management can also be facilitated through the use of mobile devices, scanners, and sensors. Some hospitals use such technologies to track patient location and status.

Input can also come from technologies that automatically sense environmental parameters. For example, the Global Positioning System (GPS) allows any device equipped with a GPS receiver to determine its geographic location within about 10 meters. All mobile phones sold in the U.S. will eventually be required to have the ability to determine their location. Various other types of sensors are capable of measuring parameters such as temperature, speed, direction, orientation, and heart rate.

While this section has summarized a variety of interaction methods for input on mobile devices, it is important to remember that each has its pros and cons. The suitability of any one method can depend on the organizational task that a mobile device is supporting and the needs and preferences of the people performing that task. Furthermore, one device and/or application may be used for multiple tasks and by different people. Thus, evaluating the suitability of different mobile form factors and input mechanisms for organizational purposes can be quite challenging.

2.2. Output interaction

Output interaction concerns the ways in which users receive information, prompts, or the results of a command. Technologies used for output interaction with mobile devices include liquid crystal display (LCD) screens (for visual output), speakers (for auditory output), and vibration (for tactile output). These different output methods fit different organizational task and work contexts.

The LCD screen is the primary technology used to produce output in the form of images and text on current mobile devices. Screen size can vary greatly from one type of device to another. Mobile phones might have one or two small (1" to 2" square) screens that can display a dozen or so lines of alphanumeric characters and limited amounts of graphical output. Handheld devices such as PDAs have relatively larger screens (about 3" by 4") that are more suitable for graphics as well as text, but can still be limited by low screen resolutions (usually 240 by 320 pixels). Most phones and handhelds have color screens, which helps increase device usability.

The screen size and resolution limitations of many mobile devices make it difficult to display large amounts of text and graphic-based output (e.g., maps, charts, spreadsheets, or Web pages). Recent technological developments, however, have begun to address some of these drawbacks. Flexible screens can be rolled up and potentially folded like a piece of paper. E-Ink (www.eink.com) and Gyricon Media (www.gyriconmedia.com) are developing displays with electronic ink technology (e-paper). The screens hold an image until voltage is applied to produce a new one, using less power than LCD screens.

Monocular units or goggles can be used with magnifying glasses to enlarge small displays (less than an inch diagonal) so they appear like desktop screens. An example of a goggle-type product is Olympus' Eye-Trek (www.olympus-global.com/en/corc/history/chron/etrek.cfm). Microvision (www.mvis.com) is developing devices that project an image, pixel by pixel, directly onto the viewer's retina. These types of devices allow viewing of color images with similar sizes and resolutions as those found on desktop computers, although a potential concern with these technologies includes interference with users' other visual inputs.

Despite improvements in screen displays, they may not be appropriate or optimal for certain mobile tasks, such as conveying directions while driving or displaying text outdoors in strong sunlight. In contexts where screen displays do not work well, sound or tactile output are two other options. Sound output can range from words to music to various beeps, buzzes, and other noises. These can be created through speakers or through headphones. Sound output may be a viable interface alternative for devices without a screen, although there may be difficulties in presenting certain visual information such as graphics and photos. Voice output is also generally produced and comprehended slower than visual output. On the positive side, sound allows those users who cannot see or attend to a screen to receive output. Ultimately, it may be that multi-modal interaction, such as the combination of voice and visual output, is best suited for mobile devices [53]. One note of caution, however, is that sound (especially on a speaker) is not necessarily restricted to its intended user. When sound is not appropriate, such as in a noisy environment, tactile output (such as a vibration) might be used as a form of output to mobile device users.

2.3. Security and privacy

Technology continues to move us closer to the point of true "anywhere and anytime" access to information. While personal computers and the Internet were large stepping stones towards 24-hour access to information across the globe, mobile devices and communications networks literally allow information access from any location. We have moved from the situation where users needed to be at a point of information access, to that where users carry the access point with them. While wireless networks and mobile devices provide great potential for increased productivity, they also create a new level of security and privacy risks.

Security is critical to organizations while privacy is valued and at times, crucial, in protecting personal and organizational information such as customers' personal data and proprietary corporate information. Usually an individual or employee of a company expects reasonable access to personal and corporate information while such information is protected from access by others. Security and privacy requirements also vary based on the type of information and on the preferences of the information's owner (individual or organization) (e.g. [26]). With the trend toward ubiquitous access comes a need for increased security and privacy of organizational data available on or via mobile applications and devices. Portable devices can be more easily lost or stolen, data transmitted through the air can be intercepted with ease, and working in public places increases the risk of accidental dissemination of information to unauthorized parties.

We explore security and privacy issues in more detail in the next two sections.

2.4. Maintaining and enhancing organizational security

Security is one of the main obstacles in creating a mobile workforce. The widespread use of unsecured laptops and devices threaten organizations' networks, data and users. To successfully deploy mobile devices for information access and transaction processing in organizations, concerns related to security need to be addressed [8].

First, mobile devices are vulnerable to loss, theft, and other security breaches. Thefts of laptops, smart phones and PDAs have increased over time, due partly to the increased number of mobile devices in use. Loss of a single mobile device can result in extraordinarily large amounts of data being compromised. For example, a laptop theft resulted in the loss of veterans' personal data (including names, social security numbers, birth dates, and disabilities) maintained by the US Department of Veteran Affairs (VA) which heightened the risks of identity theft for more than 26 million US veterans [85]. Articles in trade journals and the popular press describe instances of U.S. customs agents examining, copying data from, and even seizing mobile devices from people entering the U.S. (e.g. [94]). With the increased use of mobile devices that store sensitive information, comes the need for organizations to seriously consider advanced security solutions such as data storage encryption, tools that can track lost mobile devices, and security solutions for USB ("thumb") drives. Organizations may find it worthwhile to invest in mobile devices with biometric capabilities to restrict unauthorized access to the devices if they are lost or stolen, and multiple forms of user authentication are recommended. Mobile devices can be set to time out after being idle for a set period of time, and can also be set to trigger a lockout or completely destroy the data on the device after a series of unsuccessful logins.

Second, security of wireless data transmission pathways is critical. Wireless access points are often left unsecured or poorly secured. While most corporations use virtual private networks to protect wireless data, targeted attacks on corporate networks via wireless media have become highly probable. A high-profile example of a security breach occurred when hackers broke into the unprotected wireless networks of TJX/Marshalls. They stole customers' information by pointing a telescope shaped antenna towards a Marshalls store and used a laptop to decode data streaming through the air between handheld price checking devices, cash registers, and the store's computers [62]. After breaching TJX's wireless network, the hackers gained access to servers at the company's headquarters. Thus, the use of advanced encryption solutions is crucial for protecting sensitive wireless data streams, and the use of firewalls can prevent unauthorized access to corporate servers. Some vendors offer tools that validate an access point's identity, which can help to reduce the risk of a hacker gaining network access [23]. Wireless access via a virtual private network (VPN) can also be highly effective. Once authenticated, communication takes place via an encrypted tunnel, which reduces the risk of unauthorized parties intercepting data during wireless transmissions.

Third, viruses, spyware, and malware, which have been concerns primarily to fixed corporate (and individual) computers and networks, are spreading to cell phones and other smaller mobile devices. These rogue programs can wipe out data completely, tap into data on the devices themselves, or be used to access other machines or networks. The first mobile-specific malware, a worm called "Cabir," was created in 2004 and was transmitted through open Bluetooth connections. Malware can also be transmitted via e-mail, Multimedia Messaging System (MMS), Web downloads, and the swapping of memory cards. Based on an analysis by Miller [50], three methods of enterprise security practices are essential to combat this threat: policies, procedures, and technology. Policies for securing mobile devices should include the following: (i) restricting Web downloads such as games and ring tones on corporate mobile assets; (ii) discouraging the use of MMS unless it is critical to business; and (iii) requiring up-to-date mobile security software on any mobile device synchronizing with a corporate network. Miller suggested considering the following strategies when creating organizational procedures: standardizing mobile devices, software, and applications; installing centrally-managed security and anti-virus products designed specifically for mobile devices; using a VPN; including personal firewall software on any Web-enabled mobile devices; and (perhaps most importantly) enforcing any policies [8,34]. Other technologies that organizations should consider include access controls and intrusion detection and prevention systems.

Training and educating employees on security awareness and policies is an important first step, as employees themselves can unknowingly be a major security weakness in any organization. Employees need to be aware of security threats and vulnerabilities, and instructing them on security policies and practices is critical to ensuring that they understand and abide by them. Wireless security policies and practices should be integrated into the overall enterprise IT security plan. It is essential that these security policies and practices are clearly defined and documented, made widely available and known to all employees, and are strictly enforced [8,34].

2.5. Protecting information privacy

Security and privacy of stored or transmitted data is often maintained through methods (e.g., encryption) that keep it from being read by unauthorized parties. But in a public setting, information displayed to a user may potentially be overseen by competitors or thieves. Furthermore, the classification of information as "private" may not be absolute. Privacy levels of organizational information will be dictated by company policy, while the privacy levels of personal information are customized to a user's own comfort level and requirements. This can potentially lead to conflicts when devices support both personal and business use.

Maintaining privacy in the mobile environment remains difficult because the context of a device or application can change rapidly and without notice [20]. This is in sharp contrast to a fixed environment, like an office, where people can consistently control the way that information is handled to minimize the chance of divulging sensitive information to unauthorized parties [16]. People are not intentionally careless when it comes to protecting information, but normal human behavior makes it easy for unsafe conditions to exist. For example, laptop computers are often used whenever and wherever needed or desired (e.g., in an airplane). In these situations, the user can become more focused on the task at hand rather than the fact that information might be overseen or recorded by someone close by. While current technology makes it easy to access information anywhere and anytime, it does not concurrently provide adequate protection of that information. Mobile users need usable interaction methods that work well with multiple and varied tasks, and in environments that can change rapidly and potentially be hostile. If this is not accomplished, users must accept tradeoffs between the pervasive availability of information and the potential loss of privacy and security [16].

Several hardware-based solutions have been explored to solve the problem of maintaining information privacy on mobile displays. Privacy covers have been developed for laptop screens that provide a clear view of the screen's contents to the user but obscure the view to anyone looking at the screen from an angle. Screen contents can also be blurred, readable only through devices such as special eyeglasses. While potentially valuable in protecting the privacy of information, these techniques may have potential drawbacks in terms of 1) additional cost; 2) additional weight, bulk, and power consumption; 3) increased complexity; and 4) distortion or degradation of the displayed information, which could affect performance.

To address some of these concerns, Tarasewich et al. [90] have developed a software-based solution called *privacy blinders*, which cover parts (e.g., telephone numbers, dollar amounts) of a larger document so that they are not viewable by others. Blinders can be used to provide a mixed display in which sensitive information is hidden (covered) but information not considered private is displayed normally. The user can view the sensitive information by temporarily removing the blinder. For example, blinders on a PDA might be removed by touching them with a stylus. When the stylus is removed from the screen, the blinders reappear. It is also possible to create blinders that can only be removed with a certain gesture, thereby creating a level of security along with information privacy.

Furthermore, privacy blinders can automatically respond to a predefined organizational and/or personal "privacy policy," which specifies what types of information are covered under different circumstances. An organizational policy might be dictated by the company a person works for, while a personal policy is customized to a user's own comfort level and privacy requirements. When an organizational mobile application runs on a device that can also be used for an employee's personal tasks, it should be designed to allow easy definition of a personal "privacy policy" to be used in conjunction with an organization's privacy policy – see Karat et al. [33] for a good discussion of developing privacy guidelines.

Privacy measures can also account for user context changes; if a person moves to a less public space, s/he might turn off any privacy assurance features and view all information without obstruction. Context data (such as location, co-location, and scheduled events) might be used to automatically ensure that a user is interacting with a mobile system in the safest possible manner. For example, a change in location from a private office to a public meeting room might modify privacy settings by design. Device context-awareness would potentially increase privacy management effectiveness by shifting the burden of environmental awareness from the user to the system. Such flexibility as a whole allows more rapid adaptation to the changing environment of the mobile device user.

3. Mobile interface guidelines: From individual to enterprise considerations

Although mobile devices and their desktop counterparts share common usability concerns, unique concerns emerge in the case of mobile devices and applications. The previous section highlighted how input/output technologies and security/privacy concerns differ in the two environments. Due to the unique characteristics of the mobile environment, its devices, organizations, and users [22,68], additional usability requirements may result in interface designs for mobile devices that are quite different from those used on desktop computers [75].

This section details usability requirements for mobile interaction in the context of organizational use. First presented is a synopsis of general guidelines that apply to both desktop and mobile applications, but which emphasize the more distinct usability requirements of mobile devices. Following this are more detailed guidelines that are unique to mobile interaction design. Emphasis is placed on specifically addressing the needs and concerns of the organization in the mobile environment.

3.1. General interface guidelines applicable to mobile device interaction

This section presents a brief overview of general guidelines that apply to both desktop and mobile interface design. Table 1 summarizes the guidelines and related examples. We adapt these guidelines from the context of desktop interface design highlighted by Shneiderman [74] to the context of mobile interface design. Such adaptations are necessary to account for the unique characteristics of mobile devices, mobile users, organizations, or the mobile use of technology, and to fit the characteristics of the mobile workforce prevalent in today's organizations.

Table 1
Summary of General Mobile Interface Design Guidelines

Guideline	Definition/Description	Examples/Guidance
1. Shortcuts for experienced or frequent users	Because time is often more critical to a mobile device user [65], reducing the number of operations needed to perform regular (i.e., repetitive) tasks is a key factor in the ease of use of mobile devices.	Maintain a list of frequently used documents [87]. Web pages might use the Accesskey method (www.wapforum.org/what/technical.htm) to match buttons on a mobile device to links on a Web page.
2. Provide useful feedback	Feedback must be clear and understandable by the user in his/her current situation. The challenge of determining which type of feedback is most appropriate (i.e., visual, audio, haptic) can be addressed through context-aware mobile devices [48].	A mobile device might display visual error messages in places or contexts where it is viewed frequently, such as in an office; use haptic feedback (e.g., vibrations) when physical signals are more likely to be noticed by the user than visual ones, such as while riding a commuter train (e.g., Poupyrev [65]; and use audio feedback when visual or haptic feedback are not practical, proper, or feasible.
3. Good dialog design	The sequence of actions in which a user engages while completing a task on a mobile device can be viewed as a dialog, similar in fashion to a dialog between two people (e.g. [55]).	Direct users logically through any sequence of steps, allow changes, and show users the current state of the task at all times (e.g., Excel's Chart Wizard guides users through the creation of a data chart, showing their progress at each step and allowing users to go back to a previous step).
4. Keep user in control	Mobile device users want to be in charge and have the system/device respond to their actions, rather than feeling that the system/device is controlling them. Systems should be designed such that users initiate actions rather respond to them (with the exception of emergency notifications or event notifications set up by the user).	The ability to have user control (e.g., through customization) when a mobile device provides various notifications to the user can reduce "interruption irritability and feelings of information overload" [27]. The ability to control who has access to what information affects a user's feelings of privacy [20].
5. Consistency of interface designs	Consistency takes on an additional dimension with mobile applications: the consistency across multiple platforms and devices for the same application [9]. This is important as users of mobile devices may need to switch between their desktop machines and different mobile devices frequently. Consistency also shortens learning time across devices and applications (e.g. [6,69])	Isokoski and Raisamo [30] proposed a Minimal Device Independent Text Input Method that can be used consistently across devices by creating input/output interactions that are device independent.
6. Error prevention, handling, and reversal	Given the nature of mobile computing (e.g., limited attention, changing contexts), users are more likely to make errors with mobile devices. Therefore, error prevention, handling, and reversal mechanisms are critical [68].	Consistent and intuitive mobile interface design can reduce number of errors [59]. Error prevention needs to take the physical design of mobile devices into account (e.g., poor button placement may lead to accidental power shut off).
7. Reducing short-term memory and cognitive loads	Given the limitations of a user's short-term memory, interfaces should be designed such that very little memorization or cognitive load is needed to interact with the mobile device [9]. When in the mobile environment, a user has to potentially deal with more distractions than with a desktop computer [89]. A mobile application may not be the focal point of the user's current activities [28], and a user may not be able to suspend his or her primary task to interact with the mobile device [22, 38].	Alternative interaction modes such as visual, haptic [65], or a combination of both audio and visual feedback [59] may work better for certain applications and/or contexts. Grouping information into small, homogenous chunks and displaying only one screen's worth at a time (therefore requiring no scrolling) can reduce cognitive load [71].

A user's desires to reduce the number of interactions and to increase the pace of interaction with a mobile application increase with usage rate. As time is often more critical to a mobile device user [65], reducing the number of operations needed to perform regular (i.e., repetitive) tasks is a key factor in mobile device usability. This can be addressed through the use of shortcuts to frequently used operations, documents, and information such as contact lists and Web sites.

Each user interaction with a device should be acknowledged by system feedback, such as a beep when pressing a key or an error message for an invalid input value. Such feedback should be substantial but readily understandable by the user. Feedback can take different forms (e.g., audio, visual, haptic), not all of which are suitable for all occasions. Context-aware mobile devices may help address the problem of determining which types of feedback are appropriate to different user situations.

The sequence of actions which a user employs while completing a task on a mobile device can be viewed as a dialog, similar in fashion to a dialog between two people. Designing systems and software in such a way that dialogs consist of intuitively understandable sets of actions with a clear beginning, middle and end can increase ease of use and decrease the time and cognitive load necessary to complete a task.

Users want any information system to respond to their actions, rather than feeling that the system is controlling them. Given this, systems should be designed such that users initiate actions rather than respond to them (with the exception of event notifications, e.g., the availability of an important email message). Real and perceived user control over a system affects the usability of and satisfaction with that system (e.g. [29,60]). Overall, user control is a multifaceted concept, where the human issues associated with control vary with each piece of a system or program. This makes designing mobile systems to conform to user control needs more complex.

Consistency takes on an additional dimension with mobile applications: the consistency across multiple platforms and devices for the same application [9]. Users of mobile devices may need to switch between their desktop systems and different mobile devices frequently. Consistency can also be achieved by creating input/output interactions that are device independent (e.g. [30]). In addition, consistency of design can shorten the time it takes a user to learn a system and reduce the effort required to use the system.

Preventing and handling errors on mobile interfaces becomes more critical due to the more rapid pace of events in the mobile environment. While most error prevention and handling is addressed through application software (e.g. [59,71]), good physical design of mobile devices (e.g., button size or key placement) is an important factor as well. Allowing easy reversal of actions is also critical, but may be more difficult for mobile devices because of limits on available communications bandwidth and lack of computing power [68].

Lastly, short-term memory limitations dictate interface designs that require little memorization during task performance [9]. In the mobile environment, a user has to potentially deal with more distractions than with a desktop computer [89]. A mobile application may not be the focal point of the user's current activities [28], and a user may not be able to suspend his or her primary task to interact with the mobile device [22,38]. Using alternative interaction modes such as sound or vibration may be beneficial [65].

3.2. Organizational design guidelines for mobile device interaction

Given the nature and characteristics of mobile computing and the needs of mobile workers, additional interface design guidelines should also be considered by organizations. These guidelines are discussed below.

3.2.1. Design for multiple and dynamic contexts

The contexts of computer applications used in the office, home, or similar settings are relatively stable. On the other hand, with mobile applications, there can be a significant number of additional people, objects, and activities vying for a user's attention aside from the application or computer itself [89]. Environmental conditions (e.g., brightness, noise levels, weather) can change depending on location, time of day, and season. The usability or appropriateness of an application can change based on these different context factors [35]. For example, in the presence of strangers, users may feel uncomfortable speaking input aloud, and certain places (e.g., libraries) might restrict the use of voice input. Small text sizes may work well in office conditions but become unreadable in bright sunshine or in dimly lit surroundings. In addition, one or both of the user's hands could be occupied while using a mobile device [38]. Therefore, allowing operations to be carried out with one, both, or no hands may be extremely important to the viability of certain interfaces [35]. Including voice input and/or output on devices with other modalities is one way to address the needs of changing contexts. Such "multi-modal" capabilities can also increase the productivity of organizations by allowing flexible use of a device or application (e.g., hands-free or eyes-free) based on users' needs and desires. Holland and Morse [28] investigated an audio interface for a navigation system that frees a user's eyes and hands for other purposes. It generated sounds (through a pair of headphones) that provided information about the distance from a desired destination and the direction that the user should travel to get there.

Dix et al. [15] highlighted an initial design framework for mobile applications based on taxonomies of location, mobility, population, and device awareness. This framework supports the design of interactive mobile systems where contextual information is shared across a number of mobile devices. The problem of changing contexts can be addressed by implementing context-awareness capabilities and self-adapting functionalities [24]. Specific guidelines for implementing context-awareness services are highlighted by Hakkila and Mantyjarvi [25]. González et al. [21] suggested that the design of ubiquitous computing technology should provide the means for agents to become aware of artifact locations and status to reduce the time spent searching for and gathering information. This can also reduce users' effort and frustration, and increase the usability of the applications. Usability in a dynamic environment could also be improved by devices that derive input indirectly from the user. Schmidt [70] discussed a vision of mobile computing where devices can "see, hear, and feel" through a perceptional awareness of the environment and react according to the current situational context.

Furthermore, as technology continues to advance, mobile platforms will continue to shrink in size and include items such as bracelets, rings, earrings, buttons, and key chains. New or modified interaction techniques may be necessary to overcome physical limitations of these devices. As an example, speech input is a viable alternative for devices too small for buttons. Sound can also be used for output, taking the place of text or graphics on devices without screens. While tiny devices may seem too limited at first glance to be useful, they may facilitate task performance in ways that are currently not possible.

3.2.2. Design for limited and split attention

Users of mobile devices often need to focus on more than one task [38,58], and a mobile application may not be the focal point of a user's current activities [28]. Mobile devices that demand too much attention may distract users from more important tasks. Interfaces for mobile devices should be designed to require as little of the user's attention as possible [65]. For example, this can be accomplished by designing for hands-free interaction or even eyes-free interaction. According to Gorienko and Merrick [22], eyes-free interaction provides the greatest freedom of movement during interaction, as visual attention constrains body movement. Whenever possible, it might work better to use sound or tactile output to present information instead of visual displays [65]. A nice example of a limited attention interface can be found in Pascoe et al. [61], who developed a PDA application that allowed observers (using telescopes) to count the number of bites giraffes take from tree leaves without looking away from the animals.

3.2.3. Design for speed and recovery

For mobile devices and applications, time constraints need to be taken into account in application availability and recovery speed. When time is critical, waiting a few minutes for an application to start may not be in the user's best interest. Given the different contexts under which mobile devices are used, users may need to quickly change or access functions or applications [65]. When such situations arise, a user would need to quickly and securely save any work already performed and resume it later without any loss. This would seem to be even more important at an organizational level than at a personal level, as businesses must be able to rely on the applications used in their day-to-day operations, where large volumes of repetitive tasks are more likely the norm (e.g., confirming delivery of packages by FedEx).

3.2.4. Design for "Top-Down" interaction

Mobile devices with small screens have limitations on the amount of information that can be presented at any one time. Reading large amounts of information from such devices can require large amounts of scrolling and focused concentration. To reduce distraction, interactions, and potential information over-load, a better way of presenting information might be through multilevel or hierarchical mechanisms [7]. For example, a mobile worker may not need or want the entire contents of a message. However, s/he may wish to receive a non-intrusive notification that a message is available, along with an indication of how important it is. That way, the worker can make their own decision whether or not to stop their primary task to access the contents of the message (without being forced to stop and restart the task, possibly only to receive the notification itself).

3.2.5. Design for uniqueness/personalization

Junglas and Watson [32] highlighted the importance of uniqueness or personalization in the mobile environment. Mobile devices, by their nature, are more personal. While traditional telephones and desktop computers can many times be shared among different users, a mobile device is usually carried and used by only one person. Therefore, it is more likely that a user of mobile applications will personalize the device and its applications to his or her preferences. Different users have different usage patterns, preferences, and skill levels. So it is important to allow for variations among users. For example, when visibility is good, it is reasonable to show more text on a screen. In a dark environment, bigger fonts might allow better readability. However, the interface design should not exclude the possibility that some users may always prefer larger fonts regardless of the lighting conditions.

3.2.6. Design for synchronization

Maintaining synchronization of data across multiple devices is necessary to fully capitalize on mobile computing in organizations [58]. Complete synchronization is achieved when there is complete agreement between the phonebook, calendar, to do list, and other such files across various devices such as a cell phone, laptop, and PDA [19,32,96]. In this way, information across devices is always consistent and up-to-date, and any one of these devices can serve as the point of data entry. Another added benefit or outcome is that devices serve as a backup of one another. Hence, if one device fails, work will not be disrupted as another device can replace its function.

3.2.7. Design for security at device, application, and systems levels

Given that mobile devices are more vulnerable to loss or theft than their desktop counterparts, mobile devices and applications need to squarely focus on securing data that is stored on the device, and transmitted from or received to the device [8]. This may involve data encryption, validation of the user's identity through passwords or biometric techniques, and validation of the sender or receiver's identity (in the case of transmitted data) through electronic signatures. What becomes more critical to mobile (versus desktop) application design is the implementation of features that make it difficult or impossible to access data on the device (or with the device) should the device fall into the hands of an unauthorized user. It may be in the best interest of the user (and of anyone else whose data is stored on a device) to destroy stored data or permanently disable a device if an invalid login is attempted. These types of security measures do create additional overhead for the user, so a risk analysis may be appropriate to determine the level of security desired or needed. For example, it may not make sense to encrypt data on a device that is solely being used to play games or music. But if the game is one that is under development (that is, not yet released to the public), or the music consists of new songs by an artist being considered for distribution by a record label, then security should be a major concern.

Some organizations have instituted policies such as requiring all data to be stored on servers and accessed through VPN connections or other means; no data is to be kept on the mobile device at any time. In this approach, keeping data from being stored on a mobile device requires additional features to be built into the device's interface. It would be unwise, for example, to have a device auto-connect to a remote server because the contents of that server would be available to anyone (authorized or not) who has access to the mobile device.

While organizations certainly need to be concerned with security at the device and application levels, the security of communications pathways (especially if private) and security at a systems level (that is, the use of an application by many stakeholders) can become a design concern. Implementing proper levels of security for data as it is transmitted over wireless pathways is critical. Wireless access points need to be secured. Ways to prevent and detect the viruses and spyware is important at both ends of the communication pathway, as these hazards can conceivably be introduced midstream.

Security and privacy policies for mobile device use and information access must be set and enforced (e.g. [8,34]). Security policies of organizations often have to take many stakeholder requirements into account, including customers, governments, and regulatory bodies. An example of this can be found in the brokerage industry, which requires mobile devices and applications that can not only handle sophisticated tasks, but perform those tasks without jeopardizing security and regulation compliance [5].

3.2.8. Design for privacy

Some issues of privacy can be addressed through security measures such as encrypting stored or transmitted data. What is more specific to mobile application design is ensuring that data will not be unknowingly released to a third party when using a mobile device in a public, dynamic, or unknown environment. Information that is displayed (or transmitted by auditory or even tactile channels) must be protected from being received and/or recorded by unauthorized people that may be near the user. Ways to maximize the privacy of displayed information include hardware-based screens and software-based approaches such as blinders [90].

3.2.9. Design for optimal data access

Some of the design suggestions covered earlier, especially those related to security and privacy, can interfere with a user's ability to access needed information. For example, connecting to a VPN requires additional login steps, some types of encryption might require entering passwords or performing additional steps to access data, and organization-imposed restrictions on a device might prevent employees from performing their job under certain circumstances. Mobile devices and their interfaces need to be designed in such a way as to balance data access and data security, as well as finding a middle ground between controlling and empowering employees in terms of mobile device and application use. Employees may be held accountable regarding their use of mobile devices and applications, and coordination of control efforts throughout the enterprise is desired as imbalances may lead to unsuccessful implementations [97].

One issue that requires balancing access and security is deciding how many authentication steps are required to access a device and its data. One health care company [13] found that requiring one password to log in to a mobile device and a separate password to decrypt needed data on the device was too cumbersome for users and the extra step decreased productivity. The company made the decision to switch to single sign-on, also called pass-through authentication, which requires only one password to log in to a device and decrypt data. Single sign-on reduces security, but improves usability. Each organization must make its own decision concerning this trade off. For any form of online banking in the U.S, multifactor authentication is required by law [17]. This is commonly implemented by requiring a username and password, as well as answering another question such as place of birth or favorite book. Multifactor authentication increases security, but decreases usability. Mobile devices issued to members of an organization will often have various restrictions placed on them to enhance security. These security policies control both the device and the user, and need to be carefully chosen after considering any tradeoffs between usability and data security.

3.2.10. Design for both corporate and individual use

Mobile devices used to access the information resources and systems of an organization may be used for both personal and business purposes, and may be used for multiple types of applications as well. Levels of required security and the classification of information as "private" may not be absolute. Privacy and security levels of organizational information are based on company policy, and they usually differ from privacy and security levels of personal information. Hence, conflicts can arise.

Contradictory forces between personal and business needs of mobile users may influence patterns of user behavior in the mobile environment [10]. Hence, organizations need to design applications with both the individual and the corporation in mind because traditional boundaries between work and non-work may become blurred as worker mobility increases. To maximize effective use of mobile technology and applications, and to minimize possible dilemmas faced by employees, it may become necessary to resolve any conflicting concerns of the individual and the organization. This can involve design issues such as boundary management settings between work and personal activities, and managing organizations' priorities relating to empowerment and control.

3.2.11. Maintaining consistency with organizational standards and systems

Standardization and consistency become even more important from an organizational standpoint. Mobile systems should have interfaces that look and function as closely as possible to their desktop counterparts. Devices and networks need to be standardized as well [84]. It may not work well to grant employees access to applications and networks from any mobile device [66]. Certain devices may be better suited to the desired application, or have better security features. Many people and organizations became frustrated when they hurriedly purchased iPhones and then found out that they would not work well (if at all) with many needed applications [36].

Acceptance of applications and technology is crucial, and should be thoroughly examined before adoption of a device or application. Additional technical support and expertise may be needed that currently does not exist within the organization (e.g. [40]). User training may be needed on the use of mobile devices for organizational purposes, along with education about the benefits that any new device or system is meant to provide. In some cases, the availability of mobile applications and the increased access to corporate data may even bring about fundamental changes in the way tasks are performed, or the way the organization is structured, since processes may change due to the availability of new technology. An example of this can be seen in work by Siau and Shen [79], who discuss the many challenges of mobile healthcare informatics.

3.2.12. Design to support business models and strategies

Mobile applications can be used as strategic weapons or tools by organizations [3,72]. They can be used to enhance or reshape business models, as well as support new or existing organizational strategies. Sheng et al. [72] discussed how a leading international publisher utilized a mobile application for its sales representatives to provide better customer service and enhance sales and marketing effectiveness. As another example, Nah et al. [54] studied a utility company that explored implementing mobile applications to improve operations and increase customer satisfaction. A significant challenge to organizations is in aligning mobile applications with business goals and strategies. Strategic planning for mobile applications is critical for success in enhancing business strategies or redefining the business model [4], and interfaces to mobile systems must align with business processes that support business strategies and the business model.

4. Framework for organizational mobile interface design guidelines

We have developed a framework (see Fig. 1) to summarize the guidelines presented above and show the relationship between them. The guidelines are classified into three categories: (i) general considerations; (ii) mobility considerations; and (iii) organizational considerations. The pyramid structure of the framework illustrates that mobility considerations are built upon (and should adhere to) more general design considerations, and that both of these form a foundation for organizational considerations. General considerations refer to universal principles for interface design that apply to any type of information system.

Mobility considerations take into account characteristics of the mobile environment, including the use of multi-modal interfaces to support dynamic contexts and to address potential problems caused by limited (or split) user attention. Uniqueness or personalization can be achieved based on time (e.g., alerts or notifications), identity (e.g., user device settings or software preferences), location (e.g., location-based services), or a combination of them (e.g., context-based services). Synchronization across devices ensures that users can work anytime, anywhere, and using any device. However, controls must be in place within organizations to indicate which data are to be synchronized and which (e.g., sensitive or classified data) should not. Top-down interaction design can provide more control and flexibility to users, while data access and error recovery speeds become more crucial in mobile and dynamic contexts.

Organizational considerations must take into account mobility and general considerations, as well as additional concerns with privacy and security, balancing data access trade-offs, maintaining consistency with organizational standards and systems, and supporting business models and strategies. While mobile systems can provide many advantages, they can also introduce new threats to privacy and security such as the loss of information stored on a mobile device or unauthorized people viewing sensitive information

Fig. 1. Framework for Organizational Mobile Interface Design Guidelines.

on a device used in public. Balancing corporate and individual needs can give rise to contradictory forces such as control of information and device use versus empowerment of employees to do their jobs that must be managed effectively. Maintaining consistency with corporate standards helps to improve usability issues (e.g., consistency of interfaces can decrease learning curves) and synchronization (e.g., through the use of a common IT infrastructure to support applications). Strategic planning is necessary to ensure alignment of business models/strategies of corporations with their mobile application development portfolio.

Based on the interaction concerns for mobile devices discussed above, a list of practical guidelines is provided below, which can be used when designing and implementing mobile applications for organizations:

– Provide different ways for users of at all levels of expertise to perform application functions
– Present any feedback from an application in a clear and useful manner
– Create interactions between the user and the application or device that are logical and intuitive, and make the user feel in control of the interaction
– Maintain the same "look and feel" across desktop platforms and mobile devices as much as possible
– Anticipate and prevent errors where possible, and provide ways to undo mistakes.
– Prevent simple operations from triggering potentially harmful results (e.g., power on/off)
– Rely on recognition of function choices instead of memorization of commands
– Allow users to configure output to their needs and preferences (e.g., text size, brightness)
– Provide sound and tactile output options
– Allow for single- or no-handed operation
– Have the application adapt itself automatically to the user's current environment if possible
– Minimize a mobile application's reliance on network connectivity
– Allow applications to be stopped, started, and resumed with little or no effort
– Create applications that are up and running quickly

- Present high levels of information first and then let users decide whether or not to retrieve details
- Provide users the ability to change settings to their needs or liking
- Ensure that data stays secure and private in public settings and under extreme circumstances such as loss or theft of a device
- Introduce mobile applications that are consistent with existing standards and systems
- Standardize software and devices where practical or necessary
- Create and enforce policies on device use and data privacy/security
- Address any conflicts between mobile device use and organizational needs
- Ensure integration of mobile applications into an organization's business models and strategies

5. Conclusions and future research

This paper summarizes existing mobile input/output interaction technologies, reviews organizational issues of security and privacy when using mobile technologies and applications, and presents a framework and a set of guidelines for the design and implementation of handheld mobile device interfaces and applications within an organizational context. Some of these guidelines are adapted from desktop user interfaces, while the majority of them are derived from the unique requirements for designing mobile user interfaces and applications, and on the unique needs of using mobile applications in an enterprise setting. The guidelines should be useful to organizations that develop and utilize mobile applications. In our future research, we would like to carry out case studies to assess and validate these guidelines and identify any new ones that may develop. As the mobile or nomadic environment continues to grow and evolve, we leave the reader with some additional observations of changes that may affect the use or design of mobile applications in the future.

Location-based and context-based services are emerging trends and extensions of mobile services. The role of intelligent agents and sensors will play an even more dominant role in future services. The use of these advanced technologies can bring greater concerns and issues relating to trust, security, and privacy [19,20,76–78,80,81]. Some new or pressing concerns include: Are users comfortable with mobile applications making decisions on their behalf as part of context-based services? Are tougher security measures needed as more personal and sensitive information about users and their surroundings are gathered due to tracking of their mobile devices? How much of a concern is privacy to users if a complete trace of their whereabouts and surroundings is available at all times? How can we incorporate appropriate design features into mobile devices to provide users with the control and flexibility needed to deal with these issues? These questions will need to be addressed for enterprise-wide adoption of such services to be successful, and may be further complicated by conflicting personal and organizational objectives and policies.

The ultimate future of mobile services potentially lies with *ubiquitous services* [44], which extend beyond location-based and context-based services by offering ubiquity, universality, unison (i.e., synchronization), and uniqueness [32]. Ubiquity refers to people being reachable anytime, anywhere because computers and networks are accessible by everyone at all times. Universality refers to the elimination of incompatibility problems caused by lack of standardization; hence, devices stay connected at all time regardless of geography. Unison refers to seamless integration of data across all applications so there is always a consistent view of information regardless of which device is the "point of contact" with users. Uniqueness suggests that users can be uniquely identified and services can tailor to their preferences, surroundings, and whereabouts. Design principles will continue to adapt and evolve as advanced ubiquitous services are being developed and the technologies supporting these services advance. Lyytinen et al. [44] highlighted the design and implementation challenges of ubiquitous computing environments while [43] identified a list of research issues and questions relating to them.

Other research questions and their corresponding theoretical perspectives relating to mobile interface design include: (i) trust in technology; (ii) personalization-privacy paradox; (iii) utilitarian versus hedonic systems; (iv) aesthetic design; and (v) context/situational dependency.

5.1. Trust in technology

Trust is an important antecedent to adoption [37,39,41,47] and trust in using mobile technology can be fostered through good interface design that can be tailored to the mobile context [80,82,95]. To understand trust in mobile technology, interface design of mobile devices and websites, as well as quality of wireless services, must be considered [80]. Usability of mobile interface design is key to building a user's trust [80]. However, which aspects of mobile interface design influence the user's trust? In short, there is a lack of research, theory and empirical studies to explain the relationship between mobile interface design and user's trust in using mobile technology.

5.2. Personalization-privacy paradox

This paradox refers to the trade-off between the degree of service personalization provided to a user and the amount of privacy that is given up in return for these benefits [2,73]. Privacy has been examined and studied from various theoretical perspectives, including privacy calculus [12,14], information exchange [51], consumer/user control and awareness [52], social contracts [63], social exchanges [1], and multi-level (individual-socio-technical) [19,20] perspectives. Awad and Krishnan [2] drew on utility maximization theory to study this paradox while Sheng et al. [73] examined the trade-off between personalization and privacy concerns. Future research is warranted to investigate ways in which customers' overall utility can be maximized through design mechanisms to minimize customers' privacy concerns while maximizing the benefits they receive. This will assist organizations in capitalizing on the richness of customer information, such as location and identity.

5.3. Utilitarian versus hedonic systems

Organizations need to prioritize two important aspects of interface design for their mobile systems: utilitarian design versus hedonic design. Utilitarian systems focus on increasing the user's task performance and efficiency, while hedonic systems focus on making interaction fun and enjoyable [93]. These two aspects are not mutually exclusive, as systems that are fun and enjoyable to use can lead to a higher degree of usage over time, and hence, higher utilitarian benefits. The design objective for utilitarian systems is *productive* use, while that for hedonic systems is to encourage *prolonged* use [93]. For example, a decision support system requires a higher level of hedonic quality as compared to a transaction processing system since extensive exploration of various options is desired in organizational decision making. Thus, different mobile systems may take on different priorities depending on their purposes. Sun and Zhang [86] studied utilitarian systems and found that although perceived enjoyment of using utilitarian systems does not directly influence intention to use, the impact is mediated via perceived ease of use and usefulness. Hence, perceived enjoyment of a utilitarian system will increase its perceived ease of use, leading to prolonged usage of the system. Organizations' utilitarian and hedonic priorities for mobile systems can impact the amount of effort needed for their implementation, the form factors that are appropriate for such systems, and system usage patterns. To help determine the degree of utilitarian and hedonic priorities on mobile systems, a value-focused thinking approach can be used to identify the fundamental objectives for implementing a portfolio (or a specific type) of mobile systems [54,81]. The desired utilitarian and hedonic values of the systems can be determined from the list of fundamental objectives that are derived using this approach.

5.4. Aesthetic design

Due to the inherent characteristics and limitations of mobile devices and the pervasive nature of mobile computing, the aesthetic quality of mobile interface design takes on even greater importance. Mobile interface designers therefore need to pay more attention to aesthetic quality than in traditional systems. Aesthetic quality of mobile interface design is one important aspect of hedonic systems. By designing mobile systems that are pleasing and enjoyable to use, usability (or perceived ease of use) is greatly increased as well as usage behavior. Aesthetic quality/design is also related to affective quality or emotional design [57,98]. In the context of interaction with mobile systems, affective quality refers to the ability to cause a change in the user's affect [98]. The key research question here is: What are the design guidelines for developing aesthetic/affective mobile systems? Tractinsky [92] posed a similar question for designing aesthetic IT systems and provided a general framework to study this question. As suggested by Norman [56], positive affect can enhance creative, breadth-first thinking and exploration, while negative affect focuses cognition by enhancing depth-first processing and minimizing distractions. Hence, it is possible that positive versus negative (or neutral) affect could be triggered by mobile interface design to encourage user exploration or exploitation. Norman's conjecture can lead to an interesting stream of research on aesthetic, emotional, or affective design, especially in the context of mobile interface design.

5.5. Context/situational dependency

Sheng et al. [73] and Pica and Sørensen [64] have shown that the intention to adopt and use a mobile application depends on the context, thus the term 'situation dependency' is used to describe this contingency. Situation dependency in the context of mobile application adoption can be defined as comprising three dimensions: identity, location, time [73]. Such context-related information can also be used to design context-awareness systems to better meet the needs of users in different contexts [48,83]. However, research on the design of context-aware systems and the technology to support them is still at an early stage, and more research is needed before context-awareness systems are widely implemented, deployed, and adopted by organizations.

In conclusion, more empirical research is needed to develop an integrated theoretical foundation to guide organizations in the design and implementation of mobile systems, interfaces, and technologies [18]. The research questions and theoretical perspectives discussed above provide a starting point and direction on some of these issues that warrant further research. As we progress toward a nomadic and ubiquitous working environment, these issues become increasingly important over time, and organizations would benefit from the empirical findings and theoretical understandings generated from these research streams.

Acknowledgements

The authors would like to thank Dan Xiang at Suffolk University for her contributions to the background research for this paper.

References

[1]   E.B. Andrade, V. Kaltcheva and B. Weitz, Self-disclosure on the web: The impact of privacy policy, reward, and company reputation, in: *Advances in Consumer Research*, (Vol. 29), S.M. Broniarczyk and K. Nakamoto, eds, 2002, pp. 350–353.

[2]   N.F. Awad and M.S. Krishnan, The personalization-privacy paradox: An empirical evaluation of information transparency and the willingness to be profiled online for personalization, *MIS Quarterly* **30**(1) (2006), 13–28.

[3]   R. Basole, Transforming enterprises through mobile applications: A multi-phase framework, *Proceedings of the Americas Conference on Information Systems* (2005), 1935–1939.

[4]   R. Basole, Strategic planning for enterprise mobility: A readiness-centric approach, *Proceedings of the 2007 Americas Conference on Information Systems*, 2007.

[5]   M. Bienfang and B. Egan, Handheld device trends in the US retail brokerage advisory industry, *TowerGroup Research*, Available at: itresearch.forbes.com/detail/RES/1167062441_284.html, 2006.

[6]   A. Blackler, V. Popovic and D. Mahar, The nature of intuitive use of products: an experimental approach, *Design Studies* **24**(6) (2003), 491–506.

[7]   S. Brewster, Overcoming the lack of screen spaces on mobile computers, *Personal and Ubiquitous Computing* **6** (2002), 188–205.

[8]   P. Britt, Mobile security for those on-the-go, *Information Today* **23**(9) (2006), 32. Retrieved November 20, 2007, from Academic Search Premier database.

[9]   S. Chan, X. Fang, J. Brzezinski, Y. Zhou, S. Xu and J. Lam, Usability For mobile commerce across multiple form factors, *Journal of Electronic Commerce Research* **3**(3) (2002), 187–199.

[10] K.C. Cousins and D. Robey, Human agency in wireless world: patterns of technology use in nomadic computing environments, *Information and Organization* **15** (2005), 151–180.

[11] P. Crosman, The BlackBerry as workhorse – To increase productivity, Merrill Lynch, Blackstone Group and others are putting more mission-critical applications on handheld devices, *Wall Street & Technology* **25**(7) (2007), 147.

[12] M.J. Culnan and P.K. Armstrong, Information privacy concerns, procedural fairness, and impersonal trust: An empirical investigation, *Organization Science* **10**(1) (1999), 104–115.

[13] J. Cummings, Mobile device lockdown, *Network World* **24**(11) (2007), 40–44.

[14] T. Dinev and P. Hart, An extended privacy calculus model for e-commerce transactions, *Information Systems Research* **17**(1) (2006), 61–80.

[15] A. Dix, T. Rodden, N. Davis, J. Trevor, A. Friday and K. Palfreyman, Exploiting space and location as a design framework for interactive mobile systems, *ACM Transactions on Computer-Human Interaction* **7**(3) (2000), 285–321.

[16] P. Dourish, R.E. Grinter, J.D. de la Flor and M. Joseph, Security in the wild: User strategies for managing security as an everyday, practical problem, *Personal and Ubiquitous Computing* **8** (2004), 391–401.

[17] FFIEC, Authentication in an electronic banking environment. Available at: www.ffiec.gov/pdf/pr080801.pdf, 2001.

[18] E.R. Fontana and C. Sørensen, From idea to BLAH! Understanding mobile services development as interactive innovation, *Journal of Information Systems and Technology Management* **2**(2) (2005), 101–120.

[19] H. Galanxhi-Janaqi and F. Nah, U-commerce: emerging trends and research issues, *Industrial Management and Data Systems* **104**(9) (2004), 744–755.

[20] H. Galanxhi and F. Nah, Privacy issues in the era of ubiquitous commerce, *Electronic Markets* **16**(3) (2006), 222–232.

[21] V.M. González, M.E. Tentori, E.B. Moran, J. Favela and A.I. Martinez, Understanding mobile work in a distributed information space: Implications for the design of ubicomp technology, *Proceedings of the 2005 Latin American Conference on Human-computer Interaction* (2005), 52–63.

[22] L. Gorienko and R. Merrick, No wires attached: Usability challenges in the connected mobile world, *IBM System Journal* **42**(4) (2003), 639–651.

[23] G. Gross, Are security threats really overhyped? *PC World*, Available at: pcworld.about.com/news/Jun132005id121364.htm, 2005.

[24] K. Hinckley, J. Pierce, M. Sinclair and E. Horvitz, Sensing techniques for mobile interaction, *Proceedings of the 13th Annual ACM Symposium on User Interface Software and Technology*, (2000), 91–100.

[25] J. Hakkila and J. Mantyjarvi, Developing design guidelines for context-aware mobile applications, *Proceedings of the 3rd international conference on Mobile technology, applications & systems* (2006), 1–7.

[26] K. Hawkey and K.M. Inkpen, Keeping up appearances: understanding the dimensions of incidental information privacy, *Proceedings of CHI 2006* (2006), 821–830.

[27] J. Ho and S.S. Intille, Using context-aware computing to reduce the perceived burden of interruptions from mobile devices, *Proceedings of the SIGCHI conference on human factors in computing systems* (2005), 909–918.

[28] S. Holland and D.R. Morse, Audio GPS: Spatial audio in a minimal attention interface, *Proceedings of Human Computer Interaction with Mobile Devices* (2001), 28–33.

[29] E.A. Inglis, A. Szymkowiak, P. Gregor, A.F. Newell, N. Hine, P. Shah, B.A. Wilson and J. Evans, Issues surrounding the user-centred development of a new interactive memory aid, *Universal Access in the Information Society* **2**(3) (2003), 226–234.

[30] P. Isokoski and R. Raisamo, Device independent text input: a rationale and an example, *Proceedings of the Working Conference on Advanced Visual Interfaces AVI2000* (2000), 76–83.

[31] P. Johnson, Usability and mobility: Interactions on the move, *Proceedings of the 1st Workshop on Human Computer Interaction for Mobile Devices*, 1998.

[32] I. Junglas and R. Watson, The u-constructs: Four information drives, *Communications of AIS* **17** (2006), 569–592.

[33] C.-M. Karat, J. Karat, C. Brodie and J. Feng, Evaluating interfaces for privacy policy rule authoring, *Proceedings of CHI* (2006), 83–92.

[34] J. Kavanagh, Plans into action, *Computer Weekly* (13 September 2005), 52–54.

[35] H. Kim, J. Kim, Y. Lee, M. Chae and Y. Choi, An empirical study of the use contexts and usability problems in mobile internet, *Proceedings of the 35th Hawaii International Conference on System Sciences* **5** (2002), 132.

[36] R. King, Corporate e–mail on the iPhone, *Business Week Online*, 29 August 2007.

[37] S.Y.X. Komiak and I. Benbasat, The effects of personalization and familiarity on trust and adoption of recommendation agents, *MIS Quarterly* **30**(4) (2006), 941–960.

[38] S. Kristoffersen and F. Ljungberg, Making place to make IT work: Empirical explorations of HCI for mobile CSCW, *Proceedings of the International ACM SIGGROUP Conference on Supporting Group Work* (1999), 276–285.

[39] K.S. Lee, H.S. Lee and S.Y. Kim, Factors influencing the adoption behavior of mobile banking: A south Korean perspective, *Journal of Internet Banking & Commerce* **12**(2) (2007), 1–9.

[40] Y.C. Lu, J.K. Lee, Y. Xiao, A. Sears, J.A. Jacko K. Charters, Why don't physicians use their personal digital assistants? *Proceedings of the AMIA Annual Symposium* (2003), 405–409.

[41] J. Lu, C.-S. Yu and C. Liu, Facilitating conditions, wireless trust and adoption intention, *Journal of Computer Information Systems* **46**(1) (2005), 17–24.

[42] J.M. Lyons, C. Chan and N. Tetsutani, MouthType: text entry by hand and mouth, *Extended Abstracts of CHI 2004* (2004), 1383–386.

[43] K. Lyytinen and Y. Yoo, Research commentary: the next wave of nomadic computing, *Information Systems Research* **13**(4) (2002), 377–388.

[44] K. Lyytinen, U. Varshney, M.S. Ackerman, G. Davis, M. Avital, D. Robey, S. Sawyer and C. Sørensen, Surfing the next wave: design and implementation challenges of ubiquitous computing environments, *Communications of the Association for Information Systems* **31** (2004), 697–716.

[45] I.S. MacKenzie, Mobile text entry using three keys, *Proceedings of the 2nd Nordic Conference on Human-Computer Interaction* (2002), 27–34.

[46] I.S. MacKenzie and R.W. Soukoreff, Text entry for mobile computing: Models and methods, theory and practice, *Human-Computer Interaction* **17** (2002), 147–198.

[47] P. Mahatanankoon, H.J. Wen and B.B.L. Lim, Evaluating the technological characteristics and trust affecting mobile device usage, *International Journal of Mobile Communications* **4**(6) (2006), 662–681.

[48] J. Mathew, S. Sarker and U. Varshney, M-commerce services: Promises and challenges, *Communications of the Association for Information Systems* **14** (2004), Article 26.

[49] A.S. McAlearney, S.B. Schweikhart and M.A. Medow, Doctors' experience with handheld computers in clinical practice: A qualitative study, *British Medical Journal* **328**(7449) (2004), 1162–1166.

[50] S.K. Miller, Defending mobile devices from viruses, spyware, and malware, *TechTarget*. Available at: www.bitpipe.com/detail/RES/1167560102_718.html, 2007.

[51] G.R. Milne, Privacy and ethical issues in database/interactive marketing and public policy: A research framework and overview of the special issue, *Journal of Public Policy and Marketing* **19**(2) (2000), 238–249.

[52] G.R. Milne and A.J. Rohm, Consumer privacy and name removal across direct marketing channels: Exploring opt-in and opt-out alternatives, *Journal of Public Policy and Marketing* **19**(2) (2000), 238–249.

[53] F. Nah and S. Davis, HCI research issues in electronic commerce, *Journal of Electronic Commerce Research* **3**(3) (2002), 98–113.

[54] F. Nah, K. Siau and H. Sheng, The value of mobile applications: A study on a public utility company, *Communications of the ACM* **48**(2) (2005), 85–90.

[55] J. Nielsen, Traditional dialogue design applied to modern user interfaces, *Communications of the ACM* **33**(10) (1990), 109–118.

[56] D.A. Norman, Emotion and design: Attractive things work better, *Interactions Magazine* **ix**(4) (2002), 36–42.

[57] D. Norman, *Emotional design*, New York: Basic Books, 2004.

[58] A. Oulasvirta and L. Sumari, Mobile kits and laptop trays: Managing multiple devices in mobile information work, *Proceedings of the SIGCHI conference on Human factors in computing systems* (2007), 1127–1136.

[59] S. Oviatt, Human-centered design meets cognitive load theory: designing interfaces that help people think, *Proceedings of the 14th Annual ACM International Conference on Multimedia* (2006), 871–880.

[60] J. Paradise, E.D. Mynatt, C. Williamsand J. Goldthwaite, Designing a cognitive aid for the home: A case-study approach, *Proceedings of the 6th international ACM SIGACCESS conference on Computers and accessibility* (2004), 140–146.

[61] J. Pascoe, N. Ryan and D. Morse, Issues in developing context-aware computing, *Proceedings of the 1st International Symposium on Handheld and Ubiquitous Computing* (1999), 208–221.

[62] J. Pereira, How credit-card data went out wireless door, *Wall Street Journal – Eastern Edition* **249**(104) (4 May 2007), A1–A12.

[63] J. Phelps, G. Nowak and E. Ferrell, Privacy concerns and consumer willingness to provide personal information, *Journal of Public Policy and Marketing* **19**(1) (2000), 27–41.

[64] D. Pica and C. Sørensen, On mobile technology in context: Exploring police work, *Journal of Computing and Information Technology* **12**(4) (2004), 287–295.

[65] I. Poupyrev, S. Maruyama and J. Rekimoto, Ambient touch: Designing tactile interfaces for handheld devices, *Proceedings of the 15th Annual ACM Symposium on User Interface Software and Technology* (2002), 51–60.

[66] P. Rysavy, Device diversity, *Network Computing* **15**(7) (2004), 36–50.

[67] K.S. Saidi, C.T. Haas and N.A. Balli, The value of handheld computers in construction, *Proceedings of the 19th International Symposium on Automation and Robotics in Construction* (2002), 557–562.

[68] M. Satyanarayanan, Fundamental challenges in mobile computing, *Proceedings of the Fifteenth Annual ACM Symposium on Principles of Distributed Computing* (1996), 1–7.

[69] J.W. Satzinger and L. Olfman, User interface consistency across end-user applications: the effects on mental models, *Journal of Management Information Systems* **14**(4) (1988), 167–193.

[70] A. Schmidt, Implicit human computer interaction through context, *Personal Technologies* **4**(2) (2000), 191–199.

[71] D.S.S. Seong, Usability guidelines for designing mobile learning portals, *ACM international conference proceeding series: Proceedings of the 3rd international conference on mobile technology, applications & systems* **270** (2006).

[72] H. Sheng, F. Nah and K. Siau, Strategic implications of mobile technology: A case study using value-focused thinking, *Journal of Strategic Information Systems* **14**(3) (2005), 269–290.

[73] H. Sheng, F. Nah and K. Siau, (forthcoming). An experimental study on u-commerce adoption: Impact of personalization and privacy concerns, *Journal of Association for Information Systems*.

[74] B. Shneiderman, *Designing the user interface-strategies for effective human-computer interaction*, Reading, MA: Addison-Wesley, 2004.

[75] B.P. Shoemaker, Designing interfaces for handheld computers, *Extended abstracts of CHI 1999* (1999), 126–127.

[76] K. Siau, E. Lim and Z. Shen, Mobile commerce: Promises, challenges, and research agenda, *Journal of Database Management* **12**(3) (2001), 4–13.

[77] K. Siau and Z. Shen, Building customer trust in mobile commerce, *Communications of the ACM* **46**(4) (2003), 91–94.

[78] K. Siau and Z. Shen, Mobile communications and mobile services, *International Journal of Mobile Communications* **1**(1/2) (2003), 3–14.

[79] K. Siau and Z. Shen, Mobile healthcare informatics, *Medical Informatics & the Internet in Medicine* **31**(2) (2006), 89–99.

[80] K. Siau, H. Sheng and F. Nah, Development of a framework for trust in mobile commerce, *Proceedings of the Second Annual Workshop on HCI Research in MIS (HCI/MIS)* (2003), 85–89. Available at: sigs.aisnet.org/sighci/Research/ICIS2003/HCI03_14.pdf.

[81] K. Siau, H. Sheng and F. Nah, The value of mobile commerce to customers, *Proceedings of the Third Annual Workshop on HCI Research in MIS*, Washington, D.C., 2004, 5–69.

[82] K. Siau, H. Sheng, F. Nah and S. Davis, A qualitative investigation on consumer trust in mobile commerce, *International Journal of Electronic Business* **2**(3) (2004), 283–300.

[83] M.B. Skov and R.T. Høegh, Supporting information access in a hospital ward by a context-aware mobile electronic patient record, *Personal and Ubiquitous Computing* **10**(4) (2006), 205–214.

[84] C. Sørensen and D. Gibson, Ubiquitous visions and opaque realities: Professionals talking about mobile technologies, *INFO – The Journal of Policy, Regulation and Strategy for Telecommunication, Information and Media* **6**(3) (2004), 188–196.

[85] B. Sullivan, All veterans at risk of ID theft after data heist. Available at: www.msnbc.msn.com/id/12916803, 2006.

[86] H. Sun and P. Zhang, Causal relationships between perceived enjoyment and perceived ease of use: An alternative approach, *Journal of the Association for Information Systems* **7**(9) (2006), 618–644.

[87] J.C. Tang, J. Lin, J. Pierce, S. Whittaker and C. Drews, Recent shortcuts: using recent interactions to support shared activities, *Proceedings of the 2007 SIGCHI conference on human factors in computing systems* (2007), 1263–1272.

[88] P. Tarasewich, Wireless devices for mobile commerce: user interface design and usability, in: *Mobile commerce: Technology, Theory, and Applications*, B.E. Mennecke and T.J. Strader eds, Hershey, PA: Idea Group Publishing, 2002, pp. 25–50.

[89] P. Tarasewich, Designing mobile commerce applications, *Communications of the ACM* **46**(12) (2003), 57–60.

[90] P. Tarasewich, J. Gong and R. Conlan, Protecting private data in public, *Adjunct proceedings of CHI 2006* (2006), 1409–1414.

[91] G. Thomas and R.A. Botha, Secure mobile device use in healthcare guidance from HIPPA and ISO17799, *Information Systems Management* **24**(4) (2007), 333–342.

[92] N. Tractinsky, Toward the study of aesthetics in information technology, *Proceedings of the Twenty-Fifth International Conference on Information Systems,* Washington, D.C., 2004, 11–20.

[93] H. Van der Heijden, User acceptance of hedonic information systems, *MIS Quarterly* **28**(4) (2004), 695–704.

[94] J. Vijayan, Five things to know about U.S. border laptop searches, *PC World*, Available at: www.pcworld.com/businesscenter/article/142429/five_things_to_know_about_us_border_laptop_searches.html, 12 February 2008.

[95] Y.D. Wang and H.H. Emurian, Trust in e-commerce: Considerations of interface design factors, *Journal of Electronic Commerce in Organizations* **3**(4) (2005), 42–60.

[96] R.T. Watson, U-commerce: The ultimate, *Ubiquity*. Available at: www.acm.org/ubiquity/views/r_watson_1.html, 2000.

[97] G.O. Wiredu and C. Sørensen, The dynamics of control and mobile computing in distributed activities, *European Journal of Information Systems* **15**(3) (2006), 307–319.

[98] P. Zhang and N. Li, The importance of affective quality, *Communications of the ACM* **48**(9) (2005), 105–108.

[99] C.M. Zimmermann and R.S. Bridger, Effects of dialogue design on automatic teller machine (ATM) usability: transaction times and card loss, *Behaviour & Information Technology* **19**(6) (2000), 441–449.

Peter Tarasewich is an Associate Professor of Information Systems and Operations Management at the Sawyer Business School, Suffolk University. He received his Ph.D. in Operations and Information Management from the University of Connecticut, his MBA (focusing on Management Information Systems) from the University of Pittsburgh, and dual degrees in Electrical Engineering and Computer Science from Duke University. Dr. Tarasewich's research interests include human-computer interaction with mobile devices, text entry, information display, privacy/security of information, mobile commerce, ubiquitous computing, product design, aesthetics of information systems, and Web engineering. He has published his research in journals including *Communications of the ACM*, *International Journal of Human Computer Interaction*, *IEEE Transactions on Engineering Management*, *Communications of the AIS*, *Internet Research*, *Quarterly Journal of Electronic Commerce*, *Journal of Computer Information Systems*, *IIE Transactions*, *European Journal of Operations Research*, *International Journal of Production Management*, *International Journal of Production Economics*, and *Journal of Case Research*, as well as in the proceedings of conferences such as CHI, UbiComp, and Mobile HCI. Dr. Tarasewich serves as a track chair for the annual Association of Information Systems' (AIS) Americas Conference on Information Systems (AMCIS) conference, and on the Program Committee for the annual AIS pre-ICIS (International Conference on Information Systems) HCI/MIS Workshop.

Jun Gong is a Software Engineer whose work includes improving Web search user interfaces at Google, Inc. He recently received his Ph.D. in Computer Science from Northeastern University, and before that his M.S. in Computer Science from Northeastern University and his B.S. in Computer Science from Fudan University, Shanghai, China. Dr. Gong's research interests include various areas of Human Computer Interaction, including text entry, artificial intelligence, natural language processing, and interface design for mobile devices. He has presented several papers over the past few years at the Association of Computing Machinery's (ACM) annual SIG CHI conference, and was awarded first place in the Student Research Competition at the 9th International ACM SIGACCESS Conference on Computers and Accessibility (Assets07).

Fiona Fui-Hoon Nah is an Associate Professor of Management Information Systems (MIS) at the College of Business Administration, University of Nebraska – Lincoln. She received her Ph.D. in MIS from the University of British Columbia, and her M.S. and B.S. (Honors) in Computer and Information Sciences from the National University of Singapore. Her research interests include human-computer interaction, 3-D virtual worlds, computer-supported collaborative work, knowledge-based and decision support systems, enterprise resource planning, and mobile and ubiquitous commerce. She has published her research in journals such as *Communications of the ACM*, *Journal of the Association for Information Systems*, *Communications of the Association for Information Systems*, *International Journal of Human-Computer Studies*, *Journal of Strategic Information Systems*, *Journal of Information Technology*, *Electronic Markets*, *Information Resources Management Journal*, among others. Dr. Nah received the

University of Nebraska – Lincoln College of Business Administration Distinguished Teaching Award in 2001, the Best Paper Award at the 2003 Pre-ICIS HCI Research in MIS Workshop, the Outstanding Service Award from the Association for Information Systems Special Interest Group on Human-Computer Interaction (AIS SIGHCI) in 2005, and the University of Nebraska – Lincoln College of Business Administration Research Award in 2006. She is an Associate Editor of *Journal of Electronic Commerce Research* and she serves on the Editorial Board of eleven other MIS journals. She has served as a guest editor for various special issues including *Journal of Management Information Systems, International Journal of Human-Computer Studies, International Journal of Human-Computer Interaction,* and *IEEE Transactions on Education.* Dr. Nah is a co-Founder and Past Chair of AIS SIGHCI. She was previously on the faculty of School of Computing, National University of Singapore, and the Krannert School of Management, Purdue University.

David DeWester is a Ph.D. student in Management Information Systems at the College of Business Administration, University of Nebraska – Lincoln. He received his B.S. in Mathematics from Colorado State University and his M.A. in Mathematics from Central Michigan University, where his thesis was nominated for Best Thesis of the Year. After moving to Nebraska, he received an M.S. in Computer Science and an M.B.A. with specialization in International Business. His research interests include human-computer interaction, Web usability, mobile and ubiquitous commerce, and 3-D virtual worlds. He has several years of work experience in information technology related areas from help desk support to e-commerce consulting.

Information Knowledge Systems Management 7 (2008) 145–158
IOS Press

A comparative anatomy of mobile enterprise applications: Towards a framework of software reuse

Patrick D. Brans[a,*] and Rahul C. Basole[b]

[a]*42 Rue de la Greniere, 38180 Seyssins, France*
E-mail: Pat_Brans@hotmail.com
[b]*Tennenbaum Institute, Georgia Institute of Technology, 760 Spring Street NW, Atlanta, GA 30332, USA*
E-mail: rahul.basole@ti.gatech.edu

Abstract: While more and more enterprises are making use of mobile technology to enable field workers, in many cases a mobile solution is built from the ground up for use by a single company. This is costly, both in terms of development and support resources. By achieving higher reuse of software components these costs can come down. This paper develops a methodology for identifying re-usable components; and using this methodology several re-usable components are listed. As a by-product of this research we develop a taxonomy of mobile applications. We suggest the new term *field office* applications to describe applications used by mobile workers.

Keywords: Mobile enterprise applications, field office, taxonomy, software reuse, enterprise mobiling, wireless applications

1. Introduction

Many companies are deploying mobile enterprise applications to improve productivity of their mobile workforce. There is a sufficient number of case studies demonstrating the business value of such technology, and providing some idea about the time to investment payback (e.g. [2,3,6,20,22,28]). In many cases, the applications are bespoke. This is costly and time-consuming, since an entire application must be developed only for use within that one company according to specific user requirements. While large companies have the resources – financial, knowledge, and human – to have software developed exclusively for their own needs, small- and mid-sized companies are frequently left without a solution. Evidence to this phenomenon can be found in the adoption and implementation statistics of mobile enterprise solutions [8,31].

In order to overcome this gap, organizations, software vendors, and programmers have been searching for ways to develop software applications faster, cheaper, and better [30]. One approach that addresses these objectives – and that has found significant traction – is software reuse [13]. Software reuse is a process through which developers and organizations identify common functionality elements among applications and develop reusable components to benefit future development efforts. Software reuse has

---

*Corresponding author.

been shown to increase software system quality and decrease time and costs with software development and maintenance. Indeed, software reusability is viewed widely as a major opportunity for improving software productivity [11,32].

The concept of software reuse is particularly attractive for mobile application development due to evolving user needs and a great variety of different target devices with different capabilities, features, and functionalities [6]. Furthermore, reuse will make it feasible to develop and deploy some of the applications that have so far not made economic sense for enterprises. Previous research of software reuse in the mobile domain, however, is very limited [10,25]. This study aims to provide a first step in closing this scholarly gap.

Specifically, the objective of this research is to identify the benefits and develop a framework that can lead to a higher degree of software reuse in the development of mobile applications. In order to do so, the paper will (i) describe the forces shaping mobile enterprise applications development, adoption, and implementation; (ii) identify and characterize common functional elements of these applications, and (iii) make recommendations as how a higher degree of reusability can be achieved, by drawing on the extant software engineering and growing mobile business literature. As a by-product of this exploration, this research identifies salient dimensions and proposes a taxonomy for classifying mobile enterprise applications. In addition to the commonly identified application categories (*front-office*, *back-office*), this research introduces and develops the concept of *field-office* applications, describing applications supporting workers in the field, a characteristic specific to the mobile domain.

While software reuse can be beneficial to all types of mobile applications and user profiles, our research limits its focus on applications that support categories of mobile workers that are accessible by wide area networks [3]. These type of workers include **off-site rovers** – those who work off-site mainly away from their offices, but sometimes at their desks (e.g. consultants), **road warriors** – those who work mainly outside the company (e.g. account executives, field engineers, truck drivers), and **global cruisers** – those who often travel between different companies, customer, and locations (e.g. corporate executives) [33].

The remainder of the paper is structured as follows. The following three sections provide a background on the evolution of enterprise applications, in general, the forces shaping mobile enterprise applications, and a brief review of the benefits of software reuse. Section 5 develops a taxonomy of mobile enterprise applications. Section 6 identifies common components across mobile enterprise applications. In section 7, the paper provides recommendations for future research and implications for practitioners. Section 8 concludes the paper.

2. Background

Enterprises first began using software to automate processes and meet the needs of workers in the back office. Examples include software supporting personnel in accounting, order processing, and procurement. This was followed by a trend to deploy systems meeting the needs of workers in the front office, sales and marketing in particular.

Practitioners and research alike used a loose classification of these big enterprise applications. They were often placed into categories such as Enterprise Resource Planning (ERP), Supply Chain Management (SCM), and Manufacturing Resource Planning (MRP) for *back-office applications*; and Customer Relationship Management (CRM) and Sales Force Automation (SFA) for *front-office applications*.

While these systems were a major improvement in consolidating enterprise data – for example, the accounting department could work off the same instance of customer information as the sales department – reality often proved that data integration was not effective in many ways [5]. The accounting department, for example, might have a preference for a particular application that expects customer data to be in a format that turns out to be inconsistent with the format expected by one or more application in the sales department.

This is particularly true when different applications are purchased from different vendors. It can also happen when the different application are from the same vendor, but are of different release cycles. For example, the accounting department might have bought an application from Company X a year before the sales department bought a sales application from Company X, and during that year, Company X changed the schema representing the customer.

To some extent these applications are shrink wrapped, but in reality each customer implementation ends up being different. Nevertheless, a degree of reusability has been achieved through standardization as well as techniques and software platforms commonly referred to as enterprise application integration (EAI). For example, a messaging bus might be used to allow applications from different vendors to communicate. As long as each application understands the interface to the bus, the bus platform provides a medium for communication.

These large enterprise applications were made possible by advances in technology – or more accurately, by packaging of advancing technology and techniques, local area networks (LAN), client/server, and databases in particular:

- **LAN**: Internet protocol (IP) as a standard allowed application developers to make assumptions about communication between machines. This also provided an infrastructure for a distributed database that while dispersed, provided a logically unified view to applications.
- **Client/Server**: This provided a more powerful model than thin-clients running screens for applications on a central computer. The ever-increasing CPU power and memory technology (both primary and secondary storage) on the desktop made it possible to make more and more powerful enterprise applications.
- **Database**: Relational database technology allowed application developers to query and update data in a logical fashion and to provide different views to different applications. Structured Query Language (SQL) provided a standard interface between applications and databases.

Since then, wireless communications technology and powerful handheld computing devices have made possible a new computing paradigm [21]. Mobile applications need to suit the needs of workers in the field office. Technology now makes this possible and a lot of workers actually spend their time either on their way to the field office or in the field office [19].

This scenario has brought about a new computing paradigm with several new features. First, company data is far away and accessible by relatively slow networks – or sometimes not accessible at all, for example, when a network is not present. Second, the user is not within company premises and is not sitting behind a desktop computer; so security risks are higher, and the way the user interfaces with the application is different. A third new feature is that the mobile user expects the application to fit into his work life in a different way.

Indeed mobile applications have a different flow and take into account the job function of the mobile worker. Some examples of business processes followed by mobile workers illustrate this point:

- A technician working in the field needs to receive a dispatch. He can accept the order, reject it, or assign it to somebody else. He needs to retrieve a more detailed explanation of the problem and some history of the equipment in question. He needs a map or directions to get to the site. He needs to fill out time and materials. He may need to order parts and he may need to generate an invoice.

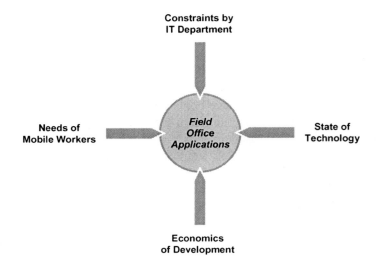

Fig. 1. Forces Shaping Field Office Applications.

– Drivers performing direct store delivery need route information in the morning, they need an inventory of what is on their truck, and they need to be prepared to deliver a different number of products than planned to a given customer. The driver might also do a pick up, in which case he would have to add records to track the item picked up.
– Construction site inspectors are required to inspect scaffolding after every shift. This information must be stored in a central location for immediate retrieval in case there is an accident. These inspectors go to the site at the end of each shift, fill out forms on a handheld computer, take pictures, and capture a signature. The information is uploaded to the central server at some point later in the day.

These business processes are completely different from those of workers sitting at a desk within company premises [6,15,16]. If we follow the naming convention of back-office applications then front-office applications, we would call this new class of applications *field-office applications*.[1] In summary, field-office applications meet the needs of workers who are away from the office, and generally rely on technology while working directly with customers.

3. Forces shaping field office applications

As shown in Fig. 1, the nature of *field-office applications* is driven by a) needs of mobile workers, b) constraints IT department must place on any solution, c) the state of the underlying technology, and d) economics of developing an application.

3.1. Needs of mobile workers

We can list needs of mobile workers based on what they are doing when they are mobile. While this list is not exhaustive, the categories provided sufficiently represent the behavior we wish to illustrate:

---

[1]The authors developed this term after discussions with Kevin Benedict, CEO of MobileDataforce.

- *Selling*: When performing this task, a worker needs information on product features, pricing, and discounts. She needs customer contact information and a history of touch points. She may need to take an order, and she may need to take notes on customer interaction.
- *Consulting*: When performing this task, a worker needs knowledge in one or more subject areas. She needs to be able to contact others in the company to ask questions. She may need to fill out expense reports and time and materials reports.
- *Fixing something*: When performing this task, a worker needs to receive a trouble ticket; and she needs to be able to reassign trouble tickets. She needs technical information on products. She may need to order parts. She may need to record time & materials information and/or generate an invoice.
- *Inspecting something*: Here a worker needs to fill out a checklist and report it back to the enterprise.
- *Collecting information*: Here are worker needs to take a reading or make an observation and report this back to the enterprise.
- *Taking payment*: When performing this task, a worker needs to take payment information and feed it back to the enterprise for a check. The enterprise then responds with acceptance or rejection. (This transaction needs to be secure. We cover security in the section "Constraints by IT Department" below.)
- *Transporting something*: The worker needs routing information and needs to have inventory of what is being transported.
- *Traveling*: The worker needs business metrics and key performance indicators. She needs to be in touch with other employees, clients, and business partners. She needs to do time and expense reports.

Information is an essential ingredient in all these tasks; and how that information is provided on the mobile device is a critical feature of any mobile application. Taking these information needs at an abstract level we get just four basic access modes:

1. **Read**: for example, while selling workers need price information, while transporting workers need routing information.
2. **Create**: for example, when fixing something workers need to create new information on time & material to generate an invoice; when selling, workers need to create new orders.
3. **Update**: for example, when inspecting we need to update a check list; when transporting something, workers need to update on-truck inventory.
4. **Alert**: for example, when fixing something, workers need to be dispatched, when traveling we need to know when somebody wants to reach us.

3.2. Constraints by IT department

The mobile enterprise brings about a computing paradigm with a new set of challenges for the IT department [21]. In the mobile scenario, workers are away from company premises; and they are carrying small computing devices that might be lost or stolen. Furthermore, it is frequently the case that workers targeted for mobile enterprise applications are not those accustomed to using computer technology as part of their jobs. Now they are being asked to use small computers with constrained user interfaces.

To mitigate the risks inherent to this environment, the IT department has to place restrictions on applications being deployed for use by mobile workers. In some cases it is a matter of having the application fit into a framework for security and device management; in other cases, the application itself has to behave differently.

IT professionals need to be able to track the software and hardware that belongs to the company. They need to be able to perform automatic backup on behalf of users. They need to be able to update applications and data on devices according to category of user. Finally, they need to be able to perform remote troubleshooting. To meet these requirements, all mobile applications have to fit into the appropriate device management framework for a given enterprise.

There are heightened security concerns given the nature of the mobile enterprise. A device can be lost or stolen. For this reason, IT departments want protection in the form of encryption of data on the device – and maybe even a way of automatically clearing data from a device thought to be lost or stolen.

The IT department needs to know who is using a given device, and grant or restrict access to various information resources accordingly. In order to minimize the risk that a user gains access to information he is not supposed to view, the IT department might mandate that data be partitioned – data is only distributed to devices where it can be viewed. This requires special functionality when data is synchronized in the mobile enterprise.

Application gateways or synchronization servers need functionality to partition the data according to roles. Different users might have different views of the data – and the actual content might be different all the way down to the user level.

IT department might also require functionality in the synchronization process to guarantee data consistency. If a data object is changed on a mobile device, and then during synchronization, the data connection is lost after only part of the change was posted, the partial change must be rolled back to prevent leaving the data in an inconsistent state.

Another concern is that of conflicting updates. When multiple workers make offline updates to the same data – and those updates are subsequently synchronized with back-end systems – special care must be taken to achieve the desired result with minimal user intervention.

When a user creates a new record offline – and that record has a field where the value must be unique – special care must be taken by the application to ensure uniqueness even though there is no way of knowing if another user is trying to insert a record with that same value.

In summary, the needs of the IT department impose the following additional requirements on mobile applications:

- Minimal incremental burden on users to perform IT tasks.
- Encryption of data on the device and functionality to clear data from a device if it is suspected stolen.
- Partitioning of data based on user or user role.
- Special synchronization logic to maintain data consistency, resolve conflicts, and ensure uniqueness in a way that is transparent to the user.

3.3. State of technology

As shown in Fig. 2, there are numerous technology areas that enable field office applications. Basole [3] coined these areas as the mobile DNA – mobile devices (D), wireless networks (N), and applications (A) [4]. Field office applications are shaped in part by the nature of the underlying technology:

3.3.1. Mobile devices (D)

The mobile worker is stuck with a constrained computer with a constrained user interface. Furthermore, the industry is still fragmented, resulting in a situation where there are still a lot of form factors, different operating systems, and different user interfaces [6].

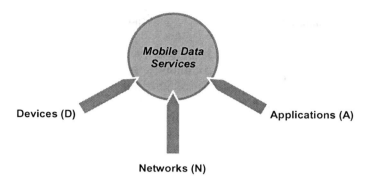

Fig. 2. Enabling Technology Areas of Mobile Data Services.

Because a mobile device has limited battery life, all software running on the device must use resources economically. Furthermore, different devices have different battery lives, adding still another dimension of variability.

Because of the variation in device types – and because companies change device preferences over time – a successful mobile application should be designed in a way that abstracts the hardware and user-interface layers. When there is a change in device type – or when a new generation of the same device is released – it should not be necessary to redevelop the application from the ground up.

3.3.2. Wireless networks (N)

Even though we have seen vast improvements, wireless links will always provide lower bandwidth than fixed line connections. There will also be more dropped connections; and less than ubiquitous coverage [6].

The user should not be bothered with these peculiarities. Mobile applications have to minimize the inconvenient of wireless networks to the user.

3.3.3. Applications (A)

Software running on constrained computers, but sometimes with requirements just as rigorous as those of desktop applications. Underlying software tools need to be present on the device, such as a relational database management system to organize data in a way that reflects business objects and eliminates redundant representations of the same data.

In summary, software must compensate for shortcomings in the underlying technology:

- Applications must provide a user-friendly interface even though the device on which they operate is constrained in computing power and user interface.
- Applications must continue to function even when there is no wireless connection. Whether the device is online or offline should be transparent to the user of the application.
- Applications must have some of the rich features of their desktop counterparts. For example, mobile applications must be able to organize large amounts of data.

3.4. Economics of developing mobile applications

There are two extreme cases of software development [7,29]. The first, which we might refer to as one-size-fits-all, is the case where an application is developed once and then used in exactly the same state by all users. At the other extreme lies the case where an application is developed from the ground up for one customer.

In the one-size-fits-all case, development, support, and maintenance costs are spread out over a larger user base. Users benefit from the larger user community because they can share ideas on how to use the application. The more prevalent the application is, the bigger the ecosystem that develops around it. For example, other applications from other vendors might develop interfaces to it, or systems integrators might train staff and develop skills to install, configure and run the application. In all these ways, the larger user base brings down the total price for a given customer.

In the case where an application is developed just for one customer, all costs are higher. Furthermore, the team developing the application usually moves on to develop another application for another customer; and it becomes much harder to retain the knowledge base needed to make sensible modifications to the application.

Unfortunately, the latter case is still quite prevalent when applying mobile technology for enterprise use. This is true for several reasons, including the following:

– Back-end systems are different from enterprise to enterprise.
– Work processes are different from enterprise to enterprise.
– There is a large variety of devices to select from; so from one enterprise to another, there may be an entirely different set of device types and operating systems.
– The industry has not yet gained the momentum required for software re-use to be achieved on a large scale.
– Customers have not yet gained the expertise required to make good choices on components of mobile solutions.

Because reuse has not been achieved on a large scale, customers are paying a higher price.

4. Software reuse

Software reuse has been a topic of interest to researchers and practitioners for a number of years [13,18]. Software reuse is a process through which developers and organizations identify common functionality elements among applications and develop reusable components to benefit future development efforts [1, 17]. The application of the software reuse process has been shown to lead to reduction in software development costs and cycle time [9] as well as in improvements in software reliability and quality [13]. Indeed, by using a component-based approach to key features and functionalities, products and services can be created easier and faster. Software reuse not only has advantages to developers, but also for users. The reuse of generic components allows users to have a more harmonized and standardized interaction with multiple applications [26]. It may also lead to applications that are more tailored towards their needs. Examples of software reuse can be found in a variety of software domains, including enterprise resource planning, appliance software, and video game development.

There are several steps involved in planning for software reuse [27]. Broadly, these steps can be categorized as domain analysis, reuse component integration, validation, and knowledge feedback implementation [12,14,24]. In this study, we focus our efforts on the first step, domain analysis, as it is generally considered the most difficult step particularly for new applications domains. Readers interested in the other steps of software reuse are referred to the following sources [13,18].

During domain analysis, developers identify common concepts, such as objects and operations (i.e. tasks), that will form the basis for creating reusable software components. In other words, domain analysis is a process performed to better understand the application domain and gather salient

Table 1
Dimensions for Classification

Dimension	Possible Values	Mutually Exclusive?
Connectivity	– **Online Constant**: The device is always connected. – **Online On Demand**: The device gets connected when the application requests connection. – **Online When Available**: The application uses a connection whenever one is available. Otherwise, it manages without. – **Offline**: All work is done without a wide-area wireless connection. Once or twice a day, the device is connected through a fixed-line or WiFi link.	Yes
Access	– **Read**: The device needs to read recent information. – **Create**: The device needs to be able to create new data entries. – **Update**: The device needs to be able to post updates to the enterprise. – **Alert**: The device needs to be able to receive alerts.	No
Data Size	– **Large**: The amount of data entries required by the application is in the thousands or more. – **Small**: The number of data entries required by the application is in the hundreds or fewer.	Yes
Content Type	– **Structured**: The information is in a format that is easily interpreted by an application (for example: a text file or a relational database). – **Unstructured**: At least some of the information is in a format that cannot easily be interpreted by an application (for example: a picture or a video).	Yes
Location	– **Yes**: The application requires location information. – **No**: The application does not need to be aware of location.	Yes

information for the design of reusable components. Since the domain of interest in this study is to support mobile workers, we need to identify common elements that characterize mobile enterprise applications. The following section elaborates on this further.

5. A taxonomy of mobile enterprise applications

One way of finding re-usability is to classify mobile enterprise applications according to a formal taxonomy. Some researchers have suggested classification along the lines of the interface between the user and the application [23]. For enterprise applications this is a useful way of finding repeatable solution areas – i.e. similarities in the problem domain –; but to find repeating elements in the solution domain, one must classify applications in terms of functional elements. In this paper, we will develop a taxonomy along the lines of functional elements. We suggest a taxonomy of *field office applications* along the dimensions described in Table 1.

Based on these dimensions, we can classify a variety of mobile enterprise applications as shown in Table 2. Of course there is some variation in what is needed for a given application. For example, some enterprises want location information for field service; others do not. For our purposes, it is best to assume a full set of features – that is, we will take the greatest common denominator –, as this allows us to pick out possible functional components.

6. Common components of mobile applications

Given the preceding discussion, we can now identify common elements of field office applications. Presumably, these common elements do not have to be developed for each application; rather, they can be built once, and re-used by any application needing one or more of them.

The common elements can be divided into the five categories, namely (1) device portability, (2) on-device application logic, (3) synchronization, (4) device management, and (5) security. We elaborate on these further:

Table 2
Classification of Enterprise Applications

Application	Connectivity	Access	Data Size	Content Type	Location
Field Service	Online On Demand	Read, create, update, alert	Large	Unstructured	Yes
Field Sales	Online When Available	Read, create, update	Large	Structured	No
Inspection	Offline	Update	Small	Structured	No
Email	Online On Demand	Read, create, update, alert	Large	Unstructured	No
Delivery	Offline	Read, create, update, alert	Large	Structured	Yes
Meter Reading	Offline	Read, update	Large	Structured	No
Home Healthcare	Offline	Read, update	Large	Structured	Yes

6.1. Device portability

Successful mobile applications will easily adapt to new device types. Different devices have different screen sizes, different input mechanisms, different battery lives, and different peripheral hardware. There is also variation in the operating system run on different devices. As shown by our taxonomy, many field office applications require location information. This requires applications to interface with on-device GPS systems. Furthermore, some applications require access to other device functions, such as barcode readers and cameras. Since mobile devices have limited battery life, software running on the device should monitor battery power and reduce functionality accordingly.

By providing an abstraction of the hardware to the application, middleware running on the device can help us achieve a degree of re-usability. This is relatively easy to do for functions such as checking the remaining battery, or detecting the presence of a network connection. Adapting content to screen size is also something that is relatively common. In the Composite Capability/Preference Profile (CC/PP) recommendations, W3C provides a framework for servers and devices to exchange information – and for the server to then choose formats appropriate for the device.

Adapting an application to a different operating system and running on a different CPU is where most of the difficulty in device portability lies. One approach is to write applications to run on Java Virtual Machines (JVMs). However, running an application in a virtual machine in an already-constrained computing environment tends to slow things down to the limits of usability.

6.2. On-device application logic

Application developers choose between two extreme models: thin client versus thick client. In the former case, the device simply displays data provided by the server. In the latter case, the device actually runs a substantial amount of application logic. Since our taxonomy shows that none of the field office applications requires *online* connectivity – and only two require *online on demand* connectivity –, field office applications have to run logic on the client. The thick client model is required.

Applications might need a large amount of data formatted in a way that optimizes search time, minimizes redundancy, and that allows access through queries that reflect business entities – Standard Query Language (SQL). Relational database management systems do exist for handheld devices; and indeed a high degree of re-use can be achieved simply by using an existing RDMS.

Our taxonomy shows that most field office applications require *update* access mode. Client-side software has to be capable of showing updates on the local device without first posting them to the server. The more updates that occur on the client between synchronization sessions, the trickier it gets for client side software to maintain the "illusion" to the user that the updates are confirmed. A series of dependencies could develop on the local device. This is not something that should be left to the application; this is a task best performed by client-side middleware.

Similarly, on-device data validation has to be consistent with validation that would occur when the record (or data) is actually posted to the server. The user would have trouble coping with the situation where one or more of his data entries are rejected during synchronization after having been validated during entry on the device. Again this is a task better performed by client-side middleware.

6.3. Synchronization

At the point where data from the device is synchronized with back-end systems, a number of tasks must be performed. If the user X posts an update to a field that has been modified by user Y since the last time user X retrieved the original field value, there is a conflict. A decision has to be made as to which value to keep. User X might have actually posted the update on his device before user Y posted his update; then user Y might synchronize before user X. Ideally the two users are oblivious to the synchronization schedule, so from their point of view user Y was the last to make the update. Middleware should provide mechanisms for conflict resolution.

As seen above, most field office applications require *create* as one of the access modes. Users frequently create records requiring one or more unique values. If the application works offline – as we have seen is the case with most field office applications – special logic has to be present to pool unique keys, so that at the time of synchronization the updates are not rejected because of non-unique values.

We have seen in our taxonomy that some field office applications require unstructured content. Ideally the middleware that synchronizes structured data is also capable of synchronizing unstructured data.

In any case where data is complex, and business objects are represented by more than one database table or data file, it is important to ensure atomicity of updates. If the synchronization process fails after one part of a business object is updated, but not the other parts, the data is left in an inconsistent state.

Our taxonomy reveals that almost all of field office applications have *large* data size. This generally means business objects are represented by more than one table or file. In order to ensure atomicity of updates, the concept of transactions must be implemented. In the event where one element of the business object is not updated, the entire update must be rolled back. Anything less than this will leave data in an inconsistent state. Transactions are something best implemented by underlying middleware.

6.4. Device management

The IT department needs to be able to control company assets in the field. This has to be done with minimal burden to users of field office applications. Data must be automatically backed up without user intervention. If a user looses a device – or if a device ceases to function – the IT department must be able to provide the user with a new device with data in a state very close to the state of the old device. The IT department must be able to define user roles and post application and file updates to users based on roles. Tools must be provided to configure devices based on roles; and there must be a way to schedule regular synchronization with minimal user intervention. These functions should not be left to an individual field office application. These are functions common to mobile applications, and should be provided by middleware – specifically, a device management platform.

6.5. Security

Field office applications are by definition run outside of the company premises. This creates several security risks. A device might be lost or stolen or access control rights might be violated by unsophisticated applications. Field office applications generally require on-device encryption. Data is then decrypted as needed. This is another example of functionality best left to an underlying middleware platform. As described in the synchronization bullet point above, some mechanism must be present to ensure data partitioning. Applications cannot download all data to a given device as this would violate access control rules. Most IT departments would object to the situation where data private to one user is sent to another user's device.

7. Contributions, Practical Implications and Future Research

This study discussed the critical dimensions of mobile enterprise applications and developed an initial framework for software reuse. Based on this discussion, several important practical and theoretical implications and recommendations for implementing and deploying field office applications can be drawn.

From a research perspective, our taxonomy provides a first step in identifying the key task elements that define mobile enterprise applications and can lead to more efficient development and production. An in-depth investigation of this taxonomy, drawing on human-computer interaction and task-technology fit literature would provide a more specific differentiation of the various tasks and user requirements that need to be addressed. This exploration may also lead to the identification and development of applications not available today. Furthermore, conclusions from our study suggest that if common elements are "outsourced" to an underlying software platform, application development can be vastly improved from a quality, time, and efficiency perspective. By bringing down the costs of developing, deploying, and supporting mobile applications, new applications are made possible. These applications do not alone provide enough return to justify a mobile solution; however, when they can make use of a reusable infrastructure, they may make sense.

From an enterprise perspective, the results of our study suggest to avoid deploying bespoke applications. Enterprises should take advantage of our taxonomy to think through their current mobility needs and investigate their future needs. Drawing on the concept of reuse, enterprises should determine what the common elements are across their current and future mobile enterprise applications and ensure that application vendors and system integrators maximize this reusability. Results have shown that this will lower costs and ease solution support. More specifically, our study proposes that an underlying enterprise infrastructure should provide at least the following:

- A mechanisms for partitioning data,
- Configurable conflict resolution policy,
- Synchronization of both structured and unstructured content,
- A way of scheduling synchronization,
- A way of defining user roles and a coherent way of treating user roles,
- Automatic backup, and application and file update,
- On-device encryption and on-demand decryption,
- A mechanism for removing data from a device that is lost or stolen.

Application developers can also benefit from the findings of our study. A recommendation to this group includes the identification of software platforms that provide common elements in order to focus their main resources and efforts on the development and implementation of application logic. Application developers thus will not get bogged down trying to deal with the peculiarities of the mobile environment, but rather focus on the proper application flow. Leveraging software reuse in mobile enterprise application development enables application developers to reduce staff costs and minimize maintenance of expertise that has little to do with the business problems they are trying to solve.

8. Conclusions

Field office applications tend to be more like large ERP systems than desktop applications. A significant amount of integration work is required to get the application to interface with existing systems; and there are enough differences in the ways enterprises operate to make each case a little different. The workload can be reduced by maximizing reusability of applications components.

In this paper we have provided a methodology for abstracting common elements of field office applications - and we have applied that methodology to identify components that can be re-used. The common functions can be performed by platform or middleware software. If APIs are exposed to applications, the platform software can reduce the complexity of developing a mobile application. The middleware takes care of the peculiarities of the mobile computing environment; and if done correctly, it also keeps field office applications within the constraints imposed by the IT department (i.e. placing minimal burden on users, mitigating security risks, and ensuring data consistency).

References

[1]   U. Apte et al., *Reusability-based strategy for development of information systems: Implementation experience of a bank*, MIS Quarterly 14 1990, 421–433.
[2]   R.C. Basole, The Value and Impact of Mobile Information and Communication Technologies, *Proceedings of the IFAC Symposium on Analysis, Modeling & Evaluation of Human-Machine Systems*, Atlanta, GA, 2004.
[3]   R.C. Basole, The Emergence of the Mobile Enterprise: A Value-Driven Perspective, *Proceedings of the International Conference on the Management of Mobile Business (ICMB)*, Toronto, Canada, 2007.
[4]   R.C. Basole, Strategic Planning for Enterprise Mobility: A Readiness-Centric Approach, *Proceedings of the Thirteenth Americas Conference on Information Systems*, Keystone, Colorado, USA, 2007.
[5]   R.C. Basole and R.A. DeMillo, Enterprise IT and Transformation, in: *Enterprise Transformation: Understanding and Enabling Fundamental Change*, W.B. Rouse, ed., John Wiley and Sons, 2006,
[6]   P. Brans, Mobilize Your Enterprise: Achieving Competitive Advantage through Wireless Technology, Prentice Hall, New York, 2003.
[7]   K.H. Britton et al., Transcoding: Extending E-Business to New Environments, *IBM Systems Journal* **40**(1) (2001), 153–178.
[8]   L. Cosgrove, Applied Wireless: Making Wireless Work in the Business, *CIO Focus* (2005), 1–39.
[9]   R.G. Fichman and C.F. Kemerer, Incentive compatibility and systematic software ruse, *Journal of Systems and Software* **57** (2001), 45–60.
[10] K.G. Fouskas et al., A roadmap for research in mobile business, *International Journal of Mobile Communications* **3**(4) (2005), 350–373.
[11] W. Frakes and C. Terry, Software Reuse: Metrics and Models, *ACM Computing Surveys* **28**(2) (1996), 415–435.
[12] W.B. Frakes and C.J. Fox, Sixteen questions about software reuse, *Communications of the ACM* **38** (1995), 75–91.
[13] W.B. Frakes and K. Kyo, Software Reuse Research: Status and Future, *IEEE Transactions on Software Engineering* **31**(7) (2005), 529–536.
[14] M.L. Griss, Software reuses: from library to factory, *IBM Systems Journal* **32** (1993), 548–566.
[15] M. Kakihara and C. Sorensen, Expanding the 'mobility' concept, *ACM SIGGROUP Bulletin* **22**(3) (2001), 33–37.
[16] R. Kalakota and M. Robinson, M-Business: The Race to Mobility, McGraw-Hill, 2001.
[17] J. Karimi, An asset-based systems development approach to software reusability, *MIS Quarterly* **14** (1990), 179–198.
[18] Y. Kim and E.A. Stohr, Software reuse: Survey and research directions, *Journal of Management Information Systems* **14** (1998), 113–147.
[19] A. Kornak, J. Teutloff, M. Welin-Berger, Enterprise Guide to Gaining Business Value from Mobile Technologies, Wiley, 2004.
[20] M. Lattanzi, A. Kohonen and V. Gopalakrishnan, *Work Goes Mobile: Nokia's Lesson from the Leading Edge*, John Wiley & Sons, 2006.
[21] K. Lyytinen and Y. Yoo, The Next Wave of Nomadic Computing: A Research Agenda for Information Systems Research, *Information Systems Research* **13**(4) (2002), 377–388.
[22] F. Nah, K. Siau and H. Sheng, The Value of Mobile Applications: A Utility Company Study, *Communications of the ACM* **48**(2) (2005), 85–90.

[23] R.C. Nickerson et al., Towards a Taxonomy of Mobile Applications, *Proceedings of the Thirteenth Americas Conference on Information Systems*, Keystone, Colorado, USA, 2007.

[24] T. Ravichandran and M.A. Rothenberger, Software Reuse Strategies and Component Markets, *Communications of the ACM* **46**(8) (2003), 109–114.

[25] E. Scornavacca, S.J. Barnes and S. Huff, Mobile Business Research, 2000–2004: Emergence, Current Status, and Future Opportunities, *Communications of the AIS* **17**(28) (2006), 635–646.

[26] K. Sherif, R. Appan and Z. Lin, Resources and incentives for the adoption of systematic software reuse, *International Journal of Information Management* **26**(1) (2006), 70–80.

[27] K. Sherif and A. Vinze, Barriers to adoption of software reuse: A qualitative study, *Information & Management* **41**(2) (2003), 159.

[28] H.A. Smith, Riding the Wave: Extracting Value from Mobile Technology, *Communications of the AIS* **8** (2002), 1–30.

[29] U. Varshney, Mobile and Wireless Information Systems: Applications, Networks, and Research Problems, *Communications of the AIS* **12**(11) (2003), 155–166.

[30] U. Varshney et al., Wireless in the enterprise: requirements, solutions and research directions, *International Journal of Mobile Communications* **2**(4) (2004), 354–367.

[31] B. Worthen, Wireless Finally Connects, *CIO Magazine* (February 2004).

[32] K. Yongbeom and E.A. Stohr, Software Reuse: Survey and Research Directions, *Journal of Management Information Systems* **14**(4) (1998), 113–147.

[33] C. Zetie, *The Mobile Enterprise: Defining your Strategy*, Forrester Research 2005, 1–15.

Patrick Brans is an independent business and IT consultant based in Europe. He specializes in developing partner ecosystems to bring complete wireless and mobile solutions to enterprises. He frequently speaks on the subject at industry events and he has written several articles describing how mobile technology can be applied for business value. In previous roles, Mr. Brans was Solution Business Manger responsible for Mobile Field Sales & Sevices Solutions at Hewlett-Packard and Manger at Strategic Alliances at Sybase iAnywhere. He is author of the book *Mobilize Your Enterprise: Achieving Competitive Advantage through Wireless Technology*. He received a B.S. degree in Computer Science from Loyola University and a Masters of Science degree from Johns Hopkins in Computer Science with a specialization in telecommunications.

Dr. Rahul C. Basole is a Research Scientist in the Tennenbaum Institute at the Georgia Institute of Technology. His research focuses on modeling, visualization, and analysis of complex systems, innovation strategy and management, emerging IT, and applied decision analysis. In his current role, Dr. Basole conducts research on the complexity of value networks and eco-systems with a particular focus on the mobile business, healthcare, biotech, and services domain. Dr. Basole has received several best paper awards and his work has been extensively published in books, prestigious research journals, and conference proceedings. In previous roles, he was the CEO, Founder, and VP Research of a Silicon Valley-based wireless research and consulting firm, the Director of Research and Development at a leading software firm, and a Senior Analyst at a leading IT management consulting firm. Dr. Basole is a member of the Institute for Operations Research and Management Sciences, the Decision Sciences Institute, and the Association for Information Systems. He currently serves as a director or advisor for several technology firms. He received a B.S. degree in industrial and systems engineering from Virginia Tech, has completed graduate studies in engineering-economic systems, operations research, and management information systems at Stanford University and the University of Michigan, and received a Ph.D. degree in industrial and systems engineering from the Georgia Institute of Technology, concentrating in IT and operations management.

Information Knowledge Systems Management 7 (2008) 159–180
IOS Press

Protecting data on mobile devices: A taxonomy of security threats to mobile computing and review of applicable defenses

Jon Friedman[a],* and Daniel V. Hoffman[b]
[a]*Fiberlink Communications, 1787 Sentry Parkway West, Blue Bell, PA 19422, USA*
E-mail: jfriedman@fiberlink.com
[b]*SMobile Systems, 2020 Leonard Ave., Columbus, OH 43219, USA*
E-mail: dhoffman@smobilesystems.com

Abstract: Mobile devices such as laptops, PDAs and cell phones have become essential tools for enterprise productivity, but they are in fact significantly more vulnerable to attack than desktop computers. This paper provides a broad overview of threats to mobile devices and the data that resides on them, as well as available defenses. It provides a taxonomy that divides threats to mobile devices into seven categories: malware, phishing and social engineering, direct attack by hackers, data communication interception and spoofing, loss and theft of devices, malicious insider actions, and user policy violations. It then discusses security technologies that can be applied against each of these threat types, including firewalls, anti-virus and zero day anti-malware software, intrusion prevention systems, virtual private networks, data encryption, device control and data leak prevention technologies. It suggests how to assess priorities among the different threats and defenses, and concludes with suggestions for further research.

Keywords: Mobile computing, security threats, laptop, virus, defense mechanisms and policies

1. Introduction

We are entering the era when the mobile employee – the worker with a laptop, a cell phone and possibly a handheld device – has become the typical employee rather than the exception. One recent survey found that 81% of global executives use a mobile device, and analyst firm IDC estimates that there will be 1 billion mobile workers by 2011, including nearly 75% of the US workforce [12,18].

This evolution toward a predominately mobile workforce is being driven by lifestyle choices, productivity gains, and technology improvements. Workers are demanding the flexibility of staying at home on some workdays, as well as working at home during evenings and weekends. Businesses are seeing major productivity benefits by keeping workers fully functional on the road and at customer sites [2]. Wide-spread adoption of Wi-Fi and 3G mobile data networking technologies have facilitated global information sharing. Rapid innovation in the form and usability of mobile devices has opened fresh horizons for new types of mobile applications.

---

*Corresponding author.

1.1. Vulnerability of mobile devices

But gaps in information security could threaten the explosive growth of mobile computing. Recent losses and thefts of laptops containing confidential employee and customer data have proved extremely costly and embarrassing to leading companies and government agencies. Profit-motivated hacks and social engineering attacks have begun to target enterprise employees as avenues into the corporate data center. And since hackers and cyber-criminals gravitate toward the largest targets of opportunity, the rapid expansion of mobile computing will inevitably draw more attention to vulnerable mobile systems in the future.

Another cause for concern is the fact that laptops and other mobile devices typically are both the most vulnerable computers in the enterprise and the least well defended. There are several reasons why they are fundamentally more vulnerable than non-mobile desktop systems and servers.

1.1.1. Outside of perimeter defenses

Non-mobile and mobile systems alike are subject to many of the same security threats, including viruses, worms, Trojans and targeted attacks by hackers. But non-mobile systems are typically protected by corporate firewalls and other security measures located at the corporate perimeter, such as intrusion prevention systems (IPS) and virus scanning systems.

Mobile systems, in contrast, connect to the Internet or shared networks directly, bypassing the corporate defenses.

1.1.2. Vulnerable communications

Non-mobile systems typically use wired LANs (Local Area Networks) and tightly controlled corporate wireless networks that are relatively impervious to external penetration.

Mobile workers, however, connect to the Internet and corporate networks using Wi-Fi hotspots and other shared public access points. These communications connections are vulnerable to many types of interception and spoofing.

1.1.3. Devices easily lost or stolen

Although there are instances of computers being lost or stolen on company premises, these events are relatively rare.

In contrast, the loss and theft of laptops and other mobile devices is widespread. Indeed, now even medium-sized organizations must assume that employees will lose some laptops and mobile devices during any given month.

1.1.4. Lack of attention and budget

It is human nature to solve the easiest problems first. In many organizations this tendency has led to the lion's share of attention and security budgets going into defenses for non-mobile systems on corporate LANs, because these are within physical reach of IT staff and can be protected by well-understood technologies.

In addition, when laptops, PDAs (Personal Digital Assistants), BlackBerry® devices and smart phones are owned by the employees rather than the enterprise, IT staff members often take the view that the sole responsibility for security lies with the employees themselves.

These attitudes are understandable psychologically, but they ignore the reality that mobile devices are used for business purposes, contain critical corporate data, and are more vulnerable than non-mobile systems.

1.2. Classifying the threats

The number of attacks on mobile devices and the data they contain have proliferated to the extent that it is sometimes hard to keep track of them all.

In this paper we put forward a taxonomy of threats to mobile devices and data. We believe this will help IT professionals, executive managers, academics and others who are concerned with computing infrastructures and information security:

1. To ensure that no major class of threat is overlooked.
2. To understand the security defenses available to protect against each class of threat.
3. To assess the relative risks of the different classes of threats and set priorities for addressing them.

We will therefore proceed by looking at each of these topics in turn, first presenting a taxonomy of security threats to mobile devices, then mapping security technologies against these threat types, and subsequently presenting some thoughts on how to set priorities among potential security solutions. We will then close with some suggestions for future research on these topics.

Any framework of this sort is inherently arbitrary. Equally valid taxonomies could be created with more or fewer categories. However, the framework presented here has proven to be useful in security consulting engagements, and it can stimulate a discussion of how best to protect corporate data and how to prevent security breaches from constraining the growth of mobile computing.

1.3. Definition of mobile devices

For the purposes of this paper we define mobile devices as portable electronic systems that store and manipulate potentially confidential information. This includes laptop and notebook personal computers, handheld computers, cell phones, PDAs, BlackBerry devices, and iPod® mobile digital devices.

2. Taxonomy of security threats to mobile devices

There are many types of security threats to mobile devices, but for the practical purpose of assessing risks and setting priorities among defensive technologies they can be grouped into the following seven categories:

1. Malware
2. Phishing and social engineering
3. Direct attack by hackers
4. Data communications interception and spoofing
5. Loss and theft of devices
6. Malicious insider actions
7. User policy violations

The nature and characteristics of these categories of threats are discussed below, and the next section will outline some of the security defenses that are available to counter each type.

2.1. Malware

Malware includes worms, viruses, Trojans, bots, spyware, logic bombs and other types of malicious software that can infest computers and other electronic devices. Malware outbreaks like Mydoom, NetSky, Bagle, Sasser and Zotob have caused a great deal of damage, with costs peaking at $17.5 billion worldwide in 2004 according to one estimate [5,14].

Most enterprises have been able to curb damage from traditional worms and viruses with anti-virus and anti-spyware packages, but malware remains a threat to mobile devices for several reasons. There are new types of malware targeting laptops. Malware targeting handheld devices and cell phones are emerging. Finally, there are unique challenges to keeping malware signature files updated on roaming devices.

2.1.1. Short-span, serial variant and designer malware

Virus writers and cyber-criminals have found ways to evade signature-based anti-virus and anti-spyware technologies with new types of attacks, including:

- "Short-span attacks" designed to distribute malware to millions of networked computers within hours by using spam mailing lists and zombie networks that can broadcast millions of copies in a few hours [8].
- "Serial variant attacks" that disseminate malware with variations, so that signatures developed for the initial versions cannot be used to identify the variants. In the case of the Stratio worm (also known as Stration or Warezov) 1,000 unique variants were distributed in one month [27].
- "Designer malware" that targets a small group of firms or organizations, or even at a few individuals within a single firm, so there is no chance to identify the malware and develop a signature of the attack [19,23,26,30].

2.1.2. Malware targeting handhelds and other mobile devices

Viruses and other forms of malware targeting handhelds and other non-PC mobile devices are starting to emerge.

For example, the Backdoor.Brador.A Trojan that infects Pocket PCs allows a remote hacker to:

- List files in directories
- Obtain files from the Pocket PC
- Place files onto the Pocket PC
- Execute a process on the Pocket PC
- Display a message on the Pocket PC

Current examples of malware affecting non-laptop mobile devices includes BBProxy (targeting Black-Berry devices), WinCE_DUTS.A (targeting Pocket PCs), Liberty.A, PALM_Phage.A and PALM_Vapor.A (targeting the Palm OS), and CommWarrior.A and Cabir.A (targeting Symbian-OS cellphones). A recent news story reported the first, if relatively harmless, Trojan targeting iPhones [7].

It is also important to note that laptops, handhelds and other devices can become a vector for infecting other computers and networks. Roaming laptops can acquire malware then infect corporate networks when users return to the office and attach to the corporate LAN from inside the firewall. Users who synchronize their mobile devices between home computers and work computers can transport malware from the former to the latter.

For example, Fig. 1 shows a Palm LifeDrive PDA attempting to synch infected data to a workstation. (In this case the threat was caught, because the workstation was running an anti-virus application with real-time scanning capabilities.)

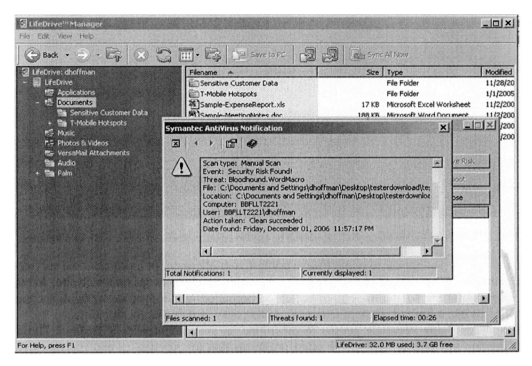

Fig. 1. Antivirus application successfully detecting infected file being synchronized between a laptop and PDA.

2.1.3. The "Mobile Blind Spot"

Keeping anti-virus and anti-spyware packages up to date with the latest signatures can be a major challenge for mobile devices. Many tools that update virus and spyware signature files operate only when a device is connected to the corporate network. However, mobile devices may travel for days or weeks, connecting to the Internet or service provider networks, but not communicating with the corporate network. In this case the virus and spyware files can become out-of-date while the device is being exposed to attacks.

This problem has been referred to as "the mobile blind spot" and it is considered a common issue for enterprises [9].

2.2. Phishing and social engineering

Phishing and social engineering attacks attempt to dupe computer users into sending confidential information to a third party, or to download a piece of malware that will find confidential information on victims' PCs and send them to the attacker.

Phishing and social engineering attacks are usually initiated by cyber-criminals motivated by profit, often acting as part of well-organized criminal groups. The flow of computer talent to cyber-crime is not surprising in that it is extremely lucrative. According to one FBI estimate cyber-crime costs businesses in the US alone $67 billion annually.

Phishing and social engineering techniques include:

– Sending emails that appear to come from a colleague, the head of human resources, an IT administrator, or some other legitimate source. The emails ask the recipients to reply with account numbers, usernames and passwords, or other confidential information.

```
msf > use ie_vml_rectfill
msf ie_vml_rectfill > show payloads

Metasploit Framework Usable Payloads
=====================================

    win32_downloadexec             Windows Executable Download and Execute
    win32_exec                     Windows Execute Command
    win32_passivex                 Windows PassiveX ActiveX Injection Payload
    win32_passivex_meterpreter     Windows PassiveX ActiveX Inject Meterpreter Payl
oad
    win32_passivex_stg             Windows Staged PassiveX Shell
    win32_passivex_vncinject       Windows PassiveX ActiveX Inject UNC Server Paylo
ad
    win32_reverse                  Windows Reverse Shell
    win32_reverse_dllinject        Windows Reverse DLL Inject
    win32_reverse_meterpreter      Windows Reverse Meterpreter DLL Inject
    win32_reverse_stg              Windows Staged Reverse Shell
    win32_reverse_stg_upexec       Windows Staged Reverse Upload/Execute
    win32_reverse_vncinject        Windows Reverse UNC Server Inject

msf ie_vml_rectfill >
```

Fig. 2. Security program Metasploit, which can be used to create exploits, such as a malicious webpage.

- Sending emails that appear to come from a contest, a publication, or a professional services organization, inviting the recipient to register with a user name and password on a web site. In some cases this information allows the hackers to access corporate computer systems or bank accounts, since most people use a limited stock of user names and passwords for many situations.
- Sending emails that persuade people to download an attachment with a Trojan. These Trojans often contain keyloggers, sniffers or other programs that log keystrokes and transmit user names, passwords and other confidential information back to the hacker.
- Sending emails that persuade people to go to a web site where a "drive-by download" installs a Trojan on the user's machine. "Drive-by downloads" can occur when hackers exploit a vulnerability in the user's browser or email system.

Some of these Phishing and social engineering attacks exhibit a startling level of ingenuity.

In one recent case cyber-criminals registered as potential hiring managers and downloaded resumes from the jobs database at Monster.com. They then used personal information from these resumes to create very convincing phishing emails to job-seekers. The emails directed the victims to a web site where they downloaded a "Monster job search tool," a file which contained a keylogger designed to capture usernames and passwords for bank accounts [6,16].

Another tactic of cyber-criminals is to send victims to a web site that downloads malware to the victims' PCs. And in some cases these malefactors magnify the effect by hacking into legitimate web sites and planting mechanisms to deceive site visitors.

For example, a group of cyber-criminals hacked into the MySpace pages of well-known rock bands and planted overlays on web pages. A cursor positioned over the overlays showed an apparently legitimate URL, but when users clicked on the links they were directed to another web site that downloaded malware to the victims' PCs [17].

The level of skill needed to perpetrate some attacks is decreasing because of tools and techniques made available on the Internet by both hackers and legitimate businesses. Figure 2 shows how the hacking tool Metasploit can be used to create malicious web pages that will infect users systems without the users having to click on links or install ActiveX controls.

Attacks that infect web site visitors are particularly dangerous to enterprises, because hackers can use the infected device to "tunnel" past corporate defenses and infect hundreds of systems on the corporate network. This process is illustrated in Fig. 3.

The risk from these attacks is particularly acute for two reasons:

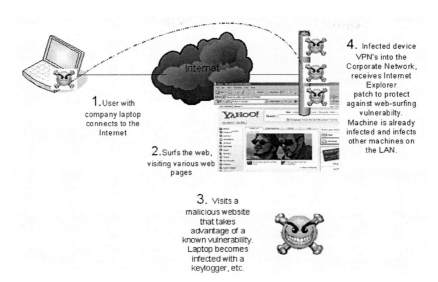

Fig. 3. Depiction of a mobile user becoming infected by surfing the Internet while missing critical patches.

- The number of compromised web sites is staggering. A study from Google titled "Ghost in the Browser" indicates that as many as one in ten of all of the URLs on the web will attempt to perform a malicious act against site visitors [20].
- Internet Explorer and other browsers are extremely vulnerable, because they suffer from many vulnerabilities and are very difficult to keep patched.

These risks are multiplied for enterprises that are unable to update and patch browsers on systems out in the "Mobile Blind Spot" we discussed earlier.

2.3. Direct attack by hackers

Direct attacks occur when a hacker identifies a particular device for attack and utilizes exploits against that specific system.

Mobile systems are especially vulnerable to direct attacks, because hackers can locate and observe potential victims in person, and have more opportunities to intercept insecure wireless network traffic.

For example, a hacker can connect to a wireless hotspot, a hotel broadband network or the Internet and use scanning or sniffing software to find the IP addresses of live hosts. These hosts can then be enumerated to find out additional information such as open ports, the operating system, and applications. After finding out information about a potential victim, a hacker can then make an educated decision on what exploits to use against the system. The attacks typically exploit a known vulnerability in the operating system, browser, or applications on the mobile system.

An extensive discussion of direct attacks can be found in Hoffman's book *Blackjacking; Security Threats to BlackBerry® Devices, PDAs and Cell Phones in the Enterprise* [11].

2.4. Data communications interception and spoofing

2.4.1. Intercepting communications
Mobile devices are particularly vulnerable because they must:

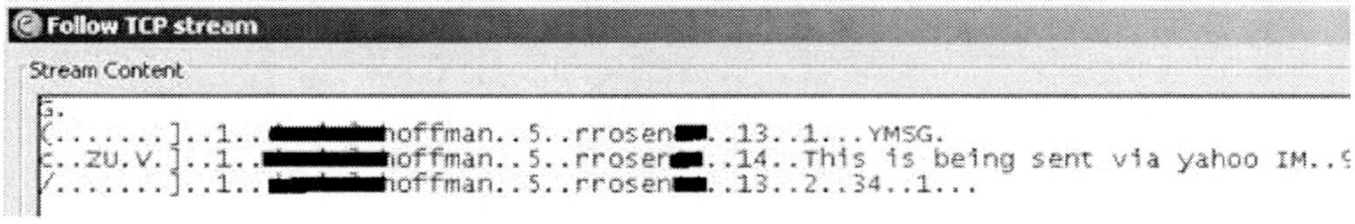

Fig. 4. Wireshark sniffing an instant messaging conversation over a wireless network.

1. Utilize wireless communications that can be intercepted.
2. Connect and authenticate to hot spots and access points that can be "spoofed" by hackers.

Many mobile devices use wireless communications for activities like browsing the Internet and checking e-mail. The plethora of free and fee-based public Wi-Fi hotspots has made this practice commonplace. The problem lies in the fact that these hotspots almost never offer any encryption capability. As a result, data is literally flying through the air, easily captured by those with malicious intent and basic computing knowledge.

For example, when mobile workers utilize applications such as Instant Messaging and e-mail when visiting public Wi-Fi hotspots without encryption, a well-known and free sniffing tool called Wireshark can be used to sniff this type of data. Figure 4 shows an instant messaging conversation that was sniffed with Wireshark over a wireless network.

This method of sniffing can also be used to do more than view data. Many PDA's and e-mail programs utilize the POP3 protocol to authenticate, check and download new e-mail. POP3 does not provide any encryption for the username and password that is being used to authenticate the user checking and downloading the e-mail messages. Because most hotspots also do not offer encryption, individual's usernames and passwords can be easily sniffed. Figure 5 is a screenshot of Wireshark sniffing an e-mail user's username and password.

2.4.2. Spoofing access points and man-in-the-middle attacks

When users log onto Wi-Fi hot spots at airports, coffee shops, hotels and retail stores they have no way of differentiating legitimate hot spots from fraudulent ones. Hackers can make their computers look like legitimate access points. This includes showing a bogus SSID (Service Set Identifier) that appears to come from a legitimate source. When users connect to these bogus hotspots, they see logon screens simulating the screens of the legitimate service providers, which then capture the users' logon information for the hacker.

Figure 6 shows a tool called Airsnarf broadcasting itself with a SSID "tmobile" and providing a realistic login page for users to enter their credentials. Figure 7 shows these credentials being written to the airsnarfs.txt file.

Another version of spoofing is the SSL Man-in-the-Middle (MITM) attack. SSL encryption is widely used by web-based merchants to protect online transactions. A knowledgeable user at a public Wi-Fi hotspot may realize that there isn't any inherent hotspot encryption provided. However, they may feel comfortable if they are visiting websites that utilize SSL encryption. An SSL Man-in-the-Middle works by sitting between that user and the banking or other secure website. In this attack, the attacker, not the trusted website, provides the end-user with the SSL (Secure Sockets Layer) certificate to encrypt the data. Having provided the certificate, the attacker can then utilize it to encrypt and decrypt the data.

Figure 8 shows how SSL works normally. Figure 9 shows how the SSL MITM attack takes place.

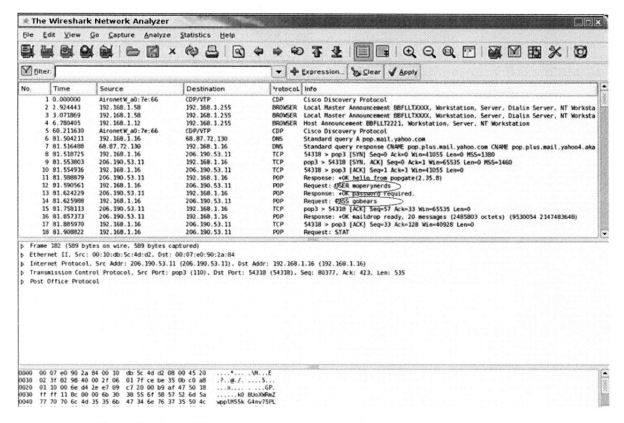

Fig. 5. Wireshark sniffing an e-mail use's username and password over a wireless network.

2.5. Loss and theft of devices

Probably no form of data breach has received more publicity over the past three years than confidential data exposed when laptops have been lost or stolen.

The most notorious example was the exposure of personal information on 26.5 million US veterans when a laptop was stolen from the home of a US Department of Veterans Affairs employee in May 2006 [28].

It is clear that laptop loss and theft is rampant, affecting every type of commercial enterprise, government agency and educational institution. A comprehensive list of data breaches, many of which are related to lost and stolen laptops, is maintained and published by the Privacy Rights Clearinghouse. According to this "Chronology of Data Breaches," the number of personal records exposed since the beginning of 2005 now exceeds 200 million [13].

The potential for losing data from mobile devices is increasing sharply for several reasons:

– More workers are becoming mobile, so more corporate data is being carried on laptops.
– More users are loading data onto USB thumb drives and other portable storage devices.
– More users are loading data onto handheld devices and even mobile phones.

One IT manager found that 80% of his company's employees were using USB storage devices, despite a clear corporate policy stating that anyone found storing data on removable devices was subject to termination [1]. Similar stories abound in the industry press [25].

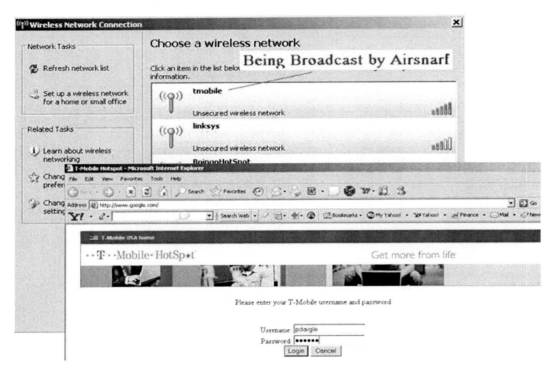

Fig. 6. Airsnarf broadcasting a froudalent 5510 and login page.

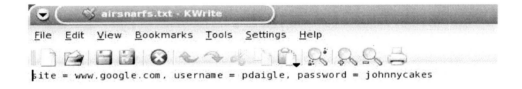

Fig. 7. Credentials being written to the airsnart.txt file.

2.6. Malicious insider actions

There are numerous examples of employees and other insiders removing confidential data or deliberating creating security vulnerabilities. In some cases these are disgruntled employees and ex-employees seeking revenge. In other cases it is employees seeking to sell information for a profit, or to bring a future employer valuable information like customer lists and engineering designs. In one notorious case, a scientist leaving a major chemical company downloaded 22,000 sensitive documents representing $400 million worth of trade secrets, then transferred 180 of the documents to a laptop owned by his new employer [10].

While disgruntled employees can obtain confidential information from many sources, laptops and other mobile devices make the job easier, since they can be used without fear of direct observation by managers, peers or IT staff members. In some cases theft can be as easy as simply retaining a company laptop and reporting it lost.

Fig. 8. A secure SSL connection.

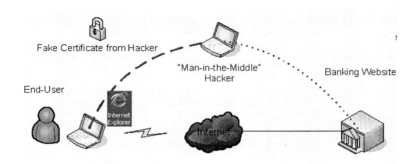

Fig. 9. A victim of an SSL Man-in-the-Middle attack, where the SSL certificate to encrypt/decrypt data is provided by a man-in-the-middle, not the banking website.

2.7. User policy violations

Unfortunately, users do not need malicious intent to create security vulnerabilities; carelessness, ignorance or indifference to corporate security policies can produce the same results.

Examples of user policy violations related to mobile devices that can undermine security include:

– Disabling firewalls, anti-virus packages and other security applications to improve performance.
– Downloading unknown applications and files that can contain malware.
– Using unauthorized software such as instant messaging and peer-to-peer file sharing programs.
– Copying files and data to USB thumb drives, handhelds and other storage and mobile devices.
– Emailing files containing confidential information to inappropriate parties.

Although these actions are usually taken to improve productivity or for some harmless motive, the effect can be severe. For example, a magazine article reported an incident in which a file with 17,000 employee records was exposed when an human resources staff member took a laptop home, her spouse loaded a peer-to-peer file sharing program on it, and other users of the peer-to-peer program were able to pull off an HR file [29].

There are even situations where users are instructed to deliberately disable their security applications, for example when getting new Internet access or installing a webcam.

And unfortunately, surveys show that a majority of employees have knowingly violated policies or seen others do so. In one survey a full third of the respondents answered in the affirmative when asked: "Do you ever feel that you need to work around your company's established security policies and procedures just to get your job done?" [24].

Table 1
Summary of threats to mobile devices and applicable defenses

Threat Category	Description	Defenses
Malware	Worms, viruses, Trojans, bots, spyware, logic bombs and other malicious software programs.	– Personal firewalls – Anti-virus – Anti-spyware – Intrusion prevention systems – Zero-day malware protection
Phishing and social engineering	Methods of duping computer users into sending confidential information to third parties or downloading malware.	– Education – Content and spam filtering
Direct attack by hackers	Hackers identify, probe and launch exploits against a specific device.	– Personal firewalls – Vulnerability and configuration management
Data communications interception and spoofing	Interception of wireless data streams and attracting users to fraudulent hot spots and access points.	– Disabling unneeded communications – Inbuilt encryption – Password encryption – Virtual Private Networks – Restricted access to hot spots
Loss and theft of devices	Loss and theft of laptops, handhelds, cell phones, USB thumb drives, and removable storage media.	– Data encryption and time bombs – Backup and recovery – Device control
Malicious insider actions	Theft of data or deliberate creation of vulnerabilities by employees and other insiders for revenge or profit.	– Identity and access management – Data leak prevention and content management – Auditing, logs and traffic monitoring
User policy violations	Creation of security vulnerabilities by users through ignorance or indifference to corporate security policies.	– Data encryption – Device control – Data leak prevention – Education and training

3. Available security defenses

Fortunately, technologies and best practices have been developed to counteract the threats described above, and we describe some of them here. The threats and defenses are summarized in Table 1.

While no security tools can be 100% effective, these defensive measures can avoid the vast majority of data breaches that are caused by known threats, ordinary hackers, and employees who violate corporate security policies through ignorance.

Applying appropriate technologies and best practices can also help meet government regulatory mandates and satisfy audits.

3.1. Defenses against malware

3.1.1. Personal firewalls, anti-virus and anti-spyware
Personal firewalls, anti-virus packages and anti-spyware packages are the first line of defense against malware.

Personal firewalls block network traffic from using unnecessary ports, and restrict the type use of protocols on ports that are in use. For example, they can restrict traffic on port 80 to Internet-related protocols such as HTTP. Personal firewalls can stop certain types of attacks from reaching devices, and block probes by hackers trying to discover weaknesses of the system. If systems are already infected, personal firewalls can sometimes prevent malware from sending information out to remote servers.

One of the major roles of firewalls on handheld devices and PDAs is to block or limit the use of Bluetooth®, Wi-Fi and phone communications. This can be extremely useful, for example by preventing hackers in public places from establishing Bluetooth connections to devices. However, IT department or the device owner must take positive actions to enable the necessary firewall features, because the default setting for firewalls on most devices is to allow all types of traffic.

Anti-virus and anti-spyware packages scan network traffic for segments of code or "signatures" that are characteristic of known malware. Most packages today can identify hundreds of thousands of instances viruses, worms, spyware and other malware.

Firewalls and anti-virus packages are now becoming available for handheld devices and PDAs as well as laptops. While anti-virus packages for handheld devices are not in wide use today, this may change as more malware appears that target these systems.

3.1.2. Limitations of firewalls, anti-virus and anti-spyware

Although necessary, personal firewalls, and anti-virus and anti-spyware packages have very significant limitations.

First, traditional firewalls usually can't block malware that goes through ports that are in use. They are like security guards who can shut unneeded doors and windows in a building, but cannot identify intruders who enter by the front door.

Second, as discussed earlier, virus writers and cyber-criminals have found ways to evade signature-based anti-virus and anti-spyware technologies using techniques like short-span attacks, serial variant attacks and designer malware.

In fact, there is evidence that the number of malware variants is simply overwhelming the capacity of anti-virus vendors and their customers to keep up. The analyst firm Yankee Group estimates that the number of unique malware variants reached 220,000 in 2007, ten times the number of variants in 2002. The firm also believes that the detection rate for new variants is less than 70%, and that most anti-virus vendors are 30–60 days behind in producing signatures for typical variants [15].

Third, signature-based technologies can lose effectiveness in the "mobile blind spot"; the area outside of the firewall where mobile devices are not connected to the corporate network and cannot receive the latest malware signature files.

3.1.3. Intrusion prevention systems and zero-day protection

Because firewalls and signature-based defenses cannot keep up with all of the malware variants being seen today, additional defenses are available based on behavioral analysis: detecting behavior or activities that are potentially harmful and stopping the source of those activities. These defenses do not require the creation and distribution of malware signatures.

Intrusion prevention systems (IPS) examine network traffic into and out of computers and to identify unexpected behavior. One technique is to utilize protocol recognition and traffic analysis techniques to identify network traffic that breaks protocol rules, for example traffic that uses a port that is non-standard for that protocol, or that sends too many header packets relative to payload packets.

Intrusion prevention systems can also identify changes in network activity. By establishing a baseline of normal traffic, the IPS can observe surges in traffic that indicate suspicious activities.

"Zero-day threat protection" or "zero-day malware protection" technologies use behavioral analysis techniques to examine the activities of software programs on computers to identify potentially harmful actions. Typically the software checks when unknown executable code is about to run and loads it into a "virtual PC" environment that simulates the memory, CPU and operating system of a PC. The zero-day software then observes the behavior of the unknown code, and notes actions that might be associated with malware, such as opening the email address book or modifying registry keys. If such actions are detected the suspicious code is quarantined or deleted.

3.2. Defenses against phishing and social engineering

3.2.1. Education
The first and best defense against phishing and social engineering attacks is education. By now most computer users know not to send bank account information to a cousin of the oil minister of a developing country. However, many don't know that an accurate looking email from their bank or credit-card issuer could be a phishing message, and even fewer realize that merely going to an unknown web site could result in a "drive-by download" of malware. Therefore some type of program that informs users of prevalent attacks and the risks of certain behaviors is essential.

3.2.2. Content and spam filtering
Content or Web Filtering programs typically maintain large black lists of web sites suspected of housing malware (or known for containing content related to pornography, gambling, drugs, job searching, games, sports, politics and other illegal or time-wasting subjects). End users can then be blocked from accessing these web sites. An even more restrictive approach is to use a "white list" to limit web access to a short list of sites that are known to be relevant to work.

Similarly, there are software programs that scan incoming email and filter out spam and phishing messages based on content and on a black list of known sources of malicious email.

Unfortunately, most content and spam filtering packages are designed to work on the enterprise perimeter, not on individual laptops or devices. This means they are effective only when the user utilizes the corporate email server and surfs the web through the corporate network (that is, when the user establishes a remote connection to the corporate network, and then goes out to the Internet through the corporate firewall and content filtering system). These perimeter-based defenses are not useful if the user utilizes a web-based email system like Hotmail or Yahoo Mail or surfs the Web through a direct connection to the Internet.

3.3. Defenses against direct attacks by hackers

3.3.1. Vulnerability and configuration management
As noted above, personal firewalls can prevent hackers from "pinging" systems and utilizing unneeded ports to probe for weaknesses and to penetrate mobile systems.

However, hackers also try to exploit known vulnerabilities in operating systems, browsers and application software. These include flaws in program code that allow hackers to slip malware onto the device, find out information about the system, or directly take control of the device.

Vulnerability management, configuration management, and software life cycle management (SLCM) programs check mobile systems for outdated versions of software programs, missing software patches, and outdated malware signature files. Some of the more sophisticated products can also check that configuration options and parameters of applications are set in accordance with corporate policies.

Some configuration management tools also have the ability to keep unwanted applications from being installed on the device, or to prevent them from executing. This eliminates the possibility that hackers take advantage of vulnerabilities in these applications. Blocking unnecessary applications can also improve employee productivity, for example by preventing workers from spending time on games.

3.4. Defenses against data communications interception and spoofing

3.4.1. Disabling unneeded communications

As discussed earlier, there are several methods hackers can use to intercept wireless communications between laptops, handheld devices, cell phones and other mobile devices. These include "sniffing" tools and "man in the middle" attacks. By intercepting communications traffic, hackers can read confidential information included in the transmissions and obtain passwords and usernames.

A first step in security communications is to disable unneeded communications methods and ports, either through firewall settings or by changing configuration settings on the system.

For example, enterprises may want to disallow the use of instant messaging, or at least to restrict IM products to types that use SSL or some other form of encryption. Similarly, it may be prudent to disable Bluetooth communications, or at least to ensure that Bluetooth-enabled systems are not "discoverable" by other Bluetooth devices.

3.4.2. Inbuilt encryption

Another key defense against these attacks is encryption of the network traffic. In many cases inbuilt encryption capabilities can be provided by software and features contained on laptops, handheld devices and cell phones using encryption algorithms such as Advanced Encryption Standard (AES) and A5 [21].

However, the IT staff must ensure that inbuilt encryption capabilities are enabled on all mobile devices, because in many cases encryption is turned off by default.

3.4.3. Password encryption

Some encryption tools allow passwords and usernames to be sent "in the clear" before an encrypted data stream is sent. Therefore it is important to use encryption tools that can encrypt authentication information. Another approach is to use protocols like APOP (Authenticated Post Office Protocol) that transmit encrypted passwords.

3.4.4. Virtual private networks

Virtual Private Networks (VPNs) combine encryption and authentication capabilities to create a secure "tunnel" over public networks. Traditional IPSec VPNs offer a very high level of security, but require an effort to place a dedicated client on each endpoint and to configure a VPN concentrator or similar device on the perimeter of the corporate network. SSL VPNs can often eliminate the need for local clients by using SSL capabilities built into browsers. However SSL VPNs require a downloadable plugin to work with some applications with non-browser interfaces.

Unfortunately, many users employ VPNs selectively to contact corporate networks but not to access the Internet from remote locations. This gives hackers a chance to capture passwords from unencrypted traffic, and use the same passwords to crack corporate networks. Therefore the most reliable security requires some that split tunneling be disabled and that the use of VPNs is enforced.

3.4.5. Restricted access to hot spots

To prevent "man in the middle" attacks, laptops and mobile devices can be configured to access only legitimate hotspots. Some wireless clients (although not all) use the Wireless Internet Service Project Roaming (WISPr) to validate hotspots. There are also network service aggregators who maintain a "phonebook" or "footprint" of legitimate hotspot addresses and distribute the phonebook to remote laptops.

3.5. Defenses against loss and theft of devices

3.5.1. Data encryption and time bombs

Many of the most highly publicized and damaging security breaches affecting both commercial enterprises and government agencies have occurred when laptops and other mobile devices have been lost or stolen.

The essential defense against the loss and theft of devices is data or disk encryption programs. These packages encrypt files as they are stored on the device and decrypt them when they are opened and used. Several different approaches to encryption are available, including "File and Folder Encryption" products that encrypt designated files and folders, "Full Disk Encryption" products that encrypt the contents of entire disk drives, and hybrid "Intelligent Encryption" products that encrypt files based on multiple criteria such as file type, storage location, and applications creating the files.

Some encryption products also include a "time bomb" capability that destroys data on the device, typically after a certain number of logon attempts have been unsuccessful.

Some handheld devices come with the ability to "wipe" data from lost or stolen units. However, this capability is not available in all situations; for example, BlackBerry devices can only be wiped if they are configured to work with a BlackBerry Enterprise Server.

3.5.2. Backup and recovery

While backup and recovery products (and managed services) are not strictly security defenses, they are often seen as a complement of encryption technologies. Backup and recovery products ensure that if a laptop or mobile device is lost or stolen the user can recovery the data and files.

3.5.3. Device control

Device control technologies can be used to prevent files from being written to USB and other external devices, or to require that files written to those devices are encrypted. For example, these packages can prevent files from being written to external disk drives, USB memory sticks, MP3 players, external hard drives, CD/DVD burner drives, digital cameras and PDAs. They can also prevent files from being transmitted using specific networking technologies such as Wi-Fi, Firewire and Bluetooth.

3.6. Defenses against malicious insider actions

3.6.1. Identity and access management controls

It is impossible to protect completely against insiders who want to steal confidential data. However, there are ways to greatly narrow the scope for action of malicious insiders and to improve the chances of detecting them.

One method for reducing the potential damage from malicious insiders is to implement identity and access management controls. These limit access to network segments and applications to specific users or user groups. Most identity and access systems are built around enterprise directories. Other tools in the identity management arsenal include provisioning, password management and single sign-on products, as well as access controls built into applications and databases.

However, a complete identity and access management infrastructure requires a great deal of effort to:

– Identify and analyze user roles and access rights
– Integrate the infrastructure with many applications, data sources and authentication points.
– Continually update the enterprise directory as employees join, leave and change roles.

3.6.2. Data leak prevention and content management

Data leak prevention (or data loss prevention) and content management technologies are relatively new security innovations that can restrict the actions of malicious insiders by blocking the transmission or copying of confidential data and files. Some of these products take the approach of tagging confidential files and then preventing those files from being emailed, transferred, copied or printed. Others scan network traffic to detect potentially confidential information, including key words and character or numerical strings typical of restricted information (for example numerical strings in the social security number format "999-99-9999").

3.6.3. Auditing, logs and traffic monitoring

The most typical way of detecting malicious insiders is through auditing and monitoring activities such as auditing transaction records, examining server and firewall logs, monitoring network traffic for suspicious patterns. These can help to detect employees trying to access servers or applications that aren't needed for legitimate activities, and employees sending files to unknown destinations.

3.7. Defenses against user policy violations

3.7.1. Data encryption, device control and data leak prevention

Most security vulnerabilities and data breaches created by end users are not caused by malicious intent, but simply through ignorance or of indifference to corporate security policies.

Several of the technologies described above can greatly reduce exposure from inadvertent user policy violations. For example, data encryption can mitigate data exposure when devices that are lost or stolen. Device control can prevent users from copying data to USB memory sticks, handheld devices and other small systems that can easily be lost. And data leak prevention and content management products can prevent users from emailing or transmitting files or information that should be kept within the corporate walls.

3.7.2. Education and training

Education and training are essential to reducing the incidence of user policy violations. Users need to be informed of security risks faced by the organization, of what actions violate corporate policies, and of the consequences of violating the policies to them and to their organization.

4. Assessing priorities

It is a maxim that the goal of IT security is to mitigate risk in a cost-effective fashion, not to eliminate risk entirely. And it should be clear from the foregoing discussion that no organization has the resources to deploy every defense needed to protect every mobile device from every type of security threat.

But how should enterprises set priorities among the threats and defenses discussed here? And what other activities must be performed to make these defenses successful?

Experience suggests that mobile security solutions should be approached using a five-step process. Some of these steps can be performed simultaneously in parallel, but none should be omitted.

The five steps are:

– Analyze information, users and risks.
– Document policies and train end-users.

Table 2
Summary of suggested priorities and activities

Step	Activities
Analyze confidential information, users and risks	– Analyze types and locations of confidential data. – Identify types of users and devices most exposed to threats. – Profile user groups based on the data they carry and exposure to risks.
Document policies and train end users	– Define, document and publish security policies. – Train end users.
Solidify the management of mobile devices	Implement an infrastructure for deploying, configuring, monitoring and updating software on mobile devices.
Deploy a set of critical baseline defenses on all laptops and mobile devices	Deploy a core set of defenses on all appropriate devices: – Personal firewall – Anti-virus package – Zero-day threat protection package – VPN client – Data encryption
Deploy advanced defenses on high-risk devices	On the most critical devices implement additional defenses such as: – Device control – Data leak prevention – Backup and recovery – Network Access Control (NAC) – Connectivity controls

- Solidify the management of mobile devices.
- Deploy a set of critical baseline defenses on all laptops and mobile devices.
- Deploy advanced defenses on high-risk devices.

A summary of the activities involved in each step are included in Table 2.
We will discuss briefly each of these steps.

4.1. Analyze information, users and risks

Organizations should survey and analyze the types of confidential information that ends up on laptops and other mobile devices. This includes not only files that are downloaded and stored on laptops, but also information contained in emails and email attachments sent to smaller mobile devices. The information should be assessed and categorized based on its importance and the potential damage if exposed. The analysis should include the types of users who use and store confidential data.

This process should also identify what types of users and devices are most exposed to threats based on factors like travel patterns, remote access methods used, and adherence to security policies.

The final result of this analysis should be profiles of user types and user groups based on both the quantity and importance of the confidential data they transport and their exposure to risk. Do sales people and field consultants regularly use Wi-Fi hot spots in airport lounges and coffee shops? Does the HR staff take home confidential employee data? Do finance executives carry sensitive financial data and business plans to countries with high crime rates and unsecure public networks?

4.2. Document policies and train end users

Security policies must be defined, documented and published to end users before they can be enforced. Policies relevant to protecting mobile data include rules on:

- Usernames, passwords and authentication methods.
- The use of data encryption.
- The use of VPNs.
- Security applications that must be installed on each type of mobile device.
- Types of mobile computing devices, storage devices and software applications that are authorized, and those that are forbidden.
- Under what circumstances new software applications can be downloaded.
- What types of information or files can be viewed and stored on mobile devices.
- What types of information or files can be emailed or transmitted to other people inside or outside of the enterprise.

Many of these policies will be dictated by government regulations like SOX, HIPAA and PCI and the UK Data Protection Act of 1998, as well as IT governance frameworks such as COBIT 4.0 and ISO 17799:2005.

Other useful guidelines can be formed simply by reading the IT industry press and observing what types of attacks are occurring and what employee actions create exposures.

As part of this process enterprises may need to rethink their approach toward handheld devices and smart phones. Many organizations allow employees to select and buy their own mobile devices. While this approach may save the enterprise money, it makes it extremely hard to define, much less enforce, a complete set of security policies.

And as mentioned earlier, enterprises must take active measures to educate their employees about security policies, and to explain the nature of security threats and why the security policies are justified.

4.3. Solidify the management of mobile devices

A very high percentage of security exposures are caused by factors like:

- Unpatched operating systems, browsers, and application software.
- Absent or out-of-date security applications and malware signature files.
- Security applications and features that are present on the device but were mis-configured or were never enabled.
- Security applications that have been mis-configured or actually shut off by end users, either by mistake or in misguided attempts to speed up system performance.

Because these types of errors are so prevalent, it is important for enterprises to develop a solid infrastructure for deploying, configuring, monitoring and updating system software and security software applications.

Enterprises willing to invest the resources can create their own platforms for managing mobile devices and mobile security applications. Most organizations, however, are better served by adopting platforms developed by security software vendors or security service providers.

A well-engineered platform for managing mobile devices has additional benefits on top of ensuring consistent deployment and patching. These include:

- Increasing the capacity of the organizations to deploy more security applications in a given timeframe.
- Reducing the cost of ongoing management.
- Providing centralized reporting to simplify management, and to document for auditors compliance with government and corporate policies.

4.4. Deploy a set of critical baseline defenses on all laptops and mobile devices

As security threats have multiplied, the number of security applications required to provide even adequate security has increased.

Today an absolute minimum set of defenses for laptops includes:

– A personal firewall.
– An anti-virus package.
– A zero-day threat protection package.
– A VPN client and a VPN enforcement mechanism.
– Data encryption.

Enterprises should use their analysis of information, users and risks to define their own package of baseline defenses that include the technologies listed above, and possibly others as well. This package should then become a required standard feature on every corporate laptop.

The baseline defenses for smaller mobile devices are more dependent on the individual device type, but in most cases these should include a firewall and some type of anti-virus or zero-day malware technology.

4.5. Deploy advanced defenses on high-risk devices

After the package of baseline defenses have been deployed on every mobile device, the enterprise can implement additional cutting-edge security technologies on the subset of devices that contain the most confidential information or are exposed to the greatest risks.

The defenses that should be considered for the high-risk devices include:

– Device Control
– Data Leak Prevention
– Backup and Recovery
– Network Access Control (NAC)
– Connectivity controls (for example controls on when Wi-Fi access can be used and restrictions to known hot spots).

5. Summary and further research

The information presented in this paper demonstrates that in the field of information security mobile devices should be considered separately from servers and desktop PCs. Unlike LAN-based systems, they move outside of the protections of perimeter defenses, rely on wireless communications, and are subject to loss and theft. Critical corporate data will be unnecessarily exposed if organizations use desktop PC defenses as a baseline and simply add a VPN client to laptops, or assume that handheld devices are the responsibility of the employees who purchase them, or treat mobile security as an afterthought. Instead, the security risks of mobile devices must be examined systematically as they apply to each organization.

Fortunately, a wide range of security technologies are available today that deal adequately with the security threats discussed here, with the exception of insider threats (which at best can only be mitigated by technology). In fact, for most organizations the challenge is not identifying useful security technologies, but assessing priorities and correctly selecting the most important defensive measures to implement first.

Finally, security for mobile devices should not be viewed as strictly a battle of technologies – the tools of hackers and cybercriminals versus security software purchased from vendors. Instead, organizations must look hard at processes and management tools so administrators can manage mobile systems effectively, and at policies and training so that end users can become allies in the fight against cybercriminals rather than bystanders or dupes.

5.1. Suggestions for further research

There is scope for a great deal of research on the details of security threats and attacks, including new and evolving types of malware, social engineering techniques, and techniques for intercepting wireless communications.

Another topic that would be of great practical value would be an examination of which attacks are in fact most prevalent and most dangerous. How can IT and security staffs separate the theoretical and exceptional threats from those that are in fact most likely to appear and cause damage?

Finally, significant research could be performed on topics related to user policy violations and what combinations of technology, training and psychology can be used to prevent them.

References

[1] Anonymous. A Fiberlink client who wishes to remain anonymous for security reasons.
[2] A. Bednarz, *Striving to keep teleworkers happy*, This article reports that forty percent of IBM's 330,000 employees work from home, on the road or at a client location on any given day, December 13, 2006, http://www.networkworld.com/news/2006/121306-striving-to-keep-teleworkers-happy.html
[3] Carneige Mellon Software Engineering Institute, with the US Secret Service and CERT® Coordination Center. (August 2004), *Insider Threat Study: Illicit Cyber Activity in the Banking and Finance Sector*, http://www. secretservice.gov/ntac/its_report_040820.pdf.
[4] Carneige Mellon Software Engineering Institute, with the US Secret Service and CERT® Coordination Center. (May 2005), *Insider Threat Study: Computer System Sabotage in Critical Infrastructure Sectors*, http://www.cert.org/insider_threat/insidercross.html.
[5] Computer Economics, Inc. (January 2006), *2005 Malware Report: The Impact of Malicious Code Attacks*, http://www.computereconomics.com/article.cfm?id=1090; Also see: Computer Economics. (June 2007). *Annual Worldwide Economic Damages from Malware Exceed $13 Billion*. http://www.computereconomics.com/article.cfm?id=1225.
[6] Computerworld. (August 20, 2007), *Identity attack spreads; 1.6M records stolen from Monster.com*, http://www.networkworld.com/news/2007/082007-monster-trojan.html.
[7] J. Dalrymple, *First Trojan reported for the iPhone*. PC World, January 8, 2008, http://www.pcworld.com/article/id,141187-page,1/article.html.
[8] O. Drori, N. Pappo and D. Yachan, *New malware distribution methods threaten signature-based AV*, 2005, http://www.commtouch.com/downloads/VBSept05_NewMalwareDistributionMethods.pdf.
[9] Fiberlink, Inc. (January 17, 2008) *As you head into 2008, don't forget to check your mobile blind spot*. Press Release. http://www.fiberlink.com/fiberlink/en-US/presscenter/releases/2008/011708.h tml.
[10] L. Greenemeier, *Massive Insider Breach At DuPont*, February 15, 2007, InformationWeek. http://www. informationweek.com/news/showArticle.jhtml?articleID=197006474.
[11] D. Hoffman, *Blackjacking; Security Threats to BlackBerry® Devices, PDAs and Cell Phones in the Enterprise*, 2007, Wiley Publishing, Inc., 2007.
[12] IDC. (January 15, 2008) *IDC Predicts the Number of Worldwide Mobile Workers to Reach 1 Billion by 2011*. Press Release. http://www.idc.com/getdoc.jsp?containerId=prUS21037208.
[13] ISACA. (October 31, 2007). *Risky Business: More Than One-third of Employees Admit to Violating Their Company's IT Policies*. Press Release. http://www.isaca.org/Content/ContentGroups/Press_Releases/2007/ISACA_ Survey_Reveals_Alarming_Computer_Behavior.htm.
[14] R. Jaques, *Cost of malware soars to $166bn in 2004*, February 1, 2005, vnunet.com. http://www.vnunet.com/vnunet/news/2126635/cost-malware-soars-166bn-2004. However, this estimate was controversial, as discussed in: *Virus Damage a Controversial Science*. Web Host Industry Review, March 12, 2004. http://www.thewhir.com/features/virus-damage.cfm.
[15] A. Jacquith, (January, 2007). *Anti-Virus Is Dead; Long Live Anti-Malware* (*Abstract*). Yankee Group Research Report. http://www.mindbranch.com/listing/product/R388-2317.html.

[16] G. Keizer, (August 22, 2007), *Monster.com Trojan recruits 'money mules' from victim pool.* Computerworld. http://www.computerworld.com/action/article.do?command=viewArticleBasic& articleId=9032278.

[17] J. Kirk, *Hackers Sneak Tricks Into MySpace Band Pages*, October 31, 2007, IDG News Service. http://www. pcworld.com/article/id,139137-pg,1/article.html.

[18] Korn/Ferry International. (August 24, 2006) *38% of Executives Surveyed Believe They Spend Too Much Time Connected to Mobile Devices.* Press Release. http://www.kornferry.com/Library/Process.asp?P=PR_Detail&CID=1743& LID=1

[19] J. Leyden, *Trojan targets UK online bank accounts*, November 12, 2004, The Register. http://www. theregister.co.uk/2004/11/12/banker_trojan/.

[20] P. Mavrommatis, D. McNamee, N. Modadugu, N. Provos and K. Wang, *The Ghost In The Browser Analysis of Web-based Malware*, 2007, First Workshop on Hot Topics in Understanding Botnets (HotBots '07). http://www. usenix.org/events/hotbots07/tech/full_papers/provos/provos.pdf.

[21] National Institutue of Standards and Technology (NIST). *Advanced Encryption Standard (AES) Questions and Answers.* http://www.nist.gov/public_affairs/releases/aesq&a.htm.

[22] Privacy Rights Clearinghouse. (2005–2008) *A Chronology of Data Breaches.* http://www.privacyrights.org/ar/ Chron-DataBreaches.htm.

[23] L. Rosencrance, January 19, 2007, *Hackers steal $35,000 from customers of federal savings plan*, Computerworld. http://www.computerworld.com/action/article.do?command=viewArticleBasic&articleId=9008619.

[24] RSA, Inc. (December 2007). *The Confessions Survey: Office Workers Reveal Everyday Behavior That Places Sensitive Information at Risk.* http://www.rsa.com/company/news/releases/pdfs/RSA-insider-confessions.pdf.

[25] T. Shifrin, July 30, 2007, *Hospital denies stolen USB stick held sensitive data*, Computerworld. http://www. computerworld.com/action/article.do?command=viewArticleBasic&articleId=9028461.

[26] Sophos, Inc., 2004, *53 arrests as Brazil cracks down on phishing Trojan authors*, Press release, http://www. sophos.com/pressoffice/news/articles/2004/10/va_brazilarrest.html.

[27] Sophos, Inc., *Sophos security threat report 2007*, Press release, 2007, (http://www.sophos.com/security/whitepapers/ sophos-security-threats-2007_wsrus.

[28] J. Vijayan, *VA installs encryption software on 15,000 laptops*, September 28, 2006, Computerworld. http://www. computerworld.com/action/articlE.do?command=viewArticleBasic&articleId=9003705.

[29] J. Vijayan, July 18, 2007, *Spouse and file-sharing program at the center of data compromise*, ComputerWorld. http:// www.computerworld.com/action/article.do?command=viewArticleBasic&articleId=9027260.

[30] J. Vijayan, October 22, 2007, *Phishers (almost) scam grocery giant out of $10 million*, Computerworld http://www. computerworld.com/action/article.do?command=viewArticleBasic&articleId=9043618.

Jon Friedman is Director of Marketing for Fiberlink Communications. Jon has over 20 years of experience with high tech companies in marketing, product marketing, sales and business planning. Jon has spoken at numerous IT conferences and has been published in trade journals including Computerworld, LinuxWorld Magazine, and Datamation. He has a bachelor's degree from Yale and an M.B.A. from the Harvard Business School.

Daniel V. Hoffman is Chief Technology Officer at SMobile Systems, Inc. He was previously a senior systems engineer at Fiberlink Communications and possesses over 13 years of hands-on remote access security knowledge. He is the author of Blackjacking: Security Threats to BlackBerry Devices, PDAs, and Cell Phones in the Enterprise (Wiley Publishing, April 2007) and Implementing NAP and NAC Security Technologies: The Complete Guide to Network Access Control (Wiley Publishing, April 2008), as well as being a frequent contributor of articles to the Ethical Hacker Network. Hoffman's live hacking demonstrations have been featured in the US Department of Homeland Security's open source infrastructure report and are regularly presented at computer conferences worldwide. He has been interviewed as a security expert by numerous media outlets around the world including Forbes, Network World, Clear Channel Communications and Newsweek.

Part IV: Strategies

Information Knowledge Systems Management 7 (2008) 183–210
IOS Press

Enterprise mobility and support outsourcing: A research model and initial findings

Christina C. Loh[a],*, Andrew D. Stadlen[b], Rahul C. Basole[c], John D. Moses[d] and
Conor Tuohy[e]
[a]*Palm Enterprise Support, 950 W. Maude Ave, Sunnyvale, CA 94085, USA*
E-mail: christina.loh@palm.com
[b]*Palm Customer Experience, 950 W. Maude Ave, Sunnyvale, CA 94085, USA*
E-mail: andrew.stadlen@palm.com
[c]*Tennenbaum Institute, Georgia Institute of Technology, 760 Spring Street NW, Atlanta, GA 30332, USA*
E-mail: rahul.basole@ti.gatech.edu
[d]*Palm Customer Relations, 950 W. Maude Ave, Sunnyvale, CA 94085, USA*
E-mail: john.moses@palm.com
[e]*Palm Marketing, 950 W. Maude Ave, Sunnyvale, CA 94085, USA*
E-mail: conor.tuohy@palm.com

Abstract: The evolution of the wireless industry and the rapid proliferation of a mobile workforce have left businesses at a disadvantage. Business customers must be creative with currently available support resources in order to address their needs. Organizations with high mobile usage maturity levels are moving towards greater device and policy standardization and are seeking a solution to their problems. Given the intrinsic gaps in current mobile network operator business models to meet business customers' wireless device support needs, and that businesses themselves are just starting to develop their capabilities in-house, this paper investigates organizational receptiveness towards outsourcing and the potentially compelling benefits that outsourcing offers.

Keywords: Support, enterprise mobility, standardization, outsourcing

1. Introduction

The global mobile workforce (e.g. mobile professionals, field workers, and telecommuters, etc.) is growing at a pace of over 5% a year. As early as 2009, it is estimated that as many as 878 million mobile workers will be toiling away on laptops, handhelds and cell phones [22].

Technology has advanced to the point where one can work from a ski slope as easily as one can from the office. Devices are capable of transmitting voice and data, accessing the Internet, and accessing enterprise applications and data. Networks enable high-speed connectivity and 3G cellular capabilities; Wi-Fi and Bluetooth networks are available in public areas.

Employers are realizing the benefits of allowing their workforce to work remotely: increased productivity and employee satisfaction, improved information capture, and lower infrastructure costs. Sun

---

*Corresponding author.

Microsystems has adopted a flexible, mobile work environment which it estimates has significantly reduced operating costs and is a major contributor to retaining talent in Silicon Valley's competitive job market [43]. British Telecom estimates that its mobile working policies and infrastructure improved employee productivity by 31% [28].

As a result of tangible benefits, businesses are investing heavily in mobility. In 2006, mobile voice and data services were over a quarter of North American business telecom budgets. In Europe, the percentage was even higher at 32% [34]. Additionally, nearly 50% of businesses are increasing their mobility budgets, and 58% state that they are planning on spending more on mobile data plans [28].

Employees are embracing technology that helps them to achieve a greater work-life balance. In fact, the number of cell phone-only households has more than tripled in the last few years. It is estimated that one-third of all American households will be cell phone-only in three years. In Europe, it is estimated that over 50% of all households are already cell phone-only [37]. Depending on a company's mobile expense policy and budget, employees may carry multiple mobile phones to satisfy their professional and personal needs.

In order to take advantage of the productivity and job satisfaction mobile devices bring to the workforce, businesses are compelled to take a greater position in managing mobile devices. IT departments are faced with supporting the devices in the field. The challenges stem from a proliferation of devices, operating system platforms, carriers, and networks, plus application integration and security concerns. In order to support mobile devices, several factors need to be taken into consideration. Notably, many of the considerations contradict each other, creating no simple or standard answer to what will work best for all businesses.

- Device Ownership – Individual ownership or corporate ownership make tradeoffs between personal choice, supportability of these devices, and the ability to leverage devices for email, business applications and security options.
- Network Coverage – Maximizing coverage for a highly dispersed workforce often requires engaging multiple carriers. Multiple carriers results in multiple plans which increases the difficulty in optimizing usage.
- Devices – Even if there is a standard device list, devices vary between carriers. If the devices are standardized, they are typically owned by the business. This model decreases support and application complexity, but increases asset management responsibilities and may adversely impact user adoption.
- Expense Management – Separating personal from business use. If service plan bills are consolidated, it requires internal resources to sift through mountains of transactions. However, expensing service plans prevents optimization of the savings a business can gain from consolidation.
- Asset Management and Support – Mobile devices become outdated quickly and are smaller, more fragile and more susceptible to loss and theft than traditional electronic assets, thus requiring significant resources to manage the deployment, replacement and return of these devices, as well as keeping up to date with the newest models and issues when manning the help desk.

In 2006, Palm conducted an internal research study on business customer needs and identified five key areas business customers were most interested in addressing (see Fig. 1). The first is mobile device deployment planning: this area is of particular interest to companies that have invested or are thinking of investing in business applications for mobile devices. They need access to experts and devices for planning and testing.

The second area is deployment. Challenges are the greatest for larger enterprises that have thousands of employees that may receive a different level of service plan and device depending on seniority or organizational group.

The third area of need is support for either their end users or advanced help desk to help desk support. Many businesses are looking to either augment existing support staff capabilities or to completely outsource the support of mobile devices.

The fourth area is in device logistics and repair. Managing device repair and replacement while minimizing the impact to end user productivity is especially challenging when there are multiple carriers, various devices and warranty considerations.

The final area of need is in control. Businesses want to be able to easily understand who has what device and what plan, feel assured that the data on those devices is secure, align carrier billing to organizational structure for charge backs and to know that their devices are being disposed of in an environmentally safe manner.

2. History and overview of the current support ecosystem

Mobile phone adoption has been mainly driven by consumers who have transformed cell phone usage from a luxury to a necessity [39]. Businesses have been slow to adopt the new technology; starting by only providing devices and covering expenses for executives or sales forces [48]. Through grassroots efforts by employees, mobile phone deployments by enterprises have proliferated. Employees at all levels now have a mobile phone – which they use for both personal and business purposes. While businesses may view the lack of a clear dividing line between personal and business as a challenge, an alternative approach could be that enterprises leverage an individual's early adoption of new technology to advance the enterprise's goals.

When mobile phones first emerged, the devices had primitive voice capabilities. Devices were typically sold through "mom and pop shops" and cellular service was provided by local wireless carriers. Both entities shared in the support of the user experience. The retailer supported device-related issues and the carrier supported service-related customer issues. This provided a hands-on support environment to consumers and small businesses that invested in these devices.

Devices got smaller and more affordable, and carriers improved their networks and service plans. Carriers started bundling devices into wireless plans as they realized that the recurring revenue far exceeded the cost of providing incentives for the device. As this occurred and carriers became retailers of mobile devices, they also became the primary providers of technical support. Additionally, carriers realized the value of developing a relationship with the customer and embraced support responsibilities as additional opportunities to up-sell or cross-sell to consumers. Since devices primarily provided only voice capabilities, support was relatively simple.

Over time, the availability of new support technologies and the rising cost of support led to a transition from US-based support centers to primitive automated call routing and offshore support centers. Customer satisfaction with carriers plummeted. From 1994 to 2001, the Council of Better Business Bureaus saw a steady increase in the number of customer complaints, which topped 2.8 million in 2000 [47]. In 2004, University of Michigan's study of its customer satisfaction index listed the mobile phone service industry as the second lowest in meeting customer satisfaction.

Market and regulatory trends, such as number portability, encouraged carriers to make investments in improving customer satisfaction, and as a result, carriers have had some success in improving this metric. In 2006, VocaLabs, an independent research company, noted that overall carrier performance has "improved over the last two years by a statistically significant amount and a greater percent of calls are now being handled entirely by automated systems" [50]. This indicates that perhaps technology has become more customer-friendly, that customers are more accustomed to automated systems and carriers have been able to create more customer-friendly processes.

However, just as carriers seem to be addressing customer satisfaction issues with basic cell phones, the last few years have seen an explosion in device capability. "Consumer expectations will continue to rise as cell phone users increasingly rely on the communication functions of their cell phones beyond voice calling," notes Kirk Parsons, Senior Director of Wireless at J.D. Power [51]. Mobile phones not only provide voice communication, but text messaging, email, web, music, camera, calendar and other data functions. Smart phones are described as "minicomputers...that support [plethora of computing-intensive] applications" [45]. With greater functionality comes greater frustration: "The proliferation of new, cutting edge features and functionalities for mobile phones have outpaced the average user's understanding and appreciation for what they can do with their handsets" [7]. As a result, the wireless industry still stands out as the top source of consumer complaints according to a 2006 report by the Better Business Bureau [17].

Putting aside customer satisfaction issues, there are inherent reasons why wireless carriers are not best suited for meeting business customers' mobile device support needs.

1. **Business customers often have contracts with several carriers**. Rarely does one carrier own an entire business customer wireless account. Employees are distributed across different regions and need a carrier that is going to provide them with the best coverage for their area.
2. **Carriers' core business is selling their network**. First, while carriers offer devices as part of their total offering, they do not possess knowledge of the devices they offer comparable to that of the manufacturer. It is also difficult to train their store and call center resources on every device as each carrier may offer over one hundred different devices from various manufactures at one time. Second, carrier investments have been heavily focused on improvements in wireless billing and network improvements, not on business customer relationship processes or systems [40,47]. Carriers do not have the systems or resources that enable them to provide business customers with tailored support that reflects a business' unique mobile environment.
3. **Carrier's main source of revenue is the consumer segment**. The majority of a carrier's business is from consumers, and therefore their systems, processes and focus are on the needs of this market. Many current carrier systems and processes are tailored to a single user or a family of users on one plan, not one administrator trying to troubleshoot or activate multiple users on multiple devices with multiple variations of service plans. Another example is that carrier billing is not aligned with a business' organization structure. For businesses that pay for employees' wireless plans, each employee's organization is often responsible for the charge back. Carrier billing is not organized in such a way that it is easy for a mobile administrator to allocate costs across the organization.

Because businesses customers are not able to meet their mobile device support needs with what is currently available in the market, there are a number of new entrants to the space that are starting to fill the gap. A web search of "mobile device lifecycle management," a term commonly used to describe mobile support services, generates the following results:

- **TEM providers**: Telecom Expense Management companies optimize a company's spend on wireless and wire line expenses. These companies have traditionally focused on wire line expenses and have expanded their services to wireless. Some examples of TEM companies are: Anchor Point, Telesoft, Rivermine, Telwares, ProfitLine.
- **Wireless Management niche players**: Companies that specialize in mobile device deployment, management and logistics. These companies are typically startups lead by entrepreneurs looking

to address market need. Some examples of companies in this space include: Movero, Integrated Mobile, Enterprise Mobile, Karbon Systems.

– **IT Service providers**: These are the most established companies in the marketplace and have traditionally focused on providing full service IT outsourcing and electronic device management. Many of these players have yet to offer services in the mobile device management space, however, as the market grows it is foreseen that these companies will move into this space. Some examples of companies in this space include: Bell Technologies, Compucom, CDW, EDS, IBM.

Additional emerging categories associated with mobile support services include:

– **In-House capabilities**: Many companies are allocating internal resources to support mobile device procurement, logistics and support for their end users.
– **OEM help desks**: Original Equipment Manufacturers are filling the gap with complimentary and paid options for their customers. For example, Palm offers MyPalm membership for individuals who want additional support and PalmES, a paid support program for enterprise customers. BlackBerry has recently launched their "Owners Lounge" resource for BlackBerry owners, which offers T-level and incident support for their business customers.

Given the needs of business customers and the current support ecosystem, this research seeks to shed light on business customers' perspectives and how receptive businesses are to the available options. In particular, this paper seeks to answer the following questions: How does a company's willingness to support mobile devices, their perception of support complexity, their satisfaction with current support sources and the strength of their internal capabilities influence their willingness to outsource? Also, what are the factors that influence a company's willingness to support mobile devices and their perception of complexity? How do factors such as the usage of advanced functionality, mobile devices providing competitive advantage, end user productivity, and the need for control ultimately influence a company's position on outsourcing?

The remainder of the paper is structured as follows. Section 2 provides a brief overview of the theoretical foundations of the paper. Section 3 presents the conceptual model and research propositions. Section 4 highlights the research approach used. Results are presented and discussed in Section 5. Section 6 concludes with a summary of findings and a discussion of future research opportunities.

3. Theoretical background

IT outsourcing has been a topic of growing interest in the information systems and strategic management literature [2,24,26,31,33]. Previous studies have examined IT outsourcing from various perspectives, including that of the client [44], the provider [12,32], and the underlying relationship [36]. In doing so, studies have identified a plethora of factors, determinants, barriers, risks, and decision making processes that shape IT outsourcing initiatives [14,16,18,20] provide a comprehensive review of this literature.

In general, IT outsourcing studies can be classified into three broad categories: the economic view, the strategic view, and the social view [10]. The economic view, largely rooted in the theories of transaction costs [3,4] and agency costs, primarily focuses on how organizations can gain cost benefits from IT outsourcing. The strategic view focuses on how organizations develop and use IT outsourcing strategies to attain competitive advantages [1,15,27,29,42]. One of the most common theories used to examine this view is the resource-based view of the firm and resource dependency theory. Organizations that perceive

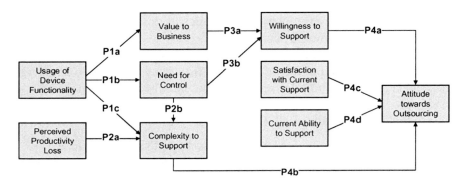

Fig. 1. Research Model of Outsourcing Determinants.

themselves to have resource and capability deficiencies related to IT are more likely to outsource that function. Resources-based theory suggests that outsourcing is fundamentally a strategic decision that helps organizations "fill gaps" in their resources and capabilities [21]. The social view tries to explain the reason why organizations enter into closer relationships with their service providers [21,24,25]. Social network theory tends to be the most common paradigm used. For a comprehensive review of theoretical foundations in IT outsourcing studies, the reader is referred to Gottschalk and Solli-Saether [19].

Lacity and Willcocks [26] argue that financial and strategic objectives drive organizations to pursue IT outsourcing initiatives. Indeed, research has shown that outsourcing enables organizations to focus on their core competencies by leveraging the expertise, experience, and resources of external entities, such as vendors, system integrators and consultants [38]. For mobile technology outsourcing decisions, issues such as data confidentiality, security, reliability, and control are particularly important.

In addition to examining the determinants of IT outsourcing, previous studies also investigated the degree of the outsourcing effort [49]. Indeed, previous studies have focused their efforts on the IT area as whole [46] or on specific IT functions [11].

Based on this brief theoretical review, this paper argues that an organization's perception, or attitude, toward outsourcing is dependent on several factors. The conceptual model is thus presented next.

4. Conceptual model and research propositions

In view of the current environment's inability to meet the needs of business customers, it can be assumed that business customers are inclined to outsource mobile device management and support. This assumption provides the basis for our research motivation, namely if business customers perceive a gap between current market, internal capability and need, do they view outsourcing as a viable alternative? If so, what are the areas that would provide them with the greatest amount of benefit? Drawing on previous work on outsourcing and IT support, we theorize that businesses traverse a complex decision space. We argue that the attitude towards outsourcing is determined and influenced by several factors and the relationships between them. Figure 1 conceptualizes these relationships.

Based on this research model, we suggest four fundamental research propositions:

Proposition 1. The more a business utilizes the functionality of mobile devices, the greater the perceived value of these devices (Proposition 1a), the greater control the business requires[1] (Proposition 1b) and the higher the complexity to support these devices (Proposition 1c).

Proposition 2. Companies that believe mobile devices have a greater impact on productivity will also perceive that mobile devices are more complicated to support (Proposition 2a). Further, the greater a company's need for control over its employees' mobile devices, the greater the complexity to support these devices (Proposition 2b).

Proposition 3. The greater the perceived value of mobile devices (Proposition 3a) and the greater control the business requires (Proposition 3b), the more likely a business is to have a support policy for mobile devices.

Proposition 4. The more willing a company is to support mobile devices (Proposition 4a), the higher the perception of complexity to support (Proposition 4b), the lower the satisfaction with current support (Proposition 4c) and the lower the current ability to support (Proposition 4d) result in a more positive attitude towards outsourcing.

5. Research methodology

The online web survey was developed to determine if there is any correlation between certain enterprise attributes and the types of mobile policies and support strategies. This directed research used a convenience sampling technique: the survey was provided to Palm's direct sales force to forward to their strategic customers, as well as emailed directly to Palm's enterprise contact database. The questions were developed based on existing instruments and keeping respondent demographics, the current mobile landscape and policies, importance of mobile devices to organizations, and areas of opportunity for increased mobility in mind. Survey length and format was designed by Palm's in-house survey resources, an organizational unit with extensive experience and education on optimizing survey responses.

The survey was implemented in Zoomerang, a professional online survey tool. An initial pilot study was conducted with internal Palm resources from customer-facing organizations, such as customer support, sales and system engineering groups, to validate the structure and flow of the survey. The survey was launched at the end of 2007 and administered for three weeks. It was sent to approximately 635,800 contacts. It should be noted that there may have been multiple contacts at one company. The enterprise contact database consists of individuals representing business entities that have requested information from Palm and have opted to allow Palm to contact them Respondents were offered a copy of the results as an incentive for survey participation. The survey instrument can be found in the Appendix.

The survey resulted in 11,121 visits (1.7% of invitees), 5571 complete responses (0.9% response rate; 50.1% of visitors completed the survey), 1121 partial responses (10.1% of visitors partially completed the survey), and 4429 abandons (39.9% abandon rate). Tables 2–6 provide a detailed breakdown of respondent demographics.

6. Analysis and discussion of results

The following section presents and discusses the results of our study.

---

[1]We define control over devices as standardization of device brands and models, corporate device ownership, and direct corporate billing or reimbursement of employees for mobile services.

Table 1
Summary of Business Customer Needs (adapted from Palm Internal Study)

Customer Need	Description	Solutions
Plan	Participate in device trials, plan your deployment with support engineers and work with software development to build custom enterprise productivity solutions	– Product Trial – Expert Services – Application Development
Deploy	Order or rent devices, train your staff, configure devices, activate service plans, and receive credit for older devices	– Online Assisted Procurement – Device Rental – Service Plan Management – Device Configuration – Kitting – Buy-Back/Upgrade – Training for IT Professionals – Training for End Users
Help	Get knowledge, tools, and support for IT and end users	– Enterprise Setup Assistance – Technical Support for IT Professionals – Technical Support for End Users – Application Support – Enterprise Support Bulletins – Support Tools and Knowledge Share
Fix	Reduce end-user downtime, eliminate logistics headaches, and improve asset life by streamlining replacement and repair processes	– Device Replacement – Device Repair – Protection – Device Insurance
Control	Manage the risk and return on your investment, and stay on top of support issues, billing, and data security	– Activity Reporting – Billing Management – Data Security – Device Recycle

Table 2
Responses by Firm Size

Firm Size	Responses
1–100	2,960 (53.1%)
101–999	980 (17.6)
1,000–9999	914 (16.4)
10,000+	717 (12.9)
Total	5,571 (100)

6.1. Usage of Device Functionality

Given the historical progression of device functionality from voice only to email, and later web access and enterprise applications, results of our survey indicate the usage of device functionality to be consistent with expectations. On average:

- 70% of respondents have most (76–100%) employees using mobile devices for voice
- 59% of respondents have most employees using mobile devices for email
- 47% of respondents have most employees using mobile devices for web
- 36% of respondents have most employees using mobile devices for enterprise applications

75% of all respondents state that some of their mobile device users are using business applications. A high percentage of businesses where their employees use mobile device applications also highly utilize email and web on their devices. Of the businesses where most employees use business applications,

Table 3
Responses by Industry Segments

Firm Size	Responses
Agriculture, Forestry, Fishing	48 (0.9%)
Automotive	84 (1.5)
Construction	149 (2.7)
Consumer Goods	52 (0.9)
Education	663 (11.9)
Energy, Chemical, and Utilities	111 (2.0)
Engineering	140 (2.5)
Financial Services	405 (7.3)
Food Services	47 (0.8)
Government	271 (4.9)
Healthcare	642 (11.5)
Computers and High Technology	482 (8.7)
Hospitality	34 (0.6)
Legal	174 (3.1)
Manufacturing	274 (4.9)
Marketing/Advertising	104 (1.9)
Media and Entertainment	113 (2.0)
Metals and Mining	12 (0.2)
Non-Profit	153 (2.7)
Professional Services	349 (6.3)
Public Sector	30 (0.5)
Real Estate	339 (6.1)
Retail	113 (2.0)
Telecommunications	224 (4.0)
Transportation	115 (2.1)
Wholesale/Distribution	107 (1.9)
Other	336 (6.0)
Total	**5,571 (100)**

Table 4
Responses by Regions of Operations

Firm Size	Responses
Asia	1,113 (19.9%)
Europe	1,333 (23.9)
North America	4,614 (82.8)
South America	801 (14.4)

88% also have most employees using email and 81% have most employees using web on their mobile devices.

Small businesses (1–100 employees) had the highest percentage of employees using business applications, with large businesses (1000+ employees) second and medium businesses (101–999 employees) last.[2]

The top three industries utilizing business applications are Real Estate, Marketing/Advertising and Professional Services.[3] The industries where cell phone functionality usage was lowest are Food

---

[2]39% of small businesses, 36% of large businesses, and 30% of medium businesses have most employees using business applications.

[3]All have 46% of respondents indicating that most employees in their organization use enterprise applications; 16% of Marketing/Advertising respondents and 15% of Professional Services and Real Estate respondents indicate that few (0–25%) employees use them.

Table 5
Responses by Department

Firm Size	Responses
Sales	923 (16.6%)
Marketing	299 (5.4)
IT	778 (14)
Finance	217 (3.9)
HR	62 (1.1)
Legal	179 (3.2)
Engineering	439 (7.9)
Operations	874 (15.7)
Security/Facilities	73 (1.3)
Other	1,727 (31.0)
Total	**5,571 (100)**

Table 6
Responses by Position

Firm Size	Responses
Owner/Principal	1,186 (21.3%)
President/CEO	388 (7.0)
General Manager	273 (4.9)
CIO/CTO	61 (1.1)
CFO/COO/Corporate Executive	136 (2.4)
IT: VP/Director	158 (2.8)
IT: Manager	334 (6.0)
IT: Staff	360 (6.5)
Business Unit: VP/Director	312 (5.6)
Business Unit: Manager	548 (9.8)
Business Unit: Staff	364 (6.5)
Other	1,451 (26.0)
Total	**5,571 (100)**

Services, Retail, Construction and Education.[4]

Proposition 1a. Do businesses that use more mobile device functionality also believe that mobile devices are more valuable to their business? Yes.

The more important mobile devices are to a company's ability to compete, the more likely users are to utilize advanced functionality. In fact, businesses that view devices as very important have more users taking advantage of voice, email, web, and business applications than businesses that consider mobile devices important; in turn, these businesses have more users leveraging each feature than those that consider mobile devices only somewhat important[5] (see Fig. 2).

Proposition 1b. Do businesses that use more mobile device functionality also believe they need greater control over mobile devices? Yes.

---

[4]Food Services: 21% have most employees and 26% have few employees using enterprise applications. Retail: 29% have most employees and 25% have few employees using enterprise applications. Construction: 30% have most employees and 31% have few employees using enterprise applications. Education: 26% have most employees and 24% have few employees using enterprise applications.

[5]78% of respondents state that mobile devices are important or very important to their company's ability to compete. Only 17% responded that mobile devices were only somewhat important and 5% responded that mobile devices were not important.

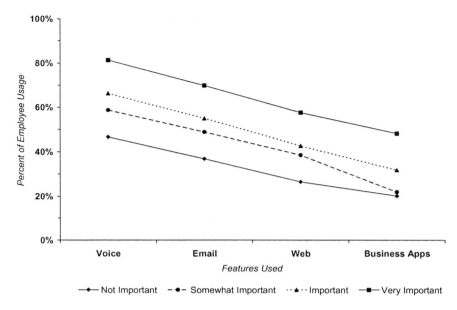

Fig. 2. Employee Usage of Mobile Device Functionality vs. Features Used.

Companies that utilize advanced mobile device functionality generally have device standards, pay for those devices, and reimburse employees for the wireless service for those devices.

6.2. Device standards

Companies where there are the highest numbers of users using advanced functionality have the most device standards. 52% of all companies have some sort of device standard, which is fairly evenly split between an approved device list (27%) and a single device standard (28%) (see Fig. 3).

The trend is that businesses are moving towards a standard device policy. 30% of companies are moving towards standard devices, whereas only 7% are moving away from standard devices.[6] Large business is moving the most towards standard devices (33%), with Medium (32%) and Small (29%) businesses close behind.[7]

6.3. Device ownership

The higher the percentage of end users that utilize advanced functionality, the higher the percentage of companies providing device reimbursement (74% of companies where most users utilize business applications reimburse, vs. 68% of all companies, on average). Overall, 68% of companies own, rent or reimburse for mobile devices.

The majority of companies have a single type of device ownership policy (92%). The remainder have a mix of policies where the employee owns their device, is reimbursed, can rent, or the business owns the device.

---

[6]Out of the 44% of companies that are staying with their current policy, 50% have an open device policy, 27% have a single device policy and 23% have a list of approved devices policy (which reflects the same breakdown as the general population).

[7]In terms of moving away from standard device policies, Medium businesses take the lead (8%), with Small (7%) and Large businesses (6%) following.

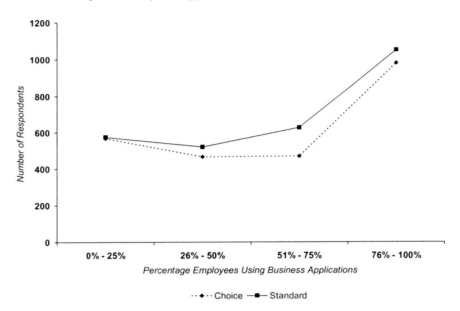

Fig. 3. Choice or Device Standard vs. Business Applications Usage.

In cases where user have their choice of device, 66% of respondents indicated that at least some devices are personally owned, and 25% indicated that at least some users are reimbursed. In cases where users can pick from a standard device list, the majority is paid for by the company.[8]

Rental is the most common in situations where there is a single device standard.[9]

6.4. Wireless plan reimbursement policy

Overall, companies with higher usage of business applications provide greater levels of reimbursement (see Table 5).

Also, companies that have a high percentage of employees utilizing business applications on their mobile device are changing their policy to provide reimbursement in the next year (see Table 6).

Proposition 1c. Do businesses that use more mobile device functionality also believe that supporting mobile devices is more complex than supporting employee PCs? No.

Companies that have most employees utilizing advanced functionality also have the highest percentage of respondents that believe that supporting mobile devices is equal in complexity to supporting laptops (46% vs. 39% average).

The majority of respondents believe that supporting mobile devices is about equal in complexity to supporting laptops. However, companies where only a small percentage (0–25%) of employees utilize advanced mobile device functionality have the highest percentage of respondents that believe supporting mobile devices is harder then supporting laptops (28% vs. 23% average). One potential explanation is that processes are not well defined, as only a small percentage of the population is utilizing advanced

---

[8]64% of companies own and distribute at least some of their employees' devices, 20% reimburse at least some employees for device purchase, and 25% require at least some employees to pay for and own their own device.

[9]45% of all rental devices are used in companies where this is a single device standard.

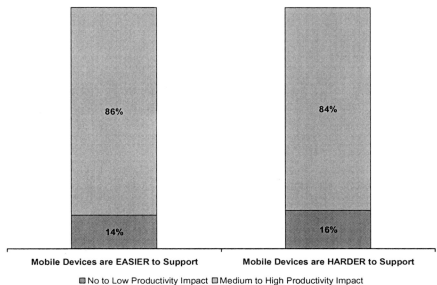

Fig. 4. Level of Productivity Impact due to Mobile Device Issues vs. Complexity to Support.

functionality. Therefore, the lack of standards to support those users makes it more difficult than if the entire population was utilizing advanced functionality. Another potential explanation is that the companies that believe supporting mobile devices is more difficult than supporting PCs have been slower to adopt advanced functionality because of these fears.

Proposition 2a. Do businesses that perceive high productivity loss when experiencing mobile device problems perceive mobile devices to be more complicated to support? No.

Companies that view mobile device problems as having a high impact on productivity are slightly more likely to view supporting mobile devices as easier than supporting PCs than those who find it harder, and companies that view mobile device support as harder than PC support are slightly more likely to view device problems as having little or no impact on productivity (see Fig. 4). This is in contrast to the original proposition, which supposes that the impact to productivity is due to the complexity and time it takes to remedy the situation when a mobile device is having problems.

One potential explanation is companies that perceive a high impact to productivity put more measures in place to ensure that supporting mobile devices is as seamless as possible. Another explanation is that companies that perceive supporting mobile devices as harder invest less in mobile devices and therefore there is less impact to productivity when they experience problems.

Overall, the majority of respondents believe that there is a medium to high impact on their productivity when users experience mobile device problems. [10]

Proposition 2b. Do businesses that have more control over their mobile devices also believe that supporting mobile devices is more complex than supporting employee PCs? No

---

[10] 39% of respondents believe mobile device problems have a high impact on productivity, 47% believe they have a medium impact, 13% believe they have a low impact, and only 1% believe they have no impact.

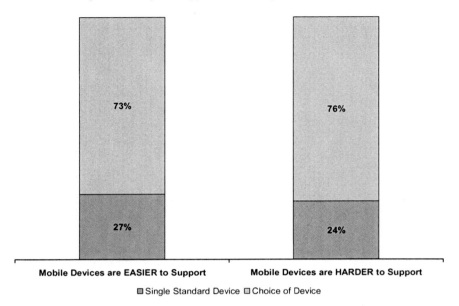

Fig. 5. Choice/Standard vs. Perceived Support Complexity.

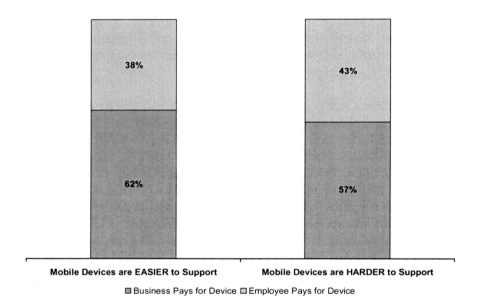

Fig. 6. Personal Device vs. Perceived Support Complexity.

The data shows that companies that don't have device standards find it more difficult to support those devices (see Fig. 5). This finding contradicts the original proposition, which assumed that with greater control comes greater complexity to manage the devices and that with less control there is less to manage.

Companies where the employees personally own their devices also find supporting mobile devices harder than businesses where the company owns the device (see Fig. 6).

This is interesting as it means that companies are attempting to support devices without exerting control

Table 7
Reimburse for Wireless Plan

Wireless Plan	Reimbursement when using Business Applications	Average Reimbursement
Voice	40%	19%
Data	45%	15%

Table 8
Companies Starting Reimbursement Next Year

Wireless Plan	Reimbursement when using Business Applications	Average Reimbursement
Voice	36%	16%
Data	33%	19%

over those devices. However, in general, companies are moving towards device standards, and we find that companies that find it harder to support mobile devices are trending slightly more towards device standards than companies that find it easier[11].

While many respondents' lack of knowledge about their companies' future policies makes it difficult to determine if companies are moving toward a corporate-owned device model,[12] there is a slight trend for companies that perceive mobile device support as easy to be moving toward a corporate-owned model (see Fig. 7).

Interestingly, companies that reimburse for the wireless plan perceive supporting mobile devices to be easier than supporting PCs (see Table 7).

Overall, the more control a company has, whether it is over devices or wireless plan, the easier the company finds it to support mobile devices.

Proposition 3a. If mobile devices are valued by a company, is it willing to support these devices? Yes

Companies that believe mobile devices are very important to their company's ability to compete also support their devices, either in house or through outsourcing (see Fig. 8).

Proposition 3b. If companies have greater control over their mobile devices, are they willing to support these devices? Yes

Among companies that support mobile devices, the majority have some form of policy regarding the devices users can choose (60%). In contrast, among companies that do not support mobile devices, the vast majority allow the use of any device (77.7%). Among those companies that do support mobile devices, there is not a significant difference in policy between those who outsource the support and those who support the devices in-house.[13]

More companies that manage their mobile devices in-house are moving towards standardization than companies that outsource their devices. Similarly, more companies that outsource their mobile device support are moving away from standardization (see Fig. 9).

---

[11] 32% of companies that find it harder to support mobile devices than PCs have device standards, vs. 31% of companies that find it easier to support mobile devices.

[12] 13% of companies are moving toward a corporate-owned model, vs. 44% moving away from a corporate-owned model. 43% of respondents do no know their company's plans.

[13] Among companies where employees must use a single device, 30% provide in-house support and 30% outsource. Among companies where employees choose devices from a list, 31% support them in-house and 30% outsource. Among companies where employees can use any device, 40% provide in-house support and 40% outsource.

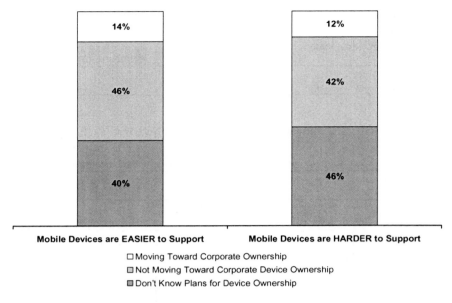

Fig. 7. Support Model Direction vs. Perceived Support Complexity.

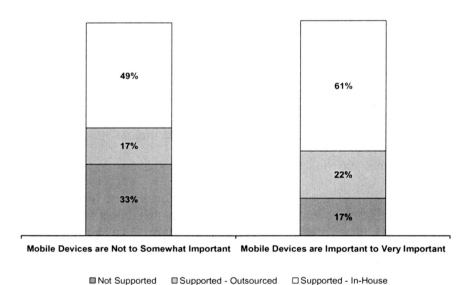

Fig. 8. Device Importance vs. Support.

This may suggest that companies are outsourcing to provide flexibility, not to just to save costs or offload work. It also suggests that outsourcers are able to provide end users with more choices than companies that support mobile devices in house.

Proposition 4a. If a company is willing to support mobile devices, is it open to outsourcing? Slightly

On average, most companies are not interested in outsourcing the support of mobile devices. However, companies that are willing to support mobile devices are slightly more interested in outsourcing than

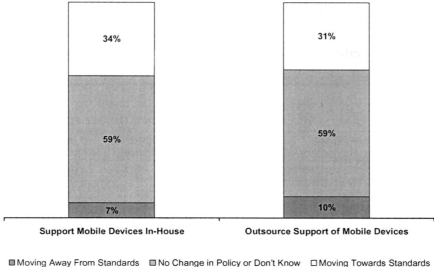

Fig. 9. Trends in Device Standards.

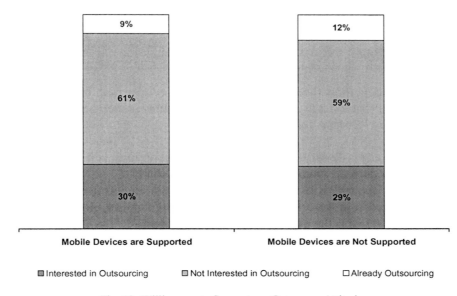

Fig. 10. Willingness to Support vs. Outsource Attitude.

companies that are not willing to support (see Fig. 10).

There is a strange discrepancy in that 12% of respondents said that they are already outsourcing their mobile device support but are not supporting it. This is perhaps due to survey participant confusion, equating "not supported" to "not supported in house".

Proposition 4b. If a company believes mobile devices are complex to support, is it open to outsourcing? Yes

In general, companies that perceive mobile device support to be harder than PC support are more likely

Table 9
Reimburse for Wireless Plan

Wireless Plan	Believe Mobile Devices are EASIER to Support	Believe Mobile Devices are HARDER to Support
Voice	66%	57%
Data	51%	42%

Table 10
Harder to Support Mobile Devices vs. Interest in Outsourcing

Function to Support	Interested in Outsourcing	Not Interested in Outsourcing
Deployment / Procurement / Logistics	21%	19%
Service Plan / Billing / Expense Management	25%	24%
Data Security	24%	29%
Training	44%	38%
Technical Support	44%	41%

Table 11
Already Outsourcing and Difficulty to Support

Function to Support	Mobile Device Support is EASIER than PC	Mobile Device Support is HARDER than PC
Deployment / Procurement / Logistics	10%	9%
Service Plan / Billing / Expense Management	10%	10%
Data Security	9%	8%
Training	8%	7%
Technical Support	10%	10%

to be interested in outsourcing most functions, except for data security (see Table 8).

Interestingly, companies that already outsource certain functions perceive supporting mobile devices to be easier than supporting PCs (see Table 9).

Proposition 4c. If a company is dissatisfied with current support options, is it open to outsourcing? Yes, regardless if the support is currently managed internally or externally.

Overall, respondents are more satisfied than dissatisfied with the support they receive. The majority of respondents receive support from the carrier and the device manufacturer, close behind is support from the company help desk, and last is the use of 3rd parties for support.[14]

Respondents that are satisfied with current support sources are most satisfied with device manufactures. Respondents that are dissatisfied with current support sources are least satisfied with carriers (see Table 10).

Companies that are dissatisfied with the external support they receive are more interested in outsourcing all functions than those who are satisfied with their external support they receive (see Table 11).

Proposition 4d. If a company does not currently have strong capabilities in supporting mobile devices, is it open to outsourcing? Yes

In all cases, companies are more interested in outsourcing functions they perceive to be weaknesses and less interested in outsourcing those functions that they view as strengths (see Fig. 11).

---

[14] 29% of respondents utilize Carrier support, 29% utilize Manufacturer support, 25% utilize Internal Help Desk support, and 16% utilize 3rd Party support.

Table 12
Support Source vs. Satisfaction

Support Source	Satisfied	Dissatisfied
Carrier	56%	33%
Device Manufacturer	61%	28%
Company Help Desk	55%	20%
3rd party Support	29%	20%

Table 13
Satisfaction with Support and Attitude Towards Outsourcing

Support Focus	Outsourcing Attitude	Satisfied	Dissatisfied
External	Interested	28%	31%
	Not Interested	63%	61%
Internal	Interested	33%	47%
	Not Interested	59%	45%

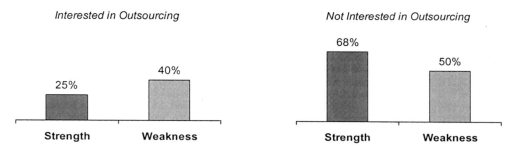

Fig. 11. Interest in Outsourcing.

In the cases where the company responded that it considered an area to be a weakness, there is a correlation with increased interest in outsourcing. The highest areas of interest are training; technical support; and service plan, billing and expense management[15].

Medium and large companies note capability in deployment, procurement and logistics as a weakness, whereas small businesses consider it a strength.[16] Smaller companies have fewer geographies, divisions, and end users to manage which make deployment, procurement and logistics easier.[17]

Large companies are least interested in outsourcing data security.[18] Medium and large companies note that data security is one of their strengths.[19]

Approximately 10% of businesses are currently outsourcing mobile device support. The services used the most are technical support; deployment; planning and logistics; and service plan, billing and expense

---

[15] Among companies that are interested in outsourcing, 65% are interested in outsourced training, 50% are interested in outsourced technical support, and 49% are interested in service plan, billing, and expense management.

[16] Among large businesses, 37% consider deployment, procurement, and logistics a weakness and 35% consider it a strength. Among medium businesses, 35% consider deployment, procurement, and logistics a weakness and 33% consider it a strength. Among small businesses, 24% consider deployment, procurement, and logistics a weakness and 34% consider it a strength.

[17] As a result, small businesses are more likely to have a neutral assessment of their capability in this area; 41% of small businesses are neutral, vs. 32% of medium businesses and 27% of large businesses.

[18] 61% of small businesses and 68% of medium businesses, in contrast to 74% of large businesses, indicated they are not interested in outsourcing data security.

[19] 47% of large companies and 37% of medium companies view data security as a strength, as compared to 29% of small businesses.

Table 14
Summary of Findings and Future Research

Proposition	Supported	Discussion and Future Research
1	1a: Yes 1b: Yes 1c: No	It was surprising to find that companies with high usage of advanced mobile device functionality do not tend to find mobile devices more complex to support than do their counterparts in businesses with lower adoption of advanced functionality. Further studies should explore the reasons for this result. For instance, comparing the support policies and processes used at companies with high vs. low usage of advanced mobile device functionality would be helpful to understand if the difference in perception of the complexity relates to whether or not a company has clearly-articulated processes for support. It would also be instructive to evaluate criteria that drive decision-makers at companies not using advanced mobile device functionality to decide against pushing for the adoption of such technology. If it proves to be the case that this decision is frequently made due to concerns over the complexity of support, a clear case for the benefits of support outsourcing may be apparent.
2	2a: No 2b: No	Further exploration is needed to understand why Proposition 2 was not valid. An assessment of why companies that perceive large productivity loss caused by mobile device problems do not find them difficult to support would help to explain this result. An analysis of support policies and processes comparing businesses that find device problems to have a high impact, versus those that perceive a low impact, would make clear if robustness in support processes has an influence on this outcome
3	3a: Yes 3b: Yes	As predicted by the model, increased perception of the value to a business of using mobile devices and an increased desire to control employees' mobile devices each lead to an increased willingness of the enterprise to provide some form of mobile device support
4	4a: Yes 4b: Yes 4c: Yes 4d: Yes	Overall, there was an increased openness to outsourcing in businesses that indicated they were willing to support devices, they found device support to be complex, they were dissatisfied with their current support, or they were currently unable to provide adequate device support However, the increased openness to outsourcing in these cases was less significant than anticipated and bears further investigation. Future studies should evaluate the specific profiles of businesses that are open to outsourcing their mobile device support to determine what factors influence this perspective. Future research should also probe the specific reasons for a general reluctance among most companies to outsource mobile device support, given that cost savings and flexibility can be increased through the use of an outsourcing partner that makes device support a core competency

management.[20] Large and small companies tend to outsource at a slightly higher rate than medium companies.[21]

7. Conclusions and future research

Overall, the data supports the hypothesis that usage of advanced mobile device functionality, the need for control, and the lack of current support capability all trend towards a willingness to outsource. There are a few exceptions in the overall model, all concerning propositions relating to how companies perceive support complexity (see Fig. 12).

The findings are summarized in Table 12.

While there is an overall reluctance for businesses to outsource their mobile device support, there is a distinct business-need profile that is receptive towards outsourcing. This overall disinterest in outsourcing is perhaps due to the backlash towards outsourcing currently prevalent in the marketplace, outsource

---

[20] 10% of businesses outsource these functions, vs. 8% of businesses outsourcing data security and training.
[21] 10% of large businesses, 8% of medium businesses, and 9% of small businesses outsource mobility support.

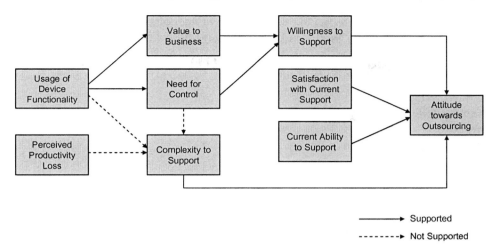

Fig. 12. Summary of Supported Research Propositions.

options still being in infancy stages or inexperience and unawareness of the complexities of supporting mobile devices. However, there are benefits to outsourcing in addition to addressing an organization's weaknesses. These benefits include the ability to provide greater choice to end users, enabling the use of advanced functionality across a diverse user group and ultimately gaining competitive advantage through the use of mobile devices.

The findings of this study are currently limited in scope because only Palm customers were surveyed. Future research to expand upon this article should strive to study a broader community of mobile device users, including those using other brands of product. Future research should strive to confirm the reasons for the deviations from the expected findings identified above, and should strive to uncover and overcome the reasons for a general reluctance of enterprises to outsource mobile device support.

Appendix

Please help us understand your company.

1. **Company Size (select one)**

   A. 0 – 49
   B. 50 – 99
   C. 100 – 249
   D. 250 – 999
   E. 1000 – 4999
   F. 5000 – 9999
   G. 10000+

2. **Industry (select one)**
   Aerospace, Agriculture / Forestry, Automotive, Business Services / Consulting, Communications / Telecom Supplier, Computer Services/Consulting, Computer Services / Technology / Manufacturer, Computer Services / Technology / Reseller, Education, Electronics, Financial / Banking / Insurance / Legal / Real Estate, Government, Healthcare / Health Services, Manufacturing Consumer Goods /

Industrial (non-computer related), Oil / Gas/ Mining / Other Natural Resources, Retail / Wholesale, Service Provider (ASP, ESP, Web Hosting), Transportation / Distribution, Travel / Hospitality / Recreation / Entertainment, Utility, VAR / VAD / Systems or Networks Integrator, Other

3. **Regions of operation (check all that apply)**

   A. North America
   B. South America
   C. Europe
   D. Asia

Please tell us about yourself.

4. **Your department (select one)**

   A. Sales
   B. Marketing
   C. IT
   D. Finance
   E. HR
   F. Legal
   G. Engineering
   H. Operations
   I. Security/Facilities
   J. Other

5. **Your position (select one)**

   A. C-Level Executive
   B. Manager
   C. Team Lead
   D. Team Member

Please tell us about how your company uses mobile devices.

6. **What percentage of employees uses a mobile device? (select one)**

   A. 0%–25%
   B. 26%–50%
   C. 51%–75%
   D. 76%–100%

7. **Among mobile users in your company, how many use the following functions?**
   Rating Scale: 0%-25%, 26%-50%, 51%-75%, 76%-100%

   A. Voice
   B. E-mail
   C. Web
   D. Business Applications

8. **What is your company's device policy? (select one)**

   A. User has their choice of any device for business
   B. User picks from an approved list of devices with devices from more than one manufacturer

C. There is a single standard device/manufacturer that the company uses

9. **Is your company's device policy moving towards or away from standards?**

   A. Moving towards standard device(s)
   B. Moving away from standard device(s)
   C. Staying with current policy

10. **Who owns the mobile devices?**

   A. The company purchases and distributes devices
   B. End users purchase their own devices and are reimbursed by the company
   C. End users personally own their devices
   D. The company rents devices from a 3rd party
   E. A combination of the above
   (a) if 10 not "A" then
   (b) **10a. Is your company planning on moving towards a corporate OWNED model in the future?**
   A. Yes
   B. No
   (c) *if 10a = "A" then*
   (d) **10b. What is the timeline for implementing a corporate OWNED policy?**
   A. 6 months
   B. 1 year
   C. 2+ years

11. **Is your company interested in renting or continuing to rent mobile devices?**

   A. Yes
   B. No

12. **Currently, what services does your company reimburse? (check all that apply)**

   A. Everyone gets voice
   B. Everyone gets data
   C. Some groups get voice
   D. Some groups get data
   E. Nobody is reimbursed

13. In the future, what services does your company plan to reimburse? (check all that apply)

   A. Everyone gets voice
   B. Everyone gets data
   C. Some groups get voice
   D. Some groups get data
   E. Nobody is reimbursed

14. **13a. What is the timeline for implementing a new reimbursement policy for mobile devices?**

   A. 6 months
   B. 1 year, 2+ years]

15. **How important are mobile devices to your company's ability to compete?**

A. Crucial
B. Advantage
C. Operational Necessity
D. Nonessential

16. **What would enable you to benefit more from mobile devices? (check all that apply)**

A. Improved mobile device functionality
B. Cheaper mobile devices
C. More reliable carrier network
D. Cheaper service plans
E. More outsourced support options
F. Greater end-user mobile device proficiency
G. Availability of off-the-shelf mobile device enterprise software
H. Other (fill in the blank)

17. **Compared to supporting employee PCs, how complex is supporting mobile devices?**

A. Much Easier
B. Easier
C. Harder
D. Much Harder

18. **Please identify the top challenges faced in supporting mobile devices? (select all that apply)**

A. Users are remote
B. Devices are outdated quickly
C. Multiple carriers
D. Multiple devices
E. No single source of support
F. Other—*Blank Write In Line*

19. **Is the majority of mobile device support within your company In-House or Outsourced?**

A. In-House
B. Outsourced

20. **Is your support offshore?**

A. Yes
B. No

21. **Who are your company's employees most likely to call for support?**

A. Company help desk / IT department
B. Carrier
C. Manufacturer
D. 3rd Party Support
E. E. Friends/Co-workers

22. **How satisfied are your company's employees with the current level of mobile device support?**

A. Dissatisfied
B. Somewhat Dissatisfied
C. Somewhat Satisfied
D. Satisfied

23. **When users have mobile device problems, how much does it impact their productivity?**

A. Debilitating
B. A Hindrance
C. Minimal Impact
D. No Impact

24. **What do you consider your company's strengths and weaknesses in supporting mobile devices?**
Checkbox: Strength, Weakness, Neutral

(a) Deployment Planning
(b) Procurement / Supply Chain
(c) Service Plan and Billing Management
(d) Technical Support for Help Desk / IT **Support Tools and Knowledge Base
(e) Technical Support for End Users, **Exec Care
(f) Enterprise Applications Support
(g) Replacement and Repair of Devices
(h) Data Security
(i) Help Desk / IT Training
(j) End User Training

25. **What areas would you be most interested in outsourcing?**
Checkbox: Interested, Not interested

(a) Deployment Planning
(b) Procurement / Supply Chain
(c) Service Plan and Billing Management
(d) Technical Support for Help Desk / IT **Support Tools and Knowledge Base
(e) Technical Support for End Users, **Exec Care
(f) Enterprise Applications Support
(g) Replacement and Repair of Devices
(h) Data Security
(i) Help Desk / IT Training
(j) End User Training

26. **Would you like to be sent a copy of this article when it is published?**

A. Yes
B. No

References

[1] S. Ang and L.L. Cummings, Strategic response to institutional influences on information systems outsourcing, *Organization Science* **8**(3) (1997), 235–256.

[2]   K.P. Arnett and C. Jones, Firms that choose outsourcing: a profile, *Information and Management* **26**(4) (1994), 179–188.

[3]   B.A. Aubert, S. Rivard and M. Patry, A transaction cost model of IT outsourcing, *Information and Management* **41**(7) (2004), 921–932, Business Wire. (June 8, 2004). Advisory experts available to discuss low ranking for customer service in mobile phone service industry. Business Wire.

[4]   B. Bahli and S. Rivard, The information technology outsourcing risk: a transaction cost and agency theory-based perspective, *Journal of Information Technology* **18**(3) (2003), 211–221.

[5]   Business Wire. (September, 9 2004). T-Mobile given highest customer satisfaction rankings in all regions surveyd; results from independent study reflect T-Mobile's Get More commitment to customers. Business Wire.

[6]   Business Wire. (January 25, 2005). T-Mobile still leading in customer service in VocaLabs' Sector Pulse report. Business Wire.

[7]   Business Wire. (March 20, 2007). Mobile Complete launches Consumer Experience Management Suite^{TM} to provide interactive online virtual phones for consumer education and support at CTIA wireless show. Business Wire.

[8]   D. Chamberlain, (November 2005). Wireless customer service: Not over the hump yet. Product #: IN0502093MCM. In-Stat.

[9]   F. Chau, (March 1, 2007). Mining customer data into intelligence: telecom carriers increasingly embrace business intelligence as a strategic tool to help them remain competitive as the focus shifts to understanding customers and their habits. Telecom Asia.

[10]   M. Cheon, V. Grover and J. Teng, Theoretical perspectives on the outsourcing of information systems, *Journal of Information Technology* **10**, 1995, 209–219.

[11]   J. Cronk and J. Sharp, A framework for deciding what to outsource in information technology, *Journal of Information Technology* **10** (1995), 259–267.

[12]   W.L. Currie and P. Seltsikas, Exploring the supply-side of IT outsourcing: evaluating the emerging role of application service providers, *European Journal of Information Systems* **10**(3) (2001), 123–134.

[13]   L. De Looff, Information systems outsourcing decision making: a framework, organisational theories and case studies, *Journal of Information Technology* **10** (1995), 281–297.

[14]   J. Dibbern, T. Goles, R. Hirschheim and B. Jayatilaka, Information systems outsourcing: a survey and analysis of the literature, *Database for Advances in Information Systems* **35**(4) (2004), 6–1026.

[15]   A. Diromualdo and V. Gurbaxani, Strategic intent for IT outsourcing, *Sloan Management Review* **39**(4) (1998), 67–80.

[16]   M.J. Earl, The risk of outsourcing IT, *Sloan Management Review* **37**(3) (1996), 26–32.

[17]   J. Gertzen, Getting satisfaction from a cell phone carrier can be a tall order. Kansas City Star (Kansas City, MO), 25, July, 2007.

[18]   R. Gonzalez and J.L. Gasco, Information systems outsourcing: A literature analysis, *Information & Management* **43** (2006), 821–834.

[19]   P. Gottschalk and H. Solli-Saether, Critical success factors from IT outsourcing theories: an empirical study, *Industrial Management and Data Systems* **105**(6) (2005), 685–702.

[20]   V. Grover, M.J. Cheon and J.T.C. Teng, A descriptive study on the outsourcing of information systems functions, *Information and Management* **27**(1) (1994), 33–44.

[21]   V. Grover, M.J. Cheon and J.T.C. Teng, The effect of service quality and partnership on the outsourcing of information systems functions, *Journal of Management Information Systems* **12**(4) (1996), 89–116.

[22]   M. Hamblen, IDC: As mobile workforce grows, IT support could lag, *Computerworld* (November 8, 2005).

[23]   M. Hancox and R. Hackney, IT outsourcing: frameworks for conceptualizing practice and perception, *Information Systems Journal* **10**(3) (2000), 217–237.

[24]   R. Kishore, H.R. Rao, K. Nam, S. Rajagopalan and A. Chaudhury, A relationship perspective on IT outsourcing, *Communications of the ACM* **46**(12) (2003), 87–92.

[25]   C. Koh, S. Ang and D.W. Straub, IT outsourcing success: a psychological contract perspective, *Information Systems Research* **15**(4) (2004), 356–373.

[26]   M.C. Lacity and L.P. Willcocks, An empirical investigation of information technology sourcing practices: lessons from experience, *MIS Quarterly* **22**(3) (1998), 363–408.

[27]   M.C. Lacity, L.P. Willcocks and D.F. Feeny, IT outsourcing: maximize flexibility and control, *Harvard Business Review* **73**(3) (1995), 84–93.

[28]   J. Lau, M. de Lussant, E. Daley, A. Carini and L. Menke, The state of European enterprise mobility in 2006. Forrester, October 13, 2006.

[29]   J.-N. Lee, S.M. Miranda and Y.-M. Kim, IT outsourcing strategies: universalistic, contingency, and configurational explanations of success, *Information Systems Research* **15**(2) (2004), 110–131.

[30]   J.-N. Lee and Y.-G. Kim, Effect of partnership quality on IS outsourcing: conceptual framework and empirical validation, *Journal of Management Information Systems* **15**(4) (1999), 29–61.

[31]   J.-N. Lee, M.Q. Huynh, R.C.-W. Kwok and S.-M. Pi, IT outsourcing evolution—past, present, and future, *Communications of the ACM* **46**(5) (2003), 84–89.

[32] N. Levina and J.W. Ross, From the vendor's perspective: exploring the value proposition in information technology outsourcing, *MIS Quarterly* **27**(3) (2003), 331–364.

[33] L. Loh and N. Venkatraman, Determinants of information technology outsourcing: a cross-sectional analysis, *Journal of Management Information Systems* **9**(1) (1992), 7–24.

[34] M.D. Lopez, E. Daley, R. Muhlhausen, The state of North American Enterprise Mobility in 2006. Forrester, December 29, 2006.

[35] F.W. McFarlan and R.L. Nolan, How to manage an IT outsourcing alliance, *Sloan Management Review* **36**(2) (1995), 9–23.

[36] K. McLellan, B.L. Marcolin and P.W. Beamish, Financial and strategic motivations behind IS outsourcing, *Journal of Information Technology* **10**(4) (1995), 299–321.

[37] J. Mara, Dumping Landline for cell a good call, *Oakland Tribune* (March 23, 2007).

[38] P.C. Palvia, A dialectic view of information systems outsourcing: pros and cons, *Information and Management* **29**(5) (1995), 265–275.

[39] B. Post, Single cell phone organisms – many think land lines defunct, *Post Bulletin, McClatch-Tribune Information Services* (September 15, 2007).

[40] P.R. Newswire, AT&T announces new offers and service improvement for business customer; $500 million investment to 'raise industry bar' on customer service; will extend corporate intranets to WiFi Hotspots at airports and hotels. PR Newswire, (June 3, 2003).

[41] P.R. Newswire, AT&T's award-winning AT&T Business Direct customer portal goes mobile. PR Newswire, (December 5, 2006).

[42] J.B. Quinn and F.G. Hilmer, Strategic outsourcing, *Sloan Management Review* **35**(4) (1994), 43–55.

[43] E. Richert and D. Rush, How new infrastructure provided flexibility, controlled cost and empowered workers at Sun Microsystems, *Journal of Corporate Real Estate* **7**(3) (2006), 271–279, Emeral Group Publishing Limited.

[44] C. Saunders, M. Gebelt and Q. Hu, Achieving success in information systems outsourcing, *California Management Review* **39**(2) (1997), 63–79.

[45] J. Smith, Setting the bar Smartphone is expected to change consumer cell phone market, but critics point out its limiations, *Rocky Mountain News* (*Denver, CO*) (June 25, 2007).

[46] J.T.C. Teng, M.J. Cheon and V. Grover, Decisions to outsource information systems functions: testing a strategy-theoretic discrepancy model, *Decision Sciences* **26**(1) (1995), 75–103.

[47] B. Trebilcock, Special report: 1-800-furious, *Good Housekeeping* (October 1, 2001).

[48] K. Wieland, Mobile lessons: mobile operators will need to bridge the 'education gap' if mobilization of the workforce is to spread beyond voice and email, *Telecommunications* (*International Edition*) (December 1, 2004).

[49] L. Willcocks, G. Fitzgerald and D. Feeny, Outsourcing IT: the strategic implications, *Long Range Planning* **28**(5) (1995), 59–70.

[50] Wireless News. (April 20, 2007). Customer Satisfaction with wireless service improves, with T-Mobile and Verizon Wireless leading the way. Wireless News.

[51] Wireless News. (April 19, 2007) VocaLabs: Wireless customer service improving with Verizon and T-Mobile leading the way. Wireless News.

Christina Loh is currently serving as the Director of Palm Enterprise Support. In this capacity she is responsible for creating, implementing and overseeing Palm's business customer support services. Palm offers a suite of premium Enterprise Support programs, called PalmES, which enable companies to get the most out of their mobile computing solutions. The PalmES program provides various offerings and levels of support to meet the needs of business customers. PalmES offerings are designed to address a range of variables such as number of mobile devices deployed, multiple handset manufacturers and wireless operators, global reach, level of corporate vs. personal ownership, need to outsource some or all support and the amount of device customization. Prior to joining Palm, Ms. Loh has over 14 years of customer experience consulting with Infosys, Accenture and Inforte. She has created and implemented customer relationship strategies for fortune 1000 clients across North America, Europe and Asia. She has a BA in Economics from University of California, San Diego and an MA in Hotel Management from Cornell University.

Andrew Stadlen is Palm's Manager of Customer Experience. In this role, he performs customer experience research and benchmarking to understand customer requirements and perceptions throughout the lifecycle of customers' relationships with Palm. Mr. Stadlen strives to identify customer experience gaps and defines and executes customer service programs to optimize experience and provide differentiation for Palm. He has seven years of consulting experience designing customer strategies and executing customer relationship management programs with Inforte. Mr. Stadlen holds a BS in Molecular Biophysics & Biochemistry from Yale.

Dr. Basole is a Research Scientist in the Tennenbaum Institute at the Georgia Institute of Technology. His research focuses on modeling, visualization, and analysis of complex systems, innovation strategy and management, emerging IT, and applied decision analysis. In his current role, Dr. Basole conducts research on the complexity of value networks and eco-systems with a particular focus on the mobile business, healthcare, biotech, and services domain. Dr. Basole has received several best paper awards and his work has been extensively published in books, prestigious research journals, and conference proceedings. In previous roles, he was the CEO, Founder, and VP Research of a Silicon Valley-based wireless research and consulting firm, the Director of Research and Development at a leading software firm, and a Senior Analyst at a leading IT management consulting firm. Dr. Basole is a member of the Institute for Operations Research and Management Sciences, the Decision Sciences Institute, and the Association for Information Systems. He currently serves as a director or advisor for several technology firms. He received a B.S. degree in industrial and systems engineering from Virginia Tech, has completed graduate studies in engineering-economic systems, operations research, and management information systems at Stanford University and the University of Michigan, and received a Ph.D. degree in industrial and systems engineering from the Georgia Institute of Technology, concentrating in IT and operations management.

John Moses is the Vice President of Worldwide Customer Relations for Palm, Inc., a global leader and innovator of easy-to-use mobile products. In this capacity, he is the executive responsible for global customer service for carrier, consumer, and enterprise customers. Mr. Moses and his teams are in charge of customer experience, contact center operations, online support, knowledge management, training, user documentation, and customer intelligence activities that are designed to help customers get the most out of their Palm mobile computing experience. Prior to joining Palm, Mr. Moses served as Vice President of Strategic Services for Inforte, a management consulting firm specializing in customer strategy and intelligence. Prior to that, he was a Manager at Accenture, one of the world's top management consulting firms. Mr. Moses has created and implemented sales, marketing, service, and operations strategies for major brands such as Alamo Rental Car, Avery Dennison, Corning, Autotrader.com, ITT Sheraton, Kimberly-Clark, Lexis-Nexis, Toshiba, Procter & Gamble, Sony, and Yahoo!. He holds a Masters of Science degree in Industrial & Organizational Psychology from San Diego State University.

Conor Tuohy is a Master's Degree candidate in Industrial and Organizational Psychology at San Jose State University, studying the application of psychology within workplace environments and organizational structures. He is currently writing a Master's thesis on the use of industrial and organizational psychology techniques to maximize the unique resources available to non-profit organizations. Previously, Mr. Tuohy was a Marketing Intern at Palm, Inc., responsible for the design and implementation of customer surveys and usability studies and the analysis of customer data. He holds a BA in Psychology from University of California, Santa Cruz.

Information Knowledge Systems Management 7 (2008) 211–224
IOS Press

Enterprise mobile product strategy using scenario planning

Sami Muneer[a] and Chetan Sharma[b,*]
[a]*Emerging Solutions, SAP, 3410 Hillview Ave. Palo Alto, CA 94304, USA*
E-mail: sami.muneer@sap.com
[b]*Chetan Sharma Consulting, 1778 12th Ave NE, Issaquah, WA 98029, USA*
E-mail: chetan@chetansharma.com

Abstract: The Mobile industry is changing at a rapid pace and so is the behavior of enterprise workforce which uses mobile technologies. When planning for a long-term product roadmap, one has to consider a myriad of evolution trends and forecasts to determine the probable list of product functionality and their introduction timing in the lifecycle of the product. One has to look at the technology trends by market, the competitive landscape, and the mobile worker adoption trends. However, one can only come up with a prioritized list of capabilities by taking into context the company's own core competencies, skill sets, and overall mission. This paper looks at how mobile product companies can use scenario-planning methodology to formulate their product strategy and roadmap.

Keywords: Mobile enterprise, scenario planning, product strategy, wireless technology, strategic framework

To create the future, a company must first be capable of imagining it.

– Gary Hamel and C.K. Prahalad, Competing for the Future, 1994

1. Introduction

The introduction of the iPhone in 2007 was a significant event in the wireless industry as it changed the mobile device paradigm. Similar to what Apple did to the digital music market with the iPod, the iPhone has already changed the mobile device industry. Earlier in the PDA world, when Apple's Newton failed, Palm's PalmPilot won rave reviews and saw significant adoption. However, only a decade later, Palm is on the verge of dissolution while RIM and Microsoft are having great success with converged devices. Motorola, having dominated the analog world, missed the digital wireless evolution, ceding market share to Nokia. Subsequently, Nokia was slow to capitalize on the flip-phone mania that led to the emergence of Korean device manufacturers – Samsung and LG. History is littered with examples where leaders and innovative players in one era did not see the next one coming. They were not completely oblivious of the emerging trends; however, they often grossly miscalculated the timing and impact of mass-market adoption growth curves.

---

*Corresponding author.

In the face of continuous uncertainty, product strategists are constantly challenged to decide the optimal product mix and release time. How does one work on a long-term product roadmap amidst so many variables and a rapidly evolving landscape? The tool of scenario planning has been used for a long time in many industries through development of various scenarios and their integration into the decision making process. Similarly, customers need to align product availability and maturity with their own business roadmap to ensure that the new technology and products benefit, and not distract, the work force.

However, external scenario assessment without a realistic due diligence of internal competencies will provide an incomplete picture for effective product strategy. Both external and internal scenarios should be designed, analyzed, and used in the same process to give the participants a complete view of pros and cons of each approach and each strategic path.

This paper looks at the scenario-based planning technique to mitigate business uncertainty as it relates to the mobile industry. We will analyze the key inputs to such a process and how they might help in developing product strategies that can carry products and services through a longer lifecycle.

2. Basics of scenario planning

Scenarios help answer the classic *"What If"* question and also help explore how the realization of any specific scenario would impact the product strategy, thus providing a comprehensive set of options of what should be done to ensure favorable outcome. Peter Schwartz, considered a pioneer in scenario planning, said in his book [8], "Scenarios are stories about the way the world might turn out tomorrow, stories that can help us recognize and adapt to changing aspects of our present environment. They form a method for articulating the different pathways that might exist for you tomorrow, and finding your appropriate movements down each of those possible paths. *Scenario planning is about making choices today with an understanding of how they might turn out.*"

Though scenario planning as a business strategy tool for organizational decision making has been in existence for a long time, its use was first brought into corporate consciousness by researchers at Shell to anticipate changes in the world and business landscapes. Starting with Pierre Wack [3,14,15] in the 1970s, a French oil executive at Shell, the oil giant has honed the art of scenario planning with an exceptionally long-term view of things to come.

While Shell focused on bigger global structural changes that might impact the energy and oil markets, and Shell in various strategic contexts, such a tool can also work well in the narrower context of an industry or a sub-segment within an industry. Several authors [1,2,5,8,13] and thinkers have provided guidance in using scenario planning tools across different industry segments such as Telecommunications, Consumer Goods, Health Care, Pharmaceuticals, Travel and Transportation, and many others.

Scenarios capture the range of plausible future conditions within which an organization might have to operate. At the corporate level, the challenge is to build an optimal strategy for each of these possible outcomes and to analyze these strategies to determine the core and contingent elements. This creates the strategic foundation and strategic options necessary for operating with true strategic flexibility [7].

While a lot of research has focused on evaluating external scenarios, as shown in Fig. 1, one must consider internal scenarios to get a complete picture that can drive effective product strategies.

Only by doing comprehensive scenario planning, can one answer big questions like, "Should we make an acquisition?" or "Do we need to hire developers with any specific skill sets?" or "Should we expand into the far-east markets?" or "Does alliance with No. 2 player in the market make sense?," etc. Then, scenarios can look at various dimensions of uncertainty and evolution while carefully limiting the scope

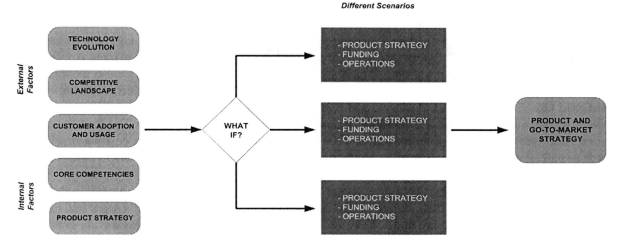

Fig. 1. Scenario planning process.

of both to get a realistic picture and have a manageable number of scenarios to work with. That is where the delicate task of scenario planning becomes important. If the planners are too conservative, they might overlook some critical emerging trends or competitors; on the other hand, if they are overly-analytical, they might waste too many resources and energy chasing evolution paths that have low probability of eventual success.

Scenario planning can help companies better prepare for uncertainties and the changing landscape of markets and global competition. In the wireless world, the convergence of different mediums namely Internet, Mobile, and TV are creating an unprecedented level of friction, introspection, fear, and opportunities (FIFO); and, if companies are not prepared to deal with the evolving marketplace, they are destined to lose market share and miss revenue opportunities on the horizon. It is not that these companies do not see these changes coming; they just have not analyzed the impact of such scenarios on their operations and thus fail to develop effective strategies to deal with the change.

3. Scenario planning in the wireless world

Researchers and planners have used the scenario planning tools in the telecom industry for looking at how technology evolution, consumer adoption, and ecosystem dynamics can play a role developing scenarios. Several organizations and industry bodies have developed "future scenarios" and "use cases" that relate to business case and technologies in the wireless world [6] including ISTAG, [1] Mobile Entertainment Forum (MEF), [2] ETSI/TIA Project MESA scenarios, [3] MIT Project Oxygen scenarios, [4] Mobile IT Forum (mITF), [5] NTT DoCoMo "Vision 2010" scenarios, [6] and Wireless World Research

---

[1] Scenarios for Ambient Intelligence in 2010, ftp://ftp.cordis.europa.eu/pub/ist/docs/istagscenarios2010.pdf.
[2] Future Mobile Entertainment Scenarios, www.boozallen.de/media/file/future_mobile_entertainment.pdf.
[3] http://www.projectmesa.org.
[4] http://oxygen.csail.mit.edu/Overview.html.
[5] http://www.mitf.org/index_e.html
[6] http://www.nttdocomo.com/pr/1999/000868.html.

Forum (WWRF) Initiative scenarios.[7]

In many cases, planners primarily focused on the evolution of information and communications technologies, and, in other cases, they focused on a specific sub-segment or technology like Broadband, MCommerce (mITF), Public Safety (MESA), Ubiquitous Connectivity (MIT Oxygen), and Applications (NTT DoCoMo). Others focused on use case scenarios and how users are likely to use technologies, applications, and services enabled by such technologies. WWRF constructed three scenarios – Blue, Red, and Green using societal, business, and regulatory trends. The Blue scenario is a world in 2010 where wireless is the dominant technology in connecting people and machines. The Red scenario is where customers are highly experimental, and the Green scenario is a world where customers primarily want to meet their basic communication needs [6]. Players across the mobile value chain have looked at market evolution scenarios to help gauge risks and opportunities.

The crucial question becomes how does one apply these scenarios in their own context, in their own industry sub-segment, and in their own product strategy and planning initiatives. This paper will examine the elements of scenario planning that help formulate product strategy in the wireless world. Though the paper is focused on enterprise mobility, these principles can be applied to consumer businesses as well.

Also, as discussed in the next section, a sound product strategy is feasible only if it factors in the internal realities of the company: competencies, skill sets, and operations.

4. The framework for scenario planning in the wireless industry

The first step is to investigate both the macro- and micro-trends in a given industry segment, in our case, the mobile enterprise market. By understanding the technology trends, evolving customer needs, and by studying the industry trends, one can form the basis of the framework.

Macro-trends

1) High broadband penetration
2) Always-on connectivity prevalent in campuses and cities, but not ubiquitous
3) Most of enterprise employees are enabled mobile workers; functions will evolve as the result of mobilization
4) Emerging economies (especially Asia Pacific-China, India) leap to mobile

Emerging customer needs

5) Large periodic usage of mobile devices for simple targeted applications - Want seamless, simple access anytime, anywhere on any device
6) Power mobile users will perform more, and more sophisticated activities
7) Increased need for organizational flexibility and differentiation

Emerging Technology Landscape

8) Powerful and diverse mobile devices
9) Flexible mobile infrastructure a necessity
10) Security is an issue of strategic importance
11) Multi access channels

---

[7] http://www.wireless-world-initiative.org/.

12) Industry standards gaining importance (OSGI, etc.)

Industry trends

13) Expansion of innovative business models and services
14) Mobile is another channel
15) Consolidation of infrastructure vendors

Why does a detailed analysis of various trends matter? It has a lot of implications on the overall portfolio and target markets of the company. For example, modeling the prevalence and rate of connectivity can influence a decision to provide an infrastructure for offline access. This adds a layer of complexity to the infrastructure since device management and security become important as well (e.g. data-laden device gets lost). Moreover, levels of connectivity also differ among different segments of the mobile population based on their universe of mobility, functional role, device usage, etc.

Another trend to model out is the possible diversity of hardware/device platforms. One cannot afford to support all platforms. Then, there are varying levels of security to consider. Alternative channels of access such as telematics can add to the complexity.

People realize that they have lost their cell phones long before they do about their wallets. This indicates how mobile devices have become a social necessity. However, mobility is more than just having a device that is connected and wire-free. It is also changing the way we do things.

While one cannot fully predict all the specific future usage of devices in the enterprise sector, one can look for clues in the consumer space for probable patterns in the enterprise space. Because more devices now have built-in cameras, taking pictures (at the point of inspiration) and sharing them has become very prevalent. Gone are the days when reporters had to find a friendly flight attendant to carry precious videotape out of the country; now satellite dishes on portable units are used to transmit text and pictures as they happen in real time. Mobile devices have further redefined the boundaries of photojournalism – this was evident when most of the pictures shown by broadcast media of the devastating tsunami of 2004 were provided by people who took pictures with the cameras on their mobile phones. In this context, the role of a journalist has evolved.

However, this is not limited to the consumer space. This is also evident in the enterprise space. Enterprise mobility is clearly on the move. With more sophisticated devices comes more evolved usage of those devices such as sales people taking product placement and promotion audits with cell-phone pictures of the grocery aisles. Built-in video devices help sales people to show off the company's latest promotions. Now, savvy companies are not only enabling their technicians (with prompts and checklists) to capture information, but also equipping them with the necessary information to sell complementary products with appropriate packages, promotions and discounts. By turning every service call into a sales opportunity, companies produce incremental revenue – at almost zero cost of sales.

Use of GPS in conjunction with corporate data is another, somewhat obvious trend. For example, in Europe, where sales people drive long distances to visit a customer, they often end up wasting a lot of "windshield time" when the customer cancels the last minute. Nowadays, with Customer Relationship Management (CRM) data uploaded through the device and with the advent of GPS, they can easily schedule meetings with other customers in the vicinity.

The above trends are the positive (or momentum) factors pushing the adoption of mobility; however, such adoption can be tempered in an organization considering security and integration issues. While there are many devices coming into the organization through the "side-door," IT departments might not support basic email connectivity to those devices. Furthermore, there are varying levels of commitment to open source. It is true that Linux is quite popular in developing economies as China, but the initial return on investment might not be as high, or worse, product capabilities can be easily copied.

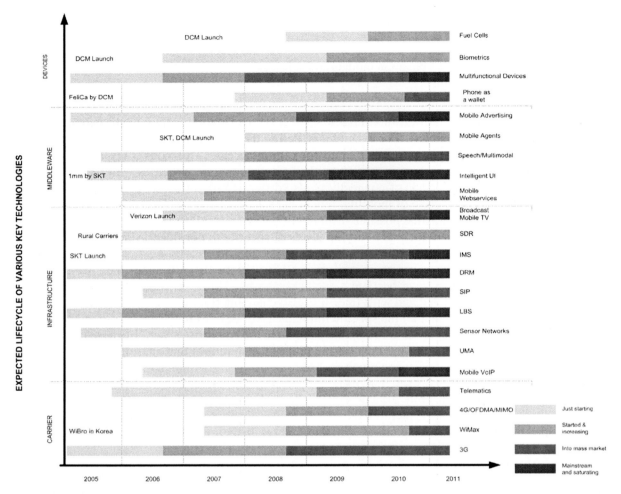

Fig. 2. Expected Lifecycle of various key technologies in North America (Source: Chetan Sharma Consulting) DCM – NTT DoCoMo, SKT – SK Telecom.

We will discuss some of the elements of the framework in a bit more detail below: Technology Evolution, Consumer Adoption and Usage, Competitive Landscape and Internal Assessment.

4.1. Technology evolution

In this section, we will discuss the specific areas that contribute to scenario planning in the mobile world. One of the most significant contributors to the process is the technology evolution path across four major areas: carrier or the network evolution, infrastructure, middleware, and devices. By studying the propensity and velocity of technology diffusion across these four areas, we can get a good understanding of how various components of the technology ecosystem are evolving.

As an example, Fig. 2 shows different technologies evolve at a different pace in North America. Similar trends exist in different countries and regions. If the product strategy does not consider such trends, it is highly likely to fail.

For example, Japan has had 3G networks since 2001 and has crossed the 80% penetration mark; but in North America, the penetration rates are over to 25% as of Q4 2007 [10]. Meanwhile, in India and China which are the two biggest growth markets, 3G spectrum hasn't been allocated yet. Therefore, if there are software products or devices that need 3G to succeed, timing the product entry into the market is essential. In the mid-nineties, Worldcom and Vulcan Ventures funded a company called Metricom, which garnered a very loyal user-base (primarily on west coast of US) for its high-speed wireless services. However, with the advent of 2.5G service, users demanded nationwide coverage and Metricom could not expand fast enough and grossly overestimated its potential subscriber base. As a result, the company shut down in 2001 after burning through billions of dollars.

Another trend that is important to the enterprise is the penetration of the converged devices or smart phones that enable mobile workers to integrate corporate applications on their devices. As of 2007, the converged device penetration in North America and Western Europe was around 12% [11]. Even though such devices constitute an increasing percentage of the new devices sold, the overall subscriber base is relatively small. If the target device for the software of an enterprise software company is a converged device, then its potential market is dictated by the growth in the converged device subscriber base. A careful assessment of the growth patterns of such devices across geographies and targeted vertical segments is critical to rolling out the respective products and upgrades. Instead of waiting, many companies have released browser-only version of their applications and, as such, are able to target a much larger audience. The obvious compromise is the user-experience – browser-based applications are typically less user-friendly than their thick-client counterparts.

4.2. Consumer adoption and usage

Next, product planners need to study the potential adoption, usage, and impact scenarios of their users. For example, let us consider a telecommunications field work force and how mobile technology might help them in their daily tasks and, consequently, affect their behaviour. By applying "A day in the life of" scenarios, one can construct use cases that describe how the user requirements, expectations, behavior and task adaptation might evolve in the future. Table 1 shows a comparative analysis of how telecommunication workers might accomplish some of their tasks in 2010 compared to 2007. Such an exercise incorporates three primary sources of input: observation of lead users behavior, usage of technology in adjacent user markets (e.g. in consumer markets) and brainstorming. This can provide valuable insights into a product's design and functional specifications.

Table 1 compares the life of a telecommunication worker in 2007 and 2010 and how one would accomplish tasks in these two scenarios. For example, such mobile workers typically receive their work instructions at the start of the day and they plan their route accordingly. As of 2007, most of this was done in a semi-automated fashion with workers picking up print outs from service depots and looking at maps to chart out their daily workflow. However, with the advent of more sophisticated devices and applications, such mundane tasks will be automated, in most cases, such that the worker does not waste time driving to the depot or figuring out the route, while the workflow will all be automated and pushed to the device. Similar automation in invoicing, troubleshooting, time management, information access, and coordination will be expected within 2–3 years.

Consumer adoption and usage process can be studied through focus groups, trials, and user-interaction. It helps in gauging and prioritizing user functionality. By laying over the user-expectations and technology evolution over a product roadmap, managers can ascertain which areas need work, in what time, and how the resources should be allocated. In 1997, Mobilestar entered the market as a wireless LAN

Table 1
Telecommunication worker task completion scenarios in 2007 and 2010

Tasks	2007	2010
Receive target list of work orders for the day	Print-out at the service depot	Download in the morning. Avoid going to the depot
Route and visit planning	Generally given the tasks in a given neighborhood. Field tech plots out their path or have maps handy	Automated and real-time route and visit planning
Look-up information on status of the line and pre-visit troubleshooting	Typically done at the depot or switch	Anywhere, anytime
Troubleshooting (in exception cases)	Call to dispatcher/depot/ colleagues	Access to drawings, etc in real-time and hence quicker resolution. Live video feed of the situation for quick consultation
Invoicing the customer	2–7 days	On the spot
Signature capture	On paper or through a non-integrated app	Integrated into application and back-end
Exception/emergency requests	Alerts, Call the field-tech to coordinate	Automated coordination
Parts lookup and ordering	Typically at depot or call to dispatcher	Real-time inventory lookup and ordering
Request capture and follow-up	Voicemail or end-of the day follow-ups	Creation, follow-up on requests in real-time
Time management	Prioritizes based on their view of the world	System helps prioritize tasks, client communication, and interactions.
Coordination with colleagues	Typically offline process that takes a long time to accomplish	Real-time look up of availability, modes of communication
Analytics to look at trends, patterns, exceptions	Typically run on PCs, not in-real-time	Graphics capability. Processing capability to run queries. Ability to share results and act on analytics result (collaboration).
Information access	End-of the day follow-up or call to office/colleagues. No real-time access to intranet	Access corporate Intranet, other nets from cell phone with capability to forward, access documents etc.
Timesheet and travel management	End-of the day or later in the week activity. Issues with entry of receipts. Prone to errors and abuse	Automated timesheet entries.
Search for information	Hard to do on mobile, typically done back at the office or call to HQ	Mobile search that returns relevant and timely results. Input can be text, picture, RFID scan, etc.
CRM	Summary information with work order	Access to all customer records
In-vehicle productivity	Primarily limited to voice. No integration with applications	Access to content using speech technology
Work-life balance	Devices and applications are not conducive to work-life balance	Efficiencies increase work-life balance
Overall User Experience	Poor. Different UI/interface for different data needs	Context driven, Push based, Great user experience

hotspot network and was funded by deep pockets like Intel and IBM, but failed to gain traction as it realized that revenue generated by tepid usage is significantly smaller than the resources required to build out a nationwide network. Similarly, Teledesic, a company focused on satellite communication, burned billions of dollars but failed to understand the simple economics that there is no demand for phone services that cost $1/minute no matter how "cool" the idea of "anywhere, anytime" communication might sound.

4.3. Competitive landscape

As we mentioned earlier, due to the forces of convergence, competition can arise from unexpected places. While product companies need to keep an eye on traditional competitors, it is more important than before to scan new upstarts or new entrants and strong financially-backed players, who could target their area of dominance in different and unexpected ways. How would one go about dealing with such unplanned strategy disruptions (for example, a startup focused on a functional niche starts to capture meaningful market share)? Does one react by building such the feature/functionality into the product or do they just buyout the company at low-cost rather than investing in their own product development? Does the competition have superior Intellectual Property or financial muscle? Telecommunication operators completely missed the Internet advertising boom while Google and the likes leveraged the operators' networks, and capitalized on the search-driven Internet economy. Now, wireless carriers, fearing that history might repeat itself with Internet brands dominating mobile advertising, are aggressively trying to wrest initiative.

Similarly, while Palm captured the initial PDA market with a simple and easy to use user-interface, it failed to recognize that users would demand more functionality that had become possible with constant improvement in device form and functionality. Some financially strong players can absorb mistakes and oversights, while others are not that lucky. For example, Microsoft is traditionally good at a "fast follower" strategy. The company missed the arrival of Internet, Search, and Advertising but has been quick to respond once it realized the evolving dynamics in the industry. Though it completely dominated the browser wars, Microsoft has been struggling to gain market share in search advertising. To challenge Google's dominance, Microsoft attempted (but failed) to acquire Yahoo, the number two player in the industry in early 2008.

Additionally, regional competitive forces help shape product strategy as well. For example, while Openwave, a company that was instrumental in getting mobile web to the market, was quite successful in the western world, it failed miserably in the two biggest growth markets, India and China. Because Openwave did not have an effective strategy against regional players, companies like Jataayu and others were able to forge closer relationships in the ecosystem, and thus, were able to effectively out-compete the company in those markets.

4.4. Internal assessment

Modeling out the macro trends is only half the issue. The other half of the puzzle is the mission and core competencies of the company. Trend assessment and analysis of the competitive landscape give one a good snapshot of the market, but how does one position oneself in that landscape? What can the company do well? And continue doing it in the face of growing competition? Does the company have enough of a differentiating "moat"? Does the company have the needed skill sets to deliver on time or much faster than the competition?

For example, today mobile has been most relevant in the revenue-generating roles (sales, management) or in the most-expensive customer-interaction roles (e.g. service). There are promises of high productivity, improved customer service, better visibility of field activities for these roles; and, moreover, some of these segments are tech-savvy, have budgets, etc. But providing mobile software for these roles is not enough. The critical missing piece is the data. Most enterprise applications are rendered useless as soon as the mobile worker steps out of the office, because much of the activity of customer-facing or mobile professionals is dependent on timely and accurate access to information and processes they need for their work. Customer organizations are spending millions of dollars on CRM systems, for example, to support the activities of sales and service people, but as these people are mostly mobile, the value of the CRM implementations is dramatically reduced without the needed mobile support. So, the mobile software needs to integrate with the backend software. Some users will have the patience to try and work with the system, but many will not after the first few initial trials. If the data is stale or incorrect, the workers will stop using the application.

Then the critical and pertinent questions become: How does one integrate this data? How easy and cost-effective is it?

Moreover, customer organizations have complex needs and require a basic foundation to build upon with more evolving mobile needs. It is not enough to have devices that provide browser access to the data. This necessitates an infrastructure. Does the company have the skill-sets or resources to build it for customers? There are many cases of companies who might be first or fast-movers, but that lead lasts only a small time when a more-resourced company copies it and does it more effectively and efficiently with a broader reach.

So, it is not enough to have a framework to model trends. It is more important to have a framework to evaluate the trends with the flexibility to accommodate changing patterns and address the following fundamental questions:

1) What is the overall mission? What drives our company?
2) Where do we want to be?

  – What significant problem are we trying to solve?
  – Why do we want to solve it?
  – What does mobile mean for us?
  – Is mobile core or an extension?

3) How will we get there?

  – Will we provide applications? Infrastructure? Hardware?
  – What are the complementary products and services needed to provide the solution? Will we be integrated or best-of-breed?
  – Do we need to work with partners? How do we prioritize them?
  – How will we go-to-market? Can we do it alone? Do we have access to the right channels?

4) Why will we be successful?

  – What can we provide the solution better than anyone else? Do we have the credibility?
  – Can we sustain the advantage over the next 3 years? 5 years? 10 years?
  – What are the major risks to this position? How will we address the different probable scenarios?

This first exercise will differ based on the size, maturity, and current business of the company. However, it is necessary to create a straw man based on an initial analysis of the needs. It can evolve and crystallize with further analysis. Usually point 4 is the hardest to address. It is human to be susceptible to heightened self-confidence and ignore some fundamental flaws in one's strategy.

At SAP, a large enterprise vendor, deliberation on point 4 was the foundation for the critical scenario planning exercise, with a prioritized focus on detailing the 3-year goals towards attaining its mission. The team knew that to be successful, in the context of the current market and evolving trends, the company had to build both applications and middleware. Moreover, the product team recognized that they could only succeed in mobile by building out a healthy ecosystem. The ecosystem expanded both horizontally and vertically along the value chain.

However, all the goals worked toward the unique traits that would make SAP successful and differentiate the company in the marketplace. These traits become the core competency. In the case of SAP, the mobile team had to ensure that this was in close alignment to the core competency of the overall organization.

Examples of competencies can be product-based as flexibility and ease-of-use or services-based. One thing was clear – that the competency had to last the test of time, at least the next 5 years, even in the midst of continuing change in a fast-paced industry such as mobile. So, the competency had to be broad enough. Moreover, scenario modeling was very pertinent. What if the industry changes in another direction? What if a competitor comes with a very different business model that could disrupt the revenue stream? For example, in the software industry, Salesforce.com was a disruptive force for incumbents like SAP and Oracle. However, as the industry soon learned, that while a subscription on-demand model keeps the costs predictable for customers, integration of data with other systems is equally important. Existing suite vendors such as SAP had the advantage of integration. Sustaining that advantage, SAP could buy itself some time to deliver an on-demand offering as well, while also providing integration, thus posing a serious competitive threat to the newcomer. In addition, every goal the team set would enhance this competency, to be better at this than anyone else. For other areas, it was acceptable to be good enough or even behind other competitors (for example, some device manufacturers might compromise on battery life for the benefit of weight).

If the competency is product-based, then the entire portfolio should inherit those characteristics. Usually these differentiating characteristics become part of the platform on which the portfolio is built. Non-core characteristics can be the basis of partnerships/outsourcing/in-sourcing agreements. Segmenting characteristics, although non-core, can help expand into new markets (for example, Tylenol Day vs. PM on the same Acetaminophen platform).

Another important variable to model out is the availability of skillsets. This decision can be very critical in building out the platform. Many software companies have learned the hard way that Java programming skillsets are not easily transferable to J2ME. Moreover, one has to also model the social factors. While J2ME skills may be found in India, attrition is a serious consideration. Hence, it is urgent to model out this constraint. Moreover, the variable might not only include availability of resources over time but the distribution of resources between platform and applications.

With the overall mission and goals set out, the next step is to define the roadmap in the following order: initial target segments, growing capabilities for those segments, and new segments. This exercise employs all the different techniques of portfolio management: strategic buckets, scoring model, 2 X 2 charts, and NPV (Net Present Value). What is important is not only to consider which is the largest and/or fastest growing market, but also where can one be both differentiating AND sustain that differentiation over time.

This might require re-evaluating the trends in the context of this information and analysis. One other facet of information is the feedback from one's customers. However, this can be a double-edged sword. It is quite common for large companies in the software industry to cater to the "long-tail." In other words, the company's portfolio includes a few large winners and a lot of niche low or negative-return businesses. This happens because large customers dictate their specialized needs into the standard products, or as is common in the software industry, the vendor productizes its custom consulting project.

Hence, it is very critical to normalize the feedback by analyzing all the win-loss statements/bug-reports/interviews/focus group feedback and compare to the trend and scenario analysis. What is most important is to be able to explain any perceptible difference with a defensible cause.

4.5. Additional factors

In addition to considering technology evolution, consumer adoption, and competitive landscape, one must consider external factors that can impact product strategy namely economic factors like inflation, political change, trade disputes; industry mergers and acquisitions (M&A) like a key partner acquired by a key competitor; awards of important patents to rivals that might hamper one's product design, etc. Such factors should be considered with a keen sense of likelihood such events might take place.

Only by understanding the complete multi-dimensional picture can one devise various scenarios and a tactical and strategic response to each plausible scenario that influences the product strategy.

While there is always a lot of uncertainty, it is a good final exercise to draw out a five-year roadmap, clearly identifying the variables, constraints, and best-and worst-case scenarios. There should also be clear KPIs (Key Performance Indicators), more transparent and measurable with time. This helps to ascertain changes in the landscape and track the variables. Clear KPIs can also bring to surface unforeseen variables.

Hence, the entire exercise is an iterative process, which includes both a framework to model trends, and has a company-specific framework to evaluate the trends that has the flexibility to accommodate changing patterns.

5. Recommendations

As we discussed in the previous section, one must take a holistic view of the potential future – both by understanding the impact of the external factors such as the technology evolution, the competitive movement, and the shifts in consumer behavior, as well as, keenly assessing the internal dynamics within a company. By having, a firm grasp on both aspects of scenario planning, executives can make much better decisions. This becomes particularly important in a rapidly changing industry landscape as communication and computing industries continue to collide, and forces of globalization render the national boundaries useless.

While scenario planning is an effective technique to help develop a solid product strategy, one must not fall in the common traps that can make the process cumbersome and ineffective. One must be cognizant of potential traps that can render the whole exercise useless.

Following are six recommendations to make your scenario planning process better:

1. **Gain management support** – Like with any other important project, scenario planning needs to have full upper management support and it should not be relegated as an exercise to keep the staff busy. The recommendations that come out of scenario planning should be seriously considered, debated, and merged into the product planning process. Scenario planning should be embraced across the chain of command.

2. **Include diverse inputs** – A scenario that merely conforms to conventional wisdom and existing thought process is of little use. Product planning and strategy should always include input from diverse teams such as product planning, development, marketing, sales, intellectual property and legal counsel, and if applicable, partners. The team should also have a good mix of management and staff. Diversity in viewpoints is necessary for good scenario planning exercise. More importantly, it can be a fatal error to limit the input to internal teams: the assumptions should be frequently and consistently tested with customers, their users and customers, industry experts, venture capitalists, researchers, etc.

3. **Have realistic goals and expectations** – Scenario planning is not a panacea that will solve all strategic problems. It is but a tool that can help in narrow down the focus by considering different inputs. It provides a framework for discussion and evaluation.

4. **Develop clear roadmaps** – The result of each scenario planning exercise is a set of requirements, specifications, and product roadmap that have a direct impact on product plans and strategy. The number of scenarios should be limited to the very relevant and plausible ones rather than considering the whole universe. Scenarios should focus on the long view and not be carried away by current events and existing marketplace.

5. **Scenario planning process should be tightly linked with product planning process** – As we discussed earlier, technology trends and competitive landscape are important inputs to the scenario planning process. If new trends emerge and the competitive activity changes, such plans and process should be adaptive enough to change and affect the product planning process. It is important to learn from scenario planning and feedback the output right into product strategy or else the process won't be efficient. The planning process should also take into consideration risks and concerns outlined by the team.

6. **Simulate, Learn, Act** – It is important for scenario planning team to come up with new and strong strategic options. With each milestone or event, company should learn and make the process of scenario planning better.

Scenario planning is a strategic conversation within a company to effectively frame the strategy and planning efforts to make cogent decisions. Managers should be willing to structure their financial resources to take into account the contingent elements and to reflect the market uncertainties, which are part of the scenario-planning framework.

6. Conclusion and future research opportunities

Mobile industry is evolving at a rapid pace and colliding with various other ecosystems (media, entertainment, online, enterprise). The pace of change itself is accelerating with each product cycle and companies need to learn to adapt in sync. Action is not just about doing. It is about being prepared to do. The most effective action will come from a state of readiness, and foresight helps create readiness. We all need to accept uncertainty. Strategy and plans are great, but surprises should be assumed. If one gets there early, one is more likely to be prepared to deal with FIFO (adapted from [4]).

By understanding the technical evolution across networks, infrastructure, middleware, and devices, by doing competitive analysis of the mobile ecosystem as well as overlapping and surrounding industries, by considering user behavior, acceptance and diffusion of technology, and by looking at external factors that could potentially change the game such as M&A, economy swings, and other events that we haven't been able to contemplate, a product strategy process can be best prepared for change and uncertainty to both tackle adverse times as well as tap into an emerging opportunities.

As discussed in the paper, external scenario assessment without a realistic internal due diligence will provide an incomplete picture and feedback into the product strategy formulation process. Both external and internal scenarios and assessments should be designed, analyzed, and used in the same process to give the participants a complete view of pros and cons of each approach and each strategic path.

The strategic framework for product strategy can be further refined by taking a look at a number of mobile enterprise product launches in different categories such as corporate email, mobile CRM and Field Force Automation (FFA) applications, mobile virus and security products, mobile middleware platforms, and others. By studying various case studies in detail, we might be able to further refine the techniques and factors discussed in this paper. Also, in each of the categories discussed (technology evaluation, customer behavior, internal assessment), one can study the best practices of success stories to further add value to the strategic framework using scenario planning.

References

[1]   L. Fahey and R. Randall, *Learning from the Future,* John Wiley & Sons, 1998.

[2]   K.V.D. Heijden, *The Sixth Sense,* John Wiley & Sons, 2002.

[3]   K.V.D. Heijden, *Scenarios, The Art of Strategic Conversation,* John Wiley & Sons, 2005.

[4]   B. Joahnsen, *Get There Early, Sensing the Future to Compete in the Present,* Institute of the Future, 2007.

[5]   M. Lindgren and H. Bandhold, *Scenario Planning – The Link between Future and Strategy,* Palgrave Macmillan, 2002.

[6]   R. Rafazolli, *Technologies for the Wireless Future,* WWRF, John Wiley & Sons, 2005, 489–512.

[7]   M.E. Raynor, *The Strategy Paradox,* DoubleDay, 2007.

[8]   G. Ringland, *Scenario Planning – Managing for the Future,* John Wiley & Sons, 1998.

[9]   P. Schwartz, The Art of Long View, Planning for the Future in an Uncertain World, *Currency Doubleday* (1991), 3–4.

[10]   C. Sharma, *Global Wireless Data Market Update,* 2007, Chetan Sharma Consulting. http://www.chetansharma.com.

[11]   C. Sharma, *US Wireless Data Market Update Q4,* 2007. Chetan Sharma Consulting. http://www.chetansharma.com.

[12]   C. Sharma and Y. Nakamura, *Wireless Data Services: Technologies, Business Models, and Global Markets,* Cambridge University Press, 2004, 333–342.

[13]   J.V.D. Veer, *Shell Global Scenarios to 2025,* Shell, 2005.

[14]   P. Wack, *Scenarios: Shooting the Rapids,* Harvard Business Review, 1985.

[15]   P. Wack, *Unchartered Waters Ahead,* Harvard Business Review, 1985.

Sami Muneer is a Sr. Director of Solution Marketing at SAP, responsible for SAP's entire mobile portfolio. Over the last 7 years at SAP, he was focused on bringing new products to market, including Duet software (in partnership with Microsoft), its xApps portfolio of composite applications and procurement software. Before joining SAP, he spent a few years with leading management consulting firms, Bain & Co. and Mitchell Madison Group, where he focused on strategic and operational issues in the wireless industry. He earned his Bachelor's and Master's degree in Economics from the University of Chicago.

Chetan Sharma is President of Chetan Sharma Consulting and is one of the leading strategists in the mobile industry. He has served as an advisor to senior executive management of several Fortune 100 companies in the wireless space. Some of his clients include NTT DoCoMo, China Mobile, Disney, KTF, Sony, Samsung, Alcatel Lucent, KDDI, Virgin Mobile, Sprint Nextel, AT&T Wireless, Qualcomm, Reliance, SAP, Merrill Lynch, American Express, and HP.

Chetan is the author of five books on the mobile industry including the two being released in 2008 – Mobile Advertising (John Wiley) and Wireless Broadband Technology: Conflict and Convergence (IEEE Press). Chetan is interviewed frequently by leading international media publications such as Time, New York Times, Wall Street Journal, BusinessWeek, and GigaOM, and has appeared on NPR and CNBC as a wireless data technology expert.

Chetan is a sought-after strategist on IP matters in the wireless industry. He has advised clients with some of the biggest patent portfolios in the world and has worked with players across the wireless value chain. He has been retained as an expert witness and advisor for some of the most prominent legal matters in front of the International Trade Commission (ITC) including Qualcomm vs. Broadcom and Ericsson vs. Samsung.

Chetan is an advisor to CEOs and CTOs of some of the leading wireless technology companies. Chetan is a senior member of IEEE, IEEE Communications Society, and IEEE Computers Society. Chetan has MS from Kansas State University and BS from the Indian Institute of Technology, Roorkee.

Part V: Cases

Information Knowledge Systems Management 7 (2008) 227–241
IOS Press

The strategic value of enterprise mobility: Case study insights

Eusebio Scornavacca[a],* and Stuart J. Barnes[b]
[a]*School of Information Management, Victoria University of Wellington, P.O. Box 600, Wellington, New Zealand*
E-mail: Eusebio.Scornavacca@vuw.ac.nz
[b]*Norwich Business School, University of East Anglia, Norwich NR4 7TJ, UK*
E-mail: stuart.barnes@uea.ac.uk

Abstract: The rapidly improving price-performance of wireless technologies is providing an unprecedented platform for the development of wireless applications for businesses. This paper aims to explore the strategic value of enterprise mobility. In order to achieve this goal, it provides an overview of the literature related to mobile business applications in the work domain and highlights the findings of four studies developed in New Zealand. The paper concludes with a discussion about present challenges and the future of the mobile enterprise.

Keywords: Mobile business, enterprise mobility, case study, strategy

1. Introduction

During the past two decades the use of technologies such as the mobile phone and the Internet have revolutionized our society [7,50]. Although, the developments of the Internet and mobile phones have followed two separate paths, only in the past eight years these technologies have converged, making possible a vast range of wireless data communication technologies such as the wireless internet [44]. As a result, the proliferation of mobile Internet enabled devices is creating an extraordinary opportunity for business to leverage the benefits of mobility [9,16,17,53,59]. This technological revolution is deeply affecting the way many organizations do business, allowing firms to expand beyond the traditional limitations of the fixed-line personal computer [8,25,28,42,44,45,47,48].

Mobile business, commonly known as m-business, is characterized as the use of wireless networks and other mobile information technologies for organizational communication and coordination, and the management of the firm [7]. There is little doubt that m-business applications are providing a significant opportunity not only to enhance organizational productivity but also to transform business practices [4, 6,14,27,49,51,54,58,59]. Jain [22] suggests that most enterprise mobile applications are likely to be motivated by the need to reduce latency, increase speed of response, enhance efficiency of operations and workforce, improve productivity, boost revenues, and increase competitive advantage. Overall, wireless data communications can provide significant business benefits for corporate infrastructure, representing the next step in the evolutionary development of information systems [21,37].

---

*Corresponding author.

This paper aims to explore the strategic value of enterprise mobility. In order to achieve this goal, it provides an overview of the literature related to mobile business applications in the work domain and highlights the findings of four studies developed in New Zealand. New Zealand is a small, developed economy with a high-level of entrepreneurship and small business. Evidence suggests that NZ businesses are among the more innovative adopters of wireless data communications [21,36,48,51,56]. In addition, New Zealand is a nation that is typically creative and receptive to new technologies and that is used as a test bed of market innovations for large corporations. For this reason, the country provides an interesting example of the use of mobile and wireless technology, and one where lessons can be translated to some degree elsewhere - especially in Western Europe and, to a certain extent, North America.

The next section provides the overview of the literature exploring the impact mobile technologies in the firm's value chain as well as on its workforce. This is followed by an examination of four studies developed in the past four years in New Zealand. The paper concludes with a discussion about present challenges and the future of the mobile enterprise.

2. Overview of the literature

This section aims to explore some relevant literature related to mobile business applications in the work domain. Scornavacca, Barnes et al. [11] point out that the body of research in m-business is heavily skewed towards business-to-consumer (B2C) applications. In their survey of the literature, mobile business-to-employee (B2E) and business-to-business (B2B) applications corresponded only to 17.4 percent of the articles found, while papers focused on consumer applications represented 55.7 percent of the sample [51].

In contrast to the shortage of research in this field, evidence suggests that business and enterprise applications are the biggest growth area in mobile business [3,32,34,36,38,56]. The following sub-section explores the potential benefits of m-business applications in the firm's value chain. This is followed by a review of the concept of enterprise mobility.

2.1. Mobilizing the value chain

There is common agreement among authors that m-business applications are providing a significant opportunity to gain competitive advantage [4,6,13,14,27,54,58,59].

Porter [40] demonstrated the value chain as the series of interdependent activities that bring a product or service to the customer. Mobile applications can provide significant business benefits for corporate infrastructure, representing the next step in the evolutionary development of IT integration in the value chain [4,37,40].

Barnes [6] presented a systematic analysis of the potential opportunities of mobile technologies in a company's value chain (Fig. 1). Figure 1 and Table 1 illustrate the standard value chain of the firm with examples of the possible impact of mobile applications for businesses.

Based on the analysis of the possible impact of a wide range of mobile applications for businesses, Barnes [6] identified eight core and not mutually exclusive benefits: business transformation, efficiency, effectiveness, flexibility, ubiquity, connectivity, interactivity and location-awareness. The first three business benefits are considered generic to most IT applications [18,31], while the remaining five are specific benefits of mobile technologies [4,6,16,60].

Barnes [6] argued that *business transformation* can happen at different levels, by automating specific business tasks, networking and sharing information, transforming sets of business processes, transforming

Table 1
Mobile applications in the firm value chain (adapted from [6])

Support activities	Impact of mobile applications
Infrastructure	Wireless networks and devices can help to strongly integrate remote, disparate or roaming employees into the corporate infrastructure.
Human resources	Handheld training devices and location aware technologies may be useful for remote or roaming workers (e.g. field and sales force automation).
Product and technology development	The impact of mobile technologies in product and technology development is quite embryonic. However, field testing and reporting is one area where it is likely to have an important role.
Procurement	Exceptional roaming employees who are involved in procurement might be aided by using mobile IT in the B2B domain.
Primary Activities	Impact of Mobile Applications
Inbound logistics	Mobile applications can accurately monitor inbound inputs to the firm. By knowing the location of 'rolling' inventory, times between transactions, manufacture and delivery can be further reduced.
Operations	The impact of mobile ICTs on the operations component of the value chain is likely to be enormous. There are many applications such as meter reading, customer alerts and credit authorization that would benefit from the mobile value propositions
Outbound logistics	Mobile ICTs – especially location technologies – can play an important part in outbound logistics. Fleet management systems help freight companies to monitor the status of deliveries and other outbound logistics activities
Sales and marketing	In many industries, the sales force is becoming increasingly mobile and teleworking is a very real part of sales activity. Mobile technologies allow strong integration of a remote sales force into ERP and other key systems. Mobile marketing is another emerging application in this area of the value chain.
Service	Similarly to the product and technology development activity, devices can be embedded in products to bring benefits to the service activity. Mobile technologies can provide information for field workers (e.g. technicians), increasing productivity and customer satisfaction.

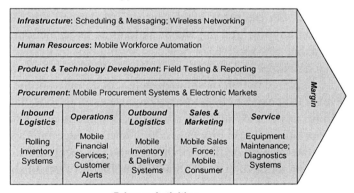

Fig. 1. Mobile applications in the firm value chain [6].

relationships with other entities, and creating new revenue streams. Westelius and Valiente [57] supported this, affirming that the core benefits of mobile technology are brought by changes to the business processes.

Efficiency is usually related to productivity gains or cost reduction achieved by process automation [2, 6,22]. Westelius and Valiente [57] noticed that processes prompted by mobile technology provide gains in efficiency. Ali and Al-Qirim [2] studied seven organizations that are currently using mobile business applications in New Zealand. They reported from these cases that efficiency gains are the principal perceived business benefits emerging from this type of technology. Other researchers also found that mobile technologies deeply affect task performance of mobile workers and promote efficiency gains [1, 12,38]. From a more strategic perspective, Chung [15] showed that mobile applications can be of great utility in supporting organizationally-interdependent decision-making.

In contrast to efficiency, *effectiveness* can be quite subjective and difficult to measure [24]. In the case of mobile business applications, gains in effectiveness have mostly being reported in conjunction with process transformation [2,6,15,22,35,37,38]. Beulen and Streng [14] and Wolf and Heinonen [58] perceived a significant influence on the nature of the task supported by mobile technology in relation to the perceived efficiency and effectiveness of mobile workers' behavior.

Flexibility refers to the high degree of adaptability and portability of mobile technologies [6,22,37, 43]. Scheepers and Steele [43] pointed out that the use of mobile devices removes a great deal of the traditional constraints associated with using information systems with stationary computers, thus providing much greater flexibility in the times at which the system may be used – e.g. it may be possible to exchange data not just at work within working hours. In addition, Jain [22] suggested that giving workers access from wherever they are, allows them to access task-critical enterprise applications in a timelier manner than having to wait until they are back at the desktop. Barnes [6] also pointed out that in some types of organizations, such as offices and supermarkets, mobile technologies allows rearranging IT equipment without significant cabling issues. Müller and Zimmermann [37] added to this point by drawing the attention to the role that passive and active tags, microprocessors, sensors and transmitters have in the convergence of physical and informational – enabling a higher level of continuous and automated information processing.

Ubiquity is frequently labelled as "mobility" [23,35,55,56]. Junglas and Watson [26, p. 578] pointed out that both terms are conceptually similar: *"Whereas ubiquity takes the lens of the environment to provide the functionality for a user to move, mobility takes on the lens of a user being active component in a ubiquitous environment"*. On the other hand, Barnes [6] defined this benefit as the capability of having data communication anytime and anywhere as long as under network coverage. Similarly, Zimmermann [61] suggested that new services or new cost saving business processes will be enabled by the development ubiquitous networks and embedded devices. Wolf and Heinonen [58] and Jarvenpaa et al. [23] reported that the implementation of some mobile technologies in the organizational domain generated a fairly high level of user expectations – based on false assumptions that this technology would enable them to "do anything, anywhere, anytime". Finally, Westelius and Valiente [57] noticed that besides the high level of expectations it also produces a high level of uncertainties among staff – perhaps caused by the novelty and/or the existing myths evolving around this technology. If this benefit becomes a widespread reality, users no longer have to think about the problems of establishing device networking, only its benefits.

Connectivity refers to the ability to transmit and receive data wirelessly [6,12,61]. Concomitantly, *interactivity* refers to the potential for complex information to be shared among devices, increasing systems interactivity [6,52]. Notice that most of the issues related to connectivity and interactivity have characteristics in common with flexibility and ubiquity.

At present, business benefits enabled by advances in location awareness can be considered much more of a promise than a reality in m-business [26]. Whereas expectations of business benefits enabled by location awareness are high, only a limited number of mobile applications have actually leveraged tangible benefits from this technology [19,20,29,30,46].

The eight benefits enabled by mobile business applications in the firm's value chain proposed by Barnes [6] have found support in the literature. There is clear empirical evidence that these technologies enhance business transformation, efficiency, effectiveness, flexibility and interactivity. On the other hand, ubiquity, connectivity and location awareness are mostly referred as *potential* benefits that, at this stage and remain bounded by the level of technological development.

2.2. Enterprise mobility

The use of mobile technologies can undoubtedly improve the efficiency of the members of an organization, especially the mobile workforce [5,13,22,32,41,56,57,59]. In several cases, as Jain [22] and Walker and Barnes [56] reported, mobile technologies replaced inefficient paper data entry processes and enabled the capture of complete and accurate data at the point-of-origin.

It is clear that different industries require distinct levels of mobility [5,22,39]. Enterprise mobility requirements can be generally divided in three categories [22]:

1. *Industries with high mobility requirements:* This group involves the organizational settings where users as well as the assets are moving constantly. Examples of such settings include shipping and trucking industries, some municipal government departments as well as law enforcement agencies. Although in agricultural and utility industries assets are fixed, these assets are spread over a wide geographic region and most tasks are accomplished in the field. For this industry group, mobile technologies are crucial as they liberate mobile employees from wired connections and enable them to accomplish IS supported tasks needs in a broader temporal and spatial boundary.
2. *Industries with medium mobility requirements:* This group involves the settings where users are highly mobile in a restricted perimeter and perform most critical tasks a "base" (e.g. office or kiosk). Examples of such settings include healthcare and university settings.
3. *Industries with low mobility requirements:* Users belonging to this category are rarely mobile and the support of mobile IS hardly influence the fulfillment of their tasks. An example of this setting would be a traditional office setting.

Undoubtedly, the nature of tasks accomplished by the mobile workforce involves a high level of geographically dispersed work [21,35,39,56,57]. Barnes [4,7] pointed out that "enterprise mobility" is defined by the degree to which an organization's operations and information needs, typically employee activity, are supported in a "geographically independent way". The author presented a conceptual framework for understanding the potential of mobile application in the B2E space, which he refers to as the Mobile Enterprise Model (MEM). Figure 2 shows the MEM diagram.

The axes are mobility, process and market value proposition. Notice that each axis indicates three distinct stages in relation to its dimension. Briefly, the axes can be described as follows:

Mobility describes the level of "geographic independence" of enterprise workers, enabled by the wireless data solution. The first level is *"transient"*, which describes the basic support of employees as they move from one location to another. These employees are restrained by spatially bounded mobility. The second level is *"mobile"* where employees have a much higher degree of spatial independence from the enterprise, and have spatial independence for prolonged periods of time, but they inevitably return to corporate locations to perform certain functions. Finally, the highest level of mobility is *"remote"*. At this level, employees are almost completely removed from the corporate location, being empowered with a very high degree of spatial independence.

Process describes the change in work configuration and processes resulting from the adoption of a mobile application. The first level, *"automation"*, refers to efficiency gains in existing processes

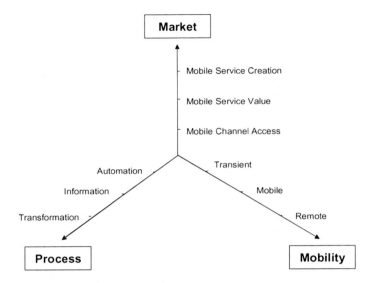

Fig. 2. Dimensions and stages of mobile enterprise model [4].

transferred to the mobile data environment. "*Decision support*" brings in a degree of effectiveness and knowledge work gains via the mobile solution. Finally, "*transformation*" describes a fundamental degree of change in organizational processes using the mobile medium. At this level, the nature of work and job roles may be transformed by the mobile medium.

Market describes the value proposition in the marketplace; typically, it refers to the alterations in products, services and relationships with customers, but it may also contain market experiences with suppliers and business partners. *Mobile channel access* – positioned at the lowest level – indicates that the mobile medium is being used largely as a conduit for information for mobile employees, without significantly different services. *Mobile service value* – positioned at the intermediate level-refers to the wireless solution is being used to add significant value to the market offering. There are specific areas where the product or service level is being significantly enhanced using mobile distributed work. *Mobile service creation* – positioned at the highest level, indicates that the wireless medium is being used to create entirely new service offerings or products.

Some of the concepts regarding business transformation presented in the MEM were also captured by Basole [13]. In addition, a few researchers applied the MEM to case studies and provided some insights on B2E mobile work solutions [4,21,56]. Three major phases in the use of mobile distributed work in organizations were identified:

Phase I: Mobile employee linkage. This phase of enterprise mobility focuses on establishing the appropriate wireless infrastructure to "link-in" transient employees, enabling access to corporate data and improving the efficiency of existing work.

Phase II: Mobile employee empowerment. In this phase, the work patterns of employees are driven by the availability of corporate knowledge via the mobile medium. In this stage, mobile employees are able to significantly improve the effectiveness of work configurations and therefore of the products or service provided.

Phase III: Mobile enterprise creation. Only in this highest phase of enterprise mobility can the organization boast truly mobile employees and services. At this level, employees can exist separately of the geographic constraints of an organization, supported by wireless solutions. The nature of

Table 2
Exploring enterprise mobility in New Zealand

Study	Focus	Type
Barnes and Scornavacca [10]	Assessment of Wireless Applications Used by New Zealand Business	Multiple Case Study and Survey
Walker and Barnes (2005)	Wireless Sales Force Automation in New Zealand	Multiple Case Study
Barnes, Scornavacca and Innes (2006)	Wireless Field Force Automation in Trade Services	Dual Case Study
Scornavacca and Herrera (2007)	Mobile Technologies in the New Zealand Real-Estate Industry	Multiple Case Study

work has been significantly transformed to take advantage of the new environment, and the roles of individuals are likely to be very different. In addition, the mobile enterprise is able to offer new and different products and services.

Most of the case studies found in the literature relating the mobile enterprise could be classified as belonging to second phase – mobile employee empowerment [2,4,13,21,22,33,35,36,38,57].

3. Evidence from New Zealand

In this section, the findings of four New Zealand based studies are examined in more detail [10,11, 48,56]. These studies are a result of an ongoing research program at Victoria University of Wellington. The results presented below are based on primary data collection. On each research project the Mobile Enterprise Model (Barnes 2003; 2004) was used as a framework of analysis. A summary of the research projects are given in Table 2.

3.1. Assessment of wireless applications used by New Zealand business

Barnes and Scornavacca [10] assessed the perceived strategic value of wireless applications use by New Zealand Business. Over 120 companies using wireless applications were identified in that study. In addition, the authors found more than thirty wireless application developers based in New Zealand. The sample was dominated by organizations utilizing mobile phones and laptops. Nearly all had mobile phones with text, a technology that has reached saturation, while more than three-quarters had phones with an Internet browser. More than 80 percent of respondent organizations were using laptops with wireless access to the principal operator networks, typically using a PC-card, while only around a third were using short-range wireless access, such as via WiFi. PDAs and smart phones with wireless access played a significant role, with around 70 percent and 50 percent of the sample respectively. Satellite navigation and RFID were less well represented, since these technologies tend to be dependent on application area; for example, navigation devices are concentrated in logistics applications while RFID-type devices are currently largely being used for asset management, tracking and supply-chain management.

The findings suggest that 72 percent of mobile business applications in New Zealand are used in a B2E and B2B context. In addition, it was found that the most popular mobile application used in the country is sales force automation (26%), followed by job dispatch/management (17%), asset management (9%), and remote office applications (9%). The dominant industries for mobile applications in New Zealand are manufacturing (19%), cultural and recreational services (14%), property and business services (13%), transport and storage (11%), and wholesale trade (9%) [10].

The research also has identified some of the organizational impact of mobile and wireless applications, in terms of benefits, strategic advantage, and barriers to adoption. Overall, while the mobility, efficiency and effectiveness benefits of the applications in use in the respondent organizations were clear, they typically did not allow a level of benefits associated with business transformation. Similarly, they typically did not enable the development of market value, such as in existing or new products or services for businesses. Thus, according to the MEM, the applications are clearly in the mobile employee empowerment phase.

3.2. Wireless sales force automation

Walker and Barnes [56] were using an exploratory multiple-case study methodology to examine the impact of wireless sales force technologies on three organizations in the New Zealand food industry.

> *Alpha* is a snack food manufacturer and employed approximately 800 people. Alpha's wireless SFA solution operates on a tablet PC. Sales people have the ability to receive and transmit information wirelessly using wireless data cards. Approximately 45 sales people are using Alpha's wireless SFA solution.
> *Beta* is the wholly-owned and independent subsidiary of a grocery distribution co-operative. They are the largest single source supply food service and route trade grocery wholesaler in the Lower North Island of New Zealand. Beta is a business-to-business operation. Beta's wireless SFA solution operates on laptop computers. The software is a replication of the company's internal order capture system. Sales people have the ability to receive and transmit information wirelessly via a hardwire connection to a mobile phone. Approximately 15 sales people are using Beta's wireless SFA solution.
> *Gamma* is a fast moving consumer goods importer and distributor with a focus on confectionary products and employed over 160 people. Gamma's wireless SFA solution operates on iPaq PDAs. Sales people have the ability to receive and transmit information wirelessly via a hardwire connection to a mobile phone. Approximately 35 sales people are using Gamma's wireless SFA solution.

The analysis of the cases was structured accordingly to the Mobile Enterprise Model [4,7].

Regarding *mobility*, all of the organizations examined have achieved and surpassed the transient level of mobility in the MEM, as the wireless SFA solutions provide more than basic support to employees as they move from one location to another. All of the solutions provide functionality that allows sales people to remain in the field for prolonged periods of time. In addition, the solutions provide sufficient geographic independence having achieved the *mobile* level of the Mobility axis on the MEM. The extent to which the organizations have reached the mobile level varies. None of the wireless SFA solutions provided sales people with enough geographic independence to be completely remote on the MEM.

The analysis of *process* identified that all of the wireless SFA solutions examined have resulted in efficiency gains in existing processes as a result of automation. Overall, wireless SFA technology has enabled improvements in the efficiency and effectiveness of sales activities. However, there is no evidence that the solutions have fundamentally transformed work configurations or processes at any of the organizations examined.

All of the factors contributing to the *market* value proposition of the solutions involve the delivery of information to employees in the field using the wireless SFA solution. All of the organizations examined have achieved the mobile channel access level of mobility in the MEM. The organizations have achieved important benefits of both mobile business and sales force automation. The solutions are providing access to real-time information at the point of need, and remote communication with back office systems. The wireless SFA solutions enabled sales people to efficiently access up-to-date information on customers, products, stock levels, pricing and promotions. None of the organizations examined were utilizing the mobile medium to create entirely new products or services. Thus, they have not yet moved to mobile service creation in the MEM.

Overall, Walker and Barnes [56] observed that sales force and overall organizational performance improved as a result of applying wireless technologies to their sales function. Several positive impacts derived from mobile channel access providing better remote access to back office systems, more efficient provision of up-to-date information, and improved ability to communicate with sales people. However, it was found that the development of mobile solutions has been limited to the improvement of existing processes, and is quite dependent on the performance of mobile networks and bandwidth availability.

3.3. Wireless field force automation

Barnes et al. [11] investigated the impact of wireless Field Force Automation (FFA) on two New Zealand trade services organizations. The study was based on an exploratory dual-case study methodology.

Case A is a leading vehicle association in New Zealand with membership totaling over one million. The organization has both commercial and non-commercial ventures, their membership only break-down assistance service comprises of around 150 service offices. This service and its associated wireless field force automation system was the focus of the case study. The wireless FFA system on Case A is based on a touch-screen laptop computer fitted in a vehicle dashboard. It is connected via a cellular network to a central dispatch centre. Job dispatch and additional information is communi-cated via the laptop, which also uses global positioning system (GPS) technology to provide a visual representation of jobs as well as the real time location of each road service officer.

Case B is a Wellington based, national supplier of glass and glazing services that operates with a network of local glaziers. It provides a wide range of flat glass solutions to home and corporate customers, it also provides nation wide glazing services for an insurance company. The system studied at Case B is based around the Kyocera 7135 smart phone and cellular network. The device is provided to the glaziers, which allow job management tasks and scheduling. The backend service application is web based and is outsourced to an Auckland supplier.

Once again, the analysis of the cases was structured accordingly to the Mobile Enterprise Model [4, 7]. Figure 3 provides a comparison between the two cases.

Case A was able to reach a higher level of *mobility* with its service officers being able to perform almost all their processes from their vehicle. Case B, with its links to the provision of a tangible good has a field force that was comparatively less mobile in nature.

Both organizations were able to achieve the level of business *process* redesign. Case A is surpassed the level of information by attributing processes that were performed elsewhere to the field force. On the other hand, the processes of Case B remained unchanged in most aspects but some capabilities are added such as for the ordering process.

The services were fairly equal in terms of the *market* axis. The addition of sales and marketing tasks to the service officers and the links to corporate customers were working towards creating more value for the organization. Case B's value came from the ties to the insurance company, which the backend of the system helped secure, and the exploration of selling the system design to other trade service organizations.

Overall, despite the two organizations differing markedly in size, business model, and operations, they both experienced similar levels of benefits derived from the implementation of wireless FFA systems.

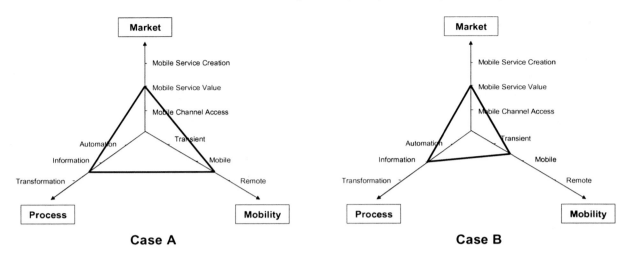

Fig. 3. Comparison of mobile field force automation [11].

3.4. Mobile technologies in the real-estate industry

Scornavacca and Herrera [48] investigated the perceived strategic value of mobile technologies in the New Zealand Real-estate industry. The Real-estate industry plays a significant role in a country's economy. Traditionally, the industry has made its contributions through the ability of handling and transferring Estate specific knowledge and information. This traditional model is being challenged by the threat of disintermediation, brought on by the emergence of new technologies, like the Internet.

The study followed a multiple qualitative case study method. In order to capture different perspectives within the industry, a total of six organizations were selected were for this study: one representing the industry association (participant 1), another representing a telecommunication provider (participant 2) and four organizations representing Real-Estate agencies (participants 3–6).

The Mobile Enterprise Model [4,7] was used for the analysis of the cases. Figure 4 provides a comparison of distinct perceptions among the participants. Participants 1 and 2 are represented by the solid line while participants 3–6 are indicated by the dashed line. It is clear from the illustrations that participants 1 and 2 have a more positive perception of the strategic value of mobile technologies.

It was found among the participants distinct perception in regards to *mobility*. Participants 1 and 2 believed that the level of geographic dependence for the agents is extremely low and salespeople have the ability to be almost completely removed and independent from the office. Mobile technologies can provide agents with remote linkages into corporate information systems allowing higher degrees of freedom form the office. However, from the branch manager perspective, mobile technologies are allowing salespeople to have geographic independence for prolonged periods of time – however there is still a need of "a base of operations" for a number of business processes.

Within *process* the NZ Real-estate industry appears to have barely reached the "information level". Developments such as the use of mapping systems to enable remote agents to access and display properties images as location could certainly support the existing processes and improve service delivery.

Regarding the market axis, participants 1 and 2 did see the potential for mobile applications to allow mobile service creation, using them to create entirely new services. However, participant 1 felt that such development may be not valued by agents. The branch managers focused on mobile channel access.

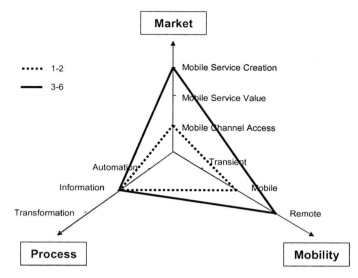

Fig. 4. Comparison of mobile field force automation [48].

However they expressed some indication of the value that new mobile services may have to their business and to gains of competitiveness.

Scornavacca and Herrera [48] found that despite the wide availability in NZ of advanced mobile technologies such as laptops with wireless capabilities, PDAs' and smart-phones, most agents are only using standard mobile phones for voice communications. The prevailing perceived business benefits derived from the ability to access the mobile channel in order to gain efficiency and improve customer service. However, there were challenges such as cost, network coverage, the identification and development of industry specific mobile application as well as nurturing partnerships across the industry value chain.

Although there was agreement that mobile technologies can enhance business processes, Scornavacca and Herrera [48] noticed a strong perception that the 'qualities of a salesperson' cannot be changed or assisted effectively through the utilization of mobile technologies. Some perceptions indicate that many agents believed that relying too much on technology could be risky. In addition, there was a clear belief that the salesperson's role is about building networks and relationships with clients and associates. Therefore the perceived strategic value and enthusiasm for adopting mobile technologies could be diminished by long standing traditions and business practices of the Real-Estate industry.

4. Conclusions

The wide spread adoption of wireless technologies is providing an unprecedented platform for business to leverage the benefits of mobility. This paper aimed to explore the strategic value of enterprise mobility in New Zealand. In order to achieve this goal, it provided an overview of the literature related to mobile business applications in the work domain and highlighted the findings of four recent studies undertaken in New Zealand.

The four research projects have provided an interesting picture of the use and strategic value of mobile technologies in NZ business. Most of the business benefits found in the studies were related to employee integration and individual performance improvement instead of product, service or organizational improvement.

Using Barnes' MEM as a framework to analyze the development of mobile distributed work and to benchmark the status of the concept in each organization, it was found across the four studies that most of the organizational focus has been predominately upon the process and mobility dimensions, rather than the market dimension. Among the three dimensions, mobility was the most highly rated dimension, and it is clear that applications did go beyond the transient employee, or temporarily mobile individual – providing significant integration of remote employees into the corporate infrastructure. The topography of New Zealand provides a significant challenge to complex communication and organizational integration; mobile and wireless applications appear to be making headway in this regard and this is emphasized in the results. Process was also seen as a significant area of impact. Many applications were focused on automating existing processes to make them faster and more efficient, with productivity being a primary goal. Job dispatch and sales force automation were typical examples. However, there was little evidence that the applications were providing transformation of business processes. Moreover, there is little indication that the applications had any impact on the value proposition.

Overall, regarding the three major phases in the use of mobile distributed work in organizations, all companies studied were clearly in the mobile employee empowerment phase. As a consequence, existing wireless applications in New Zealand have some way to go before it reaches the third phase - mobile enterprise creation. The corollary of this is that there exists significant scope for mobile enterprise applications to provide considerably more benefit for their organizations.

Any future research must continue to build on further developments in this fast-moving field of application and research. Time will tell which wireless technologies or applications become ubiquitous and dominant. However, it is clear that enterprise mobility has an important part to play in the IT strategies of many organizations.

References

[1] D. Abraham, *A Grounded Theory For the Impacts of Ubiquitous Information Systems (IS) Access on Task Performance*, Austin Mobility Roundtable, Austin, Texas, 2004.

[2] E.H. Ali and N. Al-Quirim, *Mobile Commerce Integration Across the Supply Chain in Businesses in New Zealand*, AMCIS 2003 Connect in Tampa, Florida, 2003.

[3] A.T. Kearney. (2003). The new mobile mindset. Retrieved 03.12., 2003, from http://www.atkearney.com/shared_res/pdf/Mobinet_Monograph_S.pdf.

[4] S. Barnes, *Wireless Support for Mobile Distributed Work: a Taxonomy and Examples*. 37th Hawaii International Conference on System Sciences, Big Island, Hawaii, 2004.

[5] S. Barnes and E. Scornavacca, *The Strategic Impact of Wireless Applications in NZ Business*, Hong Kong Mobility Roundtable, Hong Kong, 2005.

[6] S.J. Barnes, *Unwired Business: Wireless Applications in the Firm's Value Chain*, Sixth Pacific Asia Conference on Information Systems, Tokyo, Japan, 2002.

[7] S.J. Barnes, Enterprise mobility: concept and examples, *International Journal of Mobile Communications* 1(4) (2003), 341–359.

[8] S.J. Barnes, *mBusiness: The Strategic Implications of Wireless Communications*, Oxford, Elsevier/Butterworth-Heinemann, 2003.

[9] S.J. Barnes and S.L. Huff, Rising sun: iMode and the wireless Internet, *Communications of the ACM* 46(11) (2003), 78–84.

[10] S.J. Barnes and E. Scornavacca, Wireless Applications in NZ Business: A Strategic Assessment, *Journal of Computer Information Systems* 47(1) (2006), 46–55.

[11] S.J. Barnes, E. Scornavacca et al., Understanding Wireless Field Force Automation in Trade Services, *Industrial Management and Data Systems* 106(2) (2006), 172–181.

[12] R.C. Basole, *The value and impact of mobile information and communication technologies*, IFAC Symposium on Analysis, Modelling & Evaluation of Human-Machine Systems, Atlanta GA, USA, 2004.

[13] R.C. Basole, *Transforming Enterprises through Mobile Applications: A Multi-Phase Framework*, Eleventh Americas Conference on Information Systems, Omaha, 2005.

[14] E. Beulen and R.-J. Streng, *The impact of online mobile office applications on the effectiveness and efficiency of mobile workers. Behavior: A field experiment in the IT services sector*, International Conference on Information Systems, Barcelona, Spain, 2002.

[15] H.M. Chung, *An Enterprise Model for Mobile Application System* (*EMMAS*), Stockholm Mobility Roundtable, Stockholm, Sweden, 2003.

[16] I. Clarke III, Emerging value propositions for M-commerce, *Journal of Business Strategies* **18**(2) (2001), 133–148.

[17] Durlacher Research. (2002). Mobile Commerce Report. Retrieved 10.07., 2002, from www.durlacher.com.

[18] P.B. Evans and T.S. Wurster, *Blown to bits: how the new economics of information transforms strategy*, Boston, Harvard Business School Press, 2000.

[19] V. Gruhn, M. Hülder et al., *Mobile Communication Systems For Tuckage Companies*, Second International Conference on Mobile Business, Vienna, Oesterreichische Computer Gesellschaft, 2003.

[20] O. Henfridsson and R. Lindgren, Facilitating in-car use of multi-context mobile services: the case of mobile telephone conversations, Americas Conference on Information Systems 2003, Tampa, Florida, 2003.

[21] D. Innes, S.J. Barnes et al., The Impact of Wireless Field Force Automation on New Zealand Trade Services Organizations. *Proceedings of the Fourth International Conference on Mobile Business*. Sydney, Australia, IEEE Computer Society, 2005, 49–55.

[22] R. Jain, *Enterprise mobile services: framework and Industry-specific analysis*, Americas Conference on Information Systems 2003, Tampa, Florida, 2003.

[23] S.L. Jarvenpaa, K.R. Lang et al., Manifestations of Technology Paradoxes and Implications on the Experience of Mobile Technology Users, Austin Mobility Roundtable, Austin, Texas, 2004.

[24] L.M. Jessup and J.S. Valacich, Information Systems Today, Upper Saddle River, Prentice-Hall, 2003.

[25] I. Junglas, On the usefulness and ease of use of location-based services: insights into the information system innovator's dilemma, *International Journal of Mobile Communications* **5**(4) (2007), 389–408.

[26] I.A. Junglas and R.T. Watson, U-Constructs: Four Information Drives, *Communications of the Association for Information Systems* **17** (2006), 569–592.

[27] V. Kadyte, *Uncovering the potential benefits of mobile technology in a business relationship context: A case study*. 12th European Conference on Information Systems, Turku, Finland, 2004.

[28] R. Kalakota and M. Robinson, *M-Business: The Race to Mobility*, New York, McGraw-Hill, 2002.

[29] N.Z. Kviselius, *The Impact of Vehicle and Freight Telematics on Transportation Companies*, Austin Mobility Roundtable, Austin, Texas, 2004.

[30] M.M. Lankhorst, H. v. Kranenburg et al., Enabling Technology for Personalizing Mobile Services, 35th Hawaii International Conference on System Sciences, Maui, Hawaii, 2002.

[31] K.C. Laudon and J.P. Laudon, *Management Information Systems: Organization and Technology in the Networked Enterprise*, New Jersey, Prentice-Hall, 2000.

[32] H. Lehmann, J. Kuhn et al., *The Future of Mobile Technology: Findings from a European Delphi Study*. 37th Hawaii International Conference on System Sciences, Big Island, Hawaii, 2004.

[33] H. Liang, Y. Xue et al., PDA usage in healthcare professionals: testing an extended technology acceptance model, *International Journal of Mobile Communications* **1**(4) (2003), 372–389.

[34] J. Manget, (2002). Competitive advantage from mobile applications. Retrieved 03.12., 2003, from http://www.bcg.com/publications/files/competitive_adv_mobile_apps_ofa_feb02.pdf.

[35] J.C. McIntosh and J.P. Baron, Mobile commerce's impact on today's workforce: issues, impacts and implications, *International Journal of Mobile Communications* **3**(2) (2005), 99–113.

[36] MediaLab South-Pacific. (2003). No wires, no limits: an industry analysis of New Zealand's mobile and fixed wireless sector. Retrieved 03.12., 2003, from http://www.wirelessdataforum.co.nz/article.php?sid=855&catid=354.

[37] C.D. Müller and H.-D. Zimmermann, *Beyond Mobile: Research Topics for upcoming Technologies in the Insurance Industry*. 36th Hawaii International Conference on System Sciences, Big Island, Hawaii, 2003.

[38] M. Pesonen, M. Rossi et al., *Mobile Technology in Field Customer Service – Big improvements with small changes: Case: Amer Tobacco*, Austin Mobility Roundtable, Austin, Texas, 2004.

[39] D. Pica, C. Sørensen et al., *On Mobility and Context of Work: Exploring Mobile Police Work*. 37th Hawaii International Conference on System Sciences, Big Island, Hawaii, 2004.

[40] M.E. Porter, *Competitive Strategy: Techniques for Analyzing Industries and Competitors*, New York, Free Press, 1980.

[41] E. Rodina, V. Zeimpekis et al., *Remote Workforce Business Processes Integration Through Real-Time Mobile Communications*. Second International Conference on Mobile Business, Vienna, Oesterreichische Computer Gesellschaft, 2003.

[42] N. Sadeh, *M-Commerce: Technologies, Services, and Business Models*, New York, John Wiley & Sons, Inc., 2002.

[43] H. Scheepers and P. Steele, *The Hidden Impact of Mobile Information Systems: a case study of social interaction*. Thirteenth Australasian Conference on Information Systems, Melbourne, Australia, 2002.

[44]   E. Scornavacca, S. Barnes et al., Mobile Business Research Published in 2000–2004: Emergence, Current Status, and Future Opportunities, *Communications of the Association for Information Systems (AIS)* **17** (2006), 635–646.

[45]   E. Scornavacca and S.J. Barnes, M-banking services in Japan: a strategic perspective, *International Journal of Mobile Communications* **2**(1) (2004), 51–66.

[46]   E. Scornavacca and S.J. Barnes, Barcode enabled m-commerce: strategic implications and business models, *International Journal of Mobile Communications* **4**(2) (2006), 163–177.

[47]   E. Scornavacca and J. Cairns, *Mobile Banking in New Zealand: A Strategic Perspective*, Hong Kong Mobility Roundtable, Hong Kong, 2005.

[48]   E. Scornavacca and F. Herrera, *Unveiling the strategic value of mobile technologies in the New Zealand Real-estate industry*. International Conference on Mobile Business, Toronto, Canada, 2007.

[49]   E. Scornavacca and H. Hoehle, Mobile Banking in Germany: a strategic perspective, *International Journal of Electronic Finance (IJEF)* **1**(3) (2007), 304–320.

[50]   E. Scornavacca and S. Marshall, *TXT-2-LRN: improving students' learning experience in the classroom through interactive SMS*. 40th Hawaii International Conference on System Sciences, Hawaii, 2007.

[51]   E. Scornavacca, M. Prasad et al., Exploring the organisational impact and perceived benefits of wireless Personal Digital Assistants in restaurants, *International Journal of Mobile Communications* **4**(5) (2006), 558–567.

[52]   J. Sun and M.S. Poole, *Information Inquiry Activity in Mobile Commerce – The Behavioral Implications of IRE Approach*. Tenth Americas Conference on Information Systems, New York, 2004.

[53]   D. Tilson, *Towards a Theoretical Framework for Studying the Effect of MobileICT on Coordination*. 40th Hawaii International Conference on Systems Sciences, Hawaii, 2007.

[54]   W.W. Tollefsen, D. Myung et al., *iRevive, A Pre-Hospital Mobile Database*. Tenth Americas Conference on Information Systems, New York, 2004.

[55]   T. Tuunanen and M. Vainio, *Software Product Development Process Model: Case Studies of Mobile Software Companies Tuure Tuunanen., Marianne Vainio/cÓ*, Austin Mobility Roundtable, Austin, Texas, 2004.

[56]   B. Walker and S.J. Barnes, Wireless sales force automation: concept and cases, *International Journal of Mobile Communications* **3**(4) (2005), 411–427.

[57]   A. Westelius and P. Valiente, *Bringing the enterprise system to the frontline – Intertwining computerised and conventional communication at BT Europe*. 12th European Conference on Information Systems, Turku, Finland, 2004.

[58]   G. Wolf and K. Heinonen, *Wireless Web Strategies and Organizations*. Stockholm Mobility Roundtable, Stockholm, Sweden, 2003.

[59]   Y. Yuan and J.J. Zhang, Towards an appropriate business model for m-commerce, *International Journal of Mobile Communications* **1**(1/2) (2003), 35–56.

[60]   J.J. Zhang and Y. Yuan, *M-commerce versus internet-based E-commerce: the key differences*. Americas Conference on Information Systems 2002, Dallas, Texas, 2002.

[61]   A. Zimmermann, Context-awareness in user modelling: Requirements analysis for a case-based reasoning application, in: *Case-Based Reasoning Research and Development*, K.D. Ashley and D.G. Bridge, eds, Springer – Verlag, 2003, pp. 718–732.

 **Eusebio Scornavacca** is a Senior Lecturer in the School of Information Management at Victoria University of Wellington, New Zealand. He is interested in the business and end-user aspects of mobile and wireless technologies. He has a particular interest on mobility, user acceptance, strategy, quality and organizational/individual impact of mobile systems. Before moving to Wellington, Eusebio spent two years as a researcher at Yokohama National University, Japan. He has published and presented more than seventy papers in conferences and academic journals – including ICIS, ECIS, HICSS, Communications of AIS and Communications of ACM. Eusebio is currently on the editorial boards of the International Journal of Mobile Communications, the International Journal of Electronic Finance, Industrial Management & Data Systems, and he is the editor and founder of first online database dedicated to m-business (www.m-lit.org). In 2005, Eusebio was awarded at the prestigious MacDiarmid Young Scientists of the Year awards, and in 2006 he received a Victoria University of Wellington Research Excellence Award as well as the Victoria's Award for the best postgraduate supervisor (Faculty of Commerce) from the Postgraduate Student Association. In 2007, Eusebio received a Teaching Excellence Award from Victoria University of Wellington.

Stuart J. Barnes is Chair and Professor of Management in the Norwich Business School at the University of East Anglia. Previously he worked at Victoria University of Wellington, New Zealand, and the University of Bath. Stuart has been teaching and researching in the information systems field for over 15 years. His academic background includes a first class degree in Economics from University College London and a PhD in Business Administration from Manchester Business School. His primary research interests centre on the successful utilisation of new information and communications technologies by businesses, governments and consumers. He has published five books (one a best-seller for Butterworth-Heinemann) and more than a hundred articles including those in journals such as Communications of the ACM, the International Journal of Electronic Commerce, European Journal of Marketing, Communications of the AIS, and Information & Management.

Information Knowledge Systems Management 7 (2008) 243–271
IOS Press

Exploring enterprise mobility: Lessons from the field

Carsten Sørensen[a], Adel Al-Taitoon[a], Jan Kietzmann[b], Daniele Pica[a], Gamel Wiredu[c], Silvia Elaluf-Calderwood[a], Kofi Boateng[a], Masao Kakihara[d] and David Gibson[e]

[a]*London School of Economics and Political Science, Department of Management, Information Systems and Innovation Group London, United Kingdom*
E-mail: {c.sorensen,adel.al-taitoon-alumni,d.n.Pica,s.m.elaluf-calderwood,k.a.boateng}@lse.ac.uk
[b]*Simon Fraser University, SFU Business, Management Information Systems Burnaby, BC, Canada*
E-mail: jan_kietzmann@sfu.ca
[c]*Ghana Institute of Management and Public Administration (GIMPA) School of Technology Accra, Ghana*
E-mail: gwiredu@gimpa.edu.gh
[d]*Kwansei Gakuin University, School of Business Administration, Department of Management, Japan*
E-mail: kakihara@kwansei.ac.jp
[e]*Accenture Organisation and Change Management, Global Service Line London, UK*
E-mail: d.gibson@accenture.com

Abstract: The mobile phone has received global attention primarily as a personal consumer technology. However, we believe that mobile information technology in general will play a significant role in organisational efforts to innovate current practices and have significant economic impact. Enterprise mobility signals new ways of managing how people work together using mobile information technology and will form an integral part of the efforts to improve the efficiency and effectiveness of information work. This belief is, however, not reflected in the current selection of books and collections exploring the issue of enterprise mobility. The aim of this paper is to highlight some of the key challenges in the application of mobile information technology to improve organisational efficiency. This is accomplished through comparing and contrasting findings from a selection of 11 empirical studies of enterprise mobility with information technology conducted between 2001 and 2007. The paper argues that the debate so far has largely failed to embed glowing accounts for technological potential in a sound discussion of organisational realities. In particular, there has been a lack of balanced accounts of the implicit and explicit trade-offs involved in mobilising the interaction between members of the workforce.

Keywords: Enterprise mobility, empirical studies, critical issues, organisational efficiency

1. Introduction

Mobile technology in general and the mobile phone in particular has fuelled people's imagination by offering a rich medium for social experimentation (www.mobilelife2007.co.uk). One of the persistent issues in the use of this technology is its ability to support users in breaking down temporal and spatial boundaries, for example between home life and work life. In this sense, one of the persistent means of mobile interaction in organisations is the privately owned mobile phone. However, the challenge to the traditional division between home life and work life is only one of the barriers mobile Information

Technology (IT) require organisations and individuals to negotiate. Mobile IT is increasingly moving up on the lists of important technological concerns for organisations. This is due to the two forces of technological push whereby technological innovation provides opportunities for supporting work, and organisational pull emerging as a response to the pressures to perform and to effectivise information work [72]. This situation of technological push and organisational pull forms a rich substrate in which the technological promises can be cultivated.

When the first mobile phones were commercially introduced in the 1980s, they were only understood to be used in certain fixed locations outside the office, such as the car, a remote office or a building site [1]. What we have witnessed in the past few decades is a global experiment in joint technological sophistication and emerging interaction practices. As a result, it is almost impossible to find a business person who does not carry a mobile phone, and increasingly the phones will have personal computer capabilities, for example supporting email and web access. This technical convergence of a variety of capabilities in handsets and associated telecommunication infrastructures is the result of extensive technical innovation [60]. However, the technical convergence of capabilities must be assessed in the context of everyday use. It is not yet clear to what extent converged handsets will entirely replace diverged ones with easy user-identifiable purposes, such as notebook computer for data-intensive tasks, Blackberry for email, camera for photos and mobile phone for conversations and text messaging.

The distinguishing characteristic of this socio-technical development is the joint forces of the technology being closly associated with the body and the variety of ways it supports remote interaction with others and with informational resources. As with any new technology, organisations need to establish how using mobile technology can lead to improvements in the way work is done.

The aim of this paper is to contribute to the discussion of how mobile information technology can play a role in improving organisational efficiency. As part of a long-term research commitment to the study of enterprise mobility, we have conducted a number of in-depth studies of how organisations and individuals use mobile information technology. The research has been written up in various academic deliverables but we have so far not documented important lessons learnt across these studies. This paper, therefore, asks the question: *What are the organisational implications specifically related to the application of mobile information technology across a variety of public and private organisations?* This question is explored through cross-analysis and synthesis of results from 11 qualitative research studies conducted between 2001 and 2007. In our exploration we identify six essential aspects of organisational use of mobile information technology and discuss each in distinct Section 6. Brief vignettes and context descriptions from 7 of the 11 studies offer rich examples throughout the paper of the diversity of situations in which mobile IT can be deployed to enable organisational improvements. Due to space limitations all studies have not been included.

The article is structured as follows. Section 2 briefly outlines the research approach across the 11 studies included in the analysis. Section 3 discusses how mobile IT support changes in the way people interact, in terms of allowing work to be conducted anytime and anywhere, as well as supporting situated interaction whilst maintaining essential secondary interaction. Section 4 explores the management of work in terms of support for increased organisational control or individual discretion. Section 5 explores how enterprise mobility relates to choices between support for individual or collective working arrangements. Section 6 investigates the role of technology as being either ubiquitous or opaque to the user. Section 7 promotes the distinction between the use of mobile information technology to cultivate existing organisational practices as opposed to the transformation of these practices. Section 8 discusses how mobile IT can either facilitate encounters between people and information resources or more substantially support and mediate ongoing relationships. Section 9 concludes the paper. Appendices 1–3 present in detail more of the findings across 11 cases and 6 themes.

2. Studying enterprise mobility

LSE's Mobility Unit (mobility.lse.ac.uk) was established in 2001 and has since conducted a number of qualitative studies of how mobile technologies are used in organisations. The network has around 20 directly involved researchers and has over the years involved more than 50 MSc students. Six PhD dissertations have so far been completed and another six are in the process of completing. Common to the studies conducted within the Mobility Unit at LSE is in-depth qualitative enquiry either through interviews, direct participant observation, work document analysis, focus group discussions, or participation in projects as action researchers. The aim of the empirical efforts has been to inquire into the specifics of how work processes and supporting technologies mutually evolved over time either by investigating the established arrangements or by participating in their initiation. The closeness of mobile information technologies to the body of the user, and the the ability of the technology to converge various media, are some of the features that make processes of experimentation and complex appropriation common phenomena.

Although mobile information technology in some cases may stipulate precise work processes and thereby be less open for users engaging in experimentation, there will most often still be some room for manoeuvre as individual seek to meet their specific needs through the technology in their own preferred ways. The increased use of mobile technologies is further fuelled the discussions of technology and business innovation as conversations and networks of influence [20,23,61]. Precisely for this reason, in-depth qualitative methods can serve the valuable purpose of highlighting specific uses in order to understand more fundamental principles. If the technology was quite simple and would only be used for exactly the purposes intended by the designers, macro-perspectives emphasising general trends would be more appropriate.

For this paper, we have chosen a subset of 11 in-depth qualitative studies. Each study sought to investigate the specifics in the challenges of organisational adoption of mobile technology. Table 1 highlights the studies, which contain a variety of decisions, for example modern professionals mostly working on their own in and around Tokyo, Middle-East bankers, Black Cab drivers in London, police officers, health professionals, executives and delivery drivers. For each of the studies, key references are indicated for readers with further interest in studying the details.

Whereas each of the studies applied its own set of theoretical assumptions and associated frameworks to analyse and understand the detailed data collected, this paper will seek to draw out more general themes across these detailed studies. The aim has been to identify key-decisions of specific relevance when seeking to improve organisational performance with mobile information technology. There are of course a range of issues that always will be of interest in any type of technological intervention. As these, however, are discussed extensively elsewhere, they will not be discussed in this paper. As a result, the paper will present a fairly high-level view of very deep analyses in each study. Clearly, given this initial cross-analysis of a large number of individual research studies conducted by a group of people over a six year period, and given that the aim of this effort has been to identify major themes for discussion and not to formulate in-depth theoretical contribution, the result can be characterised as primarily representing richness of worldly realism as opposed to tightness of scientific control [41]. We have tried to draw out issues of general importance and interest to the readership of both academics and decision makers rather than focus on providing specific in-depth academic debates.

The field-studies of mobile IT outlined in Table 1 have been synthesised into distinct aspects of particular relevance for the organisational use of mobile IT. These aspects emerged from discussions of the case studies across industries. We have identified six aspects where the role of mobile information

Table 1
Characterising the 11 selected field studies

#	Workers	Year	Location	Method	Extent	Topic	References
1	Professionals	2001–2003	Japan	Interviews	63 interviews	Mobilisation of interaction for modern Tokyo professionals	(Kakihara, 2003, Kakihara and Sørensen, 2004)
2	Bank executives	2003–2005	Middle-East	Interviews	102 interviews in total for Study 2, 3 and 4	Mobile technologies for bank executives	(Al-Taitoon, 2005)
3	Mobile support centre	2003	Middle-East	Interviews & Support ticket analysis	102 interviews in total for Study 2, 3 and 4 plus 10.000 support tickets analysed	Challenges of running support function for global mobile professionals	(Al-Taitoon and Sørensen, 2004)
4	Off-premises foreign exchange traders	2004–2005	Middle-East	Interviews & observation	102 interviews in total for Study 2, 3 and 4 plus participant observation of traders	Discretion and control in mobile working for off-premises foreign exchange traders	(Al-Taitoon, 2005, Sørensen and Al-Taitoon, 2008)
5	London taxi drivers	2004–2007	UK	Interviews & video observation	35 interviews and 14 hours of video-taped observations	The choice of location as core business strategy and the role of mobile technologies in pooling resources and informing individuals	(Elaluf-Calderwood, Forthcoming, Elaluf-Calderwood and Sørensen, 2008, Elaluf-Calderwood and Sørensen, 2006)
6	Police officers	2002–2006	UK	Observation, interviews & focus group	250+ hours participant observation with 40+ officers and managers. 20+ interviews. 2 focus groups	The rhythms of interaction with mobile information technology by operational police officers	(Pica, 2006, Sørensen and Pica, 2005)
7	Health professionals	2002–2005	UK	Action research	15+ people participating in project	Supporting situated and remote learning for medical professionals (Perioperative Specialist Practitioners) with mobile information technology	(Wiredu, 2005, Wiredu and Sørensen, 2006)
8	Security guards	2004–2005	UK	Action research	350 hours of meetings, interviews and observation for Study 8 & 9	Real-life experimentation with RFID (Radio Frequency ID) enabled mobile phone technology supporting new ways of working	(Kietzmann, 2007)
9	Industrial waste management	2004–2005	UK	Action research	350 hours of meetings, interviews and observation for Study 8 & 9	Real-life experimentation with RFID enabled mobile phone technology supporting new ways of working	(Kietzmann, 2007)
10	Delivery Drivers	2006–2007	UK	Observation & interviews	50+ people participating in interviews and participant observation	Establishing IT mediated control of work tasks with low degree of discretion through enterprise infrastructure and mobile information technology	(Boateng, Forthcoming)
11	Professionals	2002	UK, USA	Interviews	16 interviews	Investigation of how mobile information technology still fails to become ubiquitous in the work of professionals	(Sørensen and Gibson, 2008)

technology must be subjected to organisational design or experimentation. These six aspects relate in general to the understanding of use, adoption, and impact of services at the individual, team and organisational level according to Lyytinen and Yoo's [37] taxonomy of research in mobile information technology. In their taxonomy, Lyytinen and Yoo [37] categorieses eight major categories of research of mobile information technology. They distinguish between the services and infrastructure levels across individuals, teams, and organisations. In terms of this classification, the six aspects can be understood as follows. (1) **Interaction** as *situated* or *mediated* by technology explores individual level services impact; (2) the **management** of activities in terms of individual *discretion* or organisational *control*, which denotes the possible conflicts between services requirement at different organisational levels; (3) organisation of **collaboration** as *individual* or *collective* work relates to individual and team-level services opportunities with mobile IT; (4) the role of **technology** in everyday use as *ubiquitous* or *opaque* is concerned with individual services use and impact; (5) the **organisational opportunities** for either *cultivation* or *transformation* of existing working practices relates to organisation level services impacts; and (6) the inherent characteristics of the **services** provided through mobile information technology as either mediating *encounters* or *relationships* investigates the IT artifact itself and as such relates more to Lyytinen and Yoo's [37] infrastructure level category of research issues. Appendix 1, 2 and 3 present more detailed findings.

3. Interaction: Mediated or situated?

This section explores interaction supported by mobile IT in terms of the distinction between on the one hand allowing activities to be carried out independent of time and space though **mediating** remote connections, and on the other supporting **situated** activities critically depending on being somewhere specific whilst still maintaining remote access to relevant people and resources.

The first element in this distinction relates to the common argument for mobile IT as a means of removing interactional constraints imposed by temporal and spatial boundaries. Paraphrasing Cairncross [9], not only distance may suffer a sudden death, time may also be a likely victim. The so-called anytime-anywhere hypothesis emphasises the technological promises of fluid interaction patterns unrestricted by the location of participants and by the necessities of synchronised interaction [26,32].

As the second part of the proposition indicates, this is only one possibility. One that is only valid to the extent that work activities indeed are independent of time, place and other situational aspects. From a phenomenological perspective, the situations people find themselves in always matter – how we feel, who we are with, what happened just before etc. [11,59]. From a pragmatic point of view, much of what goes on in organisations also depends critically on who is present, where and when the encounter takes place, and in what context. Activities can be situated, and Suchman [59, p. 48] defines this in terms of: *"action taken in the context of particular, concrete circumstances in local interactions with our environment"*. Work can be constrained in various ways, for example through the need for certain organisational resources to be available or it may need to be conducted at certain times. Spatial and temporal dependency and independency implies that embedding mobile technology in organisational contexts must consider to what extent the technological promises can be fulfilled in the particular context [66].

For all but a few of the professionals studied, our research has documented work that to some degree is bound by location and time. Police officers (Study 6) engage in incidents when called. Taxi drivers (Study 5) critically rely on understanding exactly where and when to locate customers needing cabs. Delivery drivers (Study 10) and security guards (Study 8) have very little direct control over where they

Vignette Study 1: It is 4pm in the afternoon in Japan. Hiro, the CEO of a small company developing various digital services for Internet-enabled mobile phones and television, walks down the main street in Tokyo's Akihabara district. He is engaged in one of his favourite past-times; to find inspiration for new services through immersing himself in Tokyo street-life. He observes what people do, what they buy and wear. Being in the field of the Japanese consumer is a source of inspiration to Hiro, and he characterises this behaviour as "being analogue" as opposed to surfing the Internet for inspiration. Wandering the streets of Tokyo is an important way for him to get new ideas for his company. The company only employs around a dozen people and he is the hub of most activities. Whilst traversing through Tokyo as a mobile age flaneûr he is therefore subjected to a massive amount of requests for interaction through emails and calls to his mobile phone. He uses a phone that was specially customised for him by one of his client companies and it is set up with a complex arrangement of alerts and ring-tones depending on who seeks his attention. (Study 1 in Table 1).

Context Study 1: There is a long tradition of employment in large organisations as the predominant strategy for Japanese professionals. For cultural reasons it is not seen as acceptable for individuals to unsolicitedly engage in promotion of own services. If an individual contractor needs work, the work will largely have to come through requests from others. This is quite contrary to other cultures, such as the North American, where it is seen as quite acceptable to openly offer one's services [6]. However, both cultures lead to a significant amount of time spent socialising and networking to secure future earnings [25,46]. This implies that work for small organisations and for individual professionals primarily is found through social relations and as direct results of past projects. The trend of increased flexibility for a small proportion of Japanese professionals mirrors developments seen elsewhere with organisations seeking to manage risk by relying on itinerant workers of various kinds [6,34,39]. Through a range of mobile information technologies, the 63 modern professionals studied, managed to create competitive advantage through situating themselves where work was needed at the same time as they could engage with important clients and collaborators whilst away from the office. Most of the people studied were intense notebook and mobile phone users.

work. Health professionals (Study 7) work where the patients are, waste management workers (Study 9), where the waste is, and bank executives (Study 2) occasionally where the clients are.

Mobile IT supports people engaging in rich situated interaction whilst remaining in touch with other remote contexts for their work. Even in cases where work tasks are purely informational and in principle can be conducted at anytime and anywhere, resolving mutual interdependencies still critically rely on engaging Inter-personal relationships. This makes face-to-face interaction much more effective for many situations, compared with mediated interaction – distance does matter as mediated interaction can not simply replace co-present socialisation and interaction [5,47,73].

Turning the argument around from one based on what technology can offer, namely boundary free interaction, to one emphasising what people desire, then the issue becomes much more complex. Viewed entirely from an individual point of view, the technology provides distinct opportunities for individual choice of who to interact with and from where. However, as all interaction is deeply situated in social and organisational practices, there will very seldom be an entirely free range of opportunities ahead but rather complex socially negotiated norms guiding the individual [12]. The choices are conditioned by traditions, power relations between initiator and recipient, practical concerns, the need to use organisational resources in the decision making etc.

It might be a more constructive view for the organisation to consider how the interactional context of its members can be viewed as an organisational resource of strategic importance and not merely a phenomenon accidental to practical information management constraints or individual preferences. Mobile IT implies the increased ability of organisational members to engage in mediated interaction in places of organisational importance whilst remaining in touch with necessary interactional contexts. Our study of Arabian banking executives illustrates this well (Study 2). Bank executives would frequently find themselves engaging in negotiations with high-end clients about the services rendered and the client's financial arrangements with the bank. These negotiations would most often happen at the client's site somewhere in the World. The bank executives would have direct access via Virtual Private Network (VPN) connections from their PDA's to the bank's internal systems in order to obtain up-to-date information about exactly how significant the client's involvement at that time was with the bank.

Obtaining this data provided essential information for the bank executives to get a good position for the tough negotiations with the client and allowed these to be done at the client's own location.

The distinction between situated and mediated interaction can be further qualified in distinguishing between two types of mediated interaction – local mobility and remote working. Global virtual teams or traditional telecommuters engage in remote working either across continents or from a home-office. Activities can, however, also be conducted through locally mobile working within a restricted domain [36]. Whilst the locally working person may elude fixed location, he or she will be assumed to remain within close proximity, for example in a neighbouring building. Here, the defining characteristic is the ability to contact an individual through a pager, mobile phone, tannoy system or by other means and as a result summon this person. Doctors and nurses engaged in healthcare work are a good example of local working. Study 7 illustrated how constant engaging in activities to serve the purpose of a remote quality assurance easily got in the way of this kind of working. Remote workers will be working from fixed office arrangements and will therefore typically be available through ordinary desktop communications channels such as email and telephone. Mobile working is, characterised by the combination of local mobility and remote distribution, and marks a significant increase in complexity. The mobile worker is potentially neither able to quickly be summoned, nor is he or she possible to pin down at fixed remote locations. Taxi drivers, lorry drivers, and travelling sales people are all examples of work that traditionally has been mobile seen from the perspective of others who collaborate with these.

Summarising, mobile IT support the fluidisation of time and space by offering easy mediated interaction anytime and anywhere. However, by offering mobile access to people and resources supporting work activities, the technology also makes it possible to enrich activities that inherently are situated.

4. Management: Control or discretion?

In terms of the management of work activities within the organisation, this has traditionally been conducted through combining direct observation with various systems of remote control [71]. Moble IT supports connections between remotely distributed organisational actors and can place direct access to the corporate infrastructure in the palm of their hands. The introduction of mobile IT will therefore influence the possibilities for management of remote and mobile activities. Zuboff [74] broadly characterises the effects of IT in terms of the distinction between the use of information technology as means of *automating* work processes and thereby driving discretion out of work, as opposed to *informating* work by providing rich information allowing for discretionary localised and contextualised decisions. We, therefore characterise the support for management of work through mobile IT in terms of the distinction between technology providing means for **control** as opposed to opportunities for increased individual **discretion** in decisions.

The underlying assumption of process automation is the viability of characterising work in terms of business processes that can be made explicit, negotiated, and subjected to re-design. However, some work domains, for example top-executives, professionals, and artists, are not expected to be subjected to this kind of formalisation. Here, the individual or small group of collaborators are perceived to exclusively exercise professional judgement and discretion in their decision making [55].

The literature contains extensive discussions of employee empowerment and self-organisation. While Malone [38] proposes that the cost of commnication has brought the opportunities of large-scale decentralised organisations closer, Argyris [4] argues that organisations in fact do not increasingly empower their employees. Conger and Kanungo [13] argue that there is a lack of understanding of what constitutes empowerment and how it can be promoted in organisations. Courpasson [14] points out the importance

---

Vignette Study 6: In the South of England, two police officers, John and Mary, are driving at high speed towards a domestic disturbance incident mid-morning. Whilst driving to the incident they are heavily engaged in two important tasks. One is to ensure that they arrive as fast and as safe as possible. The other is to ensure that they have as much information about the incident they very soon will be attending. They drive at high speed with the loud siren and blue blinking lights through a small town. They are in constant touch with the control room and arrange for a range of information about the incident and past incidents at the same address to be streamed from the control room to a small computer in the patrol vehicle. This enables one officer to read this information out to her colleague driving and they discuss the situation ahead trying to form a good idea of what risks may be involved and how to prioritise their effort. As they arrive at the scene, they stay in constant touch with the control room. Mary calls the neighbour reporting the incident from her mobile phone to get further information. (Study 6 in Table 1).

Context Study 6: The two-way radio system was first time used outside the military by the Chicago Police Force in the 1930s Prohibition period of emerging organised crime [1]. Since then, police forces across the World have embraced mobile voice and data-services as means of collecting intelligence, distributing information to officers in the field and for co-ordination of efforts. Most mobile IT is therefore naturally not organisationally transformative but rather finds its own place in the mobile ecosystem within the limited space of the police vehicle or on the police officers' person. Mobile IT serves an essential purpose when operational police officers engage in incidents, or rather before and during engagement. The situation ahead is often characterised by a high degree of uncertainty and the technology allows officers to draw upon mobile data and interaction with control room and others in their assessment of the risk ahead. A core consideration with time- and safety-critical work is the rhythms of interaction with technology and the right-time, right-job attitude to technology as opposed to the view that the technology is ubiquitously available and needed anytime, anywhere. Police officers need to actively engage with the incident and not stare into screens.

---

of distinguishing between operational empowerment in the the decentralised delegation of activities and the centralisation of power to set the boundaries for these activities. Kirkman and Rosen [31] study 111 teams and suggest team empowerment as a way of conceptualising the issues. We have in our studies seen a broad range of management practices from closely controlled activities to work performed exercising extensive discretion.

The independent Tokyo professionals in Study 1, the bank executives in Study 2, and the London taxi drivers in Study 5 are all examples of domains with a high degree of individual discretion [2,17,25]. The security guards in Study 8 and delivery drivers in Study 10 are examples of work with a very low degree of individual discretion where work is largely sought and stipulated in detail by procedures and supportive information technology. The highly managed work of, for example, security guards (Study 8), can be further improved by using mobile IT to speed up communication between mobile security guards and centralised management. Furthermore, the technology strengthen relationships between the physical environment and the information tasks through RFID technology automating the recording of positions converged with mobile phone technology automating the transmission of location-data [30]. We have also (in Study 10) seen how organisational infrastructures in detail organising mobile tasks centrally can support the management of mobile work activities [7].

It is, however, dangerous to assume that a particular type of work does not rely on individual discretion on a daily basis. Emerging contingencies may occur and dealt with but never reported elsewhere in the system. The formalised model collectively assumed may in fact not be an appropriate formalisation of what goes on. Localised improvisation and subtle changes to the way work is done may have altered the reality of how work is done but not the formalised assumption held about it. Schmidt [52] reports from a manufacturing study where a Kanban implementation, supposedly entirely automating the flow of parts in an assembly line, was subjected to frequent discretionary decisions explicitly breaking the principles of the formal process in order for the system as a whole to deal with emerging constraints. Kietzmann [30] documents how industrial waste management drivers (Study 9) found it problematic that management would get detailed information about the movement of waste barrels and would use this information incorrectly to derive implications for further decisions as they did not have a full overviews of loal constraints. Boateng [7] shows how delivery drivers use their initiation, judgment and negotiation

Vignette Study 10: At Foods International they distribute everything needed to run small restaurants and fast-food outlets. Jason works as a delivery driver for the company and he has, as many of his colleagues, only worked there for a relatively short period of time. However, the systems he relies on in his daily work delivering food, drinks and other goods to the customers are designed to guide him through his working day. In the course of performing his duties, Jason relies on the strength of technology mediated interaction, to update him on the readiness of customers to collect their orders and any road diversions or blocks on his routes. If he finds a customer's shop closed at the time of delivery, Jason uses the company's mobile phone to find out from Customer Service the whereabouts of the customer. The answer would determine if he will have to return at a later time with the customer's purchased order. However, sometimes when a customer is not available to take the deliveries, Jason may decide to either park near the shop and wait, or to pass by at a later point on his delivery round, by which time the shop will be open.

Context Study 10: As the example above, this one is concerned with work characterised by a low degree of discretion, which to a large extent is controlled remotely by schedules or direct managerial intervention. This study demonstrated the use of mobile IT integrated with an extensive organisational infrastructure. Mutual interdependencies between delivery drivers and those who take orders from customers, those who find the items in the warehouse, and those packing the lorry for delivery are largely mediated and stipulated by the organisational systems. This illustrates the strength of an integrated stationary-mobile work support system for not only supporting highly distributed activities but also for being a viable tool to further limit individual discretion side by side with systems-based stipulation of activities.

skills to avoid parking tickets by persuading parking attendants from issuing parking tickets in the course of delivering certain customer orders. Management have little idea as to how delivery drivers deal with such unforseen and emergent issues yet it never undermines the fact that delivery drivers are not inactive and unprepared in meeting the pragmatic exigencies relating to their work.

The business cases for mobile information technology supporting work with no discretion and for work with an abundance of discretion can be fairly straightforward. In the former the impact can be made subject of direct calculations of increased efficiency of work as it can to a large extent be externally represented. In the latter, the executives and professionals affected will be the senior decision makers and therefore not really need any business case or at least highly valued knowledge-workers whose time is considered valuable and the organisational willingness to invest in supporting works therefore quite high. The issue of understanding the value of mobile information technology is clearly in the large segment of work that both is subjected to some form of control, but which also relies on significant individual discretion. Studying operational police officers demonstrated some of the issues involved when work is a complex mixture of discretionary choices, organisational co-ordination, and occasional strong centralised control [40,46,57].

Vignette Study 4: It is 6pm somewhere in the Middle-East and one of the traders from a large Arabian bank is eating dinner with his family in a restaurant. He takes a short break from the discussion of what his child has done in school as he checks his trading pager, a Reuters SmartWatch, to see if any rate changes at the New York exchange is influencing his positions. He is one of a small group of foreign exchange traders that extend the banks' trading hours throughout the evening and night equipped with the trading pager, a mobile phone and a PocketPC with web-based trading services. The small group of traders entrusted to do off-premises trading negotiated their positions before leaving the trading floor earlier in the afternoon to get a common understanding of their limits. When trades are made, the mobile phone is used to call into an answering machine at the bank to record the transactions for back-office for further processing in the morning. (Study 4 in Table 1).

Context Study 4: The portfolio of mobile IT allows for off-premises trading and has made it possible to transform the organisation from three-shift trading to off-premises trading supplementing the normal trading day. The traders were not very happy with the three-shift system and although being granted permission to engage in off-premises trading, this still places quite strong demands on traders family life with constantly being connected. This is one of the main reasons for maintaining a light-touch with no management control during off-premises trading and traders are generally left to themselves. This, however, can lead to problematic situations if they do not at times engage in minimal co-ordination with fellow off-premises traders to negotiate trading limits.

The discussion of organisational or managerial control versus individual discretion relates to the more general concern of emerging changes to organisational arrangements in terms of centralisation versus decentralisation. Malone [38] argues that organisational forms largely depend on the cost of communicating. He argues that hierarchical and centralised communication through vertical command-and-control management is a necessity when there is a high cost associated with interaction in large organisational forms. This, Malone argues, changes when the cost of communicating drops and as a result will allow for large-scale co-ordination of activities in networks emerging through horizontal cultivation of relationships. Much has been written about shifts from hierarchical to networked organisations, and this debate is quite often based on the wrong premises that networked interrelations can occur disassociated from established structural arrangements of traditions, power, influence etc. [29]. Courpasson [14] argues that some contemporary organisational forms show the characteristics of horizontal operational co-ordination of activities in networks along with centralised control over the tactical and strategic issues of resource allocation and agenda formation. For the off-premises foreign exchange traders in Study 4 the trade-offs between organisational control to ensure proper documentation of trading versus the need for discretion features prominently. The primary mechanism to ensure this balance was the careful vetting of which pit-traders would be granted the coveted status of membership of the exclusive group of off-premises traders.

5. Collaboration: Individual or collective?

Vignette Study 5: It is early Tuesday morning and Ray has just begun working. He is one of the 40,000 licensed London Black Cab drivers. Ray has decided to start early today as he need to pick up his teenage daughter from school in the afternoon and take her to an appointment with their doctor. As he drives down Oxford Street towards Marble Arch one of his three mobile phones starts ringing. This particular phone is exclusively used for a service automatically locating an available cab nearest to the location of the caller's mobile phone. The driver answers and within five minutes the passenger is picked up at Notting Hill Gate. As he drops the passenger off in front of The Houses of Parliament one of his colleagues calls and informs him that due to a problem with one of the local train lines there is a need for a number of cabs to replace the train for a few hours. As it is good money, Ray decides to accept and sets off to the station. (Study 5 in Table 1).

Context Study 5: London Black Cab drivers have been around for 420 years and since 1851 been certified according to a strict set of exams, "The Knowledge", ensuring the driver knows over 300 routes in inner London. Drivers tend to own their own cab and work has always been conducted in a highly independent manner with each driver deciding how and when to work. This is an archetypical example of choice of work context as a strategic concern and after studying for 3-4 years for The Knowledge, drivers typically spend several years learning how to position themselves to be profitable. The mobile phone serves as a natural tool for drivers to get in touch with the rest of the world whilst driving. Colleagues may inform them about particularly profitable work or essential traffic situations. One of the computer-cab systems automatically links the nearest cab to the calling customer's mobile phone location. Competitive pressure from minicab companies without license to pick up at ranks or in the street makes closer collaboration through centralised computer dispatch systems a viable option for the independent Black Cab drivers to pool their resources. They thereby will appear as an organised unit and not individuals, but this also is associated with major discussions about the relative merits of joining the different organisations in terms of fairness of job allocation and requirements to choose a certain number of jobs from the company each month.

Mobile IT is often associated with single-user technology, for example, the mobile phone and the notebook computer. These allow the user to maintain occasional connections with other people or information resources when the resolution of mutual interdependencies are needed. Mobile IT can therefore support increased **individualisation** of work activities. At the same time, mobile IT also lowers the barrier for interaction across spatial and temporal barriers and therefore makes **collective** efforts possible where they before were not. Interestingly, the introduction of mobile IT can shift activities in both directions between these two types.

As one of the primary reasons for people working together is to negotiate their mutual interdependencies in their collaboration, an obvious concern regarding mobile information technology is to what extent it can support engaging in such negotiations. In this sense the technology can remove many boundaries to rapidly collaborating [53]. This may, for example, imply that organisational actors who previously did not have opportunities to directly negotiate their mutual interdependencies with mobile information technology can be presented with multiple means of interacting directly.

The London Black Cab drivers (Study 5) provide a clear-cut example of how mobile information technology can support an increased collectivisation of work. Individual taxi drivers owning their cab have traditionally decided entirely themselves where, when and for how long they work. Each cab is generally an independently owned business unit serving the purpose of driving people and things from A to B. Black cab drivers have traditionally engaged in the exchange of experiences and tips either when waiting at taxi ranks or when meeting for coffee or lunch, much in the same way as the engineers studied by Orr [48] exchanging important knowledge about the profession and not in a highly detailed and operative manner [19]. However, the mobile phone has made it possible for emerging and changing communities of Black Cab drivers to weave networks of mutual interdependencies, in a similar manner to the geographically situated ephemeral organisation described by Lanzara [33]. When, for example, a train operator needed many cabs to transport stranded passengers, drivers would call others to alert them of available jobs. Also, as many cab drivers will be spending some part of their working time chatting with colleagues, this would also offer opportunities of sharing a common awareness of not only emerging business opportunities but also of traffic conditions.

More fundamentally, London Black Cab drivers face competitive pressures from minicab companies who can only interact with their customers through the customer requesting their services in the minicab office, by telephone or through the Internet. As a result of this pressure, drivers increasingly join organisations facilitating the pooling of individual Black Cab resources by providing automatic, semiautomatic or manual dispatch services. This signifies not only increased opportunities for individual drivers to interact with each other but the creation of organisation where there previous was none or very little. This re-intermediation is largely dependent upon the combination of computer-cab systems and mobile phones linking the cab to the central infrastructure of the dispatch organisation.

In the case of mobile work in industrial waste management (Study 9), the introduction of stronger automated links between the work done and the systems used to monitor work implied a much smaller level of granularity in the discussions of work tasks and thereby made work more collaborative between those who worked locally, and those who managed the work remotely. This is similar to the example documented by Ciborra [10] of the product development Lotus Notes discussion groups, which in turn were read by top-executives situated remotely. As in the waste management case, this ability to remotely observe detailed work decisions led to conflict.

There was ample conflict in the health professional case (Study 7), and it was mainly related to the organisational disagreement about what working together actually meant and the relative importance of one collaborative context as opposed to another. For the local hospital where the health professionals engaged in daily training, this was the main place of collaboration. However, the responsibilty for the learning process resided in London, where students would participate in one-week sessions every nine weeks throughout a year. The ability of those responsible for the learning to centrally be able to monitor progress was deemed essential for the outcome of the project. The immediately situated concerns would frequently conflict with the demand for close documentation of the learning process imposed from London. This conflict between local and remote collaboration formed the main cause of conflict in the failure of the PDA system [68,70].

However, the use of mobile information technology can not only relate to increased collaboration. It can also be part of the opposite phenomenon of increased individualisation or segmentation of work.

Many organisations seek to manage the complexity of their business by focusing on core issues and sub-contracting or outsourcing other aspects. This relates to a variety of organisational trade-offs between managing work through social control or through economic exchange with the acquisition of commodified knowledge embedded in a product being mainly social control and the internalisation of knowledge through ongoing employment of experts [51]. Packaging of knowledge, outsourcing of activities, and sub-contracting all seek to cut or contractualise some of the mutual interdependencies within organisations and replacing them with temporary relationships or with negotiated specific contributions by individuals [6,62,67].

Modern project-workers, who do work on a contractual basis as opposed to continuing employment can, for example, spend a significant proportion of their time networking with others in order to ensure future involvement in projects [46]. We clearly found this in the study of Tokyo professionals (Study 1), especially since Japanese culture frowns upon direct solicitation of own services. Barley and Kunda [6] show how software developers use recruitment agencies as the organisational arrangement ensuring a steady stream of project engagements with clients. Although the Tokyo professionals in Study 1 often would be engaged in collaboration with others, work would most often be project based and in some cases highly individual by consisting of clearly separated modules or services. Mobile information technology supported this individualisation of work as channels by which work could be negotiated and where the work results could be disseminated.

In the case of off-premises foreign exchange traders (Study 4), their work had two distinct collaborative modalities. During the day they engaged in individual, but closely co-ordinated, trading in a stationary organisational setting. This had before been conducted as three-shift trading following the opening hours of the exchanges in Japan, Europe and USA, but trading outside normal working hours had been replaced by a selective group of trusted traders engaging in off-premises trading in their own time. As they in effect worked when off work, it was not feasible to impose the traditional requirements of collaborating and this resulted in off-premises trading largely being individual activities, which in certain situations selectively by the traders themselves could be subject to negotiation, for example off-trading limits [2,54]. Mobile information technology directly made this modality possible through the Reuters SmartWatch with market access to data and the mobile phone for documenting trades to an answer-machine for back-office processing the following day. An intermediary mode of operation had seen traders engage in trading from their desk-based PC at home, but this was equally inconvenient as three-shift trading as they were bound to their desk for trading.

6. Technology: Ubiquitous or opaque?

Not only is each mobile IT terminal normally used by one individual, the mobile phone and notebook computer being obvious examples, it also come attached with the assumption that it will dissapear for the user and become an **ubiquitous** part of their everyday activities. This was first formulated by Weiser [64, 65]. However, mobile IT can for a range of reasons easily turn into an **opaque** element demanding attention and generally being in the way of getting work done [56].

Mobile information technology is most often personal and it is always possible to physically take parts of it along as opposed to pervasive technology, which may or may not be mobile. Ubiquitous technology can be defined as the combination of technological mobility and pervasiveness, i.e, the ability of the technology to relate to its surroundings. Although most mobile technologies are exactly only that, and not particularly pervasive, the combined socio-technical relation can produce ubiquitous behaviour, for example the social use of the mobile phone as a location-based service. Although a mobile phone has quite precise information about where it is located through the cell it is registered in, this information is not normally used by its owner. However, the frequent SMS messages or brief telephone conversations stating; *"I am on my way"*; *"I'm stuck in traffic on the motorway 10 miles away"*; or *"please wave so I can see you"*, are all examples of how we can make the mobile phone ubiquitous simply because it for most people in the developed world is an individual device carried along with money and keys. As some mobile technologies, such as the mobile phone, elegantly have managed to find itself a place on or near our bodies, and others still are reserved a less close role, such as the notebook computer, it is interesting to explore the possibilities of mobile technologies becoming an ubiquitous part of work. However, just by being carried around close to our bodies does not necessarily always make a technology ubiquitously move into the background as a taken-for-granted resource. As some of the professionals in Study 11 argued, mobile technologies in general, and the mobile phone in particular, can become opaque and demanding attention, for example with the mobile phone when it has run out of battery or if someone is calling when the receiver of the call is busy concentrating on other important matters [28,35,56].

Vignette Study 7: Yin used to be a nurse, and she was very good at her job so she decided to do further specialist training for even more challenging work with patients as a specialist practitioner assisting surgeons. This involves on-the-job training for one year at the hospital she works. This morning she is following surgeons doing rounds. An essential part of her theoretical learning and practical training is done at one-week sessions every six weeks in London. Here, the main co-ordinator of the programme is keen to follow and record the progress of each of the 16 participants when they are back home. This is essential for both providing feedback on the learning and for documenting progress to ensure subsequent certification. The students are therefore provided with a personal digital assistant (PDA) with proprietary software to record conduct and outcome of each session back at their respective hospitals. Yin finds this very difficult to accomplish as the PDA constantly seems to get in the way of learning and working. The PDA, however, comes in very handy for her own personal information management and she also uses its built-in medical dictionaries frequently. (Study 7 in Table 1).
Context Study 7: The purpose of the PDA-based system, which reported to a centralised database in London was to ensure that situated learning by each of the medical professionals based around the country could be documented and subjected to assessment by the person responsible. The aim of documenting work-integrated learning at the place of work and centrally monitor and verify this did not succeed. This went far beyond the usability problems of having PDA interaction artificially interjected in situated hospital work. The conflicts between the localised control of the participants at their hospitals and the desire for centralised influence and control through the technology from the central London-based learning-centre presented a significant barrier for using the mobile technology effectively. The aims for strong local control over activities locally clashed in territorial dispute with the attempts to exercise equally strong remote control from the central learning centre. As as result, the only useful aspects of the PDA was the individual use of medical dictionaries and the personal information management functionality.

We are still far from realising the much promoted techno-optimistic vision of all matters of ubiquitous technologies like utilities of the 21st Century disappearing from our direct attention and unnoticeable becoming unconstrained resources for our immediate consumption [16,45,56,64]. The question is indeed if we ever will realise this vision, and if we do, whether or not it will be desirable. The extent to which mobile phones, for example, are constant subjects of conversation, adjustments, attention etc is a sign of the importance the users lend to this technology. It represents a means to be contacted by others and through which to reach them. The underlying 2 or 3G wireless infrastructure may only enter the user's awareness when there is no signal, much similar to other utilities such as water and electricity.

The traditional view of how information technology relates to organisational actions is one of large systems delivering a set of fairly standardised services which together forms sufficient and homogeneous support for the IT aspects of decisions [43]. The ways in which heterogeneous information services are combined and the variety of approaches adopted by individuals, indicate the need for reconsidering the role of information services in organisations. With advanced options of exporting data from one application and importing them into another is just one aspect of the ease by which users can seek their own individualised means of managing information through their selected portfolio of services and applications. Mobile services are no different and will play an increasingly important role in supporting the management of information and decision making. Modern professionals will have email at home, on their mobile phone, at the office, or indeed often anywhere with an Internet connection. The mobile phone will probably be able to download, display and maybe even support editing of attachments. So, for just the simple task of reading email, replying to them and editing sent attachments, the modern professional will have a range of options available and will often be able to combine these according to personal preferences or the situation they may find themselves in. For example, the instant availability of mobile email my lead to much more frequent checking of email [44].

In our studies we generally found that closeness of the technology to the body of the user promoted an interactive process of individual adaptation allowing the user and technology to mutually adapt. In the case of Study 4, the off-premises trading worked well because being an off-premises trader signalled status within the organisation, and because the organisation did not impose itself on the trader through the technology but instead allowed a natural flow of using the technology to support the primary tasks at hand. The London Black Cab drivers in Study 5 were experts in selecting and appropriating technology that would directly support their main task of locating customers, but also support drivers in maintaining essential social links to friends and family while driving around the streets of London. Aspects of the systems, such as the fairness of the principles they implemented for allocating jobs to drivers were of significant importance and therefore discussed intensely. For the health professionals in Study 7, using the PDA system was throughout at odds with the specific requirements of the work context and although they managed to make individual use of some features, the technology seemed to remain opaque and problematic throughout [69]. For the security guards in Study 8, the RFID-enabeled mobile phone quickly became a natural part of their work as it easily replaced the existing electronic reader. The operational police officers in Study 6 displayed, due to the extreme nature of their work, very interesting mobile technology use patterns, where there were significant variation or rhythms of interaction with the technology depending on the circumstances and on how intensively they were required to engage with the physical world of citizens embroiled in incidents [49,57].

Rather than over emphasising the challenges of making mobile technologies ubiquitously disappear in the background, it is perhaps more constructive to conceptualise mobile IT at work similar to the extreme case of the police. This makes the ability of rapidly shifting the attention from the technology to the situation or from one technology to another according to the rhythms of work much more essential. The success of the mobile phone so far is perhaps based on this criterion that the technology should be easily engaged and disengaged. This perspective of engagement and disengagement also emphasises the importance of not only using the technology but also to make it disappear in order to engage with the world around. This relates back to the initial issue of mediated or situated interaction, and the crucial role of engaging with others when it really matters. For all organisations the lessons learnt from studying the police can be valuable in terms of augmenting situations with mobile services as opposed to replacing them. The bank executives in Study 2 illustrated this very well with the entire emphasis being on intense negotiations with the client, but with relevant information for these negotiations being available when needed.

7. Organisation: Cultivate or transform?

Mobile IT can offer organisational support for the gradual **cultivation** of existing working practices and through this for example enable efficiency gains and increased flexigility. However, mobile IT also

---

Vignette Study 8: Late at night in an industrial estate in the outskirts of Manchester, the security guard Sandeep is doing his nightly round at an electronics warehouse. At each check-point he waves his mobile phone, which contains a built-in RFID (Radio Frequency Identification) reader over a tag mounted on the wall and a message is automatically sent to a central server to update his whereabouts. This is not a lot different from the previous systems where a torch-like tag reader would record each check-point. However, this would only allow data to be uploaded to the system once Sandeep was back in the office after a whole shift. Instead, the database was now immediately updated. Sandeep does not mind too much that he is a bit tighter observed as he already was so before, even if it was not in real time. (Study 8 in Table 1).

Context Study 8: The system above was part of a set of four extensive real-life experiments with RFID-reader mobile phones used to render work more effective through real-time updates within central systems of mobile work activities. The RFID reader mobile phone here enforced existing working arrangements and cultivated real-time updating of guard positioning allowing for a range of management practices operating at a finer level of granularity. As work already was characterised by a low degree of individual discretion, the technology was not seen as radically changing the conditions for work. The experiments also highlighted the added complexity of formulating systems requirements for technologies that are not only close to the human body but also directly links the physical and virtual world. Whereas end-users in other cases may be easier to circumvent, the complexity of RFID-enabling individual work processes implies the need to involve end-users and thereby also drawing them in as a significant stake-holder.

---

has the potential of being a disruptive technology [8] supporting a **transformation** of the way decisions are made, innovation carried out or services delivered.

From both an organisational and a technology vendor point of view, the aim will often be to seek to transform the organisation of work to make it more effective, innovative, profitable or whatever criterion is sought after. However, the straight-forward business cases for significant investments in mobile IT is often difficult to identify as the transformation hinges as much upon a business transformation as on technological change. Zuboff and Maxmin [75] argue that market demands from customers for increasingly individualised support will result in a demand for business transformation. Malone [38] argues from the perspective of the dropping communication costs that such scenario is practically feasible. However, these studies do not consider mobile IT and it is still somewhat unclear what role this technology can play in business transformation.

In our studies we mostly saw mobile IT supporting the step-wise cultivation of existing working practices, which is probably typical for many technologies as radical changes may only look appealing in business case texts and on spreadsheets with estimated gains or savings, but not at the coal-face of work. Furthermore, the closeness of the user and technology is in itself an experimental setting that in most cases will be needed in order to fully understand how the technology may provide transformative effects. The intensity of the human-technology relationship when the technology is constantly carried along and cared for is one that sets new issues on the innovation agenda. The user becomes an integral element in shaping the innovation and real life experimentation can be the only means by which the consequences of the innovation can be understood as the relationship between body, technology and work process becomes more and more intense [23,30].

In terms of the transformative capabilities of mobile information technology, these must be seen in the greater perspective of the overall business objectives and the role of information technology herein. Whereas the traditional role of the organisational information system was to automate back-office processes, current information technologies seek to support the organisation in for example relating to customers and business partners. The multi-faceted challenges to contemporary organisations include the ability to listen comprehensively to what products and services customers and other stake-holders desire, and to go beyond listening to also engaging various constituencies in collaborative efforts. These types of efforts are only commercially feasible through intensive use of information technology as both support for and replacement of human activities [55]. Mobile technologies will by definition follow organisational actors where they may go and as such represent the new information management boundary of the organisation. The ability of the bank in both Study 2 and 4 to extend its information services boundary beyond the walls of the organisation provided potentially transformative effects. Similarly, the ability of the police offers to gain information before and during incidents can both help protect citizens and the officers as it greatly helps transform operational uncertainties into assessed risks.

If organisations aim at softening the boundaries to customers and associates in order to better understand and involve these stake-holders, then one of the primary means may just be mobile IT. If Internet users are keen to helping companies supporting customers with deep technical questions about its products through posting their knowledge on discussion forums, some of this energy may in different forms be harnessed and adopted to the context of mobile technology use. Already now it is possible to study the phenomenon of micro-blogging, which often is done in a combined stationary and mobile manner – Twitter.com and Jaiku.com are two good examples of this. The technological convergence of various services from stationary to mobile technologies will provide interesting platforms to innovate from, for example the recent development of an affordable 3G mobile phone with Skype functionality, or the integration of GPS receivers, contact-less payment cards or general RFID readers in mobile phones.

More and more organisations understand that reaching customers on their mobile phone, if done the right way, a much stronger relationship than the one cultivated through a personal computer as it will allow much more direct access. Delivery drivers (Study 10), police officers (Study 6) and modern professionals (Studies 1, 2, and 11) alike have all experienced the importance of getting access to each other and to vital organisational resources when interacting with people at the edges of the organisation. When an airline company allows its customers to check-in from a mobile phone (for example SAS mobile check-in), it gains effectiveness in the traditional manner information technology often does, by the customer doing some, if not all, of the work [58]. However, for the customer this is not necessarily a bad idea assuming it is sufficiently simple to do. For regular customers with an account set up, it is even possible to buy ticket and check-in in one simple operation. The potential for transformation if the right conditions are present is significant as the example of the M-PESA project in Kenya where the lack of general access to banking combined with the widespread diffusion of mobile phones provided fertile soil for a mobile phone based electronic money system [24].

8. Services: Encounters or relationships?

Mobile IT can provide two different categories of information service. The first kind is comprised of information services offering technologically mediated **encounters**, and the second kind mediate ongoing **relationships** [43].

Zuboff and Maxmin [75] argue that the 21st Century is to be one characterised by individualised consumption of experiences and support more than merely the consumption of mass-produced goods. They see as one of the essential prerequisites the ability for organisations to engage in a relationship economy as opposed to the traditional transaction economy. A key element to engaging with customers and organisational partners will therefore be the ability to mediate customer relationships through information services [43]. The distinction between services offering encounters versus those mediating relationships relates to discussions of; The differences between algorithmic codification (encounters) and interactivity (relationships) [21,42,63]; the distinction between encounters and relationships in the provision of services [15,22]; and the economic development of market forces towards a relationship- as opposed to a transaction economy [75].

When a mobile phone is used for short voice calls, to send an SMS message, or for mobile email, then the phone mostly mediates encounters as any ongoing relationship is entirely managed by the people engaged in the interaction. If a series of phone conversations for participants amounts to an interesting relationship, then this is entirely constructed amongst the actors. The phone will only mediate a relationship to the extent it contains the memory of names and numbers in the log or address book. Recent services, for example on the iPhone of representing ongoing SMS messages between people as though they were instant messaging discussions will more significantly mediate the relationship [43].

Comprehensive support for mobile collaboration requires additional services supporting mutual adjustment and recording of distributed decisions beyond merely allowing people to do so themselves through instant connections. Mobile collaboration support will require support for ongoing discussions, easy sharing of workspaces, coordination of mobile activities, and establshing mutual awareness through the technology [43,63].

As an example, the reason police officers from Study 6 never disengaging their shoulder-mounted radio during incidents was that they through this kept an ongoing conversation with the control room, who could offer information and support [57]. Taxi drivers in Study 5 using a computer-cab system need some form of information service allowing them to update their recorded whereabouts in a central database at the dispatch office in order to be given jobs near where they are. The off-premises foreign exchange traders in Study 4 used a fairly simple set of information services, but the essential Reuters SmartWatch allowed an ongoing updating of the latest market information and the ways the traders set up this relationship was essential for their performance. In the mobile support centre in Study 3, the way in which the support staff managed their interaction with globally roaming bankers was through a support ticketing system – a type of CRM system – mediating the discussions of the status of submitted requests. The health professionals in Study 7 attempted to engage in a complex relationship between remote learners and a central responsible through an advanced database system being updated by each learner from their PDAs. This did, however not work and it demonstrates the complexity of establishing mobile mediated relationships. Such relationships must be constantly nurtured according to changing needs and preferences. On the other hand if too much time and effort must go into this nurturing then this may be deemed unfeasible.

9. Conclusion

We have in this paper attempted to provide some initial answer in forms of a categorisation to the question of: *What are the organisational implications specifically related to the application of mobile information technology across a variety of public and private organisations?* This was accomplished by analysing the results from a collection of 11 fieldstudies of mobile information technology use. As a result, six different challenges of seeking to gain organisational efficiency through mobile information technology there explored. The main results are summarised in Table 2 and Appendix 1–3 offers more detailed findings. The six themes unfold a complex set of relevant decisions when introducing mobile IT into an organisation and the following questions: (1) Should mobile IT through mediating remote interaction replace situated interaction or be used to make the context of situated interaction an organisational resource?; (2) Should mobile IT support increased organisational control of decisions or should it promote decentralised application of individual discretion in decision making?; (3) Should the technology strengthen mutual interdpendencies between people within the organisation and with associated partners or should it make more individualised working easier to implement?; (4) How is the technology percieved in the context of everyday activities – as ubiquitous support residing in the background and out of focus, or as an opaque reminder of itself?; (5) Should the mobile IT help the organisation engage in a transformation of existing working practices or will it support the cultivation of

Table 2

Summarising the six themes characterising enterprise mobility challenges

Theme	Question	Characteristics	Examples
Interaction	Mediate or Situate?	Mobile IT can both **mediate** remote interaction and thereby allow people to collaborate across temporal and spatial barriers – the traditional "anytime-anywhere" argument. However, mobile IT can also support **situated** interaction where the primary aim is being somewhere at some point, whilst remaining in touch with relevant people and information sources.	Off-premises traders in Study 4 could trade anytime and anywhere outside normal working hours through mediated relationship with the financial market. Hiro in Study 1 could immerse himself in Tokyo's everyday street life for inspiration whilst remaining in touch with his organisation. The senior bank executives in Study 2 likewise engaged in client negotiations and at the same time accessed essential data for the negotiation through their mobile IT.
Management	Control or Discretion?	Mobile IT support the management of work in terms of providing means for **control** for example through providing direct connections between people, and with corporate systems of control. Mobile IT can, however, also provide opportunities for increased individual **discretion** in decisions as they have access to relevant information and can implement decentralised decisions.	In several of the studies, the key issue was that of managing mobile working through mobile IT strengthening control, for example, Study 7, 8, 9 and 10, where both the health professionals in Study 7 and the waste management workers in Study 9 experienced negative aspects of increased control through mobile IT. The off-premises traders in Study 4 was each day subjected to organisational control and for the sake of offering some sort of normality when they kept trading after normal working hours, the system was mostly designed to offer support for discretionary decisions.
Collaboration	Individual or Collective?	Mobile IT can offer **individual** support for activities carried out alone, for example through offering access to information or occasional connections with colleagues or customers. Mobile IT can, however, also support distributed **collective** efforts. Interestingly, the introduction of mobile IT can shift activities between these two types.	For the off-premises traders in Study 4, the main idea was to allow highly individual working after-hours with intermittent discussions on mobile phone. For the cab drivers in Study 5, the purpose was the opposite, namely to allow highly individualised cab drivers to pool resources and compete as an organisational unit through mobile IT supporting collective response to customer demand for cab rides.
Technology	Ubiquitous or Opaque?	Much discussion of mobile IT centres on its ability to become an **ubiquitous** part of the user's activities. However, the technology can for a range of reasons also become an **opaque** element demanding attention.	For the police officers in Study 6 the main criteria for most mobile IT was to not only be ubiquitous, but at critical times to disappear entirely. The police radio was the only mobile IT close to ubiquitous. For most of the professionals in Study 11, mobile IT often would become opaque and subject of problems, such as issues when attempting establishing network connections or batteries running out. For the health professionals in Study 7, mobile IT was entirely opaque when attempted used to record learning
Organisation	Cultivate or Transform?	Mobile IT can support the organisation in **cultivating** existing practices and thereby, for example, obtain better, faster or more flexible decisions. Mobile IT can, however, also serve as one of the means of **transforming** the way decisions are made, innovation carried out or services delivered.	The security company in Study 8 experienced an incremental cultivation of existing arrangements when experimenting with RFID-enabled mobile phones as a means of recording security guard patrolling. For the bank in Study 4, the application of Mobile IT was an essential part of transforming the bank's 24-hours trading capabilities in a way that was both cost-effective, organisationally feasible, and acceptable to the individual traders. For cab drivers in Study 5, transformation with mobile IT was essential to establish coordinated organisational response.

Table 2, continued

Services	Encounters or Relationships?	Mobile IT can amplify the ability to rapidly establish technologically mediated **encounters**. Mobile IT can, however, also provide support through mediating ongoing **relationships**.	For professionals in Studies 1, 2 and 11, mobile IT was mostly supporting technologically mediated encounters supporting flexible information retrieval and decision-making. Remaining Studies 3, 4, 5, 6, 7, 8, 9, and 10 all displayed elements of mobile IT mediating a relationship – although this did not always go smoothly.

Table 3

Essential design choice of supporting encounters or mediating relationships

Type	Metaphor	Examples	Advantages	Disadvantages
Encounter	Communication Tool	Mobile voice calls, mobile email, mobile instant messaging, SMS messages	Amplifies connections in encounters Light-weight and flexible Initially easy adoption	Only scaleable through social conventions Whilst flexible in establishing communication, it essentially adds to the burden of managing interdependencies through communication
Relationship	Business Process	Coordination systems, project plans, mobile workflow management systems, radio contact to dispatch centre, etc	Amplifies collaboration in ongoing relationships and hereby reduces the complexity of negotiating interdependencies Scaleability designed into the service as it reduces the complexity of negotiating interaction	Extensive and inflexible Difficult initial adoption as it relies critically on people accepting the implied modelling of the business process

these practices?; and (6) Should the mobile technology support encounters between users and between users and informational resources, or should it mediate ongoing relationships?

Clearly, there are no straightforward answers to these six questions, but rather in each specific situation of intended organsational innovation with mobile IT, each aspect must be considered carefully and subjected to ongoing experiementation. One of the characteristics of enterprise mobility is the increased reliance on localised innovation, individual ways of appropriating the technology and the need for organisational experimentation to investigate how to yield most benefit from the technology.

The main contribution of this paper is to highlight six essential discussions of enterprise mobility consequences. This expands our theoretical knowledge about the possible consequences of enterprise mobility and sensitise managers to the key questions they need to ask in their organisation when considering implementing mobile IT. Whereas much previous research has focused on technological opportunities, this research is based on organisational realities from the 11 case studies. The practical examples presented in the vignettes and discussed in the analysis can also provide management with tangible examples of enterprise mobility placed in a theoretical context.

The obvious first consequence of the analysis presented in this paper is that there is far from a simple linear relationship between the introduction of mobile IT and the consequences in terms of increased organisational agility through enterprise mobility. Specific mobile IT can have different consequences in different settings and the analysis exactly points out that the pressure points relate to how interaction is organised, how work is managed, how collaboration is designed, how technology is assimilated, the organisational strategy for change, and the sophistication of information services.

In all of this, the application of human discretion, as opposed to the reliance on mobile IT for the control of mobile activities, is clearly one of the key issues as this was found to be one of the key differentiators in terms of the approach to support work activities. Distinguishing between work where individual discretion is essential, and work where this is not the case, will clearly be a key-decision preceeding any investment in mobile IT. In general, the distinction between mobile services supporting encounters and ones mediating relationships, offers an excellent lens through which we can discover essential archetypes of technological and organisational configurations (see Table 3 for overview).

Typically support for professional activities, such as in Studies 1, 2, 4, 5, 6 (mostly), 7, and 11 involves support for light-weight encounters through mobile phones, email, Instant Messaging and video conferencing. Here, enterprise mobility is mostly concerned with providing an open-ended light-weight platform of tools allowing individuals to exercise their discretion by essentially adopting the tools they see an immediate use for and reject those they do not [50]. The research, in particular through Studies 8, 9 and 10, saw examples of enterprise mobility where work largely was conducted according to a strictly controlled business process, and where mobile IT would stipulate and mediate the business process, and through this control the performance of mobile working. We did, however, also see clear examples where a combination of these two situations was present. In Study 5, highly independent black cab work was under transformation to introduce interdependencies formalised in dispatch systems and associated regulation enabling changes in organisational capabilities. Conversely, in the case of the police officers in Study 6, the formalised systems primarily served the purpose of providing officers with as much support in the field as possible. The increased availability of information streamed to data terminals facilitated a better foundation on which to base discretionary decisions. As illustrated in Table 3, the advantages of providing encounters are the disadvantages of mediating relationships with mobile IT and vice versa. One of the primary challenges in applying enterprise mobility is to get the balance right between the provision of discretion and the management of work through the technology.

The main challenges of determining the right enterprise mobility strategy for an organisation is to relate the available mobile IT to the overall purpose of the work conducted and determine a risk-profile, for example, in terms of how radical the organisational changes should be, how closely the business process should be aligned to the mobile IT, and how the mobile IT will not only enable more fluid interaction between users but also how it can support each of them in managing their day-to-day interaction when they experience it in abundance.

One of the reasons good business cases for enterprise mobility are difficult to establish is that such business cases are not needed for providing CxO's with mobile email and they are re-atively easy to establish for incrementally strengthening the control of routine tasks with little discretion. However, the largest group of organisational members are in situations much similar to the police officers, namely bestowed a high degree of individual discretion, but at the same time subjected to organisational control mechanisms enforcing standardisation of behaviour.

Seen in the light of increased emphasis on service delivery as opposed to product manufacturing, it is clear that developments will favour automation of what can sensibly be automated, supplemented with self-service of all aspects suitable for this approach. What is left will critically require the application of discretion. The combination of automated services, customers managing own profiles, and a high degree of discretion to solve exceptions, will be a challenge for most organisations. The application of enterprise mobility viewed in this light implies an emphasis on bringing this discretion in touch with customers when they need it – situating interaction. It also implies that although enterprise mobility is an essential part of increasing the scientific management of information workers, the challenge will be to establish support for discretion and not foremost of control.

Although substantial research has gone into our work since 2001, there is still much to do and there are still many open practical and theoretical questions in relation to the business case for enterprise mobility. As with many other technologies, mobile IT both provides the promise of radical change and of cementing sub-optimal working arrangements further through embedding them into new technological systems.

Appendix 1 – Study 1–4: Summary of themes characterizing enterprise mobility challenges

#	Workers	Interaction	Management	Collaboration	Technology	Organisation	Services
1	Professionals	Some work situated other independent of context. IT used to both maintain secondasry interaction and to conduct context independent work	IT use generally concerned with mediating participant discretion	Mobile IT makes it easier to engage in distributed collaboration	Very close relationships between professionals and technology and mobile IT generally becomes an integral and ubiquitous part of work	In most cases, mobile IT allowed for the radical organisational arrangement of individual professionals managing all aspects of their work as opposed to being part of large corporation	Mobile IT mostly supported encounters through email and mobile phone access as well as Internet searches
2	Bank executives	Critical negotiations highly situated. IT augment available information	Work characterised by a high degree of discretion and IT provides a platform to support decisions	Work highly collaborative and IT supports increased remote collaboration between executives and their colleagues	As mobile technology with relative ease can be produced and removed from negotiations, it dislays itsef in a quite ubiquitous manner	Mobile IT presented a cultivation of existing organisational arrangements	Mobile IT mostly supported encounters through mobile access to corporate databases, email and colleages
3	Mobile support centre	IT enabeled mediated remote support for mobile users	IT supports the streamlining and management of a complex distributed support process	IT enhances the opportunities for resolving technical issues in a collaborative fashion	IT supports mobile workers when they have problems with their IT and the system therefore presents itself as an opaque element in addressing these problems	Mobile IT transformed the organisation of the support function	The support system mediated a relationship between bank employees needing support and the central support function
4	Off-premises foreign exchange traders	Off-premises work not situated. IT enable trading independent of situation	IT critically allows for extensive discretion during off-premises trading as traders technically are off work	Mobile IT allows individualisation of off-premises trading with selective negotiations of mutual interdependencies	Mobile technology generally functions in an ubiquitous manner and supports the parallel conduct of private life and off-premises trading	Mobile IT critical to the transformation of 24 hour trading into the combination of day-trading and off-premises trading	Mobile IT supported ongoing relationship between the money market and the traders, as well as encounters between traders internally

Appendix 2 – Study 5–8: Summary of themes characterizing enterprise mobility challenges

#	Workers	Interaction	Management	Collaboration	Technology	Organisation	Services
5	London taxi drivers	Work situated and independent. IT supports stronger dependencies for allocation of jobs	IT exists in a setting of extreme individual discretion so individual offers of jobs can be accepted or rejected	Mobile IT supports establishing mutual interdependencies where work before was conducted highly independently	Mobile IT is an integral and ubiquitous part of the cab cockpit	Mobile IT critical element in the transformation from highly independent taxi work to organied interdependencies	Mobile IT established ongoing relationships between cab drivers and the dispatch office as well as encounters amongst drivers
6	Police officers	Work situated and IT mediate ongoing relationships between control room, colleagues and information resources.	A high degree of operational discretion is supported by IT, whilst generally allowing tactical and strategic control through traceability of actions and decisions	Work is highly collaborative and mobile IT allows for much more flexible collaboration between officers in the field and with the control room	The critical reliance of face-to-face interaction in most incidents implies that the police radio is only IT that offers sufficient ubiquity	Mobile IT supports evolution of information and interaction management in the police	Mobile IT mediated relationships between control room and officers and encounters between police officers
7	Health professionals	Work highly situated with remote control sought mediated through IT	IT failed as it sought to impose detailed control over operational activities	Mobile IT supported increased collaboration between remote professionals and the center – but failed	One factor in the failure of mobile IT was the opaque nature of the technology in many situations	The aim was for mobile IT to transform the relationship between the learning centre and the remote learners. This failed	Mobile IT failed at the intended mediation of relationships between the central management function and the distribted professionals
8	Security guards	Work situated and IT interactively records unfolding activities	Work characterised by a very low degree of individual discretion and IT emphasises this further	Work traditionally independent but mobile technology supports management's increased collaboration with and remote management of security guards	Mobile IT replaced a system not much different, form the perspective of the guards, so it rapidly gained ubiquitous status	Mobile IT signalled an incremental cultivation of existing practices	Mobile IT strengthened and mediated the relationship between the individual security guard and the central system recording activities

Appendix 3 – Study 9–11: Summary of themes characterizing enterprise mobility challenges

#	Workers	Interaction	Management	Collaboration	Technology	Organisation	Services
9	Industrial waste management	Work situated. IT mediates link to management. This causes tension	Work characterised by some discretion and tension arrise when IT makes remote control easier	Work traditionally independently conducted by teams but with mobile IT increased remote collaboration and management possible	As mobile IT allowed remote management and control previous impossible, it frequently presented itsef as in the way of getting work done	Mobile IT was aimed at incrementally cultivating existing practices but in turn transformed aspects of remote management deemed negative by workers	Mobile IT mediated and strengthened the relationship between remote waste disposal workers and central management function
10	Delivery Drivers	Work situated and IT supports remote management and support	Low degree of individual discretion and IT further strengthens the possibility for remote and systemic control	Mobile IT supports increased collaboration and remote management between drivers and central control functions. It also supports direct collaboration between drivers and customers, which can cause conflict with centralised control function	Work was very much managed and controlled through mobile IT, which therefore became integral to conducting work and therefore ubiquitous to the drivers	Mobile IT transforms the organisational capabilities for remote management of work and for tight integration between business process elements	Mobile IT mediated and strengthened the relationship between remote delivery drivers and central management function
11	Professionals	Work can be both situated and context independent. IT mediates connections to people and informational resources	A high degree of discretion where IT offers support for information management and decision-making	Work highly distributed and highly collaborative. Mobile IT enables strengthening of the remote collaborative arrangements	Whilst much of the mobile IT was ubiquitous in daily use, technical issues such as connectivity and battery life constantly made the IT a subject of discussion	Mobile IT further cultivates the abilities to engage in remote collaboration	Mobile IT mostly mediated light-weight encounters between professionals and their colleagues and clients

References

[1]   J. Agar, *Constant Touch: A Global History of the Mobile Phone,* Cambridge, Icon Books, 2003.

[2]   A. Al-Taitoon, Making Sense of Mobile ICT-Enabled Trading in Fast Moving Financial Markets as Volatility-Control Ambivalence: Case Study on the Organisation of Off-Premises Foreign Exchange at a Middle-East Bank, *Department of Information Systems,* London, London School of Economics, 2005.

[3]   A. Al-Taitoon and C. Sørensen, Supporting Mobile Professionals in Global Banking: The Role of Global ICT-Support Call-Centres, *Journal of Computing and Information Technology,* **12** (2004), 297–308.

[4]   C. Argyris, Empowerment: the Emperors New Clothes, *Harvard Business Review* (1998), 98–105.

[5]   D.J. Armstrong and P. Cole, Managing Distances and Differences in Geographically Distributed Work Groups, in: *Distributed Work,* P. Hinds and S. Kiesler, eds, Cambridge, Massachusetts, MIT Press, 2002.

[6]   S.R. Barley and G. Kunda, *Gurus, Hired Guns, and Warm Bodies: Itinerant Experts in a Knowledge Economy,* Princeton University Press, 2004.

[7]   K. Boateng, (Forthcoming) Understanding Contemporary Work Practices: On The Dynamics of Control in Technology Mediated Interaction, *Department of Management. Information Systems and Innovation Group,* London School of Economics, 2004.

[8]   J.L. Bower and C.M. Christensen, Disruptive Technologies: Catching the Wave, *Harvard Business Review,* 1995.

[9]   F. Cairncross, *The death of distance 2.0: How the communications revolution will change our lives,* UK, Texere Publishing, 2001.

[10]   C. Ciborra, ed., *Groupware and Teamwork,* Chichester, United Kingdom, John Wiley & Sons, 1996.

[11]   C. Ciborra, The Mind or the Heart? It Depends on the (Definition Of) Situation, *Journal of Information Technology* **21** (2006), 129–139.

[12]   R. Collins, *Interaction Ritual Chains,* Princeton University Press, 2004.

[13]   J. Conger and R.N. Kanungo, The Empowerment Process: Integrating Theory and Practice, *Academy of Management Review* **13** (1988), 471–482.

[14]   D. Courpasson, Managerial strategies of domination. Power in soft bureaucracies, *Organization Studies* **21** (2000), 141–161.

[15]   N.E. Coviello and R.J. Brodie, Contemporary Marketing Practices of Consumer and Business-to-business Firms: How Different are they? *Journal of Business and Industrial Marketing* **16** (2001), 382–400.

[16]   P. Dourish, *Where the action is: The foundations of embodied interaction,* MIT Press, 2001.

[17]   S. Elaluf-Calderwood, (Forthcoming) Situational and Contextual Mobile Work: Organizational Agility with Mobile ICT? The case of London Black Cab Work, *Department of Management. Information Systems and Innovation Group,* London School of Economics, 2001.

[18]   S. Elaluf-Calderwood and C. Sørensen, Organizational Agility with Mobile ICT? The Case of London Black Cab Work, in: *Agile Information Systems: Conceptualization, Construction, and Management,* K.C. Desouza, ed., Butterworth-Heinemann, 2006.

[19]   S. Elaluf-Calderwood and C. Sørensen, 420 Years of Mobility: ICT Enabled Mobile Interdependencies in London Hackney Cab Work, in: *Mobility and Technology in the Workplace,* D. Hislop, ed., London, Routledge, 2008.

[20]   E.R. Fontana and C. Sørensen, From Idea to Blah! Understanding Mobile Services Development as Interactive Innovation, *Journal of Information Systems and Technology Management* **2** (2005).

[21]   D.Q. Goldin, S.A. Smolka and P. Wegner, eds, *Interactive Computation: The New Paradigm,* Berlin, Springer-Verlag, 2006.

[22]   B. Gutek, *The Dynamics of Service,* Jossey Bass Wiley, 1995.

[23]   L. Haddon, E. Mante, B. Sapio, K.-H. Kommonen, L. Fortunati and A. Kant, eds, *Everyday Innovators: Researching the role of users in shaping ICTs,* London, Springer, 2006.

[24]   N. Hughes and S. Lonie, M-PESA:Mobile Money for the "Unbanked" Turning Cellphones into 24-Hour Tellers in Kenya, *Innovations* (2007), 63–81.

[25]   M. Kakihara, *Emerging Work Practices of ICT-Enabled Mobile Professionals,* London, The London School of Economics and Political Science, 2003.

[26]   M. Kakihara and C. Sørensen, Expanding the 'Mobility' Concept, *ACM SIGGROUP Bulletin* **22** (2001), 33–37.

[27]   M. Kakihara and C. Sørensen, Practicing Mobile Professional Work: Tales of Locational, Operational, and Interactional Mobility, *INFO: The Journal of Policy, Regulation and Strategy for Telecommunication, Information and Media* **6** (2004), 180–187.

[28]   M. Kakihara, C. Sørensen and M. Wiberg, Negotiating the fluidity of mobile work, in: *The Interaction Society: Practice, Theories, & Supportive Technologies,* M. Wiberg, ed., Idea Group Inc, 2004.

[29]   J. Kallinikos, *The Consequences of Information: Institutional Implications of Technological Change,* Cheltenham, Edward Elgar, 2006.

[30] J. Kietzmann, In Touch out in the Field: Coalescence and Interactive Innovation of Technology for Mobile Work, *Department of Management. Information Systems and Innovation Group,* London School of Economics and Political Science, 2007.

[31] B.L. Kirkman and B. Rosen, Beyond Self-Management: Antecedents and Consequences of Team Empowerment, *Academy of Management Journal* **42** (1999), 58–74.

[32] L. Kleinrock, Nomadicity: Anytime, Anywhere in a Disconnected World, *Mobile Networks and Applications* **1** (1996), 351–357.

[33] G.F. Lanzara, Ephemeral Organizations in Extreme Environments: Emergence, Strategy, Extinction, *Journal of Management Studies* **20** (1983), 71–96.

[34] R.J. Laubacher and T.W. Malone, Retreat of the Firm and the Rise of Guilds: The Employment Relationship in an Age of Virtual Business, *MIT Sloan School of Management Initiative on Inventing the Organizations of the 21st Century Working Papers,* 2000.

[35] F. Ljungberg and C. Sørensen, Overload: From transaction to interaction, in: *Planet Internet,* K. Braa, C. Sørensen and B. Dahlbom, eds, Lund, Sweden, Studentlitteratur, (2000)

[36] P. Luff and C. Heath, Mobility in Collaboration, *Proceedings of ACM 1998 Conference on Computer Supported Cooperative Work,* ACM Press, 1998.

[37] K. Lyytinen and Y. Yoo, The Next Wave of Nomadic Computing: A Research Agenda for Information Systems Research, *Information Systems Research* **13** (2002), 377–388.

[38] T.W. Malone, *The Future of Work: How the New Order of Business Will Shape Your Organization, Your Management Style, and Your Life,* Harvard Business School Press, 2004.

[39] T.W. Malone and R.J. Laubacher, The Dawn of the E-Lance Economy, *Harvard Business Review* (1998), 145–153.

[40] P.K. Manning, *Policing contingencies,* Chicago, University of Chicago Press, 2003.

[41] R.O. Mason, MIS Experiments: A Pragmatic Perspective, in: *The Information Systems Research Challenge: Experimental Research Methods,* I. Benbasat, ed., Boston Massachusetts, Harvard Business School Research Colloquium Harvard Business School, 1989.

[42] L. Mathiassen and P.A. Nielsen, Interaction and Transformation in SSM, *Systems Research and Behavioral Science* **17** (2000).

[43] L. Mathiassen and C. Sørensen, Towards A Theory of Organizational Information Services, *Journal of Information Technology* (2008), 23.

[44] M.A. Mazmanian, W.J. Orlikowski and J. Yates, Crackberries: The Social Implications of Ubiquitous Wireless E-Mail Devices, in: *Designing Ubiquitous Information Environments: Socio-technical Issues and Challenges,* C. Sørensen, Y. Yoo, K. Lyytinen and J.I. Degross, eds, New York, Springer, 2005.

[45] M. Mccullough, *Digital Ground: Architecture, Pervasive Computing, and Environmental Knowing,* Cambridge, Massachusetts, 2004.

[46] B.A. Nardi, S. Whittaker and H. Schwarz, NetWORKers and their Activity in Intensional Networks, *Computer Supported Cooperative Work* **11** (2002), 205–242.

[47] G.M. Olson and J.S. Olson, Distance Matters, *Human-Computer Interaction* **15** (2000), 139–178.

[48] J.E. Orr, *Talking About Machines: An Ethnography of a Modern Job,* Cornell University Press, 1996.

[49] D. Pica, The Rhythms of Interaction with Mobile Technologies: Tales from the Police, *Information Systems,* London, London School of Economics, 2006.

[50] M. Robertson, C. Sørensen and J. Swan, Survival of the Leanest: Intensive Knowledge Work and Groupware Adaptation, *Information Technology & People* **14** (2001), 334–353.

[51] H. Scarbrough, Blackboxes, Hostages and Prisoners, *Organization Studies* **16** (1995), 991–1019.

[52] K. Schmidt, Modes and Mechanisms of Interaction in Cooperative Work, in: *Computational Mechanisms of Interaction for CSCW,* C. Simone and K. Schmidt, eds, Lancaster, England, University of Lancaster, 1993.

[53] K. Schmidt and L. Bannon, Taking CSCW Seriously: Supporting Articulation Work, *CSCW* **1** (1992), 7–40.

[54] C. Sørensen and A. Al-Taitoon, Organisational Usability of Mobile Computing: Volatility and Control in Mobile Foreign Exchange Trading, *International Journal of Human-Computer Studies* **66** (2008), (Forthcoming).

[55] C. Sørensen and R. Gear, *Innovating with ICT: The Executive Challenge,* London, LSE – PA Consulting Group Report, 2007.

[56] C. Sørensen and D. Gibson, The Professional's Everyday Struggle to Ubiquitize Computers, in: *Computerization Movements and Technology Diffusion: From Mainframes to Ubiquitous Computing,* M. Elliott and K.L. Kraemer, eds, Medford, NJ, Information Today, 2008.

[57] C. Sørensen and D. PICA, Tales from the Police: Mobile Technologies and Contexts of Work, *Information and Organization* **15** (2005), 125–149.

[58] P.A. Strassman, *Information Payoff: Transformation of Work in the Electronic Age,* Macmillan, 1985.

[59] L.A. Suchman, *Plans and situated actions. The problem of human-machine communication,* Cambridge, Cambridge University Press, 1987.

[60] D. Tilson, K. Lyytinen, C. Sørensen and J. Liebenau, Coordination of technology and diverse organizational actors during service innovation: The case of wireless data services in the United Kingdom, *Helsinki Mobility Roundtable,* Finland, 2006.

[61] E. Von Hippel, *Democratizing Innovation,* Cambridge, Massachusetts, The MIT Press, 2005.

[62] K. Voutsina, J. Kallinikos and C. Sørensen, Codification and Transferability of IT Knowledge, in: *15th European Conference on Information Systems (ECIS),* R. Winter and H. Österle, eds, St. Gallen, 2007.

[63] P. Wegner, Why Interaction is More Powerful Than Algorithms, *Communications of the ACM* **40** (1997), 80–91.

[64] M. Weiser, The Computer for the Twenty-First Century, *Scientific American* (1991), 94–110.

[65] M. Weiser, Ubiquitous Computing. http://www.ubiq.com/hypertext/weiser/UbiHome.html, 1999.

[66] M. Wiberg and F. Ljungberg, Exploring the Vision of "Anytime, Anywhere" in the Context of Mobile Work, in: *Knowledge Management and Virtual Organizations,* Y. Malhotra, ed., Hershey, PA, USA, Idea Group Publishing, 2001.

[67] L. Willcocks and M.C. Lacity, *Global Sourcing of Business and IT Services*, Palgrave Macmillan, 2006.

[68] G. Wiredu, Mobile Computing in Work-Integrated Learning: Problems of Remotely Distributed Activities and Technology Use, *Department of Information Systems,* London School of Economics and Political Science, 2005.

[69] G. Wiredu, User Appropriation of Mobile Technologies: Motives, Conditions, and Design Properties, *Information and Organization* **17** (2007), 110–129.

[70] G. Wiredu and C. Sørensen, The Dynamics of Control and Use of Mobile Technology in Distributed Activities, *European Journal of Information Systems* **15** (2006), 307–319.

[71] J. Yates, *Control through Communication: The Rise of System in American Management,* Baltimore, The Johns Hopkins University Press, 1989.

[72] R.W. Zmud, An Examination of 'Push-Pull' Theory Applied to Process Innovation in Knowledge Work, *Management Science* **30** (1984), 727–738.

[73] R. Zolin, P.J. Hinds, R. Fruchter and R.E. Levitt, Interpersonal trust in cross-functional, geographically distributed work: A longitudinal study, *Information and Organization* **14** (2004), 1–26.

[74] S. Zuboff, *In the Age of the Smart Machine,* New York, Basic Books, 1988.

[75] S. Zuboff and J. Maxmin, *The Support Economy: Why Corporations are Failing Individuals and the Next Episode of Capitalism,* London, Penguin, 2002.

Carsten Sørensen is a Senior Lecturer in Department of Management, within the Information Systems and Innovation Group at The London School of Economics and Political Science, United Kingdom. He holds a BSc. in mathematics, an MSc in computer science and a Ph.D. in information systems from Aalborg University, Denmark. Carsten has the past 20 years studied how ICT shapes and is shaped by emerging working practices and organizational forms. He currently studies the organisational use of mobile services and the shifting role of ICT for effective information work and has published widely on this. In 2001 he initiated the mobility@lse research network in mobile interaction (http://mobility.lse.ac.uk/), which aims at drawing together academics and practitioners. Carsten has extensive EU research project experience from 1992 and international project experience from 1990. He is actively engaged with executive education and has consulted for a range of organisations, such as; Microsoft, Orange, PA Consulting, 3 UK, AXA, CA, UBS, Gartner, EDS, Siemens, KMD, and Caja Madrid.

Adel Al-Taitoon has a PhD from London School of Economics & Political Science (LSE). Adel's PhD Research was on Making Sense of Mobile ICT-Enabled Foreign Exchange as Volatility-Control Ambivalence. Adel also has BSc in Computer Engineering; and MSc in Electronics Engineering from Cardiff University (with a Distinction & Best Performance Award). Adel research is focused around organisational use of mobile ICT & information systems in the financial markets. Adel has sixteen (16) years of work experience. Over the last eight years, Adel has been working in the Arab Banking Corporation (ABC). He is currently working as a Vice President (VP) & Head of ABC Global IT Strategic Planning responsible for the selection, project management, implementation and global rollout of wide range of banking systems in different countries & financial cities in the Middle-East & North Africa (MENA), Europe & North America. Previously, Adel worked as the Head of Computer and Information Technology in Bahrain Training Institute (BTI).

Jan Kietzmann is a Lecturer at the Faculty of Business Administration, within the Information Systems Department at Simon Fraser University in Vancouver, British Columbia, Canada. Jan holds Ph.D. from the London School of Economics' School of Management (Information Systems and Innovation Group), with a focus on interactive innovation of technology for mobile work. Most recently, Jan has studied the impact of mobile work practices on the innovation of technology for mobile work, and vice versa. His interests extend to the study of pervasive technologies and discussions centred on the disappearing computer. Next, Jan will look at the role of entrepreneurs within mobile technology and service development in preparation for the 2010 Olympic Winter Games in Vancouver.

Daniele Pica is a Postdoctoral Research Fellow in Department of Management, within the Information Systems and Innovation Group at The London School of Economics and Political Science, United Kingdom. He holds a BSc in Business Administration from University Of Southern California, Marshall School of Business, an MSc in Administration, Design, and Management of Information Systems (ADMIS) and a Ph.D. in Information Systems both from The London School of Economics. Daniele has, for the past 6 years studied how Mobile ICT influence work practices and organizational forms in the public sector. He currently studies the use of mobile ICT in a variety of work settings and how the issue of convergence is reshaping the understanding of the dynamics between businesses and customers.

Gamel Wiredu is a Lecturer of Information Systems in the school of Technology, Ghana Institute of Management and Public Administration (GIMPA), Ghana. He holds BSc degree in Planning from Kwame Nkrumah University of Science and Technology, Ghana; and MSc and PhD degrees both in Information Systems from the London School of Economics and Political Science, United Kingdom. His current research examines issues of coordination and control in the implementation and management of information systems in distributed organizing. His previous research centred on mobile computing in remotely distributed activities in which he investigated the impact of motives, control, and institutional politics on mobile technology use. He has also researched into the social, cultural and organisational aspects of globally-distributed software development. His research has been published in European Journal of Information Systems, Information and Organization, and Journal of Education and Work.

Silvia Elaluf-Calderwood Computer Engineer (BSc and MSc). Worked in Telecommunications industry in the UK and the Netherlands over a period of 10 years. She has been a Cisco-Certified Network Professional (CCNP) and contributed to the Internet working groups for RIPE and the Internet Engineering TaskForce (IETF) during her telco years. She was a meta-moderator for Slashdot, and an advocate in the use of Open/Free Source Software since 1998. She has a strong technical and managerial background in the Internet and Telecoms business. Currently completing her PhD at the Information Systems Group within Department of Management at the LSE. Area of specialization: Mobile Work and Mobile technology. Her particular area of interest is the changes in working practices that mobile technology presents to mobile workers, challenging their definitions of identity and trust relationships at work. She was invited by the LSE Department of Media and Communications to work for the EU-FP6 Digital Business Ecosystem (DBE) project to define a Knowledge Base of Regulatory Issues for establishing trust in SMEs for e-business and later in the BIONETS EU funded project (www.bionets.eu). She has provided IT consultancy work for the UK Parliament. She is also a Teaching Assistant in the Department of Information Systems at the LSE for the Masters Programme "Analysis, Design and Management of Information Systems", and is an examiner for the University of London External Undergraduate Programme.

Kofi Boateng Boateng is a doctoral student in the Information Systems and Innovation Group in the Department of Management at the London School of Economics and Political Science, United Kingdom. He holds a BA (Hons) in Publishing Studies from the Kwame Nkrumah University of Science and Technology, Ghana, and an MSc in Information Systems from the London School of Economics and Political Science. Kofi's research experience has been diverse, ranging from a novel study on Pioneer Women Professionals in Ghana to the instrumentality of Information Communications Technology (ICTs) in influencing and informing the dynamics of organisational sociology in the financial sector. This includes a stint at the Central Bank of Ghana in Accra. Currently, he is engaged in the study of the varied manifestations of ICTs in organisational routines in the provision of services tailored to the specific needs of customers in a medium-size UK private company. Kofi has also participated and presented in a number of international workshops and competitions.

Masao Kakihara is a Research Scientist at Yahoo! JAPAN Research Institute, Tokyo, Japan. He has broad experiences both in industry and academia. He worked at a management consulting firm in Tokyo, Japan, for 4 years, engaging in various consulting projects for large manufacturing companies mainly in automobile, electronic appliances, and food industries. He also worked for 5 years as Assistant Professor and subsequently Associate Professor in Management Information Systems at School of Business Administration, Kwansei Gakuin University, Japan. He joined Yahoo! JAPAN Research Institute in 2008, studying economic and managerial aspects of ICT-based businesses, particularly mobile business and e-commerce. His current research projects are economic analysis of global mobile industry, strategic management of software production, and online consumer behavior. He holds B.Econ. from Kwansei Gakuin University, and M.Sc. and Ph.D. in Information Systems from London School of Economics and Political Science.

David Gibson is a Senior Consultant in the Human Performance Global Service Line and specialises in Talent and Organisation Improvement for Accenture in London. David's areas of expertise is creating talent strategies, improving customer experience, service innovation, process improvement, change management and cultural change for multi-national companies such as Shell, Microsoft, Airbus, Statoil and Telstra. He is published in INFO: The Journal of Policy, Regulation and Strategy for Telecommunication, Information and Media, as well as in an upcoming edited volume, both on the subject of optimising technology to improve knowledge worker efficiencies. Prior to joining Accenture, David worked as a consultant at a brand consultancy in London where he sold, managed, researched and wrote consumer product and service innovation studies for multi-nationals, also working at a boutique IT marketing consultancy in Singapore where he served multi-nationals operating in the pacific rim. David holds an MSc from the London School of Economics, a BA in Media Management and Journalism from the University of Calgary, Canada and Örebro Universitet, Sweden.

Author Index